Leaking Laffs
Between

PAMPERS
and
DEPENDS

He's Gonna

TOOT
and I'm Gonna

SCOOT

Living Somewhere

BETWEEN
ESTROGEN
and
DEATH

Other Books by Barbara Johnson

Where Does a Mother Go to Resign?

Fresh Elastic for Stretched-Out Moms

Stick a Geranium in Your Hat and Be Happy!

Splashes of Joy in the Cesspools of Life

*Pack Up Your Gloomees in a Great Big Box,
Then Sit on the Lid and Laugh!*

Mama, Get the Hammer! There's a Fly on Papa's Head!

I'm So Glad You Told Me What I Didn't Wanna Hear

Living Somewhere Between Estrogen and Death

Boomerang Joy

He's Gonna Toot and I'm Gonna Scoot

Leaking Laffs Between Pampers and Depends

Daily Splashes of Joy

God's Most Precious Jewels Are Crystallized Tears

Plant a Geranium in your Cranium

Carolyn Mobley —

BARBARA JOHNSON

| Leaking Laffs Between PAMPERS and DEPENDS | He's Gonna TOOT and I'm Gonna SCOOT | Living Somewhere BETWEEN ESTROGEN and DEATH |

W PUBLISHING GROUP™

www.wpublishinggroup.com

A Division of Thomas Nelson, Inc.
www.ThomasNelson.com

BARBARA JOHNSON

Leaking Laffs Between PAMPERS and DEPENDS

W PUBLISHING GROUP™

www.wpublishinggroup.com

A Division of Thomas Nelson, Inc.
www.ThomasNelson.com

What a delight for me to dedicate this book to
Larrene Hagaman,
whose clever idea adorns
the cover and whose bubbly personality
and infectious enthusiasm
have made her my
favorite co-conspirator in
Leaking Laffs
wherever we go!

CONTENTS

You shall be called the repairer of the breach. . . .
—ISAIAH 58:12 NRSV

Having a Baby Is Like Writing a Book—Lots of Whining, Begging, and Pushing

Chaos, Panic, and Disorder— My Work Here Is Done

Someone commented recently that having a baby is a lot like writing a book.[1] As a woman who has given birth to four sons and written more than a dozen books, I should know!

The baby often begins as a spark—a little twinkle in someone's eye. The same thing happens when a book is conceived—a little spark in the brain sends emotions soaring in anticipation. No doubt about it: *Conceiving* a baby—or a book—is the easiest part of the whole project!

From that tiny seed, a baby is formed inside the mother's body. In the author's mind, an idea develops into the framework of the book; a few choice thoughts slowly grow into a chapter-by-chapter outline. At this stage, we parents-to-be start having daydreams filled with precious cherubs and darling little bundles of joy snoozing sweetly in nurseries decorated by Martha Stewart. Expectant authors imagine a spellbinding book that outsells everything but the Bible.

1

Then the pregnancy is confirmed. A contract is signed, and a due date is given. (*How could anything so wonderful have an awful name like "deadline"? I wonder.*) The date seems so far off . . . a few seasons or perhaps almost a whole year away. Actually the date may seem like a cloud of fog far in the distant future. There's so much time—no need to rush things. Like Scarlett O'Hara, I push any worries aside while pulling the dessert plate closer or filling the schedule a little fuller— and trilling "fiddle-dee-dee!" all the while.

Next comes that queasy feeling in the stomach, a nauseous reminder each morning that I've made a real, almost overwhelming commitment. Suddenly I feel an urge to upchuck before breakfast, after meals, or anytime I happen to walk by the typewriter that waits, cold and silent, on the desk in my bedroom. The idea of becoming a parent suddenly takes on a more serious tone. The bare framework of the book has formed, but there's precious little hanging on it.

Then comes the stage when I feel a deep desire that this pregnancy had not happened. There are even occasional feelings of resentment toward my husband (or my publisher). Is this person intentionally trying to annoy me? Why else am I

constantly bombarded with pesky reminders and nervous questions about what I'm eating or how much I've written? And why, in the quiet darkness at midnight, do I seem to hear a clock ticking somewhere or the pages of a calendar being flipped?

Then the second three months begin, and gradually I warm to the idea again. It actually starts to seem possible that I *can* be a mother, that I *can* write a book . . . but now the IBM Selectric seems too close to my swelling abdomen and too far from my outstretched fingertips. A mysterious restlessness fills my days as I wrestle with the ideas—and the individual—churning inside of me.

Now the baby seems to intrude on everything I do, and it's not even born yet. At this stage, going out to lunch means not just squeezing my bulky form behind a tiny table at a favorite restaurant but also asking to be seated on the outside to allow room for that huge lump in front of me. It seems to be the center of attention everywhere I go. Folks who hardly know me feel free to pat my tummy or put a sympathetic arm around my shoulders and ask how far along I am. Everything centers around the baby—or the book—that is not nearly finished yet.

"That better not be my birthday present!"

As the third trimester begins, I am exhausted and sick of seeing myself in mirrors, tired of feeling so bulky. I try to type out the words, but some strange interference causes me to have to strain to get at the typewriter. Everything seems to be moving farther away from my immense middle, my book-filled brain. What an effort it takes to do anything!

The last month is the worst. I know the baby is just about due. The book is almost finished, but at this point I don't care about the ending—or the beginning or middle, for that matter. I am so sorry I ever even thought of getting pregnant, regretful that I ever had the idea of writing a book. Then the baby is born. With deep groans of agony and heaving sighs of pain, I force out the last few pages, thinking, *I JUST WANT THIS TO BE OVER!* With my last ounce of strength, I lug the manuscript to the post office and mail it off to the publisher. Returning home and collapsing into bed, I heave a huge sigh of relief when the delivery is complete.

Then there is that brief, eager time after the birth when I hold my breath and wait for the doctor's (or the publisher's) assessment—to which I respond, "What do you mean the color seems to be a little off?" "How could you possibly think this masterpiece is too lengthy?" What follows next is sometimes the most irritating part of the whole process as my book is probed and preened until I beg for mercy. I threaten to take my poor baby and move to the home for the bewildered.

Then the nurses place my sweet angel on the pillow next to me. The editors show me the cleaned-up version, and glory be! It's kinda cute. A few weeks later, it's introduced around the neighborhood—or the world—and what do you know? People ogle it and . . . why, they actually like it! Trying to be modest, I blush and smile while proudly claiming it as my own.

Then, basking in the glow of adoration and appreciation, the most amazing miracle of all happens. Somewhere inside my head, all the memories of my recent agony melt away, and there's a tiny flash of brilliant light, one bright little spark.

And somehow I have the thought that . . . well, actually, it might be nice to have another one . . .

THE FAMILY CIRCUS.   By Bil Keane

"It's better than audio books, TV or
the Internet. It's called reading."

That's exactly how this book came about. After "giving birth" to the book *Living Somewhere Between Estrogen and Death*, I was so relieved to have it finished that I actually thought of unplugging my IBM Selectric and calling it quits. After all, I'm well into retirement age, and we "mature" mothers and authors do need our rest. (By the way, you know why women over fifty don't have babies, don't you? We'd put 'em down somewhere and forget where we left them!)

After my *Estrogen* "baby" left home and went out into the marketplace, I was inundated with stories and letters from women who wanted to share their own hilarious "wonders of womanhood." They also wanted to tell me how the book had helped them laugh while they wrestled with the most heart-breaking experiences life could throw at them. One of my favorite stories came from a woman who said she had read the book aloud to her elderly mother as the loved one died of cancer. "Barb, the nurses kept coming into the room and asking what was going on. You see, they weren't used to hearing such laughter in the hospice center," she said.

That story warmed my heart! And so did a similar story shared by a woman in Chicago. She and her sister had brought along a copy of *Estrogen* when their eighty-year-old mother was hospitalized for what they feared was her final illness. Sitting in their mother's hospital room, they took turns reading the book aloud to her. She said, "Barb, I'll always be grateful to you for that cherished image: my mother, *laughing,* on her deathbed!"

"Oh," I answered softly, "when did she die?"

"Oh, she didn't die—she lived!" the woman said, laughing heartily. "That was a year ago. She's fine now. We think it was all that *Estrogen* we read to her and all that laughing!"

Another woman came to my book table at a conference and told me she had first seen *Estrogen* when she was sharing a reception area with other women awaiting radiation treatment for cancer. One of the women, she said, was reading the book and chuckling to herself. Seeing the expectant faces of the other women waiting with her, she began to read aloud. Pretty soon, the woman said as she tugged on the geranium-trimmed hat covering her bald head, "We were all roaring with laughter."

Such responses helped make *Estrogen* the number one best-selling paperback book for the whole Christian market in 1997, the year it was published![2] When the standings were announced, I thought, *This must be how it feels to be the mother of Miss America!* With the encouragement of so many readers and with an abundance of delightful new material flowing in, everyone agreed there had to be another book. But while *Estrogen* was aimed at women living somewhere "between menopause and LARGE PRINT," the material that had been shared by all the letter-writers and Women of Faith conference attendees clearly indicated that the next book would need to encompass *all* the years of a woman's life, ranging from parenting young children to parenting parents. The first seed for the title came from a gal at a Women of Faith conference somewhere who laughingly told me she was "somewhere between Pampers and Depends."

Naming the Baby

Parents know how important it is to choose the perfect name for their baby. You have to consider what words rhyme with the name so you don't choose something the poor kid can be tortured with by his or her peers. It's nice to choose a biblical name—while keeping modern trends in mind. David and Benjamin are very popular, for example, but Damaris and Boaz are less common these days. The best names bring to mind a positive image of a happy, trustworthy person.

The same is true for book titles. Authors and publishers go round and round trying to choose a name that will accurately represent the book while igniting a spark in the minds of potential readers. One of my all-time favorite book titlers is Dave Barry. A few years ago he published a book titled *Babies and Other Hazards of Sex*. Frankly, the *title* wasn't all that great, but the *subtitle* was hilarious: *How to Make a Tiny Person in Nine Months with Tools You Probably Have Around the House.*

Hoping for a phrase as clever as that one, I suggested to my publisher that the phrase "Pampers and Depends" was the heart of a great book title. At first, the W Publishing Group executives were okay with it. One W Publishing Group executive even sent me a fax, excitedly sharing that she'd found the word *pampers* in her Bible concordance: "Of course, it's not the diaper kind," she wrote, "but I thought it was funny to see it there. The reference is Proverbs 29:21: "If a man pampers his servant from youth, he will bring grief in the end."

Not being a real pious prune, I took that as a sign that God was bestowing His blessing on our next project, even if the context didn't seem to be related in any way. So we had part of a title, but we needed a verb. We'd already used *living*, so something different was needed. Someone suggested *changing*, citing all the changes we women go through—changing diapers, changing from daughters to mothers to grandmothers, going through the *change.*

But *changing* seemed so ordinary. In the middle of the night (it might have been a rainy night), the word *leaking* suddenly

**What mothers think of when someone
suggests they can change the world.**

soaked into my brain. It felt like a logical choice to me. But the
poor folks at W nearly croaked when I mentioned it!

"Oh, Barb, you don't mean it!" one of them gasped.
"Leaking diapers?"

"Barb, that's just too gross," another one moaned. (It might
have been the same one who worried a few years ago that the
Christian market just wasn't ready for the word *cesspools* in my
best-selling book titled *Splashes of Joy in the Cesspools of Life*.)

"Well," I reminded them self-righteously, "you just need to
remember Philippians 4:8 and think on things that are pure
and lovely. Obviously, you've got *your* minds somewhere
else!" (Because I've been working with these dear people for
nearly a decade, I tend to offer them a little motherly advice
and scriptural insights now and then.)

As we continued "negotiating," I sent out a short list of title
options to a couple hundred friends and supporters of
Spatula Ministries, asking their opinions. The overwhelming
response from these women was that *leaking laffs* was the best
possible choice. As one woman wrote, "The word *changing* is
boring. *Leaking* is best!"

Meanwhile, back in Nashville, the W Publishing Group

executives were probably pulling their hair out and stocking up on extra-strength Maalox.

After several weeks of whining and begging (I whined, they begged), I had just about persuaded them to let me have my way when something happened that settled the issue once and for all. To express our appreciation for the artwork Precious Moments creator Sam Butcher had generously donated to my last book, *He's Gonna Toot and I'm Gonna Scoot*, W had graciously prepared a beautifully poignant plaque to give him. The presentation was made at the Women of Faith conference in Kansas City, after which some of my favorite W executives whisked us off to lunch at a cozy restaurant where we had a special room all to ourselves.

During lunch, I waited for a quiet moment, then, with the W people listening, I casually asked Sam for his opinion on the title I was proposing for my next book. The picture below shows Sam's merry response. He burst out laughing, rocking back and forth in his chair, and then added between guffaws, "And you could have babies in diapers crawling along the bottom of the cover and call them 'little squirts'!"

My delightful friend Sam Butcher, creator of Precious Moments, loved the title I proposed for this book.

Of course, this just about sent the frazzled W folks over the edge. Judging by the stiff smiles that seemed to be frozen on their sweet faces, I thought they all might be considering a career change at precisely that moment. But when they could speak again they swallowed hard and graciously nodded their assent (probably while wondering if their therapists offered telephone counseling on Saturday).

The "baby" had been named!

Later, Sam's sharp-witted assistant, Larrene Hagaman, pulled the whole idea together by suggesting the cover illustration: the Geranium Lady riding a waterspout that's shooting up through a small boat. At one end of the boat, Sam's "little squirt" is yowling away, and at the other end there's Larrene's "little squint" (who looks a little like Mammy Yokum), enjoying the ride. When Word's artist, Dennis Hill, sent me his depiction of these little characters, I knew they were too adorable to use just once. So you'll find them popping up again in the collections of jokes and stories that close out each chapter. In fact, I've called these chapter-closing giggles "Squirts & Squints," just because the whole idea makes me laugh!

Toot 'n' *What?*

Even when I have to work hard at negotiating (begging and whining) to get the book titles I want for my "babies," I enjoy every minute of it. All the whining just makes for a better story in the end, which I love to share with folks who ask, "Where in the world did you get that title?"

It's also fun to see how the titles get mangled and twisted. For example, after *Toot 'n' Scoot* was published last year, I got an early morning call from a lady in West Virginia who said, "I heard on the radio that you have a new book out, and I wanted to read it. But it's forty miles to the nearest Christian bookstore, so I want to make sure I get the right one. It sounded like you said the title is *Poop 'n' Scoop*. Could that be right?" And at my book table somewhere, a woman said she thought the title was called *Too Pooped to Scoot!*

Another woman sent a note to my publisher that said:

Barbara Johnson will love this . . . I sent my husband to the Christian bookstore to see if they had her new book, *He's Gonna Toot and I'm Gonna Scoot.* He proceeded to go in and ask for *One More Toot and I'm Gonna Move!* (I laughed 'til I cried!)

See what fun I'd miss if I didn't insist on giving my books such zany titles? Of course, I do get a little nervous when I think of the books' foreign translations, especially after reading the long list of nightmares someone sent to me that resulted when American companies' trade names were translated overseas. One of the marketing failures supposedly occurred when a company marketed a ballpoint pen in Mexico, where its ads were supposed to say, "It won't leak in your pocket and embarrass you." Instead, due to a faulty translation, the ads said, "It won't leak in your pocket and make you pregnant"!

Leaking Laffs, Soaking Up Love
Now, isn't this just like a new mother—spilling all the gory details of labor while visitors cuddle the baby? If you're a woman, I don't think you'll mind. In fact, you may want to send

HERMAN®

"Can't you ever get sick without
bringing home one of those?"

me your own "triumphant" stories of childbirth and parenting experiences—whatever you've birthed and experienced!

And if you're a man—well, buddy, hang on to your hairpiece! If you're gonna read *this* book, you'd better prepare yourself for some mental aerobics. And your eyebrows may get a workout, too, if they're not used to frequent lifting. Don't be embarrassed; I've learned to expect some men to let their curiosity get the better of them and read my books, even when they're warned not to. After we put a "For Women Only" disclaimer on the cover of *Estrogen,* I heard from one man who joked that he'd read it by flashlight while hiding in the closet. Another man said he had propped it open in front of a newsmagazine so fellow airplane passengers wouldn't give him a hard time as he read. What a delightful picture those men must have made!

Like that famous deodorant line, this book is "strong enough for a man—but made for a woman." Whoever you are, and wherever you are along the journey from Pampers to Depends, I hope you'll come along to share some "laff leaks" in this boatload of silliness. We're gonna have a fabulous time, splashing in laughter and soaking up God's love.

"...THE ONLY REAL PROBLEM IS I KEEP GETTING HIS 'PAMPERS' MIXED UP WITH MY 'DEPENDS'..."

Used by permission of the Kansas City Star.

Unless otherwise indicated, the sources of all the "squirts and squints" in this book are unknown; people who know how much I love to laugh have sent me these little ditties in letters or faxes or passed them to me on scraps of paper at Women of Faith conferences. I'm grateful to these unnamed writers, whoever they are. Their words have touched my heart—and tickled my funny bone.

Squirts & Squints

I love deadlines.

I especially like the *whooshing* sound they make as they go flying by!

A little boy told his preschool teacher one morning, "I have a disappointment I want to talk about in circle time."

"Ohhhh," said his teacher, worried he might be planning to spill some devastating family news. "Could you tell me first?"

"No," he replied solemnly. "I want to tell everyone."

She tried to persuade him to give her a preview of his "disappointment," but he stubbornly refused to say another word until his little classmates were assembled in the sharing-time circle.

Nervously, the teacher waited. When it was his turn, the little boy took a breath and started telling about lying down on a big chair that lifted him up toward a bright light. A man wearing a mask told him to open his mouth and then tapped on his teeth with something hard, he said.

It was then that the preschool teacher realized just what the little tike was describing: his *dentist appointment*.

—JULIE HENDRY

Think it over. Of all the creatures God created, we are the only ones that have to deal with diapers. Consider the lilies of the field; they neither toil nor spin nor clean up after their junior lily offspring. . . . [Perhaps] God deliberately chose to create our babies as hygienically challenged little people who require our extremely personal service several times each day . . . to ensure that we learn to perform a selfless act on behalf of a truly helpless person who cannot even thank us, doesn't really know what we are doing for him anyway, and, more likely than not, will [wet] on us for good measure. . . .

Changing the baby is sort of like giving alms in secret, only smellier.[3]

Some time ago, a tiny three-year-old daughter used a whole roll of gold wrapping paper to wrap a present for her father. Money was tight for the family, and when the little girl brought the gift to him, her father winced to see how much of the expensive paper had been used. Then his anger flared when he found that the box, so elaborately wrapped, was completely empty.

"Don't you know that when you give someone a present, there's supposed to be something inside of it?" he snapped. "You've wasted all this paper on an empty box."

The little girl looked up at him with tears in her eyes and said, "Oh, Daddy! It's not empty. I blew kisses into the box. They're for you, Daddy."

Each of us parents has been given a gold box filled with unconditional love from our children. There is no more precious possession anyone could hold.

When it's hard to go with the flow . . .
at least try to trickle!

—PATPRINTS CALENDAR

You know you're a mother when . . .

- You have time to shave only one leg at a time.
- You've mastered the art of placing large quantities of different foods on a plate without anything touching.
- You hear your own mother's voice coming out of your mouth.
- You use your own saliva to clean your child's face.

The boss urgently needed to speak to one of his employees on a Saturday afternoon. He dialed the employee's home number and was greeted with a child's whispered, "Hello?"

"Is your daddy home?" the boss asked.

"Yes," whispered the small voice.

"May I speak to him?" the boss queried.

"No," the little kid answered.

His patience running thin, the boss asked next, "Well, is your mommy there?"

"Yes," came the whispered reply.

"May I speak to her?"

Again the small voice whispered, "No."

Perplexed, the boss asked, "Well are there any other adults there?"

"Yes," the child whispered, "a policeman."

Stunned, the boss hesitated only a moment and then asked, "Well, may I speak with the policeman?"

"No, he's busy," whispered the child.

"Busy doing what?" the boss asked.

"Talking to Daddy and Mommy and the fireman," the child replied.

"There's a policeman and a fireman there?" the boss said, now beginning to get worried. "Why are they there?"

Still whispering, the young voice replied with a muffled giggle, "They're looking for *me!*"

When my friend Roger Shouse wrote to wish me "best of luck with the new book," he struggled to find the right phrase. "With actors they say, 'Break a leg.' But what do they tell authors? 'Get a cramp in the hand?' 'Hope your mind goes blank'?"

A little girl was diligently pounding away on her father's computer. She told him she was writing a story. "What's it about?" he asked.

"I don't know," she replied. "I can't read."

A grandmother wasn't sure her granddaughter had learned her colors yet, so she decided to test her. She repeatedly pointed out things and asked the tiny girl what color it was. The girl always answered correctly. But it was fun for the grandma, so she continued the game. Finally the little granddaughter headed for the door, saying sagely, "Grandma, I think you should try to figure out some of these yourself!"

The only time a woman wishes she were a year older is
when she is expecting a baby.

A woman took her small daughter to the funeral home for the viewing of her great-grandmother. Staring, perplexed, into the casket, the little girl asked, "Mama, why did they put Great-grandma in a jewelry box?"

Someone has equated laughter with changing a baby's diaper: "It doesn't change things permanently, but it makes everything OK for a while."

A couple invited some people to dinner. At the table, the father asked their six-year-old daughter to say the blessing.

"I don't know what to say," the girl replied.

"Just say what you hear Mommy say," the dad answered.

The daughter bowed her head, heaved a little sigh, and said, "Lord, why on earth did we invite all these people to dinner?"

An old country doctor went way out into the boonies to deliver a baby. It was so far out, there was no electricity. When the doctor arrived, no one was home except for the laboring mother and her five-year-old son. The doctor instructed the child to hold a lantern high so he could see to deliver the baby. The child held the lantern, the mother pushed, and after a little while, the doctor lifted the newborn baby by the feet and swatted him on the bottom to get him to take his first breath.

Watching in wide-eyed wonder, the five-year-old shouted, "Hit him again! He shouldn't have crawled up there in the first place!"

Little kids' instructions on life:

- When your dad is mad and asks you, "Do I look stupid?" don't answer him.
- Never try to baptize a cat.
- Never trust a dog to watch your food.
- Never tell your little brother that you're not going to do what your mom told you to do.
- Remember you're never too old to hold your father's hand.

I went to a bookstore and asked the saleswoman, "Where's the self-help section?"

She said if she told me, it would defeat the purpose.

—STEVEN WRIGHT

A mom was delivering a station wagon full of kids home from nursery school one day when a fire truck zoomed past. Sitting in the front seat beside the driver was a Dalmatian dog. The children began discussing the dog's duties.

"They use him to keep crowds back," said one youngster.

"No," said another, "he's just for good luck."

A third child brought the argument to a close. "They use the dog," she said firmly, "to find the fire hydrant."

A couple of young siblings were sitting together in church. Finally, the six-year-old sister had had enough of her little brother's giggling and talking out loud. "You're not supposed to talk out loud in church," she hissed at him.

"Why? Who's going to stop me?" the little boy challenged.

The big sister pointed to the back of the church and said, "See those two men standing by the door? They're *hushers*."

A mother was preparing pancakes for her sons, Kevin, five, and Ryan, three. The boys began to argue over who would get the first pancake. Their mother saw the opportunity for a moral lesson. "If Jesus were sitting here, He would say, 'Let my brother have the first pancake. I can wait.'"

There was a pause, and then Kevin turned to his younger brother and said, "Ryan, you be Jesus."[4]

"God has made me laugh. Everyone who hears about this will laugh with me."

—SARAH, AGED WIFE OF ONE-
HUNDRED-YEAR-OLD ABRAHAM,
UPON THE BIRTH OF THEIR SON,
ISAAC (GEN. 21:6 NCV)

Who Are These Kids, and Why Are They Calling Me Mom?

Babies and Other Terrorists . . .

The Women of Faith conference rolled into Kansas City over Mother's Day weekend last year, and we opened the newspaper that Sunday morning to find a colorful article featuring profiles of the area's wackiest moms: "a motherlode of moms who keep their kids in stitches," the headline proclaimed. Reading the profiles, I felt a strong bond with these zany mamas. Even though I'd never met any of them, I had a feeling it would be fun to get together with them and trade comedy secrets.

For example, there was this story one daughter told about her laughter-loving mother: "Many years ago, my mother was in the kitchen fixing dinner, washing this raw chicken. My sister and I walked in, and she stuck her hand inside the chicken, like a puppet, and she pulled up a wing and said, 'Wave to the girls! Wave to Jane! Wave to Ellen!' And she's dancing around with this chicken. We stood there with our mouths hanging open. Now we almost can't eat chicken—it's like eating a friend."

Another girl tattled that her mother cleaned house wearing

"pink and red tutus." When the kids misbehaved, the daughter said, this mom took mug shots of them and then fingerprinted them as though she were booking them for the lockup.

As a gift for another mom's seventieth birthday her children "made up a booklet of all the goofy, weird things she's done over the years—she's pulled some real lulus." One incident described when she took her car to the mechanic because the motor was racing. That was back when cars had a manual choke knob on the dashboard. "She had pulled the choke out a foot and a half and was using it to hang her purse on," her adult son wrote fondly.

The newspaper included several more accounts by children who had written the newspaper to describe the gift of laughter their mothers had given them.[1] One daughter wrote that she had learned from her mother, "With enough practice, joy becomes as natural as breathing, and such a habit that it just comes out of your body."[2]

Reading those stories, I started to think maybe I wasn't such a weird parent after all. So what if I had joined my boys all those years ago in flicking red Jell-O on the white kitchen wall? And maybe I wasn't so odd in tricking my son Steve into thinking I'd accidentally boiled his favorite green wool sweater (I left a cute little doll's sweater, exactly the same color, in its place in his drawer).

A mother's love is one of the most important things a child can ever know. But there's another gift that enriches a child's life beyond measure. Blessed indeed are the children whose memories are filled with the familiar sound of their mother's laughter entwined with their own.

The Evolution of a Mom

As you might guess, I love to laugh. It's been one of the strongest fibers in the lifeline God has used to pull me from a variety of heartbreaking pits—my husband's devastating accident, the deaths of two sons, and the eleven-year alienation of another. If I hadn't been able to find some laughter in all these ordeals, I'd surely be making potholders today in a mental ward or bouncing around in a padded cell somewhere!

Instead, I'm blessed with a very active speaking career, in addition to my work with Spatula Ministries. As you read in Chapter 1, my "babies" these days are made of paper and ink instead of flesh and blood, but there are still a lot of similarities between becoming an author and becoming a parent. And no matter what you title *your* baby, you'll surely agree that the process of becoming a parent changes everything.

Indeed, there is an evolution to becoming a mother that is an ever-ongoing thing. Recently I saw another book that emphasized this point. It was entitled *So You Thought You Were Done with It!* and it exemplified that parenthood is never over. As I like to say, once you become a mother it's like getting a life sentence in prison with no hope of parole! And no matter how old we get, we mothers watch our kids—even when they're middle-aged—for signs of improvement. We're always hoping that something we instilled in them MIGHT show up, even when we've started to think it's too late.

Committed

Yes, becoming a parent changes everything, but parenthood itself also changes with each baby. For example, consider your wardrobe. As soon as the pregnancy home test kit confirms that you're pregnant, you head for the mall—and come home wearing a maternity outfit. With the second baby, you squeeze into your regular clothes as long as possible.

With the third baby, your maternity clothes ARE your regular clothes!

Then there's your preparation for labor and delivery. With the first baby you attend weekly classes and faithfully practice your breathing. With the second baby, you try to keep breathing when you find your two-year-old teetering at the top of the basement stairs.

With the third baby, you threaten to hold your breath indefinitely unless the doctor gives you an epidural in your second trimester!

Collecting the first baby's layette is always fun. You spend hours shopping for just the right curtains, blankets, and crib ruffle and the carefully prewash the tiny little gowns and booties with Woolite. For the second baby, you adjust the curtains and ruffles so the projectile-vomiting stains don't show and bleach everything else in hot water to disinfect it.

With the third child . . . you move to Florida so the baby needs no clothes at all—just disposable diapers.

A new baby can cause overwhelming fatigue, so parents adapt different stress-coping strategies with each child. For instance, with the first baby, you worry so much about the baby's cries that you never put the infant down—you wear her constantly in a baby carrier strapped to your chest. When the second baby cries, you pick him up only when his hysterics threaten to wake up your firstborn.

With the third child, you teach your other two kids where to look for the pacifier and how to rewind the baby swing.

Parents' dealings with baby-sitters also change. The first time you leave your baby with a sitter, you conduct a two-hour training session for the caregiver, then call home four times while you run to the post office. With the second baby, just before you walk out the door you remember to leave an emergency phone number—your neighbor's.

With the third baby, you tell the sitter to call only if someone needs stitches, splints, or an ambulance.

Baby activities change too. You take your first infant to baby swim classes, baby aerobics, and baby massage. You take your second baby to baby story hour so you can nap while the story is read.

You take the third baby to the McDonald's drive-through.

You use your time differently as each child comes along. You spend hours each day staring adoringly at your precious first infant. With the second baby, you glance in her direction occasionally as you race to stop your toddler from dropping the cat down the laundry chute.

With the third child, you train the dog to guard the baby from his siblings a few hours each day while you hide in the closet.

While I love to laugh *now* at such silly evolutions, I do remember that babies can be fabulous—and lots of fun. A baby is a small member of the family who can make the love stronger, the days shorter, the nights longer, and the bankroll

© 1999. Reprinted courtesy of Bunny Hoest and Parade magazine.

"Your father and I have *always* wanted more children. It's not a reflection on your performance."

smaller. When a baby is born, the home will be happier—even if the clothes are shabbier. The past is forgotten, and the future is worth living for. And when *more* babies come along, the work is multiplied, that's true; but so are the joy and the love.

We mothers of multiple children like to say we love all our kids equally, but in our heart of hearts, we know that's not true. It's like the mother of several children answered when a reporter asked her, "Which of your children do you love the most?"

The wise and loving mother replied, "I love the one most who is away from home until he returns; the one who is sick until he is well; the one who is hurt until the hurt disappears; and the one who is lost until he is found."[3]

Moms and Angels
Once children come along, a woman's identity is changed irrevocably. There's no feeling on earth like the twist of the

THE FAMILY CIRCUS.   By Bil Keane

Reprinted with permission of Bil Keane.

"I know why the car pool's so late, Mommy! This is OUR morning to drive!"

heart at that moment when a tiny youngster links that syllable, *Ma,* with the face of its mother. A connection is formed, and whether it evolves into the name Mom or Mama or Mother, it is a name that is as common as breath itself—and as unique as each set of two hearts it links.

Someone sent me a beautiful bookmark that says, "On the day we are born, God gives each of us a beautiful guardian angel: and as we grow, we give her a name . . . Mother."

Then there's this beautiful little essay:

The Angel

Up in heaven a child was ready to be born. The child asked God, "I know You are sending me to earth tomorrow, but how can I survive there? I am so small and helpless."

God replied, "I have chosen a special angel for you there. She will love you and take care of you."

"Here in heaven, Lord, I don't do anything but sing and smile. What will I do on Earth? I won't know how to sing the songs down there."

"Your angel will sing for you," God replied, "and she'll teach you how to sing, too. And you'll learn to laugh as well as smile. Your angel and I will take care of that."

"But how will I understand what people say to me? I don't know a single word of the language they speak!"

"Your angel will say the sweetest things you will ever hear, and she will teach you, word by word, how to speak the language."

"And when I want to talk to You . . . ?"

"Your angel will gently place your little hands together and teach you how. That's the simplest language of all. It's called prayer."

"Who will protect me there, God?"

"Your angel is soft and gentle, but if something threatens you, there is no stronger force on Earth than the power she'll use to defend you."

"I'll be sad not getting to see You anymore."

"I will always be next to you, even though you can't see Me. And your angel will teach you the way to come back to Me if you stray."

Then it was time to go. Excited voices could be heard from earth, anticipating the child's arrival. In a hurry, the babe asked softly, "Oh, God, if I must go now, please tell me my angel's name!"

And God replied, "You will call your angel . . . *Mommy.*"

—SOURCE UNKNOWN

Are You Ready for Motherhood?
Now, if you're wondering whether you have what it takes to be a *mommy,* here's a list of preparations to help you get ready for the blessed event:

Mother's Preparation for Pregnancy: From the food co-op, obtain a twenty-five-pound bag of pinto beans and attach it to your waist with a belt. Wear it everywhere you go for nine months. Then remove ten of the beans to indicate the baby has been born.

Financial Preparation: Arrange for direct deposit of your family's paycheck to be split equally between the nearest grocery store and the pediatrician's office for the next two decades.

Mess-Management Preparation: Smear grape jelly on the living room furniture and curtains. Now plunge your hands into a bag of potting soil, wipe them on the walls, and highlight the smudges with Magic Markers.

Inhalation Therapy Preparation: Empty a carton of milk onto the cloth upholstery of the family car, park the vehicle in a sunny spot, and then leave it to ripen for the month of August. Rub a half-finished lollipop through your hair, then hide it in the glove compartment.

Pain-Endurance Preparation: Collect enough small, plastic, superhero action figures to fill a fifty-five gallon drum.

(You may substitute thumbtacks.) Ask a friend to spread them all over the floor of your house after you've gone to bed, paying special attention to the stairway. Set your alarm for 2 A.M., and when it goes off, rush madly around the darkened house, trying to remember where you left the cordless phone (for the baby).

Shopping Preparation: Herd a flock of goats through the grocery store. Always keep every goat in sight and bring enough money to pay for whatever they eat or destroy.

Aerobic-Agility Preparation: Try to dress the family cat in a small pantsuit, complete with button shirt, snap-leg pants, lace-up shoes, and a bowtie while the neighbor's German shepherd barks out his encouragement from two feet away. (Make sure medics are standing by.)

Mealtime Preparation: Sit at the kitchen counter and carefully spoon strained peas and chocolate pudding into a plastic bag. When the bag is completely full, tie a knot to close it, place it on the kitchen counter at eye level about a foot from your face, then ask your spouse to smash the bag with a dictionary.

Attitude Preparation: Have a schoolteacher friend record the sounds of her second-graders scratching their fingernails across a chalkboard. Then fill a small canvas bag with ten pounds of cat litter, soak it thoroughly in water, attach the bag to a tape player with large speakers, and insert the nails-on-chalkboard recording. Beginning at 8 P.M., pick up the bag and hold it against your shoulder, play the chalkboard recording at its loudest volume, and waltz around the room with a bumping-and-swooping step. Continue for forty minutes, then gently lay down the bag and turn off the tape player. Repeat hourly until 5 A.M. Then crawl in bed, set the alarm for 6 A.M., get up and make breakfast while looking cheerful. Repeat for the next five years.

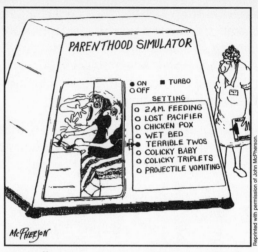

In an effort to prepare expectant parents for the challenges that lie ahead, many obstetricians' offices have installed parenthood simulators.

The funny thing about these silly preparations is that somehow all of us parents pass it when we have to. (Well, maybe not the part about looking cheerful while cooking breakfast, but the rest of it, we usually muddle through.) If you're in the middle of the "testing" period right now, remember that you're enrolled in a course that's been a perpetual requirement since Adam and Eve. You *will* get through it (unless, of course, you end up weaving doilies in the home for the bewildered first!). And *someday* you'll be rewarded. As actress Meryl Streep commented recently, "You don't really read the results of [your mothering efforts] until way late in life. Usually, it's the adult child who looks back and thinks: How did she do all of that? How did she stay in a good mood all the time? . . . If you're a mom, you know how much you're doing, but you're not going to get a lot of credit for it. Mothering is an invisible achievement."[4]

Help from Above

Mothers need all the help they can get these days to achieve their overwhelming goal, even though a recent study showed that "motherhood may actually make women smarter." The increased intellect is due to "hormones released during pregnancy and nursing [that] dramatically enrich parts of the brain involved in learning and memory."[5] When I saw that, I thought, *Wow! Just when we feel so exhausted we can hardly remember our own names, we're actually Einsteins in training!* How about that! Now if someone could just figure out how we could work on updating the theory of relativity while changing diapers, scraping *Star Wars* stickers off the car windows, and counting the sprinkles on cupcakes to make sure no one is shortchanged—we'd have it made!

No matter how smart we are, weary mothers need lots of help and encouragement—the kind that comes from family and friends, and especially the kind that comes from God. But sometimes we get so busy—and so exhausted—we forget to tap into this ultimate resource. Sometimes all it takes is a reminder. One friend of mine, the mother of two trying teenagers, bought herself a cheap digital watch that she set to softly chime every hour. "Throughout the day, whenever I heard that little beep," she said, "I paused a moment or two in whatever I was doing and whispered a little prayer on behalf of my kids."

She told her teenagers what she was doing, and the results were amazing. Her daughter, stressed out in her high school

ZITS

classroom and unable to focus on the test that lay on the desk before her, happened to look up at the clock. "It said ten o'clock, and I remembered that you were praying for me," she told her mother one day. "It was as if a very calming blanket of peace gently wrapped itself around me, and I was able to clear my head and finish the test." Her son confessed to similar results a few years later. "When I was a senior, there was one day when school was out for the day, and my buddies and I were out in the parking lot, talking about what we would do for the rest of the afternoon. They all decided that instead of going to their after-school jobs, they would hang out at the shopping mall awhile and see if there were any good-looking girls there. I was all set to go with them, but just then the bell in the church tower across the street chimed three o'clock, and I suddenly got an image of my mom, praying for me at that exact moment. I got in my car and went to work."

Last year many of us got a different kind of reminder to pray as we traveled city streets and interstate highways. The reminders were scattered all across the nation in the outdoor advertising industry's national public service campaign called "God Speaks." The messages appeared on ten thousand billboards throughout America, catching motorists' attention with their stark white letters on a solid black background. "We need to talk," one of them said. Like all the others, it was signed, "God."

The idea was started by a Florida resident who insisted on remaining anonymous but "wanted to reach people who used to go to church and for some reason don't go anymore," an advertising executive explained. Other messages in the campaign included:

- "C'mon over and bring the kids."

- "Will the road you're on get you to my place?"

- "Follow me."

- "Need directions?"

The one that touched my heart most tenderly was the one that said simply,

Tell the kids I love them.

—GOD[6]

Someone sent me a little prayer aid that's not only helpful for us parents to use but especially to teach to our children and grandchildren. It's a simple way to pray for others and ourselves by counting off the fingers of one hand. Its author is unknown, but I suspect she was a mother!

1. When you clasp your hands in prayer, your thumb is closest to you. So begin your prayer by remembering those closest to you—your children, parents, friends, and other loved ones.

2. The pointing finger is next. Pray for those who point the way for us: our teachers, ministers, mentors, and others who help us learn. Ask God to give them wisdom and courage to guide others in His truth and in His way.

3. The middle finger is the tallest one, reminding us to pray for our leaders in government, in business, and in our schools and churches. Ask God to help them heed His ways as they shape our nation and make decisions that affect all of us.

4. The ring finger is next. You might not realize it, but this finger, not the pinkie, is our weakest finger. Let it remind you to pray for those who are weak or sick or in trouble. Ask God to show them that they are weak but He is strong.

5. Then comes the smallest finger of all. This littlest finger reminds us that we are to put others before ourselves, even in prayer. By the time you have prayed for the needs of the other four groups of people—your loved ones, your teachers, your leaders, and those who

are sick and in trouble, your own needs will probably seem much less important. The little finger reminds us to pray for ourselves—and to hold to the Bible's promise that "the least shall be the greatest among you."

Whether you're reminded to pray by the beeping of a digital watch or by the sound of the phone ringing in the wee hours of the morning, if you're a mom you know prayer helps. One stage of parenting that generates *lots* of fervent prayers is surely the time when we're teaching our kids how to drive. Later—if we survive the high blood pressure and accelerated heart rates—the memories of these parent-and-teenager driving sessions can be funny, if not especially soothing. In my case, the memory of when I taught our son Tim to drive has become a cherished frozen picture in my mental scrapbook.

We went to a nearby cemetery so Tim could learn how to negotiate the narrow, curving roadway that wound through the grounds. It was the perfect place since the speed limit was about 15 and there usually weren't any other cars we could bump into. Still, there were a few screeches of the brakes and some wandering off the pavement occasionally. Now I laugh at those memories, and I'm so grateful for them when I go to that same cemetery . . . to visit Tim's grave.

Murray's Law by Leslie Moak Murray

He was teaching his daughter to drive and he froze that way.

It isn't easy being a mom, but prayer helps—and so does laughter. And sometimes it even helps to shed a cleansing tear or two. As someone said, tears are to the soul what soap is to the body. So let's end this chapter with both—jokes and tender stories about parenthood—squirts of tears and squints from the laughter.

Squirts & Squints

Bumper Sticker:
If you can't laugh at yourself . . .
I'll be glad to do it for you.

If I had my child to raise all over again,
I'd finger paint more, and point the finger less.
I'd do less correcting, and more connecting.
I'd take my eyes off my watch, and watch with my eyes.
I would care to know less, and know to care more.
I'd take more hikes and fly more kites.
I'd stop playing serious, and seriously play.
I'd run through more fields, and gaze at more stars.
I'd do more hugging, and less tugging.
I would be firm less often, and affirm much more.
I'd build self-esteem first, and the house later.
I'd teach less about the love of power,
And more about the power of love.

—Diane Loomans[7]

Things moms would probably never say:
—"How on earth can you see the TV sitting so far back?"
—"Yeah, I used to skip school a lot, too."

—"Just leave all the lights on . . . we have extra money this month for the bill."

—"Let me smell that shirt. Yeah, that's good for another week."

—"Go ahead and keep that stray dog, honey; I'll be glad to take care of it for you."

—"Well, if Timmy's mom says it's okay, that's good enough for me!"

—"The curfew is just a general time to shoot for—give or take three or four hours."

—"I don't have a tissue with me . . . just wipe your nose on your sleeve."

—"Don't bother wearing a jacket. The wind chill is bound to improve."[8]

The heart of a mother is a deep abyss at the bottom of which you will always discover forgiveness.

—HONORÉ DE BALZAC

A teacher asked her Sunday school class to draw pictures of their favorite Bible stories. She was puzzled by Jimmy's picture, which showed four people on an airplane. She asked him what story he meant.

"The flight to Egypt," Jimmy said.

"I see. And that must be Mary, Joseph, and Baby Jesus," the teacher answered. "But who's the fourth person?"

"Oh, that's Pontius—the pilot!"

More truths brought to us by children:
—Don't let your mom brush your hair when she's mad at your dad.
—If your sister hits you, don't hit her back. It's always the second person who gets caught.
—Dogs still have bad breath even after a squirt of breath freshener.
—Never hold the cat while the vacuum cleaner is running.
—When you're in trouble the best place to be is in Grandma's lap.

I note with great interest that when God made the first human being, Adam, He created him as a complete adult and thus totally bypassed diapers, colic, toddlerhood, adolescence, and driving lessons. . . .

My personal theory is that God designed parenthood, in part, as an enormous character-building exercise, and since God does not personally require character improvement, He didn't need to bother getting Adam to eat strained peas.[9]

After putting her children to bed, a mother changed into old slacks and a droopy blouse and then washed her hair in the sink and smeared her face with a slick, green moisturizing cream that hardened into a mask. As she heard the children getting more and more rambunctious, her patience evaporated. At last she threw a towel around her dripping hair and stormed into their room, threatening all sorts of dire punishments if they didn't get back into bed and go to sleep.

As she left the room, she heard a small voice whisper in the darkness, "Who *was* that?"

"I'm grounded. I said one more word to my mother."

At the end of the school year, a kindergarten teacher was receiving gifts from her pupils. The florist's son handed her a gift. She shook it, held it overhead, and said, "I bet I know what it is: some flowers."

"That's right," the boy said, "but how did you know?"

"Oh, just a wild guess," she answered.

The next pupil was the sweet-shop owner's daughter. The teacher held her gift overhead, shook it, and said, "I'll bet this is a box of sweets."

"How did you know?" the little girl asked.

"Oh, just a wild guess," the teacher answered.

The next gift was from the son of the liquor store owner. The teacher held the package overhead, but it was leaking. She touched a drop of the leakage with her finger and touched it to her tongue. "Is it wine?" she asked with a smile.

"No-o-o-o," the boy replied with some excitement.

The teacher repeated the process, taking a larger drop of the leakage to her tongue. "Is it champagne?" she asked.

"No-o-o-o-o," the boy replied again with even greater excitement.

The teacher took one more taste before declaring, "I give up. What is it?"

With great glee the little boy shouted, "It's a puppy!"

You spend a lot of parenthood on the sidelines, loving from a distance, sensing your heart twist and turn with delight and regret while your child is happily and properly oblivious of what you're enduring.

It will be like this for the next twenty years, and someday I'll probably accept it, this rule of parenthood as fixed as a law of physics: From your child's point of view, it's never okay when you leave, but it's always okay when she does.[10]

A mother watched as her daughter hopped off the school bus and scampered toward her house in a pouring rainstorm. As the little girl ran toward the house, a lightning bolt flashed and the little girl stopped, looked up toward the sky and smiled, then began running back toward the house.

Another lightning bolt flashed, and again the little girl stopped, looked toward the sky, and smiled before running once more toward the open door of her house.

When the little girl finally arrived in the house, her mother immediately asked about her strange behavior. "Why did you keep stopping and smiling at the sky?" she asked her daughter.

"I had to, Mommy," the little girl explained. "God was taking my picture."

Raising teenagers is like nailing Jell-O to the wall.

Two things every mom needs: Velcro arms and a Teflon heart.

[Moms] are the world's greatest actresses. We have to act as if our heart isn't breaking when our child comes home from school crying because he doesn't have any friends. And yet we will never receive an Academy Award. . . . We are the most overworked and underpaid occupation there is. And yet, we are the most important.[11]

You had my mother give birth to me. You made me trust you while I was just a baby. I have leaned on you since the day I was born; you have been my God since my mother gave me birth.

—PSALM 22:9–10 NCV

How to Be a Joyful Woman—
Take Up Acting

*Practicing Random Acts of Intelligence
and Senseless Acts of Self-Control*

Several friends from around the country recently sent me the same wire service article they had clipped from newspapers in their area. The first paragraph warned, "Speaking in public may be more than just terrifying. The stress may be deadly."[1] The article cited a study that had shown "public speaking is a particularly potent trigger" of a dangerous heart problem.

For some folks, the fear of public speaking may cause "risky mental stress," as the article predicts, but it just doesn't work that way for me. Once I'm onstage, I feel as if a blanket of love is surrounding me as I look out and see all those upturned faces so eagerly waiting to hear my message. Nervousness and fear just aren't a problem for me.

But there have been a few exceptions recently. For instance, last spring when I got to introduce Precious Moments creator Sam Butcher to a large audience in Kansas City, I was surprised to find my heart pounding away and my palms getting sweaty. For a moment there I even thought I felt my knees knocking together! *So this is what it feels like to be terrified in front of a microphone,* I thought.

Another time when Marilyn Meberg and I were speaking together at a conference, Marilyn kept swatting at a very persistent fly that continually buzzed around her head as she spoke. When it was my turn to speak, the same fly was doing his aerial antics in front of my face, and when I caught a big breath to join in the laughter, I sucked the little bug right down my windpipe! I coughed and sputtered—and then plucked a tiny little wing off the tip of my tongue.

Such incidents make for some memorable moments. But the real stress-maker I encounter as a public speaker doesn't occur while I'm standing on the stage. The stress comes from the problems I have trying to *get* to the stage—or to the city or the hotel or the arena. Some of the crazy escapades we've managed to survive make me agree with the guy who said, "I don't mind traveling—except when I have to be away from home!"

Here are a few glimpses into the life of this over-the-hill road warrior:

One time Bill and I were flying into Memphis, and our plane arrived hours late—after midnight. There was no transportation to the hotel—all the taxis had apparently gone to roost for the night. The only good thing that happened—and it was one of those mixed blessings—was that we had no luggage to drag around in our weary state. Our luggage was lost! By the time we got to the hotel and into our room, we were both exhausted. Still, I had trouble deciding what to wear to bed since we had no luggage. I just never was one to sleep in my underwear, so instead I wrapped a big bath towel around my torso and held it in place with three of the big, round button pins I carry with me—the ones that say, "Someone Jesus loves has AIDS." It wasn't the most comfortable night I'd ever spent, but mercifully, it was short!

The Women of Faith tour arranges contracts with local transportation companies to shuttle the conference speakers, singers, and staff members between airports and hotels in the various cities. Sometimes we ride in a van or a regular car;

other times a limo shows up. (Frankly, the limos are the vehicles I like the least. They have enough seats to haul a symphony orchestra—but only enough trunk space to accommodate the piccolos!)

The handsome young limo driver who met us at the San Antonio airport told us his "real" job as a firefighter made moonlighting for the limo service a perfect second job for him, since as a firefighter he knew the city like the back of his hand. We chatted pleasantly as he drove us to our hotel. As he whipped the big car into the hotel's circle drive, bellmen scurried to open doors and help us crawl out of the backseat. While they hurriedly began unloading the six heavy pieces of luggage belonging to Bill, my helper, and me, we hustled into the lobby to check in. The hotel was a grand old palace, with beautiful oak paneling and historic markers and all sorts of impressive fixtures. We were thrilled to get to stay in such a remarkable place!

At the front desk, I smiled at the clerk and told her my name. She typed it into her computer, frowned slightly, then typed some more.

"What did you say your name was, ma'am?" she asked.

"Barbara Johnson—I'm one of the speakers at the Women of Faith conference," I said happily, flashing her my best smile.

She typed and scowled some more.

"What conference was that again, ma'am?"

"The Women of Faith conference—we're all staying here. You should have lots of reservations for the conference. The others should already be here."

The desk clerk swallowed hard and finally raised her eyes to look carefully into my face, probably checking for signs of senility. Slowly she asked, "Ma'am? What hotel do you think you're at?"

"Why, the Hyatt!" I said confidently.

There was a pause as the poor woman arranged her face into an apologetic and sympathetic smile.

"Ma'am, this hotel is the Menger."

Our limo driver—who knew the city like the back of his hand and who, by this time, had driven off into the sunset—had left us at the wrong hotel! And there was no way our six suitcases and three hefty-size bodies would fit in an ordinary taxi to get to the Hyatt, some blocks away. So there we stood, back in the circle drive with our mountain of bags, looking like befuddled pilgrims who'd just missed the bus of life. As we waited forlornly, the bellman frantically tried to find someone who could haul us away to the Hyatt.

In Detroit, we made it to the right hotel—with our luggage—at the right time. But a primary water main had been cut, and the whole suburb was without water. Immediately, I developed an overwhelming thirst and felt myself shriveling up in what I assumed was fatal dehydration. The conference would have to be canceled, we were told. The fire marshal refused to let us occupy the arena when there was no water to fight any fires that might occur. But the prayers went up, and the blessings came down, and enough water pressure was restored just in time for the event to go on as planned. The only thing different was the signs posted in all the rest rooms, warning the women that the water in the sinks and toilets was not drinkable!

In Atlanta we were thrilled to stay on the forty-second floor of one of the tallest hotels in America—thrilled, that is, until a 911 call from a hotel guest caused the elevators to be locked down in emergency mode. It happened just as hundreds of conference women were returning to the hotel after the evening session. Luci, Patsy, Marilyn, and I walked into the lobby to be met by a huge wall of women, waiting wearily for the elevators to be turned back on. The quick-witted Luci immediately sized up the situation and shouted, "Dibs on the devo!" (We're all constantly looking for new material to go in the books of devotions—we call them "devos"—that we write together every year.)

Somehow one of the gals found an express elevator that would stop only on the upper floors, beginning with the level three floors above ours. We squeezed in, rode up, and then walked down the three flights of stairs. (Tell Luci you saw it here first!)

These are just a few of the highlights. There are many more—like the sweet, helpful hostess who showed up in a sporty two-door coupe to chauffeur my two plus-size helpers and me along with our various suitcases and boxes from the hotel to the arena. What a sight we were when it was time to unload! Folks gathered around, thinking it was one of those circus acts where assorted boxes and bags come hurtling out of a tiny Volkswagen, followed by a seemingly impossible stream of big-bodied clowns.

In another city we were assigned a thoughtful hostess who was afraid to drive in traffic, so she brought along her husband—who (like so many other husbands) refused to ask for directions and got completely lost on the way to the arena.

In Birmingham, our hostess thoughtfully whisked us out to a huge suburban shopping mall for thirty minutes of "aerobic shopping" on Friday afternoon before the conference. We were so eager to get inside and discover all there was to see, we failed to note which door we had entered! So when it was time to meet the hostess back at that same door, we had no idea where it was or even what store it was in! Completely befuddled, all I could think to tell the kind officer who tried to help us was that I vaguely remembered seeing a mannequin in a purple dress. . . .

Now, none of these incidents were any fun while we were *living* them, but it's sure fun to *relive* them now—knowing we survived! As each new travelogue misadventure unfolds, it's much easier to keep a smile on my face when I focus on the fun I'll have in telling the story—just as soon as the chaos and calamity end.

The Sandwich Stage

Whether you're a traveler or a stay-at-home woman, you probably have your own sources of stress and chaos. Some of the most overstressed women these days are those who find themselves sandwiched between the exhausting job of tending their own children while also dealing with parents who are suffering health problems or slipping into dementia—and who sometimes live hundreds or even thousands of miles away. Throw in a full-time career and/or a husband who's dealing with a similar set of parent problems, and you've got the perfect launch pad for a trip to instant insanity!

Sometimes during this stage you don't have a lot of choices about how you spend your time. You simply stumble along from one crisis to the next. There are hundreds of women out there like the one who told me her husband was out of the country on business and she had been rushing to finish a big project at work when her widowed mother, who lived a thousand miles away, required emergency surgery. The woman slept on a little cot in her mother's hospital room for several days, struggling to complete her work assignment with a laptop computer and cell phone while also tending to her mom and dealing with her two teenagers' needs—places to stay while she was away plus rides to school, church, and soccer practice—from halfway across the country. While she was there she got word that her sister-in-law, who lived alone in a city another thousand miles away, had life-threatening cancer and was also undergoing emergency surgery. Then one of her kids called and nonchalantly told her he'd gotten his tongue pierced and that the family cat had been acting strange and now refused to come out from behind the refrigerator. The refrigerator had stopped working, they hadn't heard the cat meowing in quite a while, he said, and they feared the worst.

When we're trapped in these impossible predicaments we don't have a lot of choices. Our lives seem to be controlled by whatever blow hits us next, sending us lurching from headache to heartache to horror story. But we *can* choose how we respond emotionally. We *can* choose to hold on to the One who promises never to leave us, no matter how insane our schedules get.

And we can choose to laugh.

Now, I know very well that being a joyful woman can

sometimes be a challenge. But it's like that little message someone imagined coming from God:

> I didn't say it would be easy.
> I said it would be worth it!

What I'd really like to do when the plane is late or the luggage is lost or the elevators aren't working is get upset—start whining and moaning. Other times I want to be mad; I want to raise my voice, harden my heart, tighten up my face, and unload a sharp tongue-lashing to whatever unfortunate soul happens to cross my path at that moment. But, frankly, I've tried those choices and neither one is satisfying. Oh, sure, there's a momentary release of pressure as I vent my frustration and speak my mind. But just as quickly I regret my thoughtless words and harsh remarks.

And yet, I can't remember *ever* regretting a kind word I somehow managed to share in tense times. Or a smile I forced onto my lips when I really wanted to scowl. Or a giggle that bubbled up instead of a complaint.

A Matter of Perspective

One of the people I admire most when it comes to laughing in the face of misery is my friend Joni Eareckson Tada. What a gift she has for bringing joy into the most trying situations! Paralyzed in a diving accident, Joni has spent the last thirty-plus years in a motorized wheelchair. She writes inspiring books, paints beautiful pictures, and heads a ministry called Joni and Friends, which focuses on inspiring, helping, and sharing God's love with other wheelchair-bound Christians around the world.

Thank heaven Joni was with us at a California venue when another "misadventure"—actually quite a serious problem—occurred during a Women of Faith conference. Somehow a misunderstanding had occurred, and the conference was seriously oversold. As a result, hundreds of women showed up to attend the conference—and found *other* women already sitting in their assigned seats—and holding ticket stubs to prove they were right! The conference coordinators put out a frantic call for chairs and eventually managed to borrow some narrow, hard folding chairs from a funeral home. The seats were hastily arranged in a dark basement area of the arena, and television monitors were wheeled in so the women could see—if they had really good eyes!

As you might imagine, there were quite a few impatient and disgruntled women in that crowded room! After all, they had bought tickets like everyone else, and there they sat on those cold, hard chairs. They were still muttering when the lights were dimmed and the program began. The women in the little folding chairs leaned forward, squinting to see the monitors. Joni was the first main speaker. As she sat peacefully in her wheelchair, the tiny elevator beside the stage silently lifted her up to the platform. She motored out to the center of the stage and smiled into the cameras, greeting the thousands of listeners with her melodic alto voice.

"I hear that some of you aren't too happy with your chairs tonight," she said with a warm smile. She slowly rotated her wheelchair so she could look out at the audience all the way around her. "I certainly understand your feelings," she continued, her smile never waning. "I *hate* my chair!"

There was a little collective gasp from the audience as Joni's words sank in while all eyes took in the sight of her frail, slim body strapped into the wheelchair. "And you know what?" Joni asked, her eyes twinkling merrily. "I have a thousand friends who would *gladly* change chairs with you right now!"

Suddenly the tension was eased in the vast auditorium— and in the dark, cramped basement—and twenty thousand women had a new perspective on the evening.

Joni's words that night remind me of a story someone sent to me. It described a successful young executive who tried a new shortcut on his way to work one morning and ended up getting lost in a forsaken neighborhood of abandoned storefronts and bleak-looking tenements. He was nervous about driving his sleek new sports car through the ghetto, and he

KUDZU

was frustrated because instead of saving time he now would be late for work.

Suddenly a brick sailed out from between two abandoned cars with no tires that were parked at the curb. The executive slammed on the brakes, threw the car into reverse, and angrily spun the sports car back to the spot where the brick had been thrown. A skinny adolescent stood on the sidewalk, waiting expectantly for the man to roll down the window.

"What do you think you're doing?" the man shouted angrily at the kid. Just *what* are you doing?" Building up a head of steam, he ranted on, "You just put a five-thousand-dollar dent in my new car, kid! I hope you enjoyed throwing that brick, cause it's gonna cost you a lot of money!"

"Please, mister," the boy replied. "I didn't know what else to do!"

That's when the man noticed the tears sliding down the boy's cheeks and dripping off his chin. "It's my brother, mister," he said. "We was goin' to school, but he rolled off the curb and fell out of his wheelchair behind that car there, and I can't lift him up." Now sobbing, the boy asked the executive, "Would you please help me get him back into his wheelchair? He's hurt, and he's too heavy for me."

Stunned, the young executive jumped from the sleek sports car and hurried to where the brother lay crumpled in a storm drain set into the curb. He easily lifted the young boy back into the wheelchair, a dilapidated contraption with one bent wheel and a rip in the back of the vinyl seat. He wiped the lad's scrapes and cuts with his handkerchief and gently checked him over to make sure he was okay. Once the problem was fixed, the two boys' tears evaporated. The man was amazed to hear the pair giggling and teasing each other as they prepared to resume their trip to the nearby school, a sad-looking bunker-like structure surrounded by a stark concrete playground and an eight-foot-high chain-link fence.

The man watched the younger boy push his brother down the sidewalk, stunned to hear their merry chatter resume so quickly after near-calamity had struck. As the pair turned the corner, the boy turned back to flash a bright smile at the man and wave his thanks.

It was a long walk back to the sports car. The man never did fix the dent in the door. He kept it there awhile to remind him of the new perspective the boys had given him. Eventually the thrill of driving the car evaporated, and he traded it in for a pickup. He often takes the same shortcut to work, but now he takes his time, always watching for two young boys, one pushing the other in a wheelchair. He remembers the bent wheel and the torn backrest, and if he should see them again, he wants to be ready to help.

The boys in that story gave the busy executive the same gift Joni instantly shared with all the women at the conference who found themselves in an uncomfortable situation. With a bright smile and gentle words, she showed us again how to "count it all joy."[2]

What kind of perspective do *you* bring to unpleasant situations? Do you add to the gloom or introduce joy? Do you join in the grumbling or find something to laugh about? Do you follow our Lord's example and lift the spirits of "those bent beneath their loads"?[3]

Three Little Words
One of my favorite periodicals is the wonderful little *Bits &*

Pieces booklet that comes in the mail fourteen times a year. A recent *Bits & Pieces* supplement was titled, "The Three Most Powerful Words in the English Language." Being quite a know-it-all when it comes to spiritual matters, I assumed the words were "I love you" or "God is good" or even "Please, take mine." So I was surprised to learn that the three little words that were guaranteed to "work miracles in your life" were something else entirely. They were:

ACT AS IF.

The writer explained, "Act the way you want to become, and you'll become the way you act." So if you want to *be* happy, begin by *acting* as if you're happy, even when you really feel as miserable as a moth in mud!

This idea certainly isn't new. It's the same premise behind the inspired verses that say:

Though the fig tree does not bud and there are no grapes on the vines, though the olive crop fails and the fields produce no food, though there are no sheep in the pen and no cattle in the stalls, yet I will rejoice in the LORD, I will be joyful in God my Savior. The Sovereign LORD is my strength; he makes my feet like the feet of a deer, he enables me to go on the heights.[4]

Be joyful! Even when the figs don't flower, the fields are flat, and your friends fail you, put a smile on your face and praise God. That's what we try to do on the Women of Faith tour when the water main breaks, the luggage is lost, and the elevators refuse to take us to our rooms on the forty-second floor (and that's probably why last year's tour was so appropriately titled *Outrageous* Joy).

We *can* do it. We *can* sparkle with joy in the deepest, darkest basement, because the Lord is our battery pack that empowers us to smile and laugh no matter how dire our circumstances appear to be. As someone said, "God often calls us to do things that we do not have the ability to do. Spiritual discernment is knowing if God calls you to do something, God empowers you to do it."[5]

We can act as if we're enjoying the journey, even when the road is rough, the springs in the seats are broken, and the air conditioning's best efforts produce a brisk 95 degrees. That kind of attitude was the focus of this Norman Vincent Peale story that was reprinted in the *Bits & Pieces* booklet:

> The famous religious leader John Wesley was terrified in a violent storm on the Atlantic as he sailed to America in the 17th century. But some people aboard the wildly tossing ship were calm and confident during the storm. Wesley was so impressed by their imperturbability that he asked their secret. It proved to be simply a serene faith in God's providential care. When Wesley sadly confessed that he did not have such faith, one of them said, "It is a simple secret. Act as if you do have such faith and in time faith of that character will take hold of you." Wesley followed the advice and ultimately developed such powerful faith that he was able to overcome the most difficult situations.[6]

One of the best bonuses about being—or just *acting*—joyful is that inevitably the joy we share is reflected back to us just when we need it most. For me, this principle works like a boomerang that carries giggles and all sorts of other merry tidbits to my door on a daily basis. Or sometimes it's a note scribbled on a hot dog wrapper at a Women of Faith conference and left for me at my book table. One of my favorites was an anonymous note left by a twenty-seven-year-old woman who wanted me to know how happy it made her to join me (and the other twelve thousand women at that conference) in singing "I'll Fly Away" at the end of my talk. It really *is* inspiring to hear all those voices joyfully singing, "When I die, hallelujah, by and by, I'll fly away." This woman wrote:

> Just wanted to tell you how big of a smile was on my face as we sang "I'll Fly Away." . . . Not only did I know that song, but I knew it in a way like nobody else knows it. I remember when we learned that song in church. My mom leaned over and told us the story of my grandmother singing "I'll Fly Away" at the top of her lungs. When she got to the chorus, she had forgotten the words, but that didn't stop her. She just improvised and kept right on singing. Here's her version:
>
> I'll fly away, oh glory, I'll fly away.
> *When I do, hallelujah, doo-dee-doo,*
> I'll fly away!
>
> My sisters and I will sing it that way 'til the day we "do."
> (I mean "die"!)

Since then, every time I've led audiences around the country in that rousing chorus, I imagine that spunky little grandma singing her own enthusiastic lyrics at the top of her lungs, and once again, my own heart is filled with joy.

Another joy gift came to me all the way from the Bahamas. When I opened the envelope, a piece of fabric fell out. Patterned with bright red blossoms spilling over straw hats on a black background, the fabric was attached with straight pins

**"OH, GLORY! OH, DELIGHT!
MY ESTROGEN PATCH JUST KICKED IN!"**

to a palm-size piece of dress-shaped cardboard. The writer explained that she had read my book *Stick a Geranium in Your Hat and Be Happy* and that recently she had bought the enclosed material to make herself a dress "and did not realize until I had the dress made that it had a hat on it with flowers. So I call it my 'Stick a Geranium in My Hat' dress, in honor of you."

It was just a little thing—a piece of fabric pinned to cardboard. But it brightened my day and made me smile to imagine another joyful woman, a stranger, thousands of miles away, wearing a colorful dress and thinking happy thoughts of me.

That friend's thoughtfulness reminded me of that beautiful little song I sang as a child:

> Do not wait until some deed of greatness you may do,
> Do not wait to shed your light afar,
> To the many duties ever near you now be true,
> Brighten the corner where you are.
>
> Brighten the corner where you are!
> Brighten the corner where you are!

Someone far from harbor you may guide across the bar,
Brighten the corner where you are.[7]

Injecting Joy

Recently I read someone's comment that "happiness is a talent."[8] And right after that, I came upon philosopher William James's advice that said, "If you want a quality, act as if you already have it."[9] Even if you think you don't have a talent for happiness, *act* as if you do. You'll find that joy is like a vaccine that immunizes you against all sorts of maladies. Joy opens our hearts to see God's power at work in ourselves and in our world. It helps us remember God's positive answers for all the negative things we say about ourselves, as shown in this wonderful list someone sent to me:

You say, "It's impossible." God says, "All things are possible" (Luke 18:27).

You say, "I'm too tired." God says, "I will give you rest" (Matt. 11:28–30).

You say, "Nobody really loves me." God says, "I love you" (John 3:16, 34).

You say, "I can't go on." God says, "My grace is sufficient" (2 Cor. 12:9; Ps. 91:15).

You say, "I can't figure things out." God says, "I will direct your steps" (Prov. 3:5–6).

You say, "I can't do it." God says, "You can do all things" (Phil. 4:13).

You say, "I'm not able." God says, "I am able" (2 Cor. 9:8).

You say, "It's not worth it." God says, "It will be worth it" (Rom. 8:28).

You say, "I can't forgive myself." God says, "I forgive you!" (1 John 1:9; Rom. 8:1).

You say, "I can't manage." God says, "I will supply all your needs" (Phil. 4:19).

You say, "I'm afraid." God says, "I have not given you a spirit of fear" (2 Tim. 1:7).

You say, "I'm always worried and frustrated." God says, "Cast all your cares on Me" (1 Peter 5:7).

You say, "I feel so alone." God says, "I will never leave you or forsake you" (Heb. 13:5).

Now, no one expects you to memorize all these verses overnight and make a radical change in attitude all at once. If you're like me, you'll want to taper off your whining gradually so that you don't get attitude whiplash! In the meanwhile, you might enjoy some of these silly warning signs that you've *really* reached the end of your rope:

- You don't worry when the wind blows, because you don't have anything left to blow away.

- Your dog goes home with someone else.

- You can't even afford tuition for the school of hard knocks.

- You've kept a stiff upper lip so long that rigor mortis has set in.[10]

And when the whole world seems to have turned against you, remember this advice I saw on a greeting card:

A positive attitude may not solve all your problems, but it will annoy enough people to make the effort worthwhile!

This last little quip points to the sad fact that there *are* some people living out there in the emotional tundra who just can't stand to think of anything or anyone being joyful. It's like that old joke that defined *Puritanism* as "the haunting fear that someone, somewhere, may be happy." These anti-happy people were described last year in a newspaper article that focused on a group calling itself the Secret Society of Happy People. The organization's purpose, said its founder, is "to bring happiness out of the closet." But her efforts are not always well received. In fact, the article said she had been "cursed on national television" and had even "received veiled telephone threats" from folks who just couldn't stand to be around people who are perpetually happy. Still, the lady was determined to continue her work of encouraging "the openly happy."

As an example of how the group's members spread happiness, the article described a Texas veterinarian who clips the local newspaper for photos of students honored for academic and athletic success. He then has the pictures laminated and sends them to the student's parents with "an anonymous note offering congratulations."

The man explained that "if you do something nice and the person doesn't know where it comes from, it adds a little hint of mystery."[11]

That kind of thoughtfulness was adapted by a woman who wrote to tell me that after she had read *Geranium*, she had been inspired to make Joy Boxes full of jokes, cartoons, and other laugh-getters for friends in her support group, which focused on helping its members cope with grief. "But I quickly gave you the credit for the boxes, Barb, because my name is Joy, and I didn't want them to think I was so vain I'd name this treasure box after myself!" The woman's goal is "to be a source of encouragement to others," she wrote. "I look for ways to bring cheer. I find as I lift them up I'm at the same time lifting my own spirits."

Turning Heartache to Joy
Sometimes the smallest gesture of joy can mean a lot to a person in pain. One woman wrote to say that her friend had given her a potted geranium for Christmas several years ago. The friend wanted a little something extra to go with the gift,

so she purchased a "cute little minibook" with the word *gera-nium* in the title, the woman said. That book was *Stick a Geranium in Your Hat and Be Happy.*

"The little book was intended as a joke, Barb," the woman wrote. "I don't think my friend knew anything about you at the time; she just bought the book because the title went with the gift. But God intervened, and I've been a fan of yours ever since," she added. "You have a tremendous testimony to have been through so much heartbreak and then turn it into the joy of helping others. I've thanked my friend so many times for that little book she meant as a joke."

After my friend Roger Shouse worked at my book table during the Kansas City conference, he shared another idea that he and his wife, Debbie, had used to spread *Geranium*-style joy. He made up a flyer that described "How to Host Your Own Geranium Party." It listed these six simple steps:

1. Invite several ladies from your church or neighborhood. Have each bring a favorite flower.

2. Make a few simple refreshments.

3. Share your favorite story or quote from Barbara's books.

4. Show one of Barbara's videos.

5. Discuss how the value of friends and the power of prayer can help when you are hurting.

6. Exchange flowers before everyone leaves.

No, it's not always easy being a joyful woman. Most of us are more experienced in grumbling than glowing. But to those who've learned to "count it all joy," the boomerang blessings far outnumber the bruises. When you feel as if you're wandering aimlessly in the wilderness of some grief-filled desert, look around you—and find the manna for joy that God has provided. Life isn't always what we want, but it's what we've got. So, with God's help, *choose* to be joyful.

Squirts & Squints

May your joys be added,
Your sorrows subtracted,
Your friends multiplied,
And your enemies divided.

Kinder, Gentler Ways to Indicate Stupidity:

She's a few fries short of a Happy Meal.
He has an intellect rivaled only by garden tools.
She's a few peas short of a casserole.
He's a few feathers short of a whole duck.
In her brain, the wheel's spinning, but the hamster's dead.
His antenna doesn't pick up all the channels.
Her telephone is permanently off the hook.
His belt doesn't go through all the loops.
Her slinky's kinked.

Rejected greeting card verse:
My tire was thumping; I thought it was flat;
When I looked at the tire I noticed your cat. Sorry!

Fun Things to Do in an Elevator:

1. Crack open your briefcase or purse, and while peering inside ask: "Got enough air in there?"
2. Offer nametags to everyone getting on the elevator. Wear yours upside down.
3. Stand silent and motionless in the corner, facing the wall, without getting off.

4. When arriving at your floor, grunt and strain to yank the doors open then act embarrassed when they open by themselves.
5. Greet everyone getting on the elevator with a warm handshake. Look them in the eye and say, "Welcome aboard! Just call me admiral."
6. Bet the other passengers you can fit a quarter up your nose.
7. Say "Ding!" as you pass each floor.
8. Draw a little square on the floor with chalk and announce to the other passengers that this is your personal space.

Did you ever stop to think . . .
and forget to start up again?

She who laughs last
thinks the slowest.

Sign posted on harried shopkeeper's door:
Out of my mind.
Be back in five minutes.

May God's joy shine down on you like the rays of the sun, filling your heart, soothing your spirit, and easing your pain.

(But be sure to wear some kind of joy-screen; you wouldn't want to get overjoyed.)

Success is not measured by how high you fly but how high you bounce.[12]

The flight attendant asked a passenger if he would like to have dinner.

"What are my choices?" the passenger asked.

"Yes or no," the flight attendant replied.[13]

If ignorance is bliss,
why aren't more people happy?

The young man was at the end of his rope. Seeing no way out, he dropped to his knees in prayer. "Lord, I can't go on," he said. "I have too heavy a cross to bear."

The Lord replied, "My son, if you can't bear its weight, just place your cross inside this room. Then pick out any cross you wish."

The man was filled with relief. "Thank You, Lord!" he sighed, and he did as he was told.

Inside the room, he saw many crosses, some so large the tops were not visible. Then he spotted a tiny cross leaning against a far wall.

"I'd like that one, Lord," he whispered.

The Lord replied, "My son, that's the cross you just brought in."

My next house will have no kitchen—
Just vending machines.

Oh, no! Not another learning experience!

Do you want to say you love me?
Say it now, while I can hear
Your voice, soft, low, and soothing,
Gently telling me I'm a dear.

Do you want to show you love me?
Hold my hand, caress my cheek,
And then just listen—only listen—
To my thoughts and hurts and dreams.

Age will change us, time will turn us,
Death will take us all too soon.
Do you want to say you love me?
Say it now. I'll say it too.

—ANN LUNA

Lord Jesus Christ,
You are the journey,
the journey's end,
the journey's beginning.

—DEAN MAYNE,
FORMER DEAN OF
WESTMINSTER ABBEY

The Lamb . . . will be their shepherd; he will lead them to
springs of living water. And God will wipe away every tear
from their eyes.

—REVELATION 7:17

I Finally Got My Head Together—
Then My Body Fell Apart!

I'm Just a Raggedy Ann in a
Barbie Doll World

We all felt so sorry for the clerk working the front desk at our hotel when the Women of Faith speakers checked in year before last in Charlotte. She worked very quickly to make sure our check-in went smoothly on that Thursday night before the Women of Faith conference. Her gracious greeting made us feel completely welcome. We got the feeling she'd been there a long time, because she seemed to know everything about the hotel and everyone who worked in it. But, bless her heart, she was *very* pregnant. We women groaned, thinking how her back must hurt and her feet had to swell by the end of eight hours standing behind the counter. She didn't seem a bit weary as she checked us in, though. In fact, the merriest sparkle shone out from her eyes. She seemed to constantly be on the verge of bursting out in laughter.

Yes, she was a very charming young lady, as sweet as she could be. There was just one rather tragic thing that made our hearts ache with sympathy as we watched her work. She had a *very* noticeable facial-hair problem! Above her upper lip there was a thin, dark mustache that was easily visible from across the lobby. In fact, it looked like she might have tried to trim it a little to keep the tips of the hairs out of her mouth!

What a shame! I thought. *She's such a pretty young woman— but that mustache! Someone should tell her about electrolysis or that new laser hair-removal treatment.*

I even thought about taking up a little collection from the Women of Faith folks, but I just couldn't figure out how I could present the gift to her without hurting her feelings. It just didn't seem very courteous to shove an envelope at her and say, "Here, Honey. Go get your lip waxed."

So we didn't do anything about it—except discuss how noticeable it was to us and how someone who's in front of the public all day, as she was, must surely get some rude stares and even harsh remarks. We felt sorry for her soon-to-be-born child, knowing the poor kid would be teased by insensitive classmates about having a mother with a mustache.

We didn't see her again for the rest of the visit. But when we were at the front desk again on Sunday morning, rushing to get checked out and head for the airport, there was something about the desk clerk that once again bothered me. Something I couldn't quite put my finger on. He was a young, handsome man with sparkly eyes, a bright smile, and—good grief! He had the same thin, dark mustache above his upper lip that the pregnant woman had had on Thursday!

"There you go, Mrs. Johnson. You're all set to go," he said, sliding my receipt across the counter and flashing that same bright smile his pregnant twin had given me three days earlier. My eyes must have bulged out of my head like gourds. I *know* my mouth dropped open, because he asked politely, "Is there something else?"

I gulped, wondering if I knew his mother. You see, my work with Spatula Ministries puts me in contact with the hurting families of homosexuals and other adult children whose lifestyles and escapades have splattered their parents on the ceiling. I hear from lots of brokenhearted mothers who write to tell me about their trials. Looking at the woman/man that morning in Charlotte, I assumed he had to be a cross-dresser or sex-change person, and the words I've preached to so many others suddenly came echoing back through my mind: *That poor, misguided boy is some dear mother's son!* I wanted to reach across the counter, wrap the young man in my arms, and say, "Honey, God loves you, no matter how strange you are."

But then I remembered that he had been *pregnant* on Thursday night. That's when my mind—what few brain cells were left at that point—*really* started to short-circuit.

Seeing my total bewilderment, the man's face wrinkled with sympathy; the lips under the mustache pursed into a cooing little "O," and he asked gently, "Are you okay?"

"You—you . . . on Thursday, you were . . . was that . . . were you . . . ?" I was totally at a loss to know how to ask this most personal of questions.

"That was me, all right," he said with a chuckle. "The hotel was having a costume contest for Halloween, and I won first prize!"

When I remember that creative young desk clerk and how we worried about her facial-hair problem, I can't help but wonder if there are folks out there who, when their paths cross mine as I travel the country, think, *Golly, she's such a nice lady. But can't she afford at least some costume jewelry instead of that rubber band she wears for a bracelet?* Or, *How could a woman who shares her message of hope with so many people be seen in public carrying a purse with ripped seams, using a wallet held together with staples, and wearing a dress with buttons attached with safety pins?*

Actually, I *know* people notice these fashion faux pas, because unlike my reluctance to mention the beauty problem to the hotel worker in Charlotte, they seem eager to point them out! For example, the lady sitting next to me on a plane recently looked over at me and said, "You surely don't *look* like a woman who would have a tattoo!"

I couldn't imagine what would make her say such a thing. Then I followed her gaze down to my right hand—and saw how I'd covered my palm with all the crucial numbers and details I needed to remember that day. It's such a bother, digging through my purse to find something to write on—and my hand is so, well, *handy!*

HERMAN®

10-6   © Jim Unger/dist. by United Media, 1999

"For the money I'm paying, I hope you're painting the real me."

On that day, I knew I would be needing the telephone number of the shuttle service that would take us home from the airport, so I had written it on my hand—right beside my flight number, departure gate, and the name of the shipping service that would be transporting my books to the next venue. Looking over the ink marks, I decided all the scribbles *did* look a little like a work of modern art.

And the rubber bands—I can explain that too. No, actually I can't. It's just a habit born of either frugality or laziness. Whenever I find a rubber band, I pop it onto my wrist, knowing that sooner or later I'll *need* a rubber band; I certainly don't want to waste it, and who wants to take time to find the rubber band box and put it with its stretchy brothers and sisters?

Now, my tattered tote bag . . . well, it's the perfect size and shape, and it has all these great pockets, and I've tried other styles, but they just aren't the same. You wouldn't believe how many people take pity on that tote bag—and then send me a new one, apparently thinking I can't afford a decent purse. But the thing is, I like my old tattered one best; I know right where everything is, and since the seams are ripped, it's even a little bigger now than when it was new.

And as for my wallet, yes, it has been through the mill. But I like to think the staples give it character. They certainly make it easily identifiable! Not too long ago, I lost my wallet when I was rushing through my local market picking up a few groceries. When I got to the checkout lane, I was looking for my wallet and couldn't find it. Apparently I'd laid it down in the tomatoes, where a kindhearted young couple found it wedged among the Big Boys and Beefsteaks. They turned it in to the manager just as I was entering the early stages of lost-wallet panic.

The young man and his girlfriend probably saw the worn and stained leather—not to mention the STAPLES holding it together—and thought, *Oh, some poverty-stricken and absent-minded little old lady left her pocketbook in the produce.* Then they opened it and saw my ID. When they turned it in to the store manager, the young man said, "Oh, my mom reads *all* her books!"

And then there's the matter of the safety pins that hold the buttons on some of my clothes. At one conference, a woman even offered to take my jacket and *sew* the buttons on for me when she noticed all the safety pins holding the buttons on. But I explained that on that outfit the buttons have to be taken off before it can be dry-cleaned, so I just use safety pins to make it easier!

Fashion Foibles, Beauty Bloopers

Now, the theme of this chapter is supposed to be beauty and health, describing ways women keep themselves looking good and feeling good. But as you've probably figured out already, I'm certainly not a role model for fashion statements and attention to detail! Despite my good intentions, I rarely manage to achieve that "put-together" look. And even when I do, something happens that foils my attempts.

For example, I sometimes wear false eyelashes when I'm speaking because for some strange reason when I'm wearing false eyelashes I don't cry when I tell my story describing my husband's car accident, the deaths of two sons, and the alienation of another due to his homosexuality. It must be a psychological thing: I know if I cry, the eyelashes will come off, so I don't cry.

But sometimes the eyelashes come loose anyway! For instance, last year in Orlando, when the temperature was in the high 200s and the humidity apparently was stuck on the "rain forest" setting, the glue was melting and the eyelash was curling off my eyelid as I stepped onstage. Every time I blinked, I got a glimpse of a little wisp of hairs fluttering and flapping past my eyeball. Finally, in frustration, I just reached up, ripped it off, and threw it on the stage. Any thoughts that the eighteen thousand women in the audience wouldn't notice quickly disappeared. They roared! It got such a response I just reached up, ripped off the other one, and threw it on the floor too—so the first one wouldn't be lonely, I explained.

And while I'm confessing my personal preference for comfort over fashion, I might as well include the fact that my ten-

Murray's Law by Leslie Moak Murray

dency to go for practical over pretty extends to our car. It's Bill's beloved twenty-three-year-old Volvo, and it has become a regular member of our family. Like me, it's not the snazziest thing on the road, but it's familiar and comfortable and practical—and we wouldn't think of parting with it. (Well, that's not exactly true. We've given it away twice, but like a devoted dog, it just keeps coming back to us.)

Please don't send me a new wallet or eyelashes guaranteed to stick or a notepad to wear on a string around my neck so I don't have to write on my hand. And while I appreciate the purple luggage—a complete set!—that a friend gave me last year after seeing my tattered tote bag and my dependable old black suitcase (which I've decorated with bright yellow tape so I can spot it easily on the baggage carousel), I *don't* need new stuff! I just need to be left alone to grow older with my *old* stuff!

Probably by now you've gotten the message that I won't be imparting great fashion hints and trendy beauty secrets here, but I *will* try my best to give you something that works even better to improve your appearance: a smile. And since my favorite form of aerobics is belly laughing, you'll get your exercise too. We'll throw in a quick faith lift, and before you know it, you may undergo a total-body makeover!

Let's start with these "time-tested inexpensive beauty hints" from writer Sam Levenson:

> For attractive lips, speak words of kindness.
> For lovely eyes, seek out the good in people.
> For a slim figure, share your food with the hungry.
> For beautiful hair, let a child run his fingers through it once a day.
> For poise, walk with the knowledge that you'll never walk alone.[1]

Those words describe a much better way to improve our appearance than the negative (but, I'll admit, *funny*) method someone sent to me in a card:

Remember these two simple steps to enhance your appearance:
1. Buy an expensive, full-length coat.
2. Never, ever take it off!

My philosophy is that we should just do our best—and laugh about the rest. We have to keep things in perspective. Sure we may be fat, ugly, and have the fashion sense of Phyllis Diller, but as long as our sense of humor is visible, we'll manage the rest!

Ralph

"Is your blow-dryer still broken?"

Too Big for Our Britches—and Our Dresses

Why do we complain so about our body shapes and sizes and want to keep them hidden under wraps? And anyway, how did those single-digit sizes become all the rage? Beauty seemed a lot more realistic—and attainable—when terms like *voluptuous* and *ample* were more common than the dreaded words *lean* and *firm*. For many of us, it's quite comforting to remember that Marilyn Monroe wore a size 12 and that even though there *are* a handful of supermodels who wear a size 8, there are three billion women on the planet who don't! In fact, it was reported recently that the average American woman weighs 144 pounds and wears a 12 or 14. Another survey reported that 70 percent of all adults in the United States are overweight.

It seems ironic that while the models in the fashion magazines are getting thinner, so many other things are getting bigger. Maybe it's because serving sizes in restaurants are expanding along with everything else. As one writer said about restaurant and fast-food trends, "Food is huge. A simple plate of pasta is now a trough of tortellini. . . . Bagels are the size of throw pillows."[2] Another writer suddenly realized she was eating a whole day's calories—at breakfast. After consuming a muffin the size of a cake and a "bagel on growth hormones" she could only moan, "Thank God for the hole in the middle!"[3]

Drinks are getting bigger too. Just think how soda pop servings have grown from the original six-ounce bottle of Coca-Cola. Now convenience stores offer gargantuan, sixty-four-ounce Bladder Busters that are big enough to quench the thirst of a minivan full of Boy Scouts—but are intended for just one person.

(And speaking of filling up the minivan passengers, consider the news that future cars may have everything from microwave ovens and temperature-controlled cup holders to built-in trash compactors and fold-up tray tables. Pretty soon we'll be taking our kitchens with us everywhere we go! Imagine what *that* will do to our attempts at dieting!)

Either we need to learn to eat less despite the monster-size packaging and the mobile kitchen trends, or we need to move to Africa, where in some countries "culture-conscious people . . . hail a woman's rotundity as a sign of good health, prosperity, and allure." In fact, teenage girls are sometimes tucked away in "fattening rooms" for several months where their only goal is to acquire "the traditional mark of female beauty . . . : *fat*."[4]

For most of us, moving to Africa is out of the question. Many women head instead to the plastic surgeon. Someone sent me a joke recently about a self-conscious woman in her late forties who was rushed to the hospital suffering a heart attack. Despite the medical team's best efforts, the woman's heart failed. She felt herself hurtling down a long, dark tunnel toward a piercing beam of light. At the end, she heard a voice say, "It is not your time. Go back."

"When will it be my time?" the woman asked.

"You will live another forty-three years, eight months, and seven days."

"Oh, thank you!" she cried.

Dramatically revived in the emergency room, the woman asked her doctors if she could stay in the hospital a while longer. She had more than forty-three years left to live, and she wanted to look her best. "Call the plastic surgeons," she said. "I want *everything* done!"

For three weeks she remained in the hospital and had a complete makeover: an eyelift, neck tightening, tummy tuck, thigh liposuction, bottom lift—you name it, she had it. When she finally recovered she walked out of the hospital a new woman— and was immediately struck by an ambulance and killed.

Meeting God again at the end of the tunnel, the woman fumed, "What happened? You told me I was going to live another forty-three years, eight months, and seven days!"

God shrugged and answered, "I didn't recognize you!"

The time we wish the hardest that we could make our bodies unrecognizable is when we're trying on swimsuits. The ordeal is perfectly described in this little essay by an unknown writer. While the writer's name isn't known, her attitude could be mine:

I have just survived the annual torture and humiliation of buying a new swimsuit. For generations, bathing suits for mature, "full-figured" women have been no-nonsense garments that showed an understanding that the word *full* did not mean *overflowing*. These bathing suits were boned, cupped, underwired, overwired, and reinforced— true feats of engineering rather than whims of fickle fashion. In those days, a bathing suit was built to hold up, lift up, and tuck in, and it did a darn good job.

Today's swimsuits are designed for malnourished pre-pubescent girls with pencil-shaped figures carved from granite. And even though these nymphs have no flab whatsoever, they wear swimsuits made from space-age material with enough tensile strength to launch satellites into orbit.

The mature, full-figured woman has only two options: She can either show up at the maternity department and try on a flounsey floral swimsuit with a skirt, looking like the dancing hippopotamus in Disney's *Fantasia*, or she can wander, shell-shocked, through the department store swimwear section trying to make a sensible selection from a tangled assortment of what looks like brightly colored rubber bands.

I tried my luck in the department store and thought I heard, as I neared the fitting rooms, the distinct sound of wailing and gnashing of teeth. Inside the chamber of horrors I fought my way into the swimsuit, wishing a stout girlfriend or my husband could have been there to help me wage the battle. I was exhausted by the time I finally twanged the shoulder strap into place—then gasped in horror as I turned to face the mirror. I thought I'd somehow managed to turn my head all the way around to my back: My bosoms had disappeared! Eventually I found one of them smooshed under my left armpit and, after

several minutes of searching, located the other one flattened under my ribcage at the bottom of my sternum.

Because modern bathing suits have no bra cups, the
mature, full-figured woman is forced to wear her bosoms
smashed across her chest like a speed bump. On the other
hand—or perhaps I should say the other *end*—it takes no
time at all to find the mature, full-figured woman's hips
and thighs. They ooze out from beneath the bottom of the
swimsuit like a box of lard that's been sat on. Sighing, I
realigned my speed bump, snapped the Spandex over the
escaping cellulite, and braced myself for another look in
the mirror.

Actually, the suit fit perfectly. That is, it perfectly fit
those parts of me that were willing to stay inside. The
rest of me peeked out rebelliously from top, bottom, and
sides like curious children. I resembled a lump of bread
dough wrapped with garters, a tablecloth pulled through
a napkin ring. . . .

Then I tried on a bright pink number with a top that
resembled a cleric's collar attached to suspenders. Not

"If only I were as young as my mirror thinks I am!"

only did it leave 90 percent of me exposed above the waist, it had such a high-cut leg I thought I would have to wax my eyebrows to wear it.

Finally I found a swimsuit that fit. It's a simple, two-piece style with a shorts-style bottom and a halter top. It was affordable, comfortable, and flab-flattering, so I bought it.

Then I got it home and read the label, which explained why this perfect suit for mature, full-figured women had languished on the rack. The tag said, "Material may become transparent in water."

This woman's comments about what happens to her "bosoms" when she stuffs them into a Spandex swimsuit reminded me of another funny description of one of a woman's most dreaded ordeals: the mammogram.

A mammogram is an x-ray that has its own name because no one wants to actually say the word *breast*. Mammograms require your breasts to do gymnastics. If you have extremely agile breasts, you should do fine. But most breasts, however, pretty much hang around doing nothing in particular, so they are woefully unprepared. But you can prepare for a mammogram right at home with these simple exercises.

Exercise 1: Refrigerate two bookends overnight. Lay one of your breasts between the bookends and smash the bookends together as hard as you can. Do this three times daily.

Exercise 2: Locate a pasta maker or old wringer washer. Feed the breast into the machine and start cranking. Repeat twice daily.

Exercise 3 (more advanced): Situate yourself comfortably on your side on the garage floor. Place one of your breasts snugly behind the rear tire of the family van. When you give the signal, hubby will slowly ease the car into reverse. Hold for five seconds and repeat on the other side.[5]

IF WOMEN CONTROLLED MEDICINE

Now, just let me pass along one more observation some insightful woman made about breasts before we move on to other beauty tips and quips. This lady said:

I have found at my age that going braless pulls all the wrinkles out of my face.

If you *do* wear a bra, you'll want to make sure you choose the type that's right for you. It's really very simple:

- The Catholic type supports the masses,

- The Salvation Army type lifts up the fallen, and

- The Baptist type makes mountains out of molehills.

No matter what kind of bra you wear—or *if* you wear a bra at all!—the most important wardrobe you can possess is the one described in the apostle Paul's letter to the Colossians:

Therefore, as the elect of God, holy and beloved, put on tender mercies, kindness, humility, meekness, longsuffer-

ing; bearing with one another, and forgiving one another.
. . . But above all these things put on love.[6]

A kind friend sent me a beautiful little story about the wardrobe Paul describes, and she even illustrated the story for me. She's allowed me to adapt it to share with you here. I hope you enjoy it as much as I did.

The apostle Paul listed garments of the Holy Spirit in his letter to Colossian believers. First on his list is tender mercies. Also known as compassion, tender mercies are acts of empathy for weak or hurting people. They are usually motivated by feeling the same kind of pain as others or being able to imagine it. I call tender mercies the underwear of God's wardrobe—personal and next to the skin. They are the foundation for everything that goes on the outside.

Next on Paul's list is kindness—a warm-hearted deed as simple as a smile. But kindness is more than that. It's an attitude that involves treating others with honor and significance. The attitude of kindness is everyday stuff like a great pair of sneakers. Not frilly. Not fancy. Just plain and comfortable.

Humility is next. No matter how much we win or lose in life, God wraps us in a beautiful cloak of grace. When we're humiliated, He loves us exactly as we are. When we're in the limelight, we understand the big part He played in our success.

Meekness is one of my favorite things to wear. Some people think it's non-descript, but I disagree. Meekness makes it possible to endure difficult circumstances and poor treatment at the hands of others. It is a durable garment with interesting textures. And meekness looks different on everyone!

How about long-suffering? Sometimes I wish that old rag would just wear out so I could get something more glamorous and colorful. But I know God has fashioned even this to enhance my life. There are times when long-suffering is the only appropriate thing to wear for a particular occasion—and then I'm glad it's in the closet.

Bearing with others and forgiveness are the outerwear of God's designs. They are the things we wear on top of everything else before we go out into the world. Without them we would get awfully cold. They protect us from the harsh elements and keep icy wind from blowing down our necks. As we face difficult circumstances, we button them up often and keep on trudging.

Above all else, Paul says, put on love. Without love, we are never fully dressed in Christ's wardrobe. You might think of love as your best hat or the jeweled pin on the lapel of life. It is that one essential accessory you should never leave behind. Never go anywhere without love![7]

Squirts & Squints

I have a great diet.
You're allowed to eat anything you want,
but you must eat it in the company of naked fat people.

The second day of a diet is always easier than the first.
By the second day you're off it.

A preacher visited an elderly woman from his congregation. As he sat on the couch he noticed a large bowl of peanuts on the coffee table. "Mind if I have a few?" he asked.

"No, not at all," the old woman replied.

They chatted for an hour, and as the preacher stood to leave, he realized that instead of eating just a few peanuts, he had emptied most of the bowl. "I'm so sorry for eating all your peanuts," he said. "I really just meant to eat a few."

"Oh, that's all right," replied the woman. "Ever since I lost my teeth all I can do is suck the chocolate off them."

I don't mind the rat race,
but I could do with a little more cheese.

Amazing! You just hang something in your closet for a while, and it shrinks two sizes.

Despite the cost of living, have you noticed how it remains so popular?

I have a friend who is fifty years old but she tells folks she's sixty—because she looks great for sixty and *awful* for fifty!

Beauty Tip: Beware of tucking your dress into the back of your underwear after using the rest room. You'll know this personal grooming error has occurred when you hear snickers from the people you pass on the street. Another giveaway will be the draft you feel on the back of your thighs.

Let the beauty that you love be what you do.
There are hundreds of ways to kneel and kiss the ground.

—THIRTEENTH-CENTURY POEM

The Greek word for chocolate is *theobroma,*
which means "food of the gods."

If we are what we eat
then I'm easy, fast, and cheap.

SHOE

A balanced diet is a cookie in each hand.

A greeting card verse we'll probably never see:
You had your bladder removed,
now you're on the mends.
Here's a bouquet of flowers
and a box of Depends.

There are two kinds of women who will pay big bucks for a makeup mirror that magnifies their faces. The first are young models who need to be sure to cover every eyelash and define their lips. The second group are women who, without their glasses, can't even *find* their faces.

The colorful way some men describe maturing women:
    Girls start out as beautiful little buds.
    Next they blossom into womanhood.
    Then they go on to become blooming idiots!

The easiest way to lose weight is to check it as airline baggage.[8]

If I had a beauty shop I'd name it this:
Curl Up and Dye

A telephone greeting I hope I never hear:
    "Thank you for calling Incontinence Hotline. Can you hold please?"

Medical Daffinitions

Artery: the study of paintings

Bacteria: back door to cafeteria

CAT scan: search for kitty

Dilate: to live long

Hangnail: what you hang your coat on

Node: was aware of

Outpatient: a person who has fainted

Recovery room: place to do upholstery

My sister and I bought fake fur coats on sale at the same time. If we looked like two polar bears on a Klondike bar, no one ever mentioned it.

There are many women like me who talk about cosmetic surgery, but our philosophy prevails:
No guts—live with the ruts.

When we were in Dallas, I saw many women wearing shirts identifying themselves as S.H.E.E.P. from the Garland, Texas, Tree of Life Church. I knew I would fit right in when one member told us the letters stand for "Sisters Helping, Encouraging, *Eating,* and Praying."

I like to think Psalm 16:6 (KJV) is talking about laugh lines and good genes rather than land boundaries: "The lines are fallen unto me in pleasant places; yea, I have a goodly heritage."

We Started Out with Nothing— and Still Have Most of It Left

Martha Stewart Doesn't Live Here— Thank Goodness!

Like many couples whose children are no longer living at home, Bill and I looked around one day and realized it was time to "downsize" our household in proportion to our shrinking family. We no longer needed a house big enough to accommodate the two of us plus four sons. It was time to move on.

Someone had told me about an attractive adult community of mobile homes approximately twenty-five miles from our house, but Bill was adamant that he would never live in a "trailer camp." Still, the descriptions I'd heard of the place seemed so appealing that I kept whining until Bill finally gave in. He agreed that we could stop by the place on our way home from church one Sunday, but he warned me we wouldn't be there long because it would be a waste of time.

We pulled in the entrance and saw a sparkling lake with ducks swimming peacefully and large fountains spraying water. Then we drove down a couple of quiet streets bordered by manicured grounds that looked like the well-tended landscaping at Disneyland. An agent showed us one of the models—and within half an hour we'd bought a new home! Even more incredible, Bill refused to leave! He bought a cot and a television and "moved in" *himself* that very day, noting it was closer to his work and that he was sure I'd be able to pack up our house and get it sold faster if he wasn't "underfoot." This picture of leisurely living with a pool and Jacuzzi a few feet away really enticed him.

We bought the new place in May, and by September I had sold our home in West Covina and was ready to join Bill in his beautiful "trailer camp." It was hard to leave the house we'd lived in for thirty years; after all, we'd shared years of good times in that home with our four rambunctious boys. But there had been bad times too—really sad times as we struggled to deal with the aftermath of Bill's accident, the deaths of two sons, and having a third son move out and disown us after we argued about his homosexuality.

Major life changes—like moving out of the family home—can be traumatic for anyone. But I didn't want to be one of those women who get so stubbornly attached to a structure of boards and nails that they cause headaches for their children. We know too many of these older folks who refuse to leave the place where they've lived for decades, even if the roof is about to fall in and the stairs are too steep to climb. We wanted a place where we could enjoy life without having to worry about mowing the grass or cleaning the pool. And now, more than twenty years later, we've had no regrets about our decision to move; we've thoroughly enjoyed our "mobile home" (actually,

Rhymes with Orange

it's not mobile at all but *modular)*. There's a convenient recreation center nearby, friendly neighbors, and very little upkeep. We love it.

Still, the experience taught me firsthand about the hassles of moving. How you military families and "upwardly mobile" couples do it so frequently is beyond my comprehension! Moving is one headache I hope never to repeat again. The only place I'm moving to is my mansion in heaven or the Home for the Bewildered down the street—either way I don't expect to do any of the heavy lifting!

When we moved, Bill and I both thought we got the hardest jobs. My job during all those months of getting things ready was to keep the house clean for visits by prospective buyers and handle the paperwork and financial matters. For Bill, our move meant hauling thirteen carloads of stuff from West Covina to La Habra. Now, I didn't really think that was too big a deal; if that had been *my* job, I would have just carried armloads of clothes, books, or whatever to the car, shoved everything in and held it until I could get the doors closed, then dumped it out in one huge pile when I got to my destination. But Bill is an engineer. So each item in each of those thirteen loads was carefully packed, precisely loaded, methodically sorted, perfectly labeled, and then systematically deposited in exactly the right place at the new house. It's a wonder we *still* aren't in the midst of moving at the rate he was going!

But his efforts certainly paid off. By the time I moved in, he had lined every drawer in the house with Armstrong vinyl sheeting, precisely cut so there were no bulges or upturned edges, and he had carefully placed all our things in perfect order throughout the house. (Of course, that didn't last long once I was there, with my rather casual housekeeping philosophy, but still, it was nice for the one day it lasted.)

It's not that I dislike organization. It's just that I am not a fanatic about housekeeping. My philosophy is: Why put something away when you're just gonna have to get it out again in a day or two? And besides, when I'm cleaning, I get distracted by every little thing. I might notice a magazine article I want to read and sit down to scan it—until a letter lying on the desk catches my eye. I move over there to see who it's from, maybe carrying it to the kitchen where the light is better. Standing in front of the sink, I notice the jagged edges of the coffeecake we shared for breakfast—and of course have to slice away just a sliver to make it look neat (and pop the trimming in my mouth, of course). You can see how difficult it is for me!

When I'm cleaning the bathtub, I might see the new bath-oil beads someone gave me and decide right then and there to see how quickly they dissolve. The next thing you know, I'm up to my chin in a bubble bath! When I do manage to stick to the task at hand, I usually try to think up ways to make it fun. Sometimes I sing silly songs or make up rhymes like this one:

> Sing a song of dustballs,
> A corner full of mold,
> Four and twenty cobwebs,
> Swinging to and fro. . . .

Apparently I'm not the only one whose mind is nudged to nonproductive creativity when it comes to doing household cleaning. Recently I saw these silly definitions and thought I should have invented them:

FRUST (n.)—The small line of debris that refuses to be swept onto the dustpan and keeps backing a person across the room until she finally gives up and sweeps it under the rug.

CARPETUATION (n.)—The act, when vacuuming, of running over a string at least a dozen times, picking it up, examining it, then putting it back down to give the vacuum cleaner one more chance.

But no matter how silly I get, it's still *work* to try to organize the chaos that seems to build around me. When it comes to coping with clutter, I share the attitude of that astronaut husband and his wife at the beginning of the movie *Apollo 13*. They've just given a wild party, and they're sitting in the backyard in the midst of the debris left by the partyers, looking up at the moon. "I can't deal with cleaning up," the wife moans, collapsing into a lawnchair. "Let's sell the house."

"Okay," her husband replies, never batting an eye.

That's one of the few good things about moving—the choice it gives you. You can decide to take all your clutter with you to fill up your next home, or you can leave a lot of it behind—given to friends or sold at garage sales. Of course, you may need "clutter counseling" before you can take the latter route and actually give up your priceless treasures so you can enjoy a new, streamlined lifestyle. For those of us who are organizationally impaired, there's a sense that clutter is cozy while neatness is neurotic.

One clutter-besieged woman told me she'd recently conquered this mental barrier and had gone on a clutter-clearing binge that produced "the mother of all garage sales." The woman cleaned out all the knickknacks displayed artistically throughout the house, eliminated all the extra linens she'd been hanging on to, and dug out all the toys her kids had hidden in their closets so many years ago. She'd even emptied the attic of all the old, ugly 1950s furniture she'd inherited from her mother—furniture she'd planned to use in the summer cottage she and her husband had hoped to build when their kids were younger. Truth be told, she'd always hated that orange vinyl sofa and Formica-topped coffee table.

So, in full yard-sale mode, she gleefully dragged everything out into the front lawn, sold it for pennies, and felt great about the whole endeavor—until the Sunday paper came. A headline in the lifestyle section proclaimed, "'Happy Days' Furnishings Are Here Again." She stopped reading after the sentence that said, "Plan on paying at least $2,000 for a 1950s sofa—*if* you can find one of the sleek, orange vinyl models in a vintage shop. And a hard-to-find Formica-topped coffee table, with its sleek, classic silhouette, may run almost as much."

"You bonehead! That's the same lamp we sold
at our garage sale last year for three dollars!"

Headache Hotel

It's as hard for some of us to part with clutter as it would be
for us to part the Red Sea. Let's face it. We need help.
Somehow it's comforting to us to know those old magazines,
outgrown clothes, and hand-me-down doilies are nearby in
case we ever have time to read, lose fifty pounds, or find a
naked spot on a tabletop that cries out to be dressed. While I
sympathize with this mind-set, I must admit I don't live this
way anymore. Except for my Joy Room, which is filled with
all sorts of goofy gadgets and funny plaques, my house is
pretty well organized—thanks to Bill. There are downsides to
this, of course. As a result of his zest for organization, I can't
find anything on my own. And the instant I lay something
down he snatches it up and "puts it away." If I get a glass
from the cupboard, I can't set it on the counter while I turn to
the refrigerator to retrieve the milk. Bill will put it away
before I can fill it up!

If it weren't for the fact that I'm married to this *extremely*
organized person (perhaps the only person in the world who

staples his socks together and hopes for the best before leaving them in my laundry room), my house would be furnished in a decorating style somewhere between chaos and confusion.

But Bill's anti-clutter attitude helps keep me—and all my stuff—in line. Without him, I'd be a first-rate loser. Not that it would be my fault, of course. Things simply have a way of getting away from me. When I turn my back for a mere instant, *poof!* My glasses, pocketbook, keys, and crucial bits of paper bearing absolutely necessary numbers suddenly vanish. It's so remarkable, I expect the phenomenon to be profiled someday on the *X-Files*.

"Oh that? That's so I can keep your socks
paired up in the laundry."

The fortunate thing for me, a *loser,* is that, as people often do, I married my opposite—a *finder.* Several years ago, I clipped a magazine article written by a finder about what it was like to live with a loser. One paragraph, in particular, has helped me understand what it must be like for Bill to live with me—and the last sentence keeps me striving to become less of a loser. The writer said, "I'll say this for most of the losers I know—they are optimists. Just because they can't actually put a hand on something right this minute doesn't mean it's *lost*, for heaven's sake: probably it's only teasing, and the losers are certainly not about to waste precious energy looking for it. As I ransack drawers and closets, their air of patient perplexity is a vivid reminder of how many murders are committed in the home."[1]

Decorated with Joy

Whatever you and your house are like—whether your house-keeping system is the casual stow-and-slam method or the super-organized home where even the dustballs line up evenly under the bed, the most important thing to fill your home with is *joy*. What a blessing it is to step inside a home and immediately feel surrounded by a bubble of laughter and a blanket of love. In my home, I've tried to make the colors blend and the furniture fit. But the most important thing is that wherever I look in our house, I see things that bring a smile to my face and warmth to my heart.

It's amazing to me to see the extremes some people go to under the guise of interior decorating and homemaking. You know you're in the home of a "decorating extremist" when you find a slice of lemon floating in the dog's water dish and all the table napkins, washcloths, and even the paper towels are folded in the shape of swans.

Last year an unknown writer composed a funny Martha Stewart parody describing this kind of silliness. When it circulated on the Internet, at least a dozen people sent me copies, knowing how far it was from *my* seat-of-the-pants decorating style. But the *really* funny part came later when a fictitious response was added by another mystery writer. In this version, the correspondence supposedly occurs between Martha Stewart and humorist Erma Bombeck.

Dear Erma,

This perfectly delightful note is being sent on paper I made myself to tell you what I have been up to. Since it snowed last night, I got up early and made a sled with old barn wood and a glue gun. I handpainted it in gold leaf, got out my loom, and made a blanket in peaches and mauves. Then to make the sled complete, I made a white horse to pull it from DNA that I just had sitting around in my craft room.

By then it was time to start making the placemats and napkins for my twenty breakfast guests. I'm serving the old standard Stewart twelve-course breakfast, but I'll let you in on a little secret: I didn't have time to make the table and chairs this morning, so I used the ones I had on hand.

Before I moved the table into the dining room, I decided to add just a touch of the holidays. So I repainted the room in pinks and stenciled gold stars on the ceiling. Then, while the homemade bread was rising, I took antique candle molds and made the dishes to use for breakfast. These were made from Hungarian clay, which you can get in almost any Hungarian craft store.

Well, I must run. I need to finish the buttonholes on the dress I'm wearing for breakfast. I'll get out the sled and drive this note to the post office as soon as the glue dries on the envelope I'll be making. Hope my breakfast guests don't stay too long. I have forty thousand cranberries to string with bay leaves before my speaking engagement at noon. It's a good thing!

Love,
Martha

P.S. When I made the ribbon for this typewriter, I used ⅛-inch gold gauze. I soaked the gauze in a mixture of white grapes and blackberries that I grew, picked, and crushed last week just for fun.

Dear Martha,

I'm writing this on the back of an old shopping list. Pay no attention to the coffee and jelly stains. I'm twenty minutes late getting my daughter up for school, trying to pack a lunch with one hand while talking on the phone to the dog pound with the other. Seems old Ruff needs bailing out again. Burned my arm on the curling iron when I was trying to make those cute curly fries last night. How DO they do that?

Still can't find the scissors to cut out some snowflakes. Tried using an old disposable razor—trashed the tablecloth in the process, but at least it no longer has those annoying fuzzballs that caused the water glasses to tip over.

Tried that cranberry-stringing thing, but the frozen cranberries mushed up when I defrosted them in the microwave. Oh, and here's a tip: Don't use those new chocolate-flavored Rice Krispies in that snowball recipe unless you're ready for some rather disgusting comments from your kids. I put a few too many marshmallows in mine, and they flattened out into disks I thought looked like hockey pucks—but the kids insisted were cow patties.

Gotta go. The smoke alarm is going off.

Love,
Erma

If you're not into making your own paper, mixing your own paint, firing your own pottery, or stringing your own cranberry garlands, hurray! It means you have more time to be silly and share your joy with others.

Decorating Doozies
It's incredible to realize the effort some people will make to create something unique and memorable for their homes. A friend in Florida has an extraordinary forty-foot-tall artificial tree in the atrium of her magnificent house; the tree has twenty-five thousand silk leaves, and each one was carefully glued in place by the tree's creator.

Similar treasures are being created right now by many quilting enthusiasts who are finishing up "millennium quilts" to commemorate the turn of the century. Each quilt is comprised of two thousand tiny pieces carefully stitched together. Even more mind-boggling is the goal of some quilters to have two thousand pieces cut from two thousand different fabrics! Imagine!

And it's not just our private homes that are being decorated with such amazing features. Not too long ago I saw a newspaper picture showing a huge statue of Godzilla that adorned a Tokyo hotel lobby. The ten-foot-tall monster, created by the hotel's chefs, was made from fourteen thousand pieces of bread.

The designers of the display in the baggage-claim area of the Sacramento airport may have had the same idea of using common items to create "art." When we flew into Sacramento last year, I was stunned to see a huge stack of luggage near the carousel where our bags were to arrive. And then I noticed another huge stack—and another! They were all over the place!

And there, in the middle of one stack, was *my* suitcase. Or at least I thought it was until I walked over for a closer look. Then I discovered the suitcases—hundreds of old ones, new ones, suitcases of all colors and sizes—were stuck together, piled from floor to ceiling. Talk about ways to be creative with *clutter*! Either they were using the suitcases to hold up the roof—or it was supposed to be art!

Simple Comforts

Thank heaven we *all* don't have to think up unusual ways to use stale bread and old luggage to make our homes appealing. In fact, the simplest things sometimes mean the most to guests and family members. For instance, I saw a newspaper article recently that said, "One of the greatest concerns of American families" is "running out of toilet paper."[2] Wow! How amazing to think that simply by keeping our bathrooms stocked with tissue we can wipe out all sorts of family anxieties. Not too long after that article appeared, someone sent me another item that said part of our laundry worries may be eliminated someday too. It reported that in an effort to find new ways to dispose of astronauts' dirty underwear, "Russian scientists are developing a strain of bacteria that will eat underpants."[3] Wouldn't that be wonderful?

In addition to pants-eating bacteria, all sorts of new ideas are in the works now to make homemaking and home decorating easier. For example, for those who love houseplants but can't manage to keep them alive (mine usually die in the backseat on the way home from the nursery), there's a new electronic "plant-sitter" designed to keep up to thirty plants alive. The thing costs $130 and resembles a giant squid; it might be easier to buy silk foliage.

Other technological doodads promise to make our homes intriguing, if not overwhelming, in the near future. For example, there's a new kitchen sink that comes complete with a heater underneath it, so you can cook things in it as well as clean up afterward![4] Somehow it doesn't sound all that appetizing to me, but then, nowadays all I do in the kitchen is dust, so it doesn't really matter.

Another wave of technology will have us *talking* to our alarm clocks at bedtime, telling them what to turn off, what to lock up, and under what conditions to awaken us the next morning ("If the traffic is heavy, get me up a half-hour early; if the dog's in the trash again, wake up Billy, no matter what time it is; if it snows, get Ted up so he can rev up the snowblower"). And those reminder notes we stick on our refrigerators? Someday, they'll appear as electronic marquees ("Janie, if it's four o'clock and you're reading this, you're in the wrong place—piano lesson, remember?"). That idea reminds me of the message one jokester left on his answering machine. It says, "Hi! John's answering machine is broken. This is his refrigerator. Please speak very slowly, and I'll stick your message to myself with one of these magnets."

In the future, it may even be possible to transfer phone messages to the bathroom mirror if we want. (Now, *that* would put me in a real bind, trying to decide whether I'd want to see my face at 6:00 A.M.—or a message reminding me of my pap-smear appointment.) Even our trash cans will be wired in the future. As we throw things away, they'll scan the trash and create a grocery list. And best of all, while we sleep, a quiet, sonar-guided robot vacuum cleaner will cruise through the house sucking up dog hair and Twinkie crumbs.[5]

Laugh Parade

"Hey, how about some volunteers to stay and help clean up?"

Now, while we're waiting for these space-age gizmos of the future to appear at Kmart, I'll help you pass the time by sharing two little tips for the here-and-now (just so you won't think I'm completely lost in the kitchen).

- Best Company Dessert to Serve When You Don't (or Won't) Cook: Individually wrapped ice cream bars served in an ice bucket with a big plate of cookies.[6]

- Best Way to Prevent Violence and Insanity When Trying to Find the End of the Plastic-Wrap Roll: Keep the wrap in your freezer. I don't know why it works, but it usually does.[7]

One of the easy and fun things we did to decorate when our boys were at home was to stick glow-in-the-dark stars on the ceilings of their rooms. They were barely noticeable during the day but at night emitted a soft, cheery glow. One of the first times Tim went to sleep over at a friend's house, he came home with a whole new appreciation for my decorating skills. He said, "Mom, I didn't like it over there. They didn't have any stars on the ceiling."

When we were in Memphis last year, we got a whole new perspective on home decor when our hostess took us to Graceland, Elvis Presley's estate. We had heard a lot about the outlandish decorating style "the king" had lavished on his home. And things *were* pretty amazing there. The "jungle room," for instance, not only had the green shag carpeting so many thousands of us covered our floors with in the 1970s, it also boasted a floor-to-ceiling stone *waterfall* and massive furniture upholstered with fake fur and supported by elaborately carved wooden arms and sides. Each piece looked as if it weighed a ton. The huge coffee table was made from a slice of a gigantic hardwood tree, and the gnarled base and edges were carved to make the table look as though it were a thousand years old.

The stairs leading to the basement were completely encased in mirrors, creating such an illusion of infinity that the guides warned people with vertigo and other vision and balance problems to skip that part of the tour. One basement room had three TV sets lined up beside each other on a counter. And the billiards room was swathed in nearly four hundred yards of cotton fabric bearing a busy geometric pattern that caused my astigmatism to flare up.

It was an incredible place. Many of the tourists seemed to scoff at the overdone decorating themes that grew increasingly unreal as we moved through the house, but the images that really stuck with us were created by the stories the tour guides told about the fun Elvis had enjoyed in those places. We heard about the rollicking, late-night jam sessions, the way Elvis and his daughter played in the snow, the jokes he liked to play on his friends. In the hall where his gold and platinum award records were displayed, we were told that he had sold enough records to circle the globe. But even more impressive to me was imagining "the king" sitting at the simple piano where he often played and sang beloved old gospel songs he'd learned as a boy.

As we left Elvis's mansion, our heads were buzzing with what we'd seen. But then for some reason I happened to remember a billboard back in California that advertised a local Christian bookstore. It says, "Graceland—where the KING *really* lives!" Elvis's mansion was really something, but Christians know who the *real* King is.

**"Go get the phone number of those idiots who
installed the vinyl siding."**

Decorating Our Lives

Just as we find ways to decorate our homes for personal comfort, we also decorate our lives for personal relationships. One woman wrote to tell me she had decorated her entire home with rainbows, the symbols of hope. Rainbows adorn her kitchen, bedrooms, doormats, suncatchers, stationery, bank checks, refrigerator magnets, and greeting cards, she said. And her life is decorated with hope.

Another letter-writer lost her home completely after a bitter divorce. Her daughter helped her get over it when she said, "That's OK, Mom. Jesus is working on your mansion right now."

What that daughter was saying was spelled out in another letter from a different mother. Her heart had been broken, and she had been through some extremely hard times. But she had a choice about where she was going to live now. "Thank you, Barbara," she wrote, "for showing me that I do have a choice—either to live in a pit or to climb out and open up my arms wide to God and let Him work through me."

It's a choice offered to each of us every day of our lives.

Our days are identical suitcases—all the same size—but some people can pack more into them than others.[8]

When I think of the unusual display of luggage at the airport in Sacramento, I love remembering the line from a friend's letter. She said my books were like "very large suitcases crammed full of good things, enduring things, fun things—and most of all . . . HOPE!" What a wonderful compliment!

An elderly carpenter was ready to retire after several decades of high-quality, dependable work for his contractor boss. He told his employer of his plans to leave the house-building business and enjoy a leisurely life with his wife and extended family. He would miss the paycheck, he said, but he needed to retire. They could get by.

The contractor was sorry to see his good worker go. He asked if the carpenter would build just one more house as a personal favor. The carpenter said yes. But as time went by it was easy to see that his heart was not in his work. He resorted to shoddy workmanship and used inferior materials, believing that, since it was his last house, it didn't matter if his reputation was maintained. He no longer cared.

When the carpenter finished his work, the contractor came to say good-bye. As he turned to go, the contractor handed the carpenter the key to the house he had just built. "This is your house," the boss said. "It is my gift to you."

If I live in a spotless mansion of pristine beauty with everything in its place . . .

If I have time to polish the windows, mop the floors, clean the bathroom floors—but have no time to show love . . .

If I train my children to cook and clean and mow and paint but do not teach them to love . . .

Then I am a housekeeper, not a mother; a manager, not a shepherd.

> No matter what I say, what I believe, and
> what I do, I'm bankrupt without love.
> Love never gives up.
> Love cares more for others than for self.
> Love doesn't want what it doesn't have.
> Love doesn't strut,
> Doesn't have a swelled head,
> Doesn't force itself on others,
> Isn't always "me first,"
> Doesn't fly off the handle,

Doesn't keep score of the sins of others,
Doesn't revel when others grovel,
Takes pleasure in the flowering of truth,
Puts up with anything,
Trusts God always,
Always looks for the best,
Never looks back,
But keeps going to the end.
Love never dies.[9]

HERMAN®

3-18   © Jim Unger/dist. by United Media, 1999

"Look what your stupid uncle gave us. What d'you think it is?"

Kitchen Rules

1. If a messy kitchen is a happy kitchen, my kitchen is delirious.
2. A husband is someone who takes out the trash and gives the impression he just cleaned the whole kitchen.
3. Countless people have eaten in this kitchen . . . and gone on to lead normal lives.

The nicest gift is always something you made yourself . . .
like money.[10]

Did you hear about the doorbell and hummingbird who fell
in love?
    They had a little humdinger![11]

Sign posted at a retirement village:
"LORD, PLEASE KEEP ME ALIVE WHILE I'M STILL LIVING!"[12]

Riddle:
What's gray, crispy and hangs from the ceiling?
An amateur electrician.[13]

To live in hearts we leave behind . . . is not to die.

—THOMAS CAMPBELL

I've discovered an interesting phenomenon: If you keep
microwaving bacon until it gets "real crispy" it will eventually melt down, and you will have to suck the flavor out of the
paper towel. Amazing!

Bill says, "Barb cooks for fun, but for *food* we go out."

I can't cook, hate to clean, and loathe ironing. The only thing
domestic about me is that I was born in this country.[14]

What if God had an answering machine?

"Hello, thank you for calling heaven. Please select one of the following four options: Press 1 for requests, 2 for thanksgiving, 3 to complain, or 4 for all other inquiries."

No matter what you press, you hear, "All angels are helping other members of God's family right now. Please stay on the line, and your call will be answered in the order it was received."

"To find out how many angels dance on the head of a pin, press 5.

"If you would like King David to sing a psalm for you, press 6.

"To find out if your relative is here, enter his or her date of death and then listen to the list that follows.

"To confirm your reservation, press the letters J-O-H-N and the numbers 3-1-6.

Thank goodness we have God's promise that He is THE Operator who is standing by.

Then you will call out, and the LORD will answer. You will cry out, and he will say, "Here I am."

—ISAIAH 58:9 NCV

If They Can Send a Man to the Moon . . . Why Can't They Send 'Em All?

Marriage Is a Great Institution. That's Why So Many Women End Up Institutionalized

One morning last summer when Bill was out of town I happened to be standing in the driveway when my neighbor drove by. She rolled down the window, gestured toward the pile of trash I'd put out for the garbage truck, and said sadly, "We can sure tell when Bill's not here!"

Well, you don't have to rub it in! I thought as I surveyed the untidy heap of trash bags, boxes, and newspapers I'd managed to drag out to the curb. It *did* look different from the neat, perfectly symmetrical, snowball-shaped bags that Bill usually leaves out for the trash truck. He not only flattens all the boxes, he also cuts up the milk cartons so the pieces can be stacked in neat blocks, which he binds with string before depositing them in the trash bag. He even rinses out the bottles and cans so there's no odor or stickiness. If there's one thing Bill takes pride in, it's his trash!

In contrast, I feel good if something I toss toward the trash can actually lands inside the bin. For me, life is too short to worry whether my garbage has curbside appeal. But such things are important to Bill. And when he was gone for those few days last year, I developed a new appreciation for several of his organizational eccentricities.

HERMAN®

4-1   © Jim Unger/dist. by United Media, 1999

"And another thing! I'm getting sick of you being so agreeable all the time."

He's always traveled with me for my speaking appearances around the country, and he's always been the one who makes sure the room key is handy. (Now that hotel "keys" are like credit cards, they're so easy to lose and so hard to find!) When he stays behind in the hotel room while I'm out running errands or attending meetings, he leaves the door ajar so I can get back in without digging through my purse for the key. Those things hadn't meant much to me until I had to travel alone last year while he was away.

At the hotel, for the first time in my memory (which, granted, isn't all that sharp these days, but it still seemed so strange) I had to figure out which way to slide the key into the mechanism to unlock the door to my room. Then, when I got inside, I looked around, wondering where my luggage was.

You see, when we arrive at a hotel, I usually go straight to the front desk to check in while Bill oversees the luggage handling. I was embarrassed that day to realize my suitcases were still waiting in the circle drive where the limo driver had unloaded them. As soon as the limo stopped, I had hurried off to the front desk without giving them a second thought!

The time during that trip when I missed Bill the most, however, was at bedtime. Not because of any romantic moods or lonesome thoughts—although I did miss him. No, the thing I missed was having him there to set the hotel alarm clock. Although I called the hotel operator to arrange a wake-up call, we've found that service notoriously undependable, so Bill always sets the alarm clock too. When I traveled without him on that trip, he was so sure that I, being technologically challenged, wouldn't know how to set the alarm that he called me himself at 4:00 A.M. California time to make sure I was awake at 7:00 A.M. in Detroit!

Another thing about traveling alone that made me miss Bill was the clutter in the hotel bathroom. Now, Bill never clutters anything; usually the bathroom is completely filled with all my makeup, cleansing creams, shower caps, robe, and all those other essentials we women have to travel with. The thing I missed seeing was that one little spot on the bathroom countertop where Bill would leave his neatly zippered toiletries bag. It always seems like an island of peace in a sea of chaos, and when it wasn't there, I missed it.

It does seem that the bathroom is the place where differences between men and women are most noticeable, doesn't it? Someone sent me a little quip that said a typical man has six items in his bathroom: a toothbrush, toothpaste, shaving cream, razor, soap, and a towel. The typical woman, on the other hand, has an average of 437 items in her bathroom— and most men are unable to identify 431 of them!

One of the biggest bathroom controversies, of course, is how to get men to put the seat down on the commode. Recently I was interested to see that someone in England had devised a gadget that automatically lowers the seat after the

toilet is flushed. There are rumors that the inventor is being nominated for the Nobel Peace Prize.

Husbands and wives often learn to deal with their differences as they gain greater intimacy. This funny story by an unknown writer shows just how intimate some couples can get:

A young man noticed that an elderly couple sitting down to lunch at McDonald's had ordered just one meal and an extra drink cup. As he watched, the gentleman carefully divided the hamburger in half then counted out the fries, one for him, one for her, until each had half of them. Next he poured half of the soft drink into the extra cup and set that in front of his wife. The old man then began to eat, and his wife sat watching, her hands folded demurely in her lap.

The young man decided to ask if they would allow him to purchase another meal for them so they didn't have to split theirs.

"Oh, no," the old gentleman replied. "We've been married fifty years, and everything has always been and will always be shared, fifty-fifty."

The young man then asked the wife if she was going to eat.

"Not yet," she replied. "It's his turn with the teeth."

That story always reminds me of the time Bill went down to In 'n' Out Hamburgers, just a block away, to pick up a little treat for us. When he got there, he ordered two hamburgers and two orders of french fries. But when he got the bag home, he started spreading it out and found only one hamburger and one order of fries.

"Oh," he said to me. "That's too bad. I guess they must have forgotten yours!"

Beetle Bailey

Men Are Funny

Let's face it. When men aren't making us pull our hair out, they're often making us laugh. Another story by an unknown writer described how a man with his arm in a cast could not give a convincing explanation of how he had broken his arm. He finally confessed that it had happened when his wife brought some potted plants indoors after they had been out on the patio all day. A friendly garter snake had hidden in one of the pots, and later when it slithered out across the floor the wife spotted it.

"I was in the bathtub when I heard her scream wildly," he related. "I thought she was being murdered, so I jumped out of the tub and ran to help her. I didn't even grab a towel. When I ran into the living room, she yelled that a snake was under the couch. I got down on all fours to look for it, and just then my dog came up from behind and 'cold-nosed' me. I guess I thought it was the snake, and I fainted dead away. My wife thought I'd had a heart attack and called for an ambulance. I was still groggy when the paramedics arrived. They lifted me onto a stretcher, and just as they were carrying me out, the snake came out from under the couch and obviously frightened one of the paramedics. He dropped his end of the stretcher—and that's how I broke my arm."

Men hate to admit they'd get caught in such silly scenarios. But someone out there has to do stupid things if for no other reason than to keep the rest of us entertained! Apparently, improbable acts of foolishness are more common than you would think. An article in *Newsweek* last spring listed some warnings that now appear on everyday products—apparently because enough folks have somehow used those things to hurt themselves in unimaginable ways. For example:

- On bread pudding: "Product will be hot after heating."
- On a bar of soap: "Use like regular soap."
- On a hotel shower cap: "Fits one head."
- On a package of sleeping pills: "May cause drowsiness."
- On a string of Christmas lights: "For indoor or outdoor use only."
- And best of all, this warning appeared on an iron: "Do not iron clothes on body."[1]

Now, I could be wrong about this, but somehow I just can't quite picture a woman trying to iron a blouse while she's wearing it. No, the image that comes to mind is more likely to be a man, lying down on the floor, trying to iron a crease in the legs of his trousers. Which brings to mind another ridiculous story someone sent me. It describes how a young man happened to show up at a family reunion with extremely red ears—*burned* ears, actually. In all seriousness, the man explained that it had been a long, lazy weekend afternoon when he had flipped mindlessly from one football game to another. His wife was ironing in the same room, and she had set the phone on the ironing board so she could talk to her mother while she worked.

She had left the room to carry the ironed clothes to the bedroom when suddenly the phone rang.

"I was deeply engrossed in the game at that point," the young man said. "So, keeping my eyes glued to the television, I grabbed the hot iron and put it to my ear, thinking it was the telephone."

"But how did *both* ears get burned?" someone asked.

"I hadn't any more than hung up," the man said, "when the guy called back!"

"No, dear. The phone's working fine — you just answered the TV remote."

Having to admit they are capable of doing stupid things isn't the only thing that's embarrassing for some men. One of the scariest things some of them do is accompany their wives to the mall, especially at Christmastime, when the traffic is hectic and the stores are packed. One researcher said the stress levels in some men skyrocket when they're faced with crowded stores. The scientist compared it with the heart rate and blood pressure "you would expect to find in a 'fighter pilot going into combat.'"[2]

Knowing how stressful it can be for him, I insist on driving when Bill accompanies me to the mall. I've adapted a strategic plan someone suggested for finding a parking space. What you do is hang your head out the car window . . . be very quiet . . . and listen for a motor to turn over. Then you tear across the parking lot in the direction of the sound, driving *against* the arrows, to try to get to that space first. Other than someone dying and leaving you a parking spot, I don't know of any other way to get one during the holiday rush.

NON SEQUITUR

Besides shopping, there are other things that may cause men's stress levels to rise. One stressful activity is brushing their hair and finding that they're becoming, shall we say, *folicularly challenged.* This is a devastating loss for many men. It reminds me of the quip that claims Adam was the luckiest man ever to live, in part because "if he had gone bald, no one would have known that wasn't normal."

Men may get all sorts of crazy ideas when their hair falls outs, and commercial organizations have no shame in promoting an endless variety of products aimed at camouflaging the loss. One of the more creative products combines particles of Australian sheep wool with an adhesive spray that (along with static electricity) holds them in place. One newspaper reporter described it this way:

> The stuff comes in a can that looks like a pepper shaker. You sprinkle the fibers on your head, trying not to pretend you're a pot roast, then pat your hair, apply a little Fiberhold Spray and off you go. Ta da.[3]

No sensitive woman would ever mention such a touchy subject to her husband. Experienced wives know there are certain topics that just shouldn't be brought up. The topics to be avoided depend on each couple's issues, of course. In a magazine article last year a political wife told how she'd learned to refrain from criticizing one important topic: her husband's speeches. She said that after she'd criticized one of her husband's speeches, "he came home for weeks afterward with [supporters'] letters saying it was his *best* speech ever."

Then, one night, as the politician and his wife were pulling into the driveway, he said to her, "Tell me the truth. How *was* that speech?"

She told him quietly, "It wasn't that good"—and her husband "drove right into the garage wall."[4]

The Lockhorns

"We can't agree on a long-distance provider."

And then there's the issue of how men so often refuse to stop for *anything* once they've begun any kind of trip. Have you heard the joke about what would have happened if there had been three wise *women* instead of wise *men*? They would have stopped to ask for directions, arrived on time, helped deliver the baby, cleaned up the stable, made a casserole, and brought disposable diapers and other *practical* gifts!

Along those same lines, someone came up with this goofy list of how things would be different if *men* got pregnant:

- Maternity leave would last two years—with full pay.
- There'd be a cure for stretch marks.
- Natural childbirth would become obsolete.
- Morning sickness would rank as the nation's number one health problem.
- Children would be kept in the hospital until they were potty trained.
- Men could use *their* briefcases as diaper bags.
- Paternity suits would be a line of clothing.
- They'd stay in bed for the entire nine months.

Love, Laughter, and Togetherness
With all these differences existing between millions of husbands and wives, it's a wonder the "institution" of marriage survives at all. As Bill Cosby said, "That married couples can live together day after day is a miracle the Vatican has overlooked." One reason it continues, say researchers, is simply because . . . it works. Marriage is "a glorious mess," one writer said. It "is pretty good for the goose much of the time, but golden for the gander practically all of the time." In other words, "Marriage has a beneficial effect for both men and women, but the effect is much stronger for men. . . . They may resist, they may kick and scream about getting married, but then it does them a world of good." Other studies show that

"matrimony adds more years to a man's life than it does to a woman's. . . . Marriage can even make frail men strong," researchers say.[5]

It makes sense, then, that losing a spouse "hits men harder than it does women."[6]

Perhaps that explains what happened last year when I opened an envelope that came in the mail to find a check made out to me and signed by a man. Most noticeably, at the bottom of the check the man had written, "DO NOT SELL OUR NAME TO ANY MAILING LISTS! DO NOT SEND SOLICITATIONS OR MATERIALS! DO NOT CONTACT US!"

Flabbergasted to get such a note, I noticed the phone number was printed on the check, and I decided I'd call the guy up and ask why he would write such a message!

In a cold, gruff tone, he told me his wife had attended a recent Women of Faith conference. He hadn't wanted her to go, he said, because she was in very poor health. In fact, in December her doctor had given her less than three months to live. Then, in January, some friends bundled her up in a wheelchair and took her to the conference.

"Well . . . what happened?" I asked fearfully.

"Oh, she loved it," he said, his tone warming slightly. "She came home bubbling over with all the stuff she'd seen and heard. And she asked me to send you that check to pay for books she'd gotten from your book table. She hadn't taken her checkbook and didn't have enough cash after lunch, and one of the helpers at your book table gave her the books and said she could send the money later. So she asked me to write the check. But I've heard about these Christian organizations that are always after you for money once they get your name on their mailing lists. And I don't want any part of that."

I assured him we weren't about to sell or use his name on *any* mailing lists. "Why, I've got three shoeboxes full of names of people who *want* to be on our mailing list and we can't get them on. I'm not about to add someone who doesn't want to be on it." I also gave him the address of the bulk-mail organization he could register with to get his name off junk-mail lists. (It doesn't work, but I thought giving it to him might calm him down.)

Finally, I got up the nerve to ask, "Well, how is your wife now?"

"She's here. Would you like to speak to her?" he asked.

"Oh, I'd love to speak to her!" I answered.

The man obviously left the room. I think he was embarrassed—and he should have been!

When the woman got to the phone, she said, "Oh, Barbara! I can't believe you called! Thank you so much for those books. I've already read them, and I just loved them."

She said she thought the conference was wonderful, and she remembered that I had talked about a new book I was doing about heaven called *He's Gonna Toot, and I'm Gonna Scoot*. "Oh, Barb, I'd love to read it . . . but you said it'll be three months before the book is out, and by then . . . I'll be gone."

"Yeah, you'll be gone," I agreed sadly before I realized what I was saying.

Then I had an idea: "Well, I have a rough copy of the manuscript, and I'd be glad to send it to you—to *you*, not to *him!*"

She said, "Oh, I'd just love that!"

So I sent the manuscript to her—to *her*, not to *him!*—and in a couple of days she called and said, "Barb, I'm just so happy to have that manuscript. It's going to be a wonderful book. But now I have a favor to ask of you—would you do it?"

I said, "Oh, Honey! I'd do anything for you!"

She paused a moment then said, "Well, when I'm gone, my husband is going to be so desolate and so alone. . . . Would you mind putting him on your mailing list to get your newsletter?"

Even though we poke fun at our husbands and their different way of doing things, most of us have chosen to link our lives with theirs and face whatever comes, good or bad, laughter or tears. As Thomas Merton said:

Even saints cannot live with saints on this earth without some anguish, without some pain at the differences that come between them. . . . Love is the resetting of a body of broken bones.

Murray's Law by Leslie Moak Murray

The happiest marriages are surely those where love and laughter overcome any brokenness. Between these couples, laughter is a natural part of every day. One friend sent me a packet of funny poems and stories she wanted to share. She had hoped to also send a photocopy of her favorite cartoon, titled "The Incurable Romantic." But she couldn't copy it, because her husband had *glued* it inside the door of their medicine cabinet! Instead she had to tell me what it said. The illustration, she said, showed a man climbing into bed with his wife, and saying, "The light reflected off your night cream is like moonlight on a still mountain pool, and the silver gleam of curlers under the hair net suggests dew on cobwebs in some remote glade."

Can't you just see that husband and wife, chuckling every morning when they open the medicine cabinet to reach for the toothpaste?

Other husbands may lack this guy's sense of humor but find other ways to keep a marriage alive. One woman, who fought major depression after learning her son was a homosexual, wrote to say,

There was a time when I was so sad all the time, but I can now experience joy in life in many areas. My husband gave me a wake-up call when I was so blue. He looked at me with tears in his eyes and said, "You still have *me*." That was a turning point for me. I cannot let this problem destroy my life and those around me.

This kind of "we're-in-it-together" attitude of another husband and wife was honored last year when a *Washington Post* columnist wrote about ninety-six-year-old Mike Mansfield, the former U.S. Senate majority leader. After lying about his age and joining the navy at age fourteen, Mansfield went to Montana to work in the copper mines. There he "met a young schoolteacher who recognized his exceptional qualities and encouraged him to pursue an education. After sixty-eight years of marriage to Maureen Hayes, the teacher, his devotion is undiminished."

My favorite part of the story came in the next sentence, which noted that "the Montana Legislature recently proposed erecting a statue of Mansfield in the state capitol in Helena." Mansfield's reply to the legislature was easy: "If it's just me, no; if it's Maureen and me, OK."[7]

"What I said was, 'I'm feeling *rheumatic!*'"

Another illustration of this kind of togetherness exists on Vashon Island, Washington, just south of Seattle. There a living phenomenon is becoming something of an attraction. It is the Bicycle Tree, a bit of "magic," according to writer Charis Collins, "that began when a young child leaned a little red bicycle into the tree's young, reaching crook and never returned for it. As the tree matured, it embraced the bicycle without complaint, drawing the tiny handlebars, the banana seat, the rotted tires to itself most naturally. . . . The two have become intertwined inexplicably, forever unable to separate. These days the tree literally has grown into the bicycle, and the bicycle has stretched with it, curiously raised several feet off the ground, encased lovingly by the tender, knotty trunk."

To Charis, the Bicycle Tree reminds her "of how Grandpa and Grandma's wedding rings look to me, embedded in the creases of their thick, worn fingers." It also symbolizes how she sees their marriage:

> Marriage is taking on another person in life. It is not usually planned from the beginning; you don't know who it will be when you are born . . . , but somehow the two joined become one, even if it doesn't seem likely or at all possible. If you are lucky, you grow more entangled with each passing day.[8]

Entangled is the perfect word for couples tied to each other by the bonds of matrimony. Sometimes we're wound up and crisscrossed like contestants playing the old Twister game. And other times, it feels as if we're irreparably stuck in one big knot. But without that tangled knot, I know for sure I'd be at loose ends, because there's a third strand running through our marriage that ties us, not only to each other, but also to our Creator. That strand is God's love for us.

> If two lie down together, they will keep warm. But how can one keep warm alone? . . . A cord of three strands is not quickly broken. (Eccles. 4:11–12)

Squirts & Squints

This is a rule for women that has no exceptions:
If it has tires or testosterone, you're gonna have trouble with it.

Two small cousins were straining to hear what was going on at a recent wedding. The older cousin turned to her father and asked, "Dad, what are they saying?"

"They're saying their vows," the father whispered.

The girl turned and dutifully passed on the news to her cousin: "They're saying their A-E-I-O-U's," she carefully explained.[9]

Veni, vedi, visa
Translation: I came, I saw, I did a little shopping.

I have a little red box with a little red button on it. If someone asks me what it's for, I have to tell them, "Whenever I push that button, absolutely nothing happens. It just keeps me humble!"

If men can run the world, why can't they stop wearing neckties? How intelligent is it to start the day by tying a little noose around your neck?

—Linda Ellerbee

A good way to have the last word . . .
is to apologize.

Dear Lord, prop us up in all our leaning ways.

Engraved on the tombstone of the mother of nine children:
Here Lies Mom.
Let Her R.I.P.

Wise husbands know that PMS is Mother Nature's way of saying, "Get out of the house!"

Somewhere between ice cream and being buried alive.... is........

P.M.S.

© David Horrocks, Muskrat Springs, Inc. Used by permission.

One Sunday a pastor told his congregation the church needed some extra money. He asked the people to prayerfully consider giving a little extra in the offering plate. He said that whoever gave the most would be allowed to pick out three hymns.

The offering plates were passed, and the pastor was delighted to find a check for a thousand dollars. He announced the "winner," and a quiet, elderly, saintly lady shyly made her way to the front of the church. The pastor told her how wonderful it was that she had given so much. In thanksgiving, he asked her to pick out three hymns.

Her eyes brightened as she looked over the congregation, pointed to the three handsomest men in the building, and said, "I'll take him, him, and him!"

A joke:
Do old men wear boxers or briefs?
Depends!

Bumper Sticker:
Few women admit their age.
Fewer men act it.

Man trying to meet woman: "Hey, sweetie, what's your sign?"
Woman: "Do Not Enter."

A man was walking along a California beach and stumbled across an old lamp.

He picked it up and rubbed it, and out popped a genie. The

genie said, "OK, OK. You released me from the lamp. This is the fourth time this month, and I'm getting tired of these wishes, so you can forget about getting three. You only get one wish! What is it?"

The man thought about it awhile and said, "I've always wanted to go to Hawaii, but I'm afraid to fly and I get very seasick. Could you build a bridge to Hawaii so I can drive over there?"

The genie laughed and said, "Are you crazy? That's impossible! Think of the logistics of building a bridge like that! How would the supports ever reach the bottom of the Pacific? Think of how much steel I'd need! No. Think of something else."

The man said OK and tried to think of a really good wish.

Finally, he said, "I wish I could understand women— know how they feel and what they are thinking, understand why they cry and what makes them laugh. I want to know what they really want when they say 'nothing' and how to make them truly happy."

The genie paused a moment then answered, "Do you want that bridge two lanes or four?"

Within this grave we lie,
Back to back, my wife and I.
When the last trump the air shall fill
If she gets up, I'll just lie still.

—FEARFUL HUSBAND

I wonder . . .
What hair color do they put on the driver's licenses of bald men?

There are two theories for arguing with a woman.
Neither one works.

If women ran the world . . .
> The hem of men's pants would go up or down depending on the economy.
> Men who designed women's shoes would be forced to wear them.
> Men would bring drinks, chips, and dip to women watching soap operas.
> Men would sit around and wonder what *we're* thinking.
> All toilet seats would be nailed down.

A Male-Designed Curriculum for Training Wives

1. *Silence, the Final Frontier:* Where No Woman Has Gone Before
2. *The Undiscovered Side of Banking:* Making Deposits
3. *Man Management:* Postponing Minor Household Chores 'Til After the Game
4. *Bathroom Etiquette I:* Men Need Medicine Cabinet Space Too
5. *Bathroom Etiquette II:* His Razor Is His
6. *Communication Skills I:* Tears—the Last Resort, Not the First
7. *Communication Skills II:* Thinking Before Speaking
8. *Communication Skills III:* Getting What You Want Without Nagging
9. *Driving a Car Safely:* Introduction to Parking
10. *Telephone Skills 101:* How to Hang Up
11. *Water Retention:* Fact or Fat?
12. *Cooking I:* Bringing Back Bacon, Eggs, and Butter
13. *Advanced Cooking:* How Not to Inflict Your Diet on Other People
14. *PMS:* Your Problem . . . Not His
15. *Classic Clothing:* Wearing Outfits You Already Own
16. *Household Dust:* A Harmless Natural Occurrence Only Women Notice

17. *Integrating Your Laundry:* Washing It All Together
18. *Oil and Gas:* Your Car Needs *Both*
19. *TV Remotes:* For Men Only
20. *Shortening Your Attention Span:* How to Watch Fourteen
    TV Shows Simultaneously

Tell a man there are four hundred billion stars, and he'll believe you. Tell him a bench has wet paint, and he has to touch it.

—STEVEN WRIGHT

Only two things are necessary to keep one's wife happy. One is to let her think she is having her own way. The other is to let her have it.

—LYNDON B. JOHNSON

DENNIS the MENACE

"MY DAD'S A GOOD DRIVER BECAUSE MY MOM COACHES HIM."

Man is incomplete until he is married.
Then he's finished!

A little boy asked his father, "Daddy, how much does it cost to get married?"

The father replied, "I don't know, son. I'm still paying."

A woman marries a man expecting he will change, but he doesn't. A man marries a woman expecting that she won't change, and she does.

Ah, children! A woman knows all about her children. She knows about dentist appointments and soccer games and romances and best friends and favorite foods and secret fears and hopes and dreams.

A man is vaguely aware of some short people living in the house.

A little girl was having a hard time grasping the concept of marriage. In an attempt to help, her father got out the wedding album and explained the ceremony to her.

"Oh, I see," the little girl said. "That's when Mommy came to work for us!"

My dear brothers and sisters, always be willing to listen and slow to speak. Do not become angry easily, because anger will not help you live the right kind of life God wants. . . . In gentleness accept God's teaching that is planted in your hearts, which can save you. (James 1:19–21 NCV)

When Your Road Is All Downhill . . . You're Probably Holding the Map Upside Down

God grant me the senility to forget the
people I never liked anyway, the good
fortune to run into the ones I do—and the
eyesight to know the difference.

Sometime back Bill and I were going to a retreat in Texas, and the dear gals who were to pick us up at the airport in Houston were overwhelmed by their assigned jobs and nervous about making sure everything would go perfectly. Unfortunately, almost nothing did!

The first mix-up occurred when they mistakenly thought we were flying into Houston's smaller Hobby Airport. Instead, we landed at the much larger Intercontinental. (It's so big some frequent flyers have nicknamed it Houston Intergalactic Airport.) Then, when they discovered their first mistake and arrived at the right airport, they looked at our itinerary and saw that we were flying in from Ontario—and assumed that meant we were arriving from Canada at the international terminal. Instead, we were really flying from Ontario, California!

As a result, Bill and I waited in the luggage area for an hour with no one showing up. Then, far down the corridor, we spotted two figures rushing toward us. I knew they were coming for *us*, because as they trotted down the concourse they were struggling to control huge, sombrero-sized hats with geraniums flying off them in every direction. They rushed up to us, apologizing in their charming southern accents for being so late and explaining about going to the wrong airport and then the wrong terminal in the right airport. Finally they hustled us out to the one lady's lovely new Town Car, piled our luggage in the trunk, and headed out of the parking lot on the two-hour trip to the little town about eighty miles away where the retreat was to be held.

The disaster continued.

The two hostesses, still wearing their huge hats, sat in front so Bill and I could feel as if we were being chauffeured. As we pulled out of the parking lot, the driver confessed, from beneath her sombrero, "Barb, I have NO idea where this retreat is, and I've never driven around this airport before, so I have to call my husband for directions." She explained that she would *never* have agreed to be our driver if she'd known we were flying into *this* airport instead of her familiar Hobby.

It turned out her husband was a judge in a Houston court, and she called him on her cellular phone while we drove rather aimlessly around the airport freeway system. She didn't have a pen and paper—and even if she had, of course, she couldn't write, drive, and talk on the cell phone, so I sat in the backseat, trying to interpret her deep southern drawl and write down the directions she relayed from the judge. He was quite patient but apparently realized he wasn't making any headway in relaying the directions. He directed her to pull out a map.

Her seatmate fumbled in the glove compartment, found a map, and spread it out over her lap. The driver continued relaying the judge's information to both of us, but the gal reading the map interrupted to say, "I can't find where we are or any of the roads he's describing!"

At that point, Bill, the former Eagle Scout whose motto is "Be Prepared," came to the rescue. He leaned over the seat, raised the rim of the second lady's sombrero to glance at the map, and said, "That's Mexico you're looking at. Why don't you turn it over and see if it might have Texas on the other side?"

"Oh, silly me!" giggled the navigator. She wrestled the map over to its other side and once again searched diligently for something that sounded familiar. But the printing was so small she gave up, admitting she still couldn't find anything. Once again Bill came to the rescue. He pulled out the magnifier he carries in his pocket and shoved it under the lady's hat. She took it from him with a puzzled tilt of her head and laid it down flat on the map. "Oh dear, it doesn't seem to help any, Bill," she commented, still confused.

"Lift it up!" Bill ordered.

The woman raised the magnifier a few inches from the map and exclaimed, "Oh, the words get *bigger* when you do that!"

Eventually we arrived at the little town (proving once again that God *does* answer prayer!), and the retreat was bunches of fun. But I think Bill and I have had *more* fun recalling that hilarious encounter with those two charming but confused ladies (now that it's *over!*). As we watched them fumble through one goofy mix-up after another, I was sure we were observing some classic "senior moments." And we just love seeing senior moments in folks who are obviously younger than we are! Maybe we should just remember those gals as "geographically challenged" or "hormonally oversaturated," but "chronologically advanced" is my preferred excuse.

Menopausal Moments

My friends love to tell me about their own menopausal moments when they do the silliest things. When one gal in her late forties was just tiptoeing into that hormonal cesspool, she had to drive her daughter to soccer practice several times a week. One of the intersections on the way to the soccer field was filled with fast-food places lined up next to each other, and the woman often stopped by the Burger King drive-through for her favorite sandwich after she dropped off her daughter.

One evening the drive-through was packed with a long line of cars, so the woman had to change her routine. Hurrying, she drove around the confusing collection of parking lots until she finally found a place to park and hustled inside to order.

Already frustrated by the delay and thinking about her tight schedule and many errands left to run, she was a bit crabby when she got to the cash register. A nervous-looking teenager stood behind the counter, expectantly waiting. Beside him towered the manager, trying to monitor the kid's work as he also yelled orders into the kitchen. *Great*, the woman thought. *I'm already in a hurry, and now I have to deal with a trainee.*

"I'd like a BK Broiler, no mayo, and a large Diet Coke," she ordered in her most no-nonsense tone.

The kid dropped his head and searched the cash register keyboard, obviously looking for the right button. His eyes moved left, right, up, down—and then back to the woman. "I'm sorry?" he asked.

"A BK Broiler . . . no mayo . . . and a large Diet Coke," the woman said deliberately and loudly, as though the kid had a hearing problem.

Once again the poor trainee searched the keyboard. By now completely flustered, he turned helplessly to the distracted manager while the woman rolled her eyes impatiently. The manager asked her to repeat the order one more time.

By now totally exasperated, the woman turned up the volume and enunciated slowly, "BK BROILER, NO MAYO, AND A LARGE DIET COKE!"

The manager paused only half a second before he replied deliberately, as though the woman had a mental problem, "MA'AM, THIS IS TACO BELL."

And then there was this funny story someone passed along about a sweet little lady who was well along the path to confusion corner:

Lola and Ned sat at the same bingo table and often walked home together. They took the shortcut through the adjacent cemetery.

One night Ned left early, so Lola had to walk home alone. Halfway through the cemetery she heard a faint noise—a voice calling, "Help, help." As Lola approached an open grave site, the voice was stronger. She peered down into the grave, and there lay Ned.

"Help me," he said. "I'm freezing."

Lola had a puzzled look on her face as she said to herself, *Ned is dead? I must have forgotten.* She said, "Of course I'll help you, Ned. You stay quiet while I get someone. No wonder you're cold. You've kicked off all your dirt."[1]

DENNIS the MENACE

"BOY! DAYS LIKE THIS MAKE ME FEEL YOUNG AGAIN!"

I'm Only Old on the *Outside*

It's fun to laugh at these silly senior moments—as long as the stories aren't about us! We want to believe that no matter how old and shriveled we get on the outside, our brains are still humming along like a fine-tuned engine inside. If only we could get everyone to believe us when we protest that it's not our fault when we end up in ridiculous circumstances. That was the case when two longtime schoolteachers visited a drive-through wildlife park recently to check it out and see if it might be appropriate for their third-grade classes to visit on a field trip. If you've been to one of those parks, you know you're told to keep your windows rolled up, drive slowly, and be prepared to stop your vehicle to let the animals cross the road.

That's exactly what these two smart gals did. They stopped, spellbound, as an enormous elephant strolled across the road in front of them. But the beast didn't just cross the road. It stopped, its huge body completely blocking the two ladies' view out the windshield. And then a horrible thing happened. The elephant turned around, paused a moment, then *sat down* on the hood of their car! Hearing the car's metal groan and then crease pitifully under the weight, the two ladies were horrified, and for a moment they wondered if they were about to be crushed too. But the elephant apparently found the spot too uncomfortable and within a few seconds, it got up and ambled away, leaving in its dust the shocked women—and their smashed-in car.

Luckily, the car was still drivable, and the two schoolteachers hurried out of the park. They stopped to survey the damage at the first place down the road—a restaurant. They were far too upset to eat anything, but they went inside to try to calm down. Neither woman ever drank alcohol, but they decided that just this once, a glass of wine might be a good idea.

Eventually they finished the wine and got back into the crumpled car to drive home. By this time it was dark, and they'd gone only a few miles when a policeman stopped them because their headlights were cattywampus. One was pointing skyward while the other dangled morosely out of its socket. When the driver rolled down her window, the policeman smelled wine on her breath and ordered her out of the car.

At that point, the story came pouring out of the ladies, and the two schoolteachers begged the policeman not to arrest them. They pointed to the third-grade textbooks and teaching materials in the backseat, showed him their ticket stubs to the animal park, and assured him they were telling the truth. He listened to them with amused disbelief then stood quietly surveying the scene for a moment while the ladies held their wine-ladened breaths, knowing he held their fate in his hands. In a moment he snapped the ticket book closed and told the women they could leave.

"You're not gonna give me a ticket?" the driver anxiously asked.

"Ma'am, if I put this story in my report, I'd be laughed off the police force," he said. "Please stay out of the wildlife park in the future. OK?"

Can't you just see these prim and proper schoolteachers trying to explain their fender bender—and blaming an elephant?

Age Is Important—If You're Cheese
After reading about a recent Harvard University study, I'm starting to wonder if my fondness for funny stories may be a double-edged sword. The study looked for similarities among those who live to be very old—in fact, older than one

hundred. One of the threads they found running through these "centenarian personalities" was that most of these folks who lived to be one hundred years old or older were "generally optimistic and, in most cases, funny. They use humor all the time," one of the researchers said.[2]

The report is a Catch-22 for me, because I love to laugh, but I'm also eagerly awaiting the sound of that celestial trumpet that will summon me to heaven! I'm not sure I *want* to live to be one hundred—and a lot of other people apparently feel the same way. Another recent survey reported, "The once-elusive goal of turning 100 years old is becoming more attainable every day. But a majority of Americans don't want to live that long."[3]

After all, by the time we've lived to be one hundred years old, our hearts will have beaten 3,681,619,200 times, pumping 27,323,260 gallons of blood weighing more than one hundred tons! Just thinking about it exhausts me. Even more amazing was the news story that said centenarians comprise the fastest-growing segment of the American population. And, the article adds, women in that age group outnumber men five to one![4]

But so far, old age just seems to be the direction I'm headed. Sometimes I feel like the fellow who was asked how he managed to live so long. He shrugged and replied simply, "I didn't die."

Making Each Day Matter

As long as I'm not dying, I'd like to do something productive—or at least something that makes me laugh. My mail is full of clippings friends have sent to me that describe others who share my love of life and laughter, no matter how old they are. Here's a sample:

- A ninety-eight-year-old Florida woman who goes ballroom dancing twice a week. (Her motto is, "Smile awhile, and while you smile another smiles, and soon there's miles and miles of smiles, and life's worthwhile because you smiled.")[5]

- A seventy-two-year-old Colorado runner who has been running—and winning—a ten-kilometer race at high altitude for the last seventeen years. Last year her goal was to finish in less than an hour.[6]

- A ninety-three-year-old Texas woman who recently helped paint a historical mural in her town.[7]

- A 108-year-old woman in Florida who learned to play the piano and organ at age seventy, rode a camel and hiked through Israel at age ninety-nine, and, last we heard, was enjoying reading e-mail notes sent to her web page on the Internet.[8]

- Two New York women who wrote their first book, a bestseller, *after* they were one hundred years old.[9]

- A Georgia woman who, at 101, is the oldest practicing physician in the United States.[10]

"It's not fair. Just as I'm turning into my mother, she gets to turn into a grandma."

Riding the Hormonal Hurricane

We gals have an extra road bump to deal with on our way to the golden years—menopause. We blame this hormonal hurricane for all sorts of maladies that range from hot flashes and forgetfulness to weight gain and tearfulness. How nice it is to know there are women out there who are actually celebrating this zany stage of life. In fact, 52 percent of American women between ages forty-five and sixty told a recent survey that "they consider menopause the beginning of a new and fulfilling stage."[11] *Those* are the gals *I* want to sit next to in the geriatric doctor's waiting room!

One of those optimistic gals was surely the sweet lady who gave me an adorable little doll called the Estrogen Fairy. The doll is a soft, tubby, little white-haired figure who sports a superhero's hooded cape and wings. And like a Barbie doll for middle-agers, she comes with a complete story line. The attached booklet described some of her mischievous "feats" this way:

> With a touch of her magic wand, she zaps your estrogen, taking it with her in the hope of someday using it to recapture her own long-lost youth. Now, you may ask, "How can I tell if I've been zapped by the Estrogen Fairy?" Well, if you've ever experienced one of these symptoms, you can bet she's the culprit:

> - You find yourself in the garage and don't know whether you're on your way out or you've already been there and had a good time.
>
> - You burst into tears when the traffic light turns red.
>
> - You go to bed feeling peaceful yet awaken thinking the world (and everyone in it) is falling apart and you're positive it's your fault.

The Estrogen Fairy

- The only men who smile at you are plastic surgeons.[12]

Here are some other signs that you're living somewhere between estrogen and death:

- When you do the "Hokey Pokey," you put your left hip out . . . and it stays there.

- You run out of breath walking *down* a flight of stairs.

- Classmates at your reunion think you're one of their former teachers.

As we grow older, everything slows down—including our mental processes. Bill and I have noticed this phenomenon as we enjoy one of our favorite TV game shows—*Jeopardy!* Recently I noticed I was a bit late with the answers . . . sometimes by two or three days! Then one night I was *amazed* that I knew almost all the answers. Later I realized it was a rerun from the week before!

We're all aware of the years passing by. But just when do we become *old?* How do we know when we've reached that stage? One jokester said you know you're getting old when you yearn for those blessed old hymns of days gone by, especially:

- "Go Tell It on the Mountain—and Speak Up!"

- "Nobody Knows the Trouble I Have Seeing"

- "Guide Me, O Thou Great Jehovah (I've Forgotten Where I Parked)"

It's not as if we're the only ones trying to figure out when old age hits. Awhile back when Bill had to have some medical tests, the doctor's nurse called to explain the procedure and what he needed to do before and after the tests. Knowing Bill is living somewhere between geriatric junction and heaven's pearly gates, the *real* reason for the nurse's call to me was apparently to determine whether I was capable of following her instructions and taking care of his needs. We made small talk for a minute or two before she finally drew in a breath and said, "Well, you sound pretty *spry!*"

Humorist Dave Barry says old age begins the first time you put on a pair of reading glasses. He compares this transformation to the same one Clark Kent went through, only in reverse: "He takes off his glasses and becomes Superman; you put on your reading glasses and become . . . Old Person." But this transformation doesn't happen overnight, of course. For Barry, it began in restaurants when he was forty-eight:

At first I thought that this had nothing to do with me— that, for some reason, possibly to save ink, the restaurants had started printing their menus in letters the height of bacteria; all I could see was little blurs. But for some reason, everybody else seemed to be able to read the menus. Not wishing to draw attention to myself, I started ordering my food by simply pointing to a likely looking blur.

Me (pointing to a blur): I'll have this.

Waiter: You'll have "We Do Not Accept Personal Checks"?

Me: Make that medium rare.

Pretty soon I started noticing that everything I tried to read—newspapers, books, nasal-spray instructions, the U.S. Constitution—had been changed to the bacteria-letter format. I also discovered that, contrary to common sense, I could read these letters if I got farther away from them. So for a while I dealt with the situation by order- ing off the menus of people sitting at other tables.

"I'd like to order some dessert," I'd tell the waiter. "Please bring a menu to the people at that table over there and ask them to hold it up so I can see it."[13]

"I've reached the age where
I need three pairs of glasses:
One for driving, one for reading—
and one to find the other two!"

Snappy Birthday Greetings

Many of us especially feel ourselves whizzing through the aging turnstiles when we celebrate (or endure) birthdays end- ing with zeros. Actually, these events might not seem as monu- mental to us except for the wisecracks of our so-called friends, the ones who delight in sending us those sarcastic greeting cards that start ribbing us about getting old when we first turn thirty. By the time we're forty, they're downright wicked. Author Max Lucado said he received these happy birthday wishes when he reached the big four-oh:

- You know you're getting older when you try to straighten out the wrinkles in your socks only to find you aren't wearing any.

- At twenty we don't care what the world thinks of us; at thirty we start to worry about what the world thinks of us; at forty we realize the world isn't thinking of us at all.

- I've gotten to the age where I need my false teeth and hearing aid before I can ask where I left my glasses.

- Forty is when you stop patting yourself on the back and start patting yourself under the chin.[14]

The smart-aleck cards continue for decades. And then an interesting thing happens. It would seem like a relief, except that we *know* what it *really* means when the greeting-card humor dries up. The kidding stops, and the greeting cards take on a kinder, gentler tone (with bigger, bolder letters). That's the indication that we've reached the point when it's not safe to make wisecracks because the things that were once so funny on the earlier greeting cards are now *true!*

One greeting-card company spokesman said age forty used to be the company's cutoff for printing cards with humorous slams about getting old. Now, he said, fifty-year-olds "are able to take kidding. . . . We tend to tone it down a little at fifty, but not much. At sixty, it's definitely toned down. And that's where [the company's humor division] stops doing milestone cards." Another card company follows the same philosophy. After fifty, a card company editor said, "We enter Compliment City." That's when the wisecracks turn into compliments: "You're looking marvelous" or "What a great year you've had!"[15]

Compliment City? How awful!

It's strange, isn't it, the way we look at aging? Someone sent me a little essay that notes when we're kids, we *want* to get old. In fact, kids younger than ten give their age in fractions: "I'm four and a half." We're even more forward-focused as teenagers, automatically jumping to the next number: "I'm almost sixteen." Then comes twenty-one, and we've peaked. After that, the verbs start taking on a rather negative tone as we mark each milestone:

We *turn* thirty (makes you sound like milk that turned bad). The next thing we know, we're *pushing* forty. Then we *reach* fifty, *hit* sixty, *make it to* seventy, and *live until* our eighties. After that, a strange thing happens. We start going backward, telling listeners, "I was ninety-two in April."

These stages keep coming so quickly, you may not even realize they're taking you into old age. Here's the way one writer told Ann Landers how to know you're getting old:

- The magic begins. You put your keys on the dresser, and they mysteriously wind up on top of the fridge. You lay the remote on the TV and find it later under the sofa. You slip your wallet into your purse, and the next morning it is on the front seat of your car.

- You do a lot of arithmetic. "Let's see, he died, and he was—and I am four years younger, so that means she is—and I'm—no way! Not possible." . . .

- You develop TMI (Too Much Information), a sure sign of old age. I remind myself that every happening need not be reported in endless detail.

- You laugh at yourself more. Be grateful that you can. Some people can't. If you are unable to find the humor in yourself, chances are you won't find it anywhere else. The alternative is anger and despair.[16]

That kind of attitude was expressed in the happy demeanor of an old lady in the nursing home where my sister Janet goes every week to play the piano for the residents. One week the ninety-three-year-old woman told Janet, "I get up every morning and look in the mirror, and I know who I am. And I see the calendar and know what day it is. And then I say, 'Well, praise the Lord!'"

In contrast, there was Bill Cosby's grandfather. When someone asked him, on his ninety-eighth birthday, "How does it feel to be ninety-eight?" the old man replied gruffly, "It wasn't worth the wait!"

Looking Back in Awe

Imagine what it's like for these witty elders to think back on the changes they've witnessed. When we were in Nebraska last year, an Omaha woman told me how her grandmother had marveled that she lived long enough to see covered wagons . . . and the space shuttle. Soon after that, I read a newspaper story announcing the recent death, at age ninety, of the first patient whose life was saved by penicillin back in 1942. And not long after that I saw an article that named an American company that has committed $500 million to "build a cruise ship to ferry people from Earth orbit to the moon and back" and another company that "confirmed that it is looking into the feasibility of a space hotel."[17]

Such stories reminded me of all the things we gained during the last century. But we lost some things too. When *USA Today* asked its readers last year what they would miss in this new millennium, one of the surprising things they mentioned was *stars!* Apparently many of the respondents had grown up in a more rural era, and they remembered standing in the yards of their remote farmhouses at night and seeing the beautiful canopy of the universe twinkling overhead. Now, in many places, the stars are dimmed, the writer noted, "their spectacular nightly show hidden behind the glare of city lights."[18]

This little "test" someone sent to me reminds us of some of the other things that disappeared with the turn of the century—or earlier. See which ones you remember:

1. Blackjack chewing gum
2. Little Coke-shaped bottles made of wax with colored sugar water inside
3. Soda pop machines that dispensed glass bottles
4. Home milk delivery in glass bottles with cardboard caps
5. Telephone party lines
6. Newsreels before movies
7. P.F. Flyers

8. Butch Wax

9. Telephone numbers with a word prefix (Olive 2-6933 or Tuxedo 4-9351)

10. Peashooters

11. Howdy Doody

12. 45 RPM and 78 RPM Records

13. Metal ice trays with levers

14. Mimeograph machines

15. Blue flashbulbs

16. Beanie and Cecil

17. Roller-skate keys

18. Cork popguns

19. Studebakers

20. Wringer washtubs

Count how many of these items you remember to know how old you really are:

0: You're still young.
1–10: You're getting older
11–15: Don't tell your age.
More than 15: You're older than dirt!

There probably was a time, perhaps back at the *last* turn of the century, when those wringer washtubs were considered modern miracles. One woman told me her pioneer grandmother used to regale her with stories of taking the family's clothes and bedding to the creek several times a year to do the laundry. She dipped creek water into iron kettles, built a fire, boiled the clothes, scrubbed them with homemade lye soap, and then had to wring out everything—including the heavy quilts—by hand. To those hardworking women, wringer washtubs were probably a modern miracle!

"Some would say I'm retired, but I like to think of
myself as a stay-at-home grandfather."

In the same way, we still have many advances to be thankful for, even as we lament beloved things we've had to give
up. A recent newspaper clipping reminded me of this kind of
blessing. It described a seventy-year-old woman—a woman
born long before penicillin, computers, and many other modern medical advances—who had lost almost all of her hearing
nearly twenty years earlier. Since then she had had a tiny bit
of hearing in one ear but had been functionally deaf. She used
a writing board to communicate with her family.

Then she learned of a new type of surgical technology that
would insert a tiny, computerized device in her head that
might restore her hearing. Or it might not. In fact, there was
an almost certain risk that the operation would destroy the
tiny bit of hearing she still had, so if the implanted device
didn't work she would be totally deaf. But being a courageous woman, she decided to take that risk. She wasn't just
courageous, though. She was a Christian. And on the morning of her surgery, the woman's daughter opened her book of
daily readings and was amazed to find, in that day's selec-

tion, this verse from Isaiah 48:6: "From this time forward, I will make you hear new things, hidden things that you have not known."

It took several weeks after the surgery for the incision to heal and the device to be turned on so it could begin working. And on that morning when the doctor finally attempted to activate the implant, the woman and her family rejoiced when, for the first time in two decades, she heard her loved ones' voices again.[19]

Don't you love stories like that? Courageous people of all ages are inspiring to the rest of us. But when they're seventy years old, they're more than courageous. They're heroes.

Of course, being one who loves to laugh, I can't help but throw in here the joke about the old man who had had a serious hearing loss for many years. He finally went to the doctor and was fitted for a set of hearing aids that restored his hearing completely. When the old man went back to the doctor a month later for a checkup, the doctor said, "Your hearing is perfect. Your family must be really pleased that you can hear again."

"Oh, I haven't told them yet," the old man replied. "I just sit around and listen. I've changed my will three times!"

That old guy had discovered a wonderful insight that many of us would be wise to share. Some of us, especially as we get older, seem to have no interest in *listening*. We only want others to listen to us. But if we would just stop yapping for a minute and really *hear* what our friends and loved ones are telling us, we might learn something—or maybe even something that would prompt us to change our wills!

Saturated Brain Storage

Hearing about the implant that miraculously restored the deaf woman's hearing, I can't help but wish scientists would develop some kind of brain implant we could get to ward off memory loss as we age. One comedian said that older people "lose their memory because their brains are full, often with useless data such as the name of their third grade teacher and the lyrics to 'Volare.'" Well, I can't sing "Volare," but I can name my former teachers—and I have no idea where I just left my glasses . . . or my checkbook . . . or my car keys. So maybe the comedian is right when he suggests that what we need is a form of add-on storage space for our brains, along the lines of those storage sheds people erect in their backyards. Or, he said, we might somehow "download" surplus information to our stomachs, "where there is plenty of room."[20]

Think about it. If only we had more room to store the things we want to remember, we'd actually get our money's worth from those memory-enhancing courses that are so popular now. One elderly couple, getting on in years and losing their memories, decided to take such a course. The husband was thrilled with the results; in fact, he felt the course changed his life. He and his wife met their friend Bill on the street, and the husband said to him, "Bill, you just have to take this incredible memory course my wife and I just finished. It's fantastic! You won't believe the improvement."

Bill said, "Wow! That's great. What's the name of the course?"

The husband turned to his wife and asked, "What's the name of that flower? You know, the one with the long stem and the thorns?"

"You mean a rose?" his wife replied.

"Yeah, that's it! (pause . . .) Rose, what was the name of that memory course?"

Aging Gracefully

One of the things I hope I can remember is the advice that Dear Abby columnist Abigail Van Buren gave when she celebrated her eightieth birthday. Asked to name her biggest accomplishment, she answered succinctly, "Surviving." Then she shared her advice for aging gracefully:

Fear less; hope more. Eat less; chew more. Talk less; say more. Hate less; love more. And never underestimate the power of forgiveness.

Squirts & Squints

Bumper sticker:
Jesus is coming! Look busy!

A reporter was visiting an elderly couple who had just celebrated their sixty-fifth wedding anniversary. He was touched by the way the husband continually spoke to his wife in terms of endearment, always calling her "Sweetheart," "Honey," or "Dear."

"It's so sweet, the way you address your wife in those endearing ways," the reporter said to the husband.

"Well, to tell you the truth," the old man answered, "I forgot her name about ten years ago."

I can see clearly now. My brain is gone.

Top Ten Reasons Why Heaven's Looking Good

10. You can begin the Lord's Prayer, "Our Father, who art here . . ."
9. You can find out the answer to the question "Why?"
8. Wings.
7. Soul music for eternity.
6. Real golden arches.
5. Great view.
4. "No pain, no gain" becomes "no pain, no pain."
3. When you say, "Oh, God . . ." you'll hear, "Yes?"
2. Harp lessons.

And the number one reason why heaven's looking good:
1. It's totally fat free.

—Fred W. Sanford

It is easier to get older than wiser.

Some people grow up and spread cheer . . .
Others just grow up and spread.

SHOE

© Tribune Media Services, Inc. All Rights Reserved. Reprinted with permission.

The glory of each morning
is that it offers us a chance to begin again.

As an aircraft landed at the airport, a flight attendant made
this announcement:

"Ladies and gentlemen, we have a very special person
on board this evening. He is ninety-six years old today,
and this is his very first flight. As you deplane this
evening, please stop by the cockpit and wish our captain
Happy Birthday!"

It's not the pace of life that concerns me,
it's the sudden stop at the end.

Three friends were talking about death. One of them asked, "When you are in your casket and friends and family are mourning over you, what would you most like to hear them say about you? I've been thinking about it, and I hope they'll say that I was one of the great doctors of my time—and a great family man."

The second man said, "I would like to hear them say that I was a loving husband and father, and a devoted schoolteacher who made a difference in shaping the adults of tomorrow."

The third man thought seriously for a moment and then said, "I would like to hear them say . . . 'LOOK, HE'S MOVING! HE'S STILL ALIVE!'"

Two bikers were riding down a country road on a Harley. The driver's leather jacket wouldn't stay closed because the zipper had broken, so he pulled over. "Just put your jacket on backward," his buddy suggested.

Then they zoomed off down the road, until they hit a curve at high speed and crashed. A farmer found them and called the police.

"Is either of them showing any sign of life?" asked the officer.

"Well, the first one was," replied the farmer, "until I turned his head around the right way."[21]

Have you heard about the new Barbie dolls?

Bifocals Barbie: Comes with her own set of bifocal fashion frames in six wild colors (half-frames too!), neck chain, and large-print editions of *Vogue* and *Martha Stewart Living*.

Hot Flash Barbie: Press Barbie's bellybutton, and watch her face turn beet red while tiny drops of perspiration appear on her forehead. Comes with handheld fan and tiny tissues.

Facial Hair Barbie: As Barbie's hormone levels shift, see her whiskers grow. Available with teensy tweezers and magnifying mirror.

Bunion Barbie: Years of disco dancing in stiletto heels have taken their toll on Barbie's dainty, arched feet. Soothe her sores with the pumice stone and plasters, then slip on soft terry slippers.

No-More-Wrinkles Barbie: Erase those pesky crow's-feet and lip lines with a tube of Skin Sparkle-Spackle from Barbie's own line of exclusive age-blasting cosmetics.

Post-Menopausal Barbie: She wets her pants when she sneezes, forgets where she put things, and cries a lot. Comes with micro-Depends and Kleenex.

A little boy took his pet iguana to school to show the other kids. If you've ever seen an iguana, you know it has a large flap of skin, called the dewlap, that hangs down from the neck. The kids asked what it was, and when the boy explained, a little girl said, "Oh! My grandma has one of those."

> When did my wild oats
> turn into shredded wheat?

Post Mark Twain's wisdom on your mirror and practice adding facial creases each day: "Wrinkles merely indicate where the smiles have been."

Praise the LORD, O my soul, and forget not all his benefits.

—PSALM 103:2

Sliding Down a Rainbow, into a Pool of Joy!

"That's What It's All About, Isn't It, Barb?"

When Sam Butcher, the creator of Precious Moments, gave me permission to use some of his adorable artwork in my book *He's Gonna Toot and I'm Gonna Scoot!* I was overjoyed. He even invited us to come to the fabulous Precious Moments Chapel outside Carthage, Missouri, to get better acquainted with his work—and with him. We had such a marvelous time there seeing the chapel, the breathtaking fountain event, and even his own private art gallery and visiting with Sam and his super-efficient assistant Larrene Hagaman, that I wanted to reciprocate. "You've gotta come to a Women of Faith conference," I begged, "so I can introduce you to a few thousand of *my* friends."

Larrene told "the rest of the story" about Sam's appearance at the Kansas City conference in May 1999 in an article she wrote for *Chapel Bells* magazine, and she's agreed to let me adapt it here for you to enjoy:

The mere thought of being present with over eighteen thousand women was enough to give Mr. Butcher a chill,

but when Barbara implied he might want to say something, he really got the "willies"! At first he agreed that
if my husband, Darrell, could go along, he would go and
be willing to be introduced, stand, and wave. Then he
got braver and said he would "say a little something."

Kemper Arena in Kansas City is a huge, round building, and as we met Barbara, her husband, Bill, and the
others, Mr. B said, "I really need more time to think about
what I'm going to say."

Loosely translated, I have come to know that means he
needs to pace—and I need to be sociable. I gathered with
several others in the green room and discovered that
Barbara was nearly as nervous as he was! This is not the
norm for Barbara, who will speak in over thirty cities this
year with audiences ranging from eight to twenty thousand people. But introducing Mr. Butcher made her more
nervous than if she were "introducing Billy Graham or
the Pope," she said as we left the room and began to walk
back and forth in the hallway, straining to see which
direction Mr. B had gone. It was a long, long hallway that
circled the entire building.

I tried to soothe Barbara, and we moved back into the
green room to join the others. "The neat thing about
these conferences," one of the ladies said, "is that all the
men's bathrooms are turned into women's!"

My eyes widened as that thought penetrated my brain
and I realized Mr. B *didn't know* that potentially cata-
strophic little fact! I ran out the door, grabbed Darrell
and said, "You go that way, and I'll go this way! Find Mr.
Butcher, and don't either of you go to the bathroom!"

Darrell thought I'd lost my marbles, but he dutifully
headed out, found the boss, and much to my relief, both
of them returned unscathed.

It wasn't long until we were swooped into the midst
of eighteen thousand rousing, clapping, joyous women
who were swinging with the gospel group that was leading into Barbara's segment of this whopper of a gather-

ing. Mr. B was mentally still gathering his thoughts right up until he was introduced. And, as usual, he gathered them in a way that was just right. He endeared himself to everyone when he pointed to the words he had written on his hand and shyly said, "My notes!"

Part of what he shared was a real surprise for Barbara. He announced that this year's charity doll would have a specific name for the first time, and that the proceeds would go to assist her Spatula Ministries.*

The "Barbara Charity Doll" is really a beauty. It has a straw hat with a red geranium on it, and it is holding a spatula. Barbara's best-selling book, *Stick a Geranium in Your Hat and Be Happy*, led to her being well known as the "Geranium Lady." Her ministry is to assist parents who learn something about their children that they find so shocking, they need someone to scrape them off the ceiling with a spatula of love. Barbara often receives calls and letters from parents of gays, lesbians, young people who have joined occult groups, etc. She assists in so many ways to help those who have AIDS and their families as well. In fact, each December she personally telephones hundreds who have lost a child and are struggling to survive, to tell them that she remembers and is thinking of them. That phone bill alone is well over five thousand dollars!

The W Publishing Group presented Mr. Butcher a plaque showing the cover of *Toot and Scoot* and a perfectly charming drawing of the Geranium Lady bending over to kiss Timmy the Angel. It will be hung in the gallery near the chapel for everyone to enjoy.

After the presentation, we slipped away to a lovely, historic restaurant several miles from the arena. Sue Ann Jones, Barbara's editor, explained that at the arena the night before a sweet Precious Moments collector,

* For details about ordering the Precious Moments "Barbara Johnson Charity Doll (PMC 1145)" call 1-800-445-2220 or go to www.preciousmoments.com.

Sarah Rawley, had bought a copy of *Toot and Scoot* at Barbara's book table and was so excited to learn that Mr. Butcher would be present the next day. When she asked if he was going to be signing, Sue Ann told her no, but being the kind person that she is, she offered to take the girl's book and see if Mr. B would sign it during the luncheon.

As we walked into the restaurant and made our way to a private dining room in another area, Sue Ann expressed complete surprise to find Sarah sitting in this restaurant, miles from the arena, with her friends and family. (She learned later that Sarah's mother had made *their* reservations long before the event and had no idea we would be there either!)

As we settled into our private dining room, Mr. B took off his suit coat and rolled up his shirt sleeves, grateful for a moment of "down time" after the excitement of the jam-packed arena. After Sue Ann told me about the situation with the girl out in the main dining room, I assured her that Mr. Butcher would no doubt want to sign the book for her—and deliver it personally! Such was the case! As soon as he heard about Sarah, he quickly signed a brief dedication, re-buttoned his shirt cuffs, reached for his coat, and beckoned for Sue Ann to come and point Sarah out to him. Knowing Sarah would want a photographic remembrance of the moment, he said, "Larrene, don't forget the camera!" as he headed out the door.

So we all trooped back out toward the main dining room, intending to peek around the door while Sue Ann pointed out Sarah to Sam. But as soon as their heads poked around the edge, Sarah spotted them and popped to her feet. She'd been watching that door!

With a broad smile, Mr. B presented the signed book to Sarah, then we snapped the photo shown here—and made Sarah's day!

Later, Barbara told Mr. B how special she thought it

Sam Butcher's thoughtful kindness touched Sarah Rawley's heart—and mine.

was of him to make that extra effort. His response was so typical of him. "That's what it's all about, isn't it, Barbara?" he said.

As she nodded, I thought how blessed I am to call each of them my friend.[1]

My friendship with Sam Butcher and his incredible assistant, Larrene, has been a "bath of blessings" for me. To be honest, after twenty years of working with hurting families and heartbroken parents, I thought I knew a lot about serving others through ministry. But every time I'm with Sam, I'm inspired and educated. In Kansas City when he said, "That's what it's all about, isn't it, Barb?" I saw the incredible power of his servant's heart. Sam's right. As Christians, serving others is exactly what it's all about for all of us!

By his kind thoughtfulness, Sam demonstrates the truth of the following "gift list" put together by an unknown writer:

Priceless Gifts to Give for Free

The gift of listening: No interrupting, no daydreaming, no planning your responses. Just listen.

The gift of affection: Be generous with appropriate hugs, kisses, pats on the back, and handholds. Let these small actions demonstrate the love you have for family and friends.

The gift of laughter: Share articles, funny stories, and cartoons to tell someone, "I love to laugh with you."

The gift of a written note: A brief, handwritten note may be remembered for a lifetime and may even change a life.

The gift of a compliment: A simple and sincere "You look great in red," "You did a super job," or "That was a wonderful meal" can make someone's day.

The gift of a favor: Every day, go out of your way to do something kind for someone.

The gift of solitude: There are times when we want nothing more than to be left alone. Be sensitive to those times and give the gift of solitude to others.

The gift of a cheerful disposition: The easiest way to feel good is to extend a kind word to someone, even if it's just saying hello or thank you.

The gift of a prayer: Let your friends and loved ones know you pray for them—and then do it!

Reaching Out . . .

We like to say that Spatula Ministries uses a spatula of love to scrape parents down when something about their children has caused them to land on the ceiling. Sometimes these ceiling-flattened parents are trying to cope with adult children who are struggling with AIDS, addictions, prostitution, cults, and all sorts of other problems that cause many folks, even Christians, to reject them and heap scorn upon them—and sometimes upon their parents too. That's why I was so touched last year when a friend added this postscript to her letter:

> Barbara, keep doing what you do. There are churches and Christian programs around the world that minister to the ninety-and-nine. But you are reaching out to that one lost sheep.

My friend's encouragement reminded me that it might be *my* arms reaching out to that "one lost sheep," but it's God's love flowing through me that accomplishes the healing. As someone said,

> Broken skin heals in days . . . broken bones in weeks or months . . . broken hearts and spirits sometimes in years . . . broken souls heal only by God's grace.

Sam Butcher shares my concern for the outcast. Larrene loaned me a tape of a message Sam gave recently about the story of the leper in the first chapter of the Gospel of Mark. Sam noted that the leper lived each day with three condemnations. He was condemned by his own deadly afflictions, by his friends and family, and by society and the law. In Jesus' day, lepers were totally shunned; some people feared that they might be contaminated if they even looked at a leper.

Keep this situation in mind, Sam said, as you picture Jesus surrounded by a crowd of people, all wanting something from Him. Suddenly the crowd parted as the believers pushed and shoved to keep from touching the one lone leper who was courageously making his way toward Jesus. The others struggled to get away from the leper, but Jesus remained. And then He did something that astonished those watching. The Bible says Jesus, "filled with compassion, . . . reached out his hand and touched the man."[2]

A simple touch . . . but what a difference it made.

Jesus' example shows that serving others with a humble heart doesn't mean we have to do great, extravagant things to

I know the Lord is my shepherd...

Sometimes I just really
look forward to lying down in
those green pastures by
that quiet stream, don't you?!

Art and copy by Matt Anderson. Used by permission. © DaySpring® Cards, Siloam Springs, Arkansas.

do what Jesus would do. Sometimes we can simply touch the untouchable . . . and share God's loving, life-changing grace.

We do God's work because God promises to work in us and through us. What a comfort to consider this list someone compiled of the promises He has made to us:

God's Promises

I will never leave you nor forsake you. (Josh. 1:5)

I will sustain you and rescue you. (Isa. 46:4)

I will strengthen you and help you; I will uphold you with my righteous right hand. (Isa. 41:10)

I am with you and will watch over you wherever you go. (Gen. 28:15)

I am your hiding place. I will protect you from trouble and surround you with songs of deliverance. I will instruct you and teach you in the way you should go; I will counsel you and watch over you. (Ps. 32:7–8)

Call to me and I will answer you and tell you great and unsearchable things you do not know. (Jer. 33:3)

I am with you, I am mighty to save. I will take great delight in you. I will quiet you with my love. I will rejoice over you with singing. (Zeph. 3:17)

The Smallest Gesture

After our son Steven was killed in Vietnam, he was buried with military honors in a local cemetery. My memory of that day is a blur of painful yet encouraging scenes. But the most memorable moment for me lasted no more than a second; it was a tiny gesture of respect that has comforted me for nearly thirty years. At the end of the military salute at the cemetery, the honor guard precisely folded the flag covering Steven's casket. Next it was passed to the leader of the honor guard, who turned sharply and then slowly walked the few steps to where our family was seated. It was the split-second gesture the soldier made before giving us the flag that has stayed with me all these years. He touched the folded flag to his heart, held it there for only a second, and then extended it to Bill.

You may never know who or how others will be affected by the simplest gesture of kindness or the briefest message of hope. After including in my conference message the story of how some of the Women of Faith gals had reached out to help a desperate prostitute with full-blown AIDS who had stumbled into the arena where the event was being held, someone left this note at my book table.

Dear Barbara,
    Thank you. I am a police officer and a mother of four. My 21-year-old daughter is a crack-addicted prostitute. Thank you for the hope.

You see, when I told that story to the audience of ten thousand women, I thought I was delivering a motivational message—an encouragement to those women to put the idea of

"What Would Jesus Do?" into action. But to one woman I was sharing a message of hope—the hope that somewhere out there, a kind, Christian soul might also show kindness to *her* daughter, wherever she was, and lead her to Christ.

A similar thing happened when the Women of Faith tour was in a southern city a couple of years ago. My hostess there was a wonderfully efficient professional woman who not only made the conference go smoothly for us but also gave us a delightful tour of the city and nearby plantations and shared with us the stories of her own amazing ancestors. She knew very little about my books or my ministry that reaches out to the families of homosexuals. In fact, she knew very little about "that lifestyle" at all—except, she said, she'd had a cousin, an entertainer, who'd lived a rather unusual existence.

She was driving my helpers and me from the hotel to the arena as she told us the story. Her entertainer cousin, she said, had undergone one of the first sex-change operations several years earlier. Then he had become a Christian and had had the operation reversed, all in the glare of publicity that had embarrassed his whole family. "We all knew about it," the hostess said, "but no one talked about him anymore. It was as though he didn't really exist. But he was always so dear to me. We had been friends as children, and I just loved him right up until his death a few years ago," she said sadly.

My antenna had gone up as soon as she started laying out the details of the entertainer's story. "What was his name?" I asked.

"Perry Desmond," she answered simply.

"Perry Desmond!? Perry *Desmond?* Oh, of course I knew Perry Desmond!" I exclaimed. "I loved him! He and I did some programs together. In fact, we shared a room together once. We got to the hotel somewhere, and there weren't enough rooms, and no one would share with him—you know he *was* a little strange—and I said, 'Well, I'll room with him— or her—or whatever he was at that moment.' He was so much fun, and he had so much talent. And when he died, we had a

little service for him out in California, just his close friends
and the people he had worked with. I think I've still got the
videotape we made of all the funny things and tributes his
friends made for him."

Hearing my excited babbling, the hostess burst into tears! I
couldn't imagine what I'd said that was so bad. But finally
she managed to say, "Oh, Barb! I loved Perry, and it hurt me
to see how he was treated by everyone, including his family.
You can't imagine what it means to me to know that he had
friends like you . . . that there were people out there who were
kind to him."

That's Life

"Have a nice eternity."

Having a son who's a homosexual, I know how hurtful it is
to imagine him being scorned or ridiculed. Now whenever I
see or meet a person who's obviously struggling with homosexuality or "gender identity," as they say, I no longer think,
What a strange person that is! Instead I quickly remember, *That
person is some poor mother's child.* And that attitude, I've found,
makes quite a difference in my actions. It's an idea that is expressed so beautifully in this essay by an unknown writer:

You see her, don't You, Lord Jesus? She's standing there, alone, on the edge of the playground, a forlorn little waif who's not quite right. Her clothes aren't right, her hair isn't right, and her speech . . . well, it isn't right, either.

You know her, Lord. A bypassed, misfit little duckling, standing all alone because the other ducklings say she's not quite right.

What can I do, Lord? I can't force the other kids to include her in their merry game. That would only make matters worse, turning a harsh spotlight on her misery.

Seeing her standing there, I swallow hard, bite my lip, and look away. Oh, Lord Jesus, why? Why are there outcasts on the edge of the playground, on the edge of the neighborhood, the edge of the church? If I were in charge, there'd be none of that. No one would be lonely just because her clothes weren't right, her hair was funny, and her speech came with a lisp. If it were *my* world, all the ducklings would be, well, *acceptable* . . .

But I know Your ways are not my ways, Lord. I want acceptable ducklings, while You want glorious swans. You want Your ducklings to know the infinite value of being weak, humble, and not quite "right." You want us to understand that the pain of being different just might be Your way of preparing us for greatness.

Lord, please help me to see that lonely little girl through Your eyes. Show me the promise in her humility, the talents hidden within her so that I can help her see them too. Help me to give her . . . herself.

Thank You for reminding me that no one loves the outcast more than You do, Lord Jesus. No one is more sensitive to the abandoned and the lonely than You, who stretched out Your arms on the cross to gather the outcasts, the misfits, the lepers, the maimed, and the funny-looking.

Oh, Jesus! Open Your arms again and gather in that forlorn little girl . . . and me.

Blessed to be a Blessing

As someone said, the opportunity to do good is so fleeting. It's not enough to see the little, lonely girl and have our hearts broken. We have to do more than grieve for her and pray for her. We have to *touch* her in some way, just as Jesus reached out and touched the leper.

At the National Prayer Breakfast last year, one of the speakers said, "Each one of us has a unique assignment in this world given to us by a sovereign God—to love and to serve those within our own sphere of influence. We've been blessed to be a blessing; we've received that we might give."

More times than I can recount, I know I have "received that I might give"; I've been blessed to be a blessing. Here's one way someone's gesture of kindness to me has descended through the years to be a blessing to others like a pebble dropped in a pond.

The story began in 1973 when our son Tim and another friend were in their early twenties and traveled to Alaska for one of those classic adventures of youth. They planned to just stay a short while, see the sights, and come home. But at a gas station in Anchorage, they happened to meet a friendly resident who noticed their California license plate and commented on how far they had driven. Despite my best efforts during Tim's childhood to train him not to go home with strangers, he and his friend accepted the man's invitation to go to his house for dinner. He was a youth minister, he told them, and some other young people were coming over that night for a Bible study get-together.

The boys must have enjoyed the evening. They not only stayed for dinner—they stayed two months! The thoughtful youth minister, Ted McReynolds, and his wife, Joanne, opened their home to these young adventurers so far from home. While they were staying with Ted and Joanne, Tim's life changed. He'd been raised as a Christian, but there in Alaska, with Ted and Joanne leading the way, his spiritual life ignited, and he was on fire for Jesus. While he was up there he was baptized. And he rededicated his life to the Lord.

(I was a little hurt by that. I thought, *Our church has good water down here.*) I was eager to have him come home and tell us all about his experiences.

After he'd left Alaska and was driving back to California, he called about midday from White Horse in the Yukon Territory of Canada and told me, "Mom, I have a spring in my step and a sparkle in my eye. I'll be home in five days and tell you all about it!"

We were so eager to see him and hear how God had worked in his life. But it wasn't to be. A few hours later, while we were eating dinner, we got a call from the Royal Canadian Mounted Police telling us that Tim and his friend had been killed in a crash with a drunk driver.

During the awful time after the accident, Ted and Joanne McReynolds called from Alaska. They wanted to come to California and tell us what had happened to Tim—in other words, they wanted to tell the story of Tim's experiences in Alaska that Tim himself had been so eager to tell us. After meeting them, we asked Ted to help conduct the boys' service. It was a tremendous outpouring of hope as he told the story of how Tim had dedicated his future to living for Jesus.

Inspired by Ted and Joanne's example, I resolved right then and there to reach out to other parents in pain and offer the kind of encouragement and hope they had given us. Wherever and whenever I could, I wanted to help other parents whose hearts had been broken by the loss of a child. Bill and I had already taken a few steps in that direction five years earlier when Steven died in Vietnam, but now we worked with renewed purpose. Later, when a third son, Larry, disappeared into the homosexual lifestyle, our work expanded to include *those* parents too.

Looking back now, I recognize that gift of encouragement from Ted and Joanne as the pebble tossed into a pool. Their kindness splashed over me in a ripple of love. And I have been blessed, in the twenty-six years since then, with the honor of splashing those ripples on to others. The result has been more than a dozen books—now totaling more than five million copies in print—plus several years of nationwide speaking appearances and thousands of contacts with parents who have lost their children to death or alienation due to homosexuality or other situations. In addition, I've been a guest on dozens of TV and radio shows across the land, spreading the encouraging message of hope that was handed down to me by the McReynoldses all those years ago.

One of those radio shows came back to me as a boomerang blessing last year when the Women of Faith tour was in Denver. As a result, someone else dropped in another pebble of hope to keep the blessing going. And along the way, I had a little adventure of my own!

This part of the story actually began about fifteen years ago—five years after the McReynoldses had inspired me to pass along their blessing of hope. A young doctor was driving from Houston to San Francisco. His younger brother had committed suicide, and he was on his way up there to plan the service and pull everybody together. He turned on the radio in his car on his way up there, and it happened to be playing a *Focus on the Family* program. It was actually a tape that had been made a few months earlier when I'd been a guest on the show. On the tape Dr. James Dobson was asking me, "Barb, how do you deal with the families of those who have committed suicide?"

I answered that I remind parents that when someone commits suicide he "goes out to meet a just and a loving God." And then I said some other things about counseling those families who have gone through that situation.

At the end of the program, Dr. Dobson, bless his heart, gave out my home phone number! This young doctor, driving from Texas to California, heard my number, got off the freeway, stopped at a pay phone, and called me. He said, "My brother committed suicide, and I'm on my way to organize his funeral. I've never done this before. I don't know what to say, but you were a ministering angel to me today, Barbara. Everything you said I can put together for his memorial service. I just had to call and tell you how you ministered to me today—without even knowing it."

Sometime later I visited the doctor in Houston and spoke at his church, and then he came to our home and visited us. We became friends. He would call me every few weeks and say, "I need a couple of boxes of your books. I have a lot of patients who have problems!"

So, over the next fifteen years, we kept him supplied with books for his patients. Then, just a few years ago, he moved to the Denver area.

When the Women of Faith tour was in Denver last fall, our MC, Mary Graham, became incapacitated with severe leg cramps. When I heard about it, I rushed to Mary's room, took one look at her, and even though it was eleven o'clock at night, I called my doctor friend, Doug.

Right away he said, "Barbara, what can I do for you? You've been a ministering angel to me for all these years. Can I be your ministering angel *now?*"

"Oh, yes!" I answered. "I need help, because this woman, Mary, is not only my dear friend, she's in charge of this whole conference! And she can hardly walk. She's having terrible trouble, and oh, I hope you can help her. But I've already called two or three drugstores, and there's nothing open around here this late at night. I can't even get aspirin!"

He said, "You just hang on. I'll call her and make sure I understand what her problem is. Then I'll call a Walgreen's that's open all night. It's not in the safest area, Barb, but if you can get over there, they'll have the prescriptions waiting for you."

I said, "Doug, I've already gone to bed. I've got no car or anything. How am I gonna get over there?"

He said, "Oh, you'll figure that out, Barb. I know you. Now, I'll call in the prescriptions, but I also want you to get her some ripe bananas. She needs to eat something with this medication, and bananas would be best."

Ripe bananas? At eleven o'clock at night when I can't even find a drugstore, I had to find ripe bananas too? But I called a cab and rushed downstairs. In the lobby I met Liz, a Campus Crusade worker who helps with the conferences. She was just coming in from the airport. She took one look at me—I was wearing Bill's shirt over my slacks, had on no makeup, and hadn't fixed my hair since getting out of bed—and said, "Barb! What's wrong?"

I told her the whole story, and she said, "I'll take you to Walgreen's."

"They say it's in a dangerous part of town," I warned.

Liz answered, "That's OK. Let's go."

The hotel desk clerk drew out a little map to show us how to get to the drugstore, but we went a few blocks and realized we didn't know where we were or where we were going. In other words, we were lost. So we turned the dome light on and stopped the car to look at the hand-drawn map again. Just then a man's face appeared right at my door, pressed up against the window! He was wearing a ski cap pulled low over his head, and he just about scared me right into eternity. I yelled, "Liz, let's go! Just pull away. Go! Let's get out of here!"

We finally got to the drugstore and picked up the prescriptions. And on the way back, I said, "Now, Doug said to get some ripe bananas. But there's nothing open; everything's closed." Then, down the road, we saw a big, bright sign with just one four-letter word on it: "F-O-O-D." That's all it said, "FOOD," as though God were trying to keep things simple for us.

We pulled into the parking lot, and I told Liz, "Honey, you park by the door. You're young and cute, and I'm old and fat, so no one will bother me. Keep the motor running, keep the lights on, and lock the doors." (I don't have much faith. I've got a lot of joy, but you can't have every gift.) I told Liz to "stay right here by the door so nobody can get in or out. And if I'm not out in five minutes, you honk that horn and get the police."

So I went in, and right in front of me was a huge table filled with beautiful, yellow, ripe bananas! I couldn't believe it! That was the biggest miracle of all. So I shoved seven or eight bananas in a sack, paid the guy, jumped back in the car, and we were on our way back to deliver our emergency supplies to Mary.

The next morning Doug called and said, "I was just wondering how your big-shot friend is doing."

"Oh, she's doing fine!" I told him. "She's moving around and handling the whole thing just fine. Thanks so much, Doug. You *were* a ministering angel to all of us."

He paused a moment and said, "Barbara, I've been thinking. You know what I'd like to do, if you could help me? I'd like to start a ministry for people like you—for missionaries and Christian speakers who are on the road and get a sore throat or leg cramps. They could call a number and get a Christian doctor who could help them—give them suggestions and call in a prescription to wherever."

"Oh, Doug, that would be wonderful!" I exclaimed.

And the ripples in the pond just keep spreading outward . . .

A Blessing Phenomenon

There's another phenomenon that happens when we pass on a blessing to someone else. It may defy the laws of physics; I don't know. But I'm convinced it happens. While a blessing of kindness ripples outward to others, it boomerangs right back to the one who threw the pebble. As one brokenhearted mother wrote in a letter to me, "God will take care of me, and I will do for others while God does for me. A great way to beat the blues is to do something for someone else." And another Christian wrote, "Those of us who have been saved should always be prepared to throw others a rope."

This isn't just the view of believers; it's been proved by scientific research. One report said recently that research had found that "doing for others . . . infuses people with vitality, purpose, happiness and health to heretofore unrecognized degrees."[3] It was a lesson illustrated by the loving actions of an eighty-eight-year-old mother who, every Sunday, pushed her fifty-year-old disabled son's wheelchair down the center aisle of a church to the front row where they sat so they could both hear. Every week an usher or friend offered to push the son's wheelchair for the old woman, and every week she politely declined the help. "No, thank you," she would say. "You see, I hold on to Michael's chair to keep *myself* from falling."

To paraphrase Proverbs 11:25, as we help others, we ourselves are helped.

She who waters others will also be watered herself.
(Prov. 11:25 adapted)

There are so many ways we can follow Jesus' example and be a servant to others. Sometimes we provide a gift of encouragement simply by doing ordinary work with cheerfulness. A friend's letter reminded me of that fact. She wrote to tell me about the death of her uncle.

He was a Christian. Hadn't had any serious illness. He and his wife . . . went to a Hardee's drive-through, and he ordered their breakfast. They ate there often, and the boy who took their order recognized my uncle's voice. The boy said, "Come on up, partner, we are waiting for you." Just then, my uncle grabbed his chest and said to his wife, "I'll see you in heaven!" And he was gone.

My aunt guided the car to a stop, and the boys at the counter came running out to help, but he was already gone . . .

At my uncle's funeral the minister said, "The voice over the speaker may have been the order-taker's, but it was a message straight from Jesus: 'Come on up, partner; we're waiting for you.'"

Isn't that sweet? So, it has been a great comfort to us to know our beloved uncle was welcomed home by Jesus—*over the speaker at Hardee's!*

If you thought your words would be the last earthly thing someone heard, would it make a difference in what you said or how you said it? In today's troubled world it's easy to be a pessimist. Anyone can spread that kind of message of gloom—"like clouds and wind without rain," as Proverbs 25:14 says. Instead, Christians need to be like the clouds that bring showers of blessings and encouragement to those who are struggling through a desert of despair.

The Best Gift of All

When we're thinking of ways we can follow Jesus' example and show a servant's heart to those in need, there's no better gift we can give them than the hope of heaven! Many times, the only lifeline I've had to hang on to when I've landed in one of life's cesspools is the assurance that "this too shall pass"! We're only pilgrims here, not settlers, and the heavenly home we're promised will have no pain, no misery—nothing but joy! Hallelujah! As one friend said, "If we knew what God knows about heaven, we would clap our hands when a Christian dies."

The best illustration of the future that we Christians are promised is the following story by an unknown writer:

There was a woman who had been diagnosed with a terminal illness and had been given three months to live. So, as she was getting her things in order, she contacted

THE FAMILY CIRCUS.   By Bil Keane

"Grandma's right. There ARE lots of
people dying to get to heaven."

her pastor and had him come to her house to discuss certain aspects of her final wishes.

She told him which songs she wanted sung at the service, which Scriptures she would like read, and which
outfit she wanted to be buried in. The woman also
requested to be buried with her favorite Bible. Everything was in order, and the pastor was preparing to leave
when the woman suddenly remembered something very
important to her.

"There's one more thing," she said excitedly.

"What's that?" came the pastor's reply.

"This is very important," the woman continued. "I
want to be buried with a fork in my right hand."

The pastor stood looking at the woman, not quite
knowing what to say.

"That surprises you, doesn't it?" the woman asked.

"Well, to tell you the truth, I *am* puzzled by the request," said the pastor.

The woman explained, "In all my years of attending church socials and potluck dinners, I always remember that when the main course was being cleared away, someone would inevitably lean over and say, 'Keep your fork.' It was my favorite part because I knew that something better was coming . . . like velvety chocolate cake or lemon meringue pie. Something wonderful was coming, something with substance! So I just want people to see me there in that casket with a fork in my hand, and I want them to wonder, 'What's with the fork?' Then, I want you to tell them: 'Keep your fork. The best is yet to come.'"

The pastor's eyes welled up with tears of joy as he hugged the woman and said good-bye. He knew this was one of the last times he would see her. He also knew that this parishioner had a clear and insightful vision of heaven. She *knew* that something better was coming.

At the funeral, people were walking by the woman's casket and they saw the pretty dress she was wearing and her favorite Bible. That made sense. Then they saw the fork in her right hand. Over and over the pastor heard the question, "What's with the fork?" and over and over he smiled.

During his message, the pastor told the people of the conversation with the woman shortly before she died. He told them the fork story and what it meant to her.

So the next time you reach down for your fork, let it remind you, oh, so gently, that the best is yet to come!

The wonderful "fork story" always reminds me of another favorite line, one a friend included in a recent letter. She said, "Barb, after reading about some of your funny ways of looking at death, I came up with one of my own for my epitaph."

It's the perfect parting gift all Christians could give their loved ones, a reminder that we're enjoying the "dessert" of eternity:

> Don't cry for me.
> I'm finally where I want to be.

This dear woman has an eagerness for heaven that I share. The only thing different is that I may not have a tombstone to engrave. Bill and I want to donate our bodies to the local university—if they'll have us!

Rubes

**"I always thought that one day I'd donate my body to science,
but I was kind of hoping it would be after I was dead."**

Billy Graham has also made it clear that he's enthusiastically looking forward to spending eternity in heaven. The last words in the book *Billy Graham: God's Ambassador* convey this enthusiasm in a most dramatic way. In script across the inside back cover of the book are these words:

Someday you will read or hear that Billy Graham is dead. Don't you believe a word of it! I shall be more alive then than I am now. I will just have changed my address. I will have gone into the presence of God.[4]

A friend sent me a card last year that said, "When I was growing up in an East Texas farming community, we had an old-fashioned custom of 'walking a piece of the way home' with our visitors. Guests who walked to our house were accompanied halfway home after their visits. As a little girl, I welcomed this extra time I could spend with a cherished friend. Often these were the most delightful moments of all. I'm a good deal older now, and life's day is growing shorter. I am nevertheless comforted that I have walked at least part of the way home with a Friend—One who walks with me always, everywhere."

Now imagine the joy of passing along that blessing and walking someone else "halfway home" to heaven. Wouldn't it be marvelous to join that heavenly throng and have someone say, "Because of YOU, I accepted Jesus' invitation to spend eternity with Him"? It would be almost as wonderful as hearing the Savior say these words of gracious welcome:

> Come, you who are blessed by my Father; take your inheritance, the kingdom prepared for you since the creation of the world.
>   For I was hungry and you gave me something to eat,
>   I was thirsty and you gave me something to drink,
>   I was a stranger and you invited me in,
>   I needed clothes and you clothed me,
>   I was sick and you looked after me,
>   I was in prison and you came to visit me. . . .
>   Whatever you did for one of the least of these brothers of mine, you did for me.[5]

If I've managed to earn the gift of hearing those marvelous words someday, I can just imagine that my friend Sam Butcher's reminder will be ringing through my memory next, saying, *That's what it's all about, isn't it, Barb?*

Acknowledgments

If your heart has been touched or your day has been brightened by reading this book, credit is due to the many friends of Spatula Ministries who sent jokes, stories, poems, and zany insights to be shared with you for just this reason. We have made diligent effort to identify the original sources of this material, but sometimes this goal was impossible. Other times our research turned up multiple sources for the same item. Whenever the source of an unattributed item in this book can be positively identified, please contact W Publishing Group, P.O. Box 141000, Nashville, TN 37214, so that proper credit can be given in future printings.

Grateful acknowledgment is also given for:

The mammogram essay on page 75 from *And How Are We Feeling Today?* by Kathryn Hammer © 1993. Used with permission of NTC/Contemporary Publishing Group.

The wonderful artwork and enduring patience of artist Dennis Hill.

The delightfully creative illustrations and story related to Colossians 3:12–14 by Marcey Hripak.

"If I Had My Child to Raise Over Again" by Diane Loomans. From the book *Full Esteem Ahead* © 1994 by Diane Loomans with Julia Loomans. Reprinted by permission of H. J. Kramer, P.O. Box 1082, Tiburon, CA. All rights reserved.

Endearing stories and incidents shared by Evelyn Maxey, Julie Hendry, Elizabeth Dent, and Sarah Rawley.

"Top Ten Reasons Why Heaven's Looking Good" by Fred Sanford. Used by permission.

"Parallels between writing a novel and having a baby," by Ed Stewart, writing for Tyndale House Publishers' "Page Turner's Journal," in Spring 1999, which I adapted for chapter 1.

NOTES

Chapter 1: Having a Baby Is Like Writing a Book—Lots of Whining, Begging, and Pushing

1. The idea for this comparison came from Ed Stewart's essay, "An Author Speaks: Ed Stewart describes some parallels between writing a novel and having a baby," which appeared in "The Page Turner's Journal," an editorial/advertising newsletter by Tyndale House Publishers included in *Marriage Partnership*, spring 1999, and in *Today's Christian Woman*, March/April 1999. Used by permission.

2. "*CBA Marketplace's* Top 10 Best-Selling Nonfiction Books of 1997," *CBA Marketplace*, February 1998, 12. *Estrogen* was still making appearances on the bestseller list in 1999 while I was working on this book.

3. Dave Meurer, *Boyhood Daze: An Incomplete Guide to Raising Boys* (Minneapolis: Bethany House, 1999), 17–18.

4. Adapted from "Gladly," Faith & Values Section, *Minneapolis Star Tribune*.

Chapter 2: Who Are These Kids, and Why Are They Calling Me Mom?

1. Dru Sefton, "The Wonderful and the Wacky: Here's a motherlode of moms who keep their kids in stitches," *Kansas City Star*, 9 May 1999, G1–2.

2. Linda Davenport, "Dancing with Mom," *Kansas City Star Magazine*, 9 May 1999, 13.

3. Original source unknown. Adapted from Alice Gray, *Stories for a Woman's Heart* (Sisters, Oreg.: Multnomah: 1999), 63.

4. Meryl Streep, quoted in Steve Persall, "Mother of Invention," *Tampa Tribune*, 18 September 1999, D-1.

5. Robert Lee Hotz, "Pregnancy may increase brain power," *Los Angeles Times*, reprinted in the *Tampa Tribune*, 11 December 1998.

6. Caryle Murphy, "Motorists see signs from 'God,'" *Washington Post*, reprinted in the *Denver Post*, 9 July 1999, 1.

7. Diane Loomans, "If I Had My Child to Raise Over Again," *Full Esteem Ahead: 100 Ways to Build Self-Esteem in Children and Adults* (Triburon, Calif.: H. J. Kramer, 1994). Used by permission.

8. Mike Atkinson, Mikey's Funnies, Youth Ministry on the Net: http://www.Youthspecialties.com.

9. Meurer, *Boyhood Daze*, 13.

10. Mary Jo Malone, "Of love and leave-taking: Does it ever get easy?" *St. Petersburg Times*, 6 April 1999, B1.

11. Barb Greco, in a letter to Oprah Winfrey on *The Oprah Winfrey Show*, 14 July 1999.

Chapter 3: How to Be a Joyful Woman—Take Up Acting

1. Associated Press writer Daniel Q. Haney, "Study: Mental stress can cause long-term damage to the heart," *The Register*, 10 March 1999, 7.

2. "My brethren, count it all joy when ye fall into divers temptations; knowing this, that the trying of your faith worketh patience" (James 1:2–3 KJV).

3. Psalm 145:14 TLB.

4. Habakkuk 3:17–19.

5. Suzanne Farnham, founder of the Listening Hearts ministry in Baltimore, quoted in Ed Stannard, "The Spirit speaks to us, if we can learn to listen," *Episcopal Life*, February 1999, 16.

6. Norman Vincent Peale, *Enthusiasm Makes the Difference*. This excerpt, along with the discussion of "act as if," is adapted from Rob Gilbert, Ph.D., "The Three Most Powerful Words in the English Language," a *Bits & Pieces* booklet published by The Economics Press, 12 Daniel Road, Fairfield, NJ 07004-2565.

7. Charles H. Gabriel, "Brighten the Corner Where You Are," 1913.

8. George F. Will, "Pithy words of wisdom to Class of '99," *Tampa Tribune*, 10 June 1999, A15.

9. William James, quoted in Gilbert, "The Three Most Powerful Words in the English Language," 5.

10. Source unknown.

11. David Flick, "Don't Worry About Being Happy," *Dallas Morning News,* July 1999.

12. *Bits & Pieces,* 15 July 1999, 7.

13. Ibid., 23.

Chapter 4: I Finally Got My Head Together—Then My Body Fell Apart!

1. Sam Levenson, *In One Era and Out the Other* (New York: Simon and Schuster, 1973), 176–77.

2. Doreen Iudica Vigue, "Americans' appetite grows for all things gargantuan," Boston Globe, reprinted in *Memphis Commercial Appeal,* 18 April 1999, A18.

3. Ellen Goodman, "Americans grow into their food in giant economy-size portions," *Boston Globe,* published in the *Tampa Tribune,* 3 March 1999, 15.

4. "For some Nigerians, womanhood begins in 'fattening room,'" *Los Angeles Times,* published in *St. Petersburg Times,* 16 October 1998, 21A.

5. Kathryn Hammer, *And How Are We Feeling Today?* (Chicago: Contemporary Books, 1993), 72–73. Used by permission.

6. Colossians 3:12–14 NKJV.

7. Thanks to Darcey Hripak, Port Washington, New York, for sharing this delightful story and the accompanying illustrations.

8. Adapted from Peggy Ryan, quoted in Roz Warren, ed., *Women's Lip* (Napierville, Ill.: Sourcebooks, 1999), 24.

Chapter 5: We Started Out with Nothing—and Still Have Most of It Left

1. Jane Clapperton, "Finders Weepers," *Woman's Day,* 2 October 1984, 138.

2. "Don't leave the market without it," *St. Petersburg Times,* 7 August 1999, Home and Garden section, 1.

3. "Strangers in Strange Lands," *Arkansas Democrat Gazette,* 10 January 1999, H1.

4. "Objects of Desire: Sink Job," *Denver Post*, 5 June 1999, Scene section, 1.

5. Dave Gussow, "High tech @ home," *St. Petersburg Times*, 21 June 1999, Tech Times section, 11.

6. Judy Stark, ed., "No-dish Dessert," *Tampa Tribune*, Homes 1, 22 May 1999.

7. Mary Hunt, "Tiptionary," *Cheapskate Monthly*, February 1999, 7.

8. *Bits & Pieces*, 6 November 1997, 15.

9. 1 Corinthians 13:1–8, *The Message*, with added paraphrase.

10. Tal D. Bonham and Jack Gulledge, *The Treasury of Clean Senior Adult Jokes* (Nashville: Broadman, 1989), 121.

11. Ibid., 103.

12. Ibid., 18.

13. Doc Blakely, "Laughter, the Best Medicine," *Reader's Digest*, August 1999, 89.

14. Adapted from Phyllis Diller, quoted in Warren, *Women's Lip*, 53.

Chapter 6: If They Can Send a Man to the Moon . . . Why Can't They Send 'Em All?

1. George F. Will, "The Perils of Brushing," citing a report by *American Enterprize* magazine in *Newsweek*, 10 May 1999, 92.

2. Psychologist David Lewis, cited in "Loose Change: Shopping. It's War," *St. Petersburg Times*, 17 January 1999, Money & Business section, 1.

3. Tom Zucco, "Wild & Wooly," *St. Petersburg Times*, 19 February 1999, Floridian section, 1.

4. Laura Bush, quoted in *Redbook*, August 1999.

5. Jeffery Sobal, Cornell University, quoted by Natalie Angier, New York Times Syndicate, reprinted in "Marriage maxim adjusted," *Denver Post*, 8 July 1998, 3F.

6. Maradee A. Davis, University of California at San Francisco, cited by Angier, "Marriage maxim adjusted," ibid.

7. David Broder, *Washington Post* Writers Group, "An unmatched American life," *St. Petersburg Times*, 21 March 1999, 7A.

8. Charis Collins, "Serendipitous but eternal enmeshment," *Oregonian*, First Person Singular, 14 February 1999, L3.

9. Adapted from *Episcopal Life*, March 1999, 2.

Chapter 7: When Your Road Is All Downhill, You're Probably Holding the Map Upside Down

1. Betty Boyd Eigenauer, "Good Times Await Seniors," letters to the editor, *Orange County Register,* undated clipping.

2. Associated Press, "Study finds similarities among people who live past 100," *Tampa Tribune,* 20 April 1999, 8A.

3. Stephaan Harris, "Most reject the growing opportunity to live to 100," *USA Today,* 26 May 1999, D1.

4. Knight Ridder Newspapers, "More Americans reaching 100, and they're healthier," *St. Petersburg Times,* 18 August 1999, 4A.

5. Associated Press, "98-year-old dance student doesn't miss a single beat," *Tampa Tribune,* 31 August 1998.

6. Rick Folstad, "A Class by Herself," *Denver Rocky Mountain News,* 30 May 1999, 40R.

7. Anne Dingus, "Small Town Heroes," *Texas Monthly,* March 1999, 144.

8. Associated Press, "At 108, woman recalls momentous, mundane," *St. Petersburg Times,* 26 April 1999, 5B.

9. Eric Deggans, "Tale of two remarkable sisters," *St. Petersburg Times,* 18 April 1999, 8F.

10. Advertisement, "At 101 years old, Leila Denmark, M.D., is the oldest practicing physician in the U.S.," *Wall Street Journal,* 15 September 1999, B5.

11. Associated Press, "Study: Women find menopause a fulfilling stage," *St. Petersburg Times,* 5 September 1997, 4A.

12. "The Estrogen Fairy Tale," a product of DonEl, Pittsburgh, Penna.

13. Dave Barry, *Dave Barry Turns 50* (New York: Crown, 1998), quoted in Dave Barry, "Can You See Turning 50? Or, Turning 50, Can You See?" *Dallas Morning News,* 27 September 1998, F1, 7.

14. Max Lucado, *A Gentle Thunder* (Nashville: Word, 1995), 60.

15. Michael Precker, "At What Year Should Those Birthday Messages Turn Kinder and Gentler?" *Dallas Morning News,* 27 September 1998, F1, 9.

16. This item appeared in the Ann Landers column, Creators Syndicate, 14 May 1999.

17. "LifeWatch" column, *Philadelphia Inquirer,* 3 October 1999.

18. Craig Wilson, "The good old days, we hardly knew you," *USA Today*, 3–6 September 1999, 1.

19. Sue Landry, "A whole new world, in a sense," *St. Petersburg Times*, 18 April 1999, F1.

20. Steve Martin, *Pure Drivel* (New York: Hyperion, 1998), quoted in Curt Schleier, "Two wild and crazy guys," *St. Petersburg Times*, 27 September 1998, 6D.

21. "Laughter, the Best Medicine," *Reader's Digest*, August 1999, 88.

Chapter 8: Sliding Down a Rainbow, into a Pool of Joy!

1. Adapted from Larrene Hagaman's column "From the Chapel," in *Chapel Bells* magazine, Vicki Cash, editor, Fall 1999, 6–7. Published by Precious Moments, P. O. Box 802, Carthage, MO 64836.

2. Mark 1:41.

3. "Successful Aging: A Lifestyle Choice," a report on the MacArthur Foundation Study of Aging in America, *St. Louis Times*, August 1998, 7.

4. *Billy Graham: God's Ambassador* (New York: Time-Life, 1999).

5. Matthew 25:34–36, 40.

BARBARA JOHNSON

Waiting for Gabriel's Horn

W PUBLISHING GROUP™

www.wpublishinggroup.com

A Division of Thomas Nelson, Inc.
www.ThomasNelson.com

This book is lovingly dedicated to my good friend Samuel J. Butcher, the talented creator of Precious Moments.

Through his art, his message, and his many creations—especially the beautiful Precious Moments Chapel and the awe-inspiring Fountain of Angels in Carthage, Missouri—Sam shares the gospel with millions from all over the world.

It is such an honor for me to be able to include several of his adorable Precious Moments figures as illustrations. Copying from his original figurines, Sam did the line drawings just for me—and for you, the reader—when we were visiting the Precious Moments Chapel recently. Just as we were leaving, Sam dashed up to us and said he'd been unable to sleep the night before because he was so excited about this project. (We hadn't slept either from all the excitement of being there!) He was so delighted, just like a little child, as he showed us two variations he had drawn in the line drawing of "This World Is Not My Home," shown above. The two additions are things I talk about a lot, but they don't appear on the collectible figurine. Can you find them? (The answer is on page 157.)

Thank you, Sam!

Contents

Just a few more weary days and then,
I'll fly away;
To a land where joys shall never end,
I'll fly away.[1]

We've Got a One-Way
Ticket to Paradise!

When Bill and I moved into our California mobile home several years ago, we quickly discovered a potential problem we'd overlooked during our prepurchase visits. As soon as the movers had left and the dust had settled, things gradually became quiet—except for the sound of airplanes flying nearby. We found we were under the approach path for Los Angeles International Airport!

For a day or two, we thought the noise would be a real nuisance, but it wasn't long until we stopped noticing it altogether. And eventually I even came to like this aspect of our neighborhood a few miles east of LAX. As strange as it may sound, I sometimes enjoy standing outside at night and watching the planes approaching at five-mile intervals. Sometimes when I'm able to see the lights of four to six planes, all lined up across the sky from as far as forty miles away, all sorts of heavenly images flood my mind.

In my imagination, those planes aren't just vehicles carrying passengers from Boston or Bangkok; they're not cargo jets hauling oranges to Oakland or pecans to Peoria. Instead, in my mind, the planes are full of joyful Christians, soaring upward, climbing through the night skies, bound for heaven itself.

Sure, it's just my imagination playing games. But isn't that a wonderful image? Just think of the joy those planes would carry if each one was packed with hundreds of heavenbound Christians! That's such a happy picture. It's certainly a contrast to the one that filled my imagination when I first moved to California many years ago. Back then I was so homesick for Michigan, where I grew up, that every time I saw an airplane I imagined it was going home to Michigan—and I wanted to go too! Since then I've met many others who have also longed to go home, wherever that might be—anyplace from Kansas to Korea, Colorado to Cuba.

Now I watch the airplanes flying overhead, and I'm homesick all over again. But it's not Michigan I long for these days. At this stage of my life, I'm homesick for my REAL home—heaven! Standing outside on a moonlit night, imagining those planes flying away to paradise, I have a frozen picture in my mind of all the wonders awaiting us there, and before I know it, I'm almost overwhelmed by the awesome promises of God. (When my neighbors call to ask if I'm all right, I tell them I'm just getting in a little rapture practice!)

A Joyous Preoccupation

Maybe it's just a hormone thing (after all, my last book *was* titled *Living Somewhere Between Estrogen and Death*), but lately, thoughts of heaven have completely absorbed me. It's become such a joyous preoccupation for me that I've collected an amazing assortment of quips, quotes, inspiring stories, motivating ideas, Scripture insights, gospel song lyrics, and funny cartoons about our eternal life in heaven—a collection too good to keep to myself. And the proof that W Publishing Group apparently agrees with me is right here in your hands.

This book is intended as a joyful reminder of the wonderful life awaiting us in heaven. In these pages I hope you'll find encouragement (a word that means to *"fill* the heart") as you

"YOU CAN FLY"

Used by permission of Samuel J. Butcher, creator of Precious Moments.

struggle through difficulties, renewal when you find yourself sinking in the spiritual doldrums, and laughter when you think you'll never laugh again. This is a book that, I hope, will reaffirm for every Christian the words to that beautiful chorus:

> I'm going higher, yes, higher some day,
> I'm going higher to stay;
> Over the clouds and beyond the blue sky,
> Going where none ever sicken or die—
> Loved ones to meet in that "Sweet by and by,"
> I'm going higher some day.[2]

And it's a book that should show nonChristians what they're missing. Like someone said, if you want to dwell in the Father's house you have to make your reservation in advance!

Including this introduction, there are seven chapters in this book—because seven is the perfect number, and heaven is perfect. The stories, quotes, and inspiring messages are loosely grouped around my favorite heavenly themes: music, bells, crowns, mansions, angels, and inheritances, along with the "fly away" fun we'll focus on here in chapter 1.

And just like the rest of my books, each chapter ends with a collection of zany jokes and wisecracks, silly poems and touching stories that have made me laugh. As Christians, one of the things we're uniquely qualified to laugh about is death, so I hope you won't mind if we poke a little fun at the Grim Reaper now and then. We're calling the collections "Cloud Busters" because of something I read somewhere. It was an essay that described clouds as "those sorrows . . . which seem to dispute the rule of God."[3] But Jesus "busted" right through that idea when He said we would see Him "coming on the *clouds* of the sky." Another Scripture verse says, "Behold, he cometh with *clouds.*"[4]

Oswald Chambers said that instead of contradicting God's presence, clouds are actually "a sign that He is there." They are "the dust of our Father's feet," he wrote.[5] Now *that's* an image that makes me smile—God kicking up dust as He strides across the skies! And the thought that we'll someday be soaring upward, blasting right through those "dust clouds" on our way to heaven, certainly brings laughter to my heart. Until then, I hope the little gems at the end of each chapter will keep you smiling until your time on earth is finished and you blast off to do some "cloud-busting" of your own!

The Route I'm Hoping For

A friend once closed a letter to me with the quip "Until He comes or until I go!" Given a choice, many of us would agree with Joni Eareckson Tada's eighty-year-old friend who said she was eagerly anticipating heaven but hoped to "stay around for Jesus' return" because, she said, "I never like to miss a good party."[6] Like this woman, most of us probably agree that the BEST way to get to heaven will be if Jesus comes again while we're still alive. Then we can skip death, rendezvous with our Savior in the clouds, and "party" with Him as we enter the gates of heaven. *That's* the route I want to take, just the way the beautiful old hymn describes it:

> Oh, joy! Oh, delight! Should we go without dying,
> No sickness, no sadness, no dread and no crying.
> Caught up through the clouds with our Lord into
>   glory,
> When Jesus receives His own.[7]

This part of Christ's second coming is what biblical scholars call the rapture. The apostle Paul said it will happen like this:

> The Lord himself will come down from heaven, with a loud command, with the voice of the archangel and with the trumpet call of God, and the dead in Christ will rise first. After that, we who are still alive and are left will be caught up together with them in the clouds to meet the Lord in the air. And so we will be with the Lord forever.[8]

"JOY TO THE WORLD"

Or, as we who are a little less sophisticated in spiritual matters put it: *He's gonna toot, and we're gonna scoot!*

A lot of people are saying "toot 'n' scoot" day may not be far off. As one writer suggested, "By every indication which we can gauge, the rapture seems near. Certainly each day that passes brings it twenty-four hours nearer, and each trend that develops points to its coming."[9]

The rapture can't come soon enough for me! I'm ready right now! So if I sometimes seem a little distracted these days, it's not because of advancing age or approaching senility (even though my *next* book will be titled *Living Somewhere*

Between Pampers and Depends). It's because I keep one ear tuned toward heaven, listening for the sound of that trumpet announcing Jesus' return! That's when *I'll* be a soaring cloud buster, myself!

We're Outta Here!

Just think of what that day will be like. Well, actually, it won't be a *day*. First Corinthians 15:52 says it'll happen "in a flash, in the twinkling of an eye." He's gonna blow that trumpet and *poof!* We're outta here!

Someone gave me a darling T-shirt that gives us a glimpse of what this scene may be like. It's a pair of running shoes with little jet trails rising out of them as their Christian owner is zapped up to heaven.

In a Moment...
in the twinkling of an eye. . . .
1 *Corinthians* 15:52

© Danny Loya

Of course, imagining this scene is one thing—but I don't want to be left here to see it in person! That kind of nightmare was described in the bestselling novel *Left Behind*. Soon after the story begins, the rapture occurs, and the people left behind feel bewildered. The main character is the captain of a commercial airliner making a transatlantic flight when the chief flight attendant tells him, "I'm not crazy! See for yourself! All over the plane, people have disappeared."

"It's a joke," he replies. "They're hiding, trying to—"

"WHO'S GONNA FILL YOUR SHOES?"

"Ray! Their shoes, their socks, their clothes, everything was left behind. These people are *gone!*"[10]

It's true. We won't need our earthly shoes in heaven, where, if the old spiritual hymn is accurate, we'll be walking streets of gold in "dem golden slippers"!

The Shoes of the Sailors

Such thoughts remind me of a trip Bill and I made to Hawaii recently. At Pearl Harbor, we visited the somber memorial to the USS *Arizona*, which sank in 1941 during the surprise attack that pushed America into World War II. The ship now rests on the bottom of the harbor, a sad monument to the 1,177 men who died when it went down.

In my current state of heavenly fixation, the part of the *Arizona*'s story that touched me most poignantly was a detail one of the tour guides shared. He said the contents of the great battleship had been left intact and that divers who visited the ship recently were surprised to find, more than fifty years after the disaster, that the sailors' shoes were still there, right where the brave men had died. Some were under the table where the sailors were playing cards. Others were left beside the bunks where the men were sleeping or by the ship's signal light where they stood watch. Hearing this description, I couldn't help but think that's the way it will be for us when we fly away to heaven.

Someone shared a wonderful story with me about heavenly footwear recently. In the story, a harried woman rushes to a discount store to pick up some last-minute Christmas gifts. The store is packed, the lines are long, and her patience is frayed.

She pushes her piled-high cart into a checkout lane behind two small children. Seeing the little girl's tangled hair and her older brother's shirt with the two buttons missing, the woman wonders where their mother is. The children are almost giddy with excitement as they repeatedly examine the item they are holding: a package containing glittery gold, adult-size, fold-up house slippers.

Finally it's the youngsters' turn to pay, and the boy—he's probably eight or nine—pulls a wad of balled-up dollar bills from his pocket. Carefully he smooths them onto the counter. There are four of them. The clerk rings up their purchase and announces the total: six dollars and thirty-six cents.

The little boy's shoulders sag. Again he digs deep into the pockets of his tattered jeans and pulls out a dime and a penny. There is an awful moment of silence as the little boy looks up at the clerk, perhaps hoping there's been a mistake. "You need two more dollars and two more quarters," she states matter-of-factly.

"Sorry, Lizzie," the little boy says, gently pushing the gold house shoes back across the counter toward the clerk. "We'll have to wait awhile. We gotta save up some more money."

"But Jesus will LOVE these shoes!" wails Lizzie, starting to cry.

The shopper, pushed out of her exhausted numbness by the girl's cry, quickly sizes up the situation and fumbles in her purse. Without a word, she hands three dollar bills to the clerk with a little smile.

"Thank you, lady!" the little boy exclaims.

"Thank you, lady!" the little girl repeats.

"We just *had* to get these shoes for our mama," the boy explains. "She's real sick. Daddy says she's going to heaven soon. He says heaven has streets of gold and Jesus is there. So we wanted to get Mama these shoes. We thought Jesus would smile when He saw 'em on Mama's feet 'cause they'd be like the gold streets."

Imagine yourself and your loved ones walking the streets of gold in matching gold slippers. Won't we be a sight to behold? And if there *are* golden slippers awaiting us in heaven, they sure won't be the discount-store variety!

Filled with Hope for the Sweet By and By

Sad events in our lives here on earth make us long for that day when we'll "meet on that beautiful shore" in the "sweet by and by," as the beautiful old hymn describes heaven. The hope of heaven sustains us in our earthly struggles and pushes us closer to God. As Joni Eareckson Tada said,

> Suffering hurries the heart homeward.[11]

For Christians, *home* is *heaven!* That's our eternal home as well as our enduring hope, a hope someone defined as

> **He**
> **Offers**
> **Peace**
> **Eternal.**

The hope of heaven, the knowledge that we'll someday enjoy "peace eternal," means we can face *anything* here on earth as long as we focus on the joy that's waiting for us in heaven. We cling to this hope as a constant reminder in good times and in bad. As the psalmist wrote, "I will *always* have hope."[12]

Meet Me at the Pearly Gates

One especially powerful aspect of our heavenly hope is knowing that loved ones who have died are not just "gone" but they've "gone on ahead" to wait for us there. Often this belief is the only thing that can sustain us as we grieve for those we hold dearest. That's something I know from painful experience!

After our son Steve was killed in Vietnam and his things were shipped home to us, we found, in the jacket he had been wearing the day he died, a letter I had written him. It was stained with water from the rice paddy where he had fallen and was black with mold. But the lipstick kiss I'd put on it was still visible. Usually I wrote Steve letters full of jokes or funny tales about his three brothers' latest shenanigans. But something—actually it was Someone—moved me to write a different letter that day. It said:

> Steve, today I felt a special need to reaffirm our faith in eternal life and being prepared to meet God. I particularly wanted to assure you that whether you are at home here in West Covina or over there in Vietnam you are still SAFE in God's hands . . . and even if your life would be sacrificed for us in Vietnam, EVEN THEN, Steve, you are safe in the arms of Jesus. . . .
>
> Somehow today, I wanted to get all this on paper to you to think about . . . and to let you know we are proud and thankful for you, especially for your faith in what we believe also, because it seems to be so important now.
>
> Even death, should it come to us—ANY of us— brings us just a step closer to God and to eternity, because we have placed our faith in Jesus Christ.

What comfort it brought Bill and me to know those thoughts were precious enough to Steve that he defied orders not to carry personal items and tucked that letter into his pocket on the morning he was killed. One of his friends told us later that Steve had shared the letter with him, and he had told Steve, "Man, you gotta keep this one!" And he did.

His death was a terrible loss for us. And so was the death of a second son, Tim, just five years later in a car crash with a drunk driver on his way home from Alaska. In that heart-breaking time, another letter consoled us. It was one Tim had written to a girlfriend describing the wonderful change that had occurred in his life in Alaska. He had recommitted his life to the Lord, he said, and he was eagerly anticipating God's glorious gift of eternal life.

"Time is short," he wrote. A few days later, he was killed.

The only way we survived the deaths of our sons was know-ing that both Steve and Tim's final exits here were their grand-est entrances there. Now we cherish the knowledge that they're waiting for us just inside the pearly gates—our deposits in heaven. Oh, how eagerly we await that glorious reunion!

Fly Away Home
Holding this rock-solid belief about the glory to come for us and our loved ones not only empowers Christians here on earth to endure tough times, it also inspires us to accomplish great things. For example, songwriter Albert Brumley dreamed of flying away to heaven as he toiled at picking cotton in 1928. The result was Brumley's simple but classic hymn "I'll Fly Away," which opens this chapter.

It's a simple song with a powerful message, and it has been recognized as the "most recorded gospel song in history."[13]

Of course, this idea of flying away to heaven wasn't born in Albert Brumley's mind as he picked cotton anymore than it was an original idea when it landed in my mind as I watched the LAX traffic fly overhead. It's an ancient image described in Scripture:

> The years of our life are three score and ten, yet their span is but toil and trouble; they are soon gone and *we fly away.*[14]

At the end of our lives here on earth, as Christians, our souls "fly away" to heaven. When we think of "R.I.P." carved on a Christian's tombstone, we don't think "rest in peace" but "rejoicing in paradise"!

A touching story reminded me of that promise last year when Swissair Flight 111 crashed off the coast of Nova Scotia. One of the 229 passengers killed in the crash was Jonathan Wilson, a twenty-two-year-old man who was heading for Geneva to work for Youth With a Mission, a ministry that trains young people for outreach mission work around the world. The parting words Jonathan spoke to his family when he left Florida would later take on a double meaning that reminded them he had flown away—not to Europe but to heaven. He told his family he would "be there until the Lord called him home."[15]

This remarkable story proves the point of a little clipping someone sent me recently. To nonbelievers, it's just a joke. To Christians, it's glorious truth.

> When traveling by plane, the Christian said, "If we go down, I go up."

Now we know that young Jonathan—and thousands of other children and moms and dads—are up there, rejoicing along with Steve and Tim. Picturing the happy reunion we'll have someday in that "land beyond the river that we call the sweet forever"[16] brings tears of joy to my eyes. And I like to think that Christian parents and others who've shed so many tears of anguish here on earth may have an even greater capacity for rejoicing up there. As Randy Alcorn said, "All of us will be full of joy in heaven, but some may have more joy because their capacity [has] been stretched through their trust in and obedience to God in this life."[17] How comforting to know the hole left by the loss of our loved ones will be filled in heaven with "joy, joy, joy, joy down in our hearts!"

Whenever this image comes to my mind, such feelings of anticipation sweep over me that I feel like a young child, eagerly awaiting Christmas morning. I can hardly wait!

Toot 'n' Scoot Traffic Goes *Up*

Of course, even though we hope the Lord will return for us soon, there's no way we can know for certain *when* the rapture will occur. So we have to be ready to fly away to heaven at any moment, because, as someone said, the trumpet hasn't sounded yet but the trumpeter is surely warming up!

For that reason (and a few others!) I won't be making reservations with the company in Seattle that's selling tickets for a rocketship ride in the year 2001. The newspaper clipping describing this crazy caper (sent to me by a friend who knows my longing to "fly away" and who suggested this was one way I could do it) says that, on the first day reservations were accepted, fifteen people plopped down a five-thousand-dollar deposit for the three-hour trip, which will ultimately cost each passenger nearly one hundred thousand dollars.[18]

While those daredevils will fly sixty-two miles above the earth, the journey I'm dreaming of will take me much farther than that; I'm heading all the way to eternity! But one thing we'll have in common is that we'll both be headed *up*. (Of course, I won't be coming back *down* like those rocketship passengers!)

While we're not really sure where heaven is, the Bible often refers to it as being *up* or *above*. That produces one of the "side effects" of heavenly thinking. When we're focusing on the joy we'll know in heaven, our thoughts turn heavenward—that's upward. Our hopes rise, and life down here is more bearable.

Recently I saw this story about how a doctor's friends created a touching tribute for him by their upward thinking:

> A doctor who had devoted his life to helping the poor lived over a grocery store in the ghetto of a large city. In front of the grocery store was a sign reading, "Dr. Williams Is Upstairs."
>
> When he died, he had no relatives, and he left no money for his burial. He had never asked for payment from anyone he had ever treated.
>
> The doctor's friends and patients scraped enough

money together to bury the good doctor, but they had no money for a tombstone. It appeared that his grave was going to be unmarked until someone came up with a wonderful suggestion. They took the sign from in front of the grocery store and nailed it to a post over his grave. It made a lovely epitaph: *Dr. Williams Is Upstairs.*[19]

My friends share these little stories with me, knowing how things that touch my heart or make me smile are always welcome in my mailbox. Fortunately, they understand that my sense of humor is a little warped. That's why, after hearing me complain recently that someone's behavior had nearly sent me to the home for the bewildered, a friend sagely remarked:

Barbara, some people are only alive because it's illegal to kill them!

Waiting, Waiting, Waiting . . .
It's true. We have all sorts of problems—and problem people—to contend with while we're waiting for God to take us home. And for people with an impatient temperament, the waiting itself is hard enough to contend with!

We all seem to struggle with impatience. A newspaper article recently reported that the lack of patience has become such a problem that "it wouldn't be surprising if a 12-step program were introduced any day now. Call it IA—Impatience Anonymous."[20] Some folks I know won't even buy frozen dinners if they take longer than five minutes in the microwave!

Here in Southern California, one of the places where we have to do a lot of waiting is in traffic jams. The only good thing about going nowhere on one of our multilane freeways is that it gives me a good excuse to let my mind wander. (Of course, it sometimes wanders off completely, leaving me sitting there wondering where it's wandered to—and wondering where I was going when I got started!)

Here I am, waiting on hold . . .
waiting to speak to a human being . . .
waiting for the Lord to return . . .

I wonder which will happen first?

Whenever I'm stuck in traffic or forced to do some waiting, I head off on a different path—mental path, that is. My favorite "mind trips" take me right up to heaven. I love thinking about what it will be like when the trumpet toots and we scoot out of here. Even though millions of us will be flying away to meet Jesus in the clouds, isn't it nice to think there will be no traffic jam in the sky, no lines to stand in, and no car problems to contend with? That thought gives us the endurance we need to cling to the *first* part of Psalm 27:14 while enduring the *second* part:

> Be strong and take heart
> and wait for the LORD.

Someone pointed out that we're not the only ones who have to wait. God is also experienced at waiting. When we're struggling through problems here on earth, trying to cope with the trials that block our way home, He longingly waits for us to turn to Him. He watches our stories unfold and waits for us to acknowledge His plan for our lives. He counts our tears and waits for us to cry out to Him. God is there with us wherever we are on the road of life. He is our comfort today as well as our hope for tomorrow. "This is a strange journey we walk," one friend wrote to me, "full of peaks and valleys. But since God is in both places, we walk unafraid."

Frederick Buechner said, "We are as sure to be in trouble as the sparks fly upward, but we will also be 'in Christ.' . . . Ultimately not even sorrow, loss, or death can get at us there."[21] And Billy Graham wrote, "There is no greater joy than the peace and assurance of knowing that, whatever the future may hold, you are secure in the loving arms of the Savior."[22]

What could be better than knowing we're "leaning on the everlasting arms" of Jesus? What could be more encouraging than remembering that we're loved by the almighty One who created us—and died for us! What could be more rewarding than the knowledge that the Carpenter from Nazareth has built mansions for us in heaven! And those inspiring facts are just *part* of the reason why heaven will be so wonderful. The real reason is much simpler. As Charles Dickens wrote:

> You never can think what a good place Heaven is without knowing who He was and what He did.

Dickens's words remind me of the *real* reason why heaven will be so glorious: because in heaven we'll be with Jesus.

> When Christ shall come
>   with shout of acclamation
> And take me home,
>   what joy shall fill my heart!
>
> Then I shall bow
>   in humble adoration
> And there proclaim,
>   my God, how great Thou art![23]

Cloud Busters

Frankly, I'm fed *up* with *up*. From the moment I wake *up* in the morning, it seems I'm playing catch-*up* with *up* until I think I'll wind *up* locked *up* in a mental ward.

At straight-*up* seven o'clock, I lock *up* the house, start *up* the car, and hurry *up* to get to the office. At work I'm either looking *up* some facts, speaking *up* at a meeting, or standing *up* for what I believe in. I know it's *up* to me to hold *up* the truth. When my allotted time is *up* and I've finally used *up* every opportunity to stir *up* enthusiasm for my *up*standing position, I give *up* and hope those others aren't mixed *up* about the points I've brought *up* for discussion.

Then I lock *up* the office and head home to brighten *up* my family's evening by stirring *up* something for dinner, knowing they've worked *up* an appetite.

My husband says I'm too worked *up* about *up*. He'd really like me to shut *up* and stop being so *up*set. I'm trying, but every time I give *up*, *up* pops *up* again!

Up is really starting to get me down!

Ann Luna

Always read books that will make you look good if you die in the middle of it.[24]

Epitaph over a dentist's grave:
He is filling his last cavity.[25]

© Bil Keane

Experience is something you don't get until just after you need it.[26]

Bumper Sticker: When you do a good deed, get a receipt—in case heaven is like the IRS.

Bishop Fulton Sheen once went shopping at a department store. He got on an elevator at the fifth floor and pushed the button for the sixth. Before the doors closed, a woman rushed on, and as the elevator rose, she said, "I didn't want to go up. I wanted to go down."

She turned to Bishop Sheen and added, "I didn't think I could go wrong following you."

"Madam," replied the bishop, "I only take people up, not down."[27]

Bumper Sticker: Rapture *Ready!*

Oh, that I had the wings of a dove!
I would fly away and be at rest.[28]

A man had just undergone surgery, and as he
came out of the anesthesia, he said, "Why are all the
blinds drawn, Doctor?"

"There's a big fire across the street, and we didn't
want you to wake up and think the operation was a
failure."[29]

"Hey, Annette! Put this on! He should
be coming to any minute!"

Under His wings I am safely abiding;
Though the night deepens and tempests are wild,
Still I can trust Him: I know He will keep me;
He has redeemed me and I am His child.

Under His wings, under His wings,
Who from His love can sever?
Under His wings my soul shall abide,
Safely abide forever.[1]

Transposed by Music

It was a scene right out of *I Love Lucy*, that episode where Lucy's working in the chocolate factory, frantically assembling boxes of truffles—and stuffing her mouth full of the "extras" she can't catch before they move on down the assembly line. In one of my first jobs as a teenager I, too, worked on a conveyor belt. But instead of chocolates, I repeatedly braced myself for an avalanche of dimpled, white Walter Hagen golf balls.

When my coworker yelled, "Let 'em roll!" the jaws of a large chute would open wide, emptying hundreds of golf balls onto the fast-moving belt. My job was to scoop up the balls at lightning speed, a dozen at a time, arrange them in boxes like egg crates, and then rotate the balls so that the stamped name of Walter Hagen was on top and would be visible when the carton was opened. The trick was to get all the balls safely inserted into their little carton before the chute opened again and another batch came tumbling down the line.

At first the job was simply stressful. Then it became stressfully boring. Sometimes, standing there waiting for the chute to

open, I felt like one of the contestants on the *Gong Show*, ready
to be "gong-ed"—or like Mr. Green Jeans on *Captain Kangaroo*
when that feisty Bunny Rabbit showered him every day with
ping-pong balls. I spent so much time scooping up the dimpled
golf balls I dreamed of drowning in a sea of mothballs. And
Walter Hagen's name appeared before my eyes so many times,
I swore I'd never play golf—and never name a son Walter if I
ever had one! It could have been worse, I suppose, if I'd been a
dimple counter. A regulation golf ball has 336 dimples!

The only thing that saved my sanity in that place was
music, surely a gift from heaven! Being a pastor's daughter
who'd been singing "specials" during church services for
years, I'd usually focus on gospel songs. Waiting for the golf
balls to rain down on me, I'd sing "Showers of Blessings."
Standing there beside the conveyor belt, I'd hum "Standing on
the Promises." Grabbing the golf balls before they were "lost,"
I'd sing "Bringing in the Sheaves" and "Rescue the Perishing."

Now, to be honest, gospel songs weren't the only things
that came to my mind. Sometimes a tune of popular music
would get stuck in my head, and I'd sing it over and over all
day long. Unfortunately, the one that seemed to stick most
steadfastly was a ridiculous tune that said, "You can have her,
I don't want her, she's too fat for me. Yes, she's too fat for me."

Golf ball-grabbing was just one of the "exciting " jobs that
music helped me endure. Another job that ranked low in status and high in tedium was my employment at a dry cleaner's,
where my assignment was to snip the buttons off clothes that
came in for cleaning. Back in those days, dry-cleaning equip-
ment couldn't handle buttons—they would either break or
melt during the process. So the buttons had to be snipped off
and put into a little envelope stapled to the cleaning tag. Then
they were sewn back on the garment after it had been cleaned.
Actually, I was glad to be the snipper instead of the stitcher;
sewing is not my gift, and I'm great at losing buttons!

Working there, I'd sing, "What can wash away my sin?
Nothing but the blood of Jesus!" and "Have Thine Own Way,
Lord," especially the beautiful line that says, "Whiter than

snow, Lord, wash me just now, while in Thy presence, humbly I bow." Of course, there, too, stupid lyrics sometimes wedged themselves firmly in my mind. The worst ones were:

> Blest be the tie that binds
> This collar to this shirt.
> For underneath this collar
> Is a tiny speck of dirt.

Whether it was gospel hymns or silly tunes, music was the lifesaver ring I clung to as I bobbled along, enduring these dreary jobs. And while my mindless work at golf ball-grabbing and button-snipping was pretty dull, neither of these summer jobs could hold a candle to the job I still consider the lowest of the low: staple-straightening.

RALPH

"OKAY, THINK DEEPLY AND HOLD IT!"

After I acquired some business skills and had another summer vacation from college, I was hired to be the secretary for a hospital administrator. Friends had told me this particular person was a real jerk to work for and had gone through several secretaries who had left his employment in tears. Since I was considered to be versatile, I was to do a monthly hospital newsletter (that's probably where I got the experience for what I *now* do) and keep the administrator from upsetting the doctors on the staff (he was such a perfectionist that he was known to frequently cause problems).

Whatever his problems were, I figured I could certainly tolerate him for one summer. The fact was, I needed a good-paying job so I could return to college in the fall. So on the first day I put on my most business-like dress and arrived early to impress him. Straightening my desk and putting a new ribbon in the IBM Selectric, I was all set to be his secretary.

The day had only been going a few minutes when he called me into his office to explain my duties. He said that since he was new there, too, he wanted to start out by having me arrange his files the way he'd had them organized in a previous hospital. (Later I learned that he had worked in *several* hospitals in the past and had always left on bad terms.)

So my first assignment, which he wanted done immediately, was to take all the previous administrator's files and "correct" the papers that were stapled with the staple going diagonally across the corner. He wanted me to restaple all the papers so that the staple was *parallel* to the top of the page. To be certain that his instructions were followed *exactly*, he gave me several boxes of special staples that had little zigs and zags in them. They weren't smooth like the ones I had always used in the past.

The job seemed a little ridiculous, but since this was my first day and I was eager to get off to a good start, I hurried to follow his instructions. After I had completed the drawerful of files, I proudly took them back so he could check them. He thumbed through them for a minute then pointed to four more big drawers of files that he wanted restapled! What I wanted to do at that point was staple HIM to the wall!

But I was determined to last out the summer, so I did what was requested of me that day and every day, although most of my assignments were similarly ridiculous. It was challenging trying to satisfy such a jerk, but I learned to discipline myself and get the job done. And in the process I learned a lot about myself and how much I could endure. Then, a few months after the summer ended and I'd gone back to college, I learned that the administrator was in another hospital. But this time he hadn't been *hired*; he'd been *committed*—to a mental hospital! Upon hearing the news, I thanked God that I had done my job without a fuss, so I knew it wasn't ME who had put him there! And I was grateful it wasn't a reverse situation—that he hadn't sent *me* to the home for the bewildered!

In that job, too, I tried to fill my head with comforting gospel songs. (But I must admit, a lot of the time the hymns had titles like "Master, the Tempest Is Raging" and "Out of My Bondage.") The thing about that job that makes me laugh today is that when my husband, Bill, a perfectionist himself, hears me talk about it, he doesn't understand why it's funny! It makes perfectly good sense to him that someone would want to fix all those "incorrect" staples!

A Heavenly Gift from God

In good times and bad, music has always been a part of my life flowing through the laughter as well as the trials. To me, it is a gift from God—a bit of heaven He loans to us while we live on earth to help us survive the hard times, to celebrate the good times, and especially to praise Him in a way no other method can match.

Music has been a golden thread woven through the tapestry of my life, bringing joy into the dark areas. Music reminds me that God's enduring love runs throughout my life and into eternity, a symbol of His promise that someday I'll be rejoining my loved ones in heaven to sing praises to our Lord in person. Whenever I hear especially beautiful gospel music, I imagine that I'm hearing a broadcast performance direct from my eternal home where angelic hymns will be the "Muzak" of heaven!

Singing lifts our spirits. It's just plain good for us. Whether we sing with trained voices that bring thundering applause or off-key screeching, by the time our songs of praise reach heaven they're all equally beautiful. That's what I had to keep telling myself a few years ago when the Billy Graham Crusade came to Anaheim, near our home.

The crusade asked for hundreds of volunteers to enlist in the huge choir that would perform during the event. Because I knew choir members were guaranteed good seats, I was eager to participate. But during rehearsals I realized that choir members would have to be at the stadium much earlier than the audience members, and I knew Bill would want us to attend the event together. So I signed him up, too, although he couldn't stay on key if his life depended on it! (I felt sure the Lord would forgive me this one little bit of deception, because I knew He wouldn't want me to face that crusade traffic alone!)

During rehearsals, I "encouraged" Bill to keep quiet and just mouth the words so his lack of singing ability wouldn't be discovered. Everything went according to plan until the night the crusade began. Then, swept up in all the excitement of the event, with tens of thousands of folks all joining in to sing along with the choir, Bill joined in too. There wouldn't have been a thing wrong with his participating except for one little thing: He was carrying a little tape recorder in his shirt pocket so we could enjoy all the music and messages again later on. That meant he recorded himself loudest of all! And let me just say as kindly as I can: It WASN'T something you'd want to hear again!

Bill has taken a lot of kidding about that recording. But he just says it's not his singing that's off key, it's our ears that are out of tune!

Marvelous Music

Just as music has helped me endure monotonous jobs during my life, it has also encouraged and inspired me in other situations over the years. In times of despair, music has provided

soothing comfort. In happy times, it has inspired me to even higher realms of joy. In times of loneliness, it has brought abundant comfort. Truly, it is a gift of heaven on earth!

For example, whenever I hear the hymn "Constantly Abiding" my mind immediately fills with a precious memory

"MAKE A JOYFUL NOISE"

that reminds me of a cherished loved one in heaven. As a small child accompanying my dad to his tent-meeting revivals, I would sometimes perform this song for the crowd. My dad would place a chair on the sawdust floor and lift me up on it so the audience could see me, a cute little girl wearing a bright red dress with its sharply pleated skirt, white, lace stockings, black patent leather shoes, and a big bow holding back the bangs of my Buster Brown haircut. Then, as I sang, my dad would stand beside me, beaming proudly. Sometimes we sang his favorite song, "Under His Wings," together. But whether I was performing solo or with him, his arm was always around me, holding me securely as I stood on the chair and belted out the words.

My dad died suddenly when I was twelve, and I was allowed to choose the music for his funeral service, including "Under His Wings" and "Constantly Abiding."

> There's a peace in my heart that the world never gave,
> A peace it cannot take away;
> Tho' the trials of life may surround like a cloud,
> I've a peace that has come there to stay!
> Constantly abiding, Jesus is mine;
> Constantly abiding, rapture divine;
> He never leaves me lonely, whispers, O, so kind:
> "I will never leave thee," Jesus is mine.[2]

Hearing those hymns now triggers a bittersweet memory—a happy period of my life, which ended with an unhappy experience—that now brings incredible comfort. They instantly transport me back more than half a century to one of those tent meetings somewhere; I can smell the sawdust shavings on the floor and, best of all, remember the comfort of my dad's arm holding me secure.

The Music of Heaven

What a powerful gift music is! Even without words, a familiar melody can bring tears to our eyes or a smile to our lips—

sometimes both. As I arrived at the funeral of a friend recently I was shocked to see in the funeral leaflet that one of the songs to be sung was "If You Could See Me Now." Immediately I imagined Kathie Lee Gifford standing at the railing of a Carnival cruise ship, belting out the company's theme song. Instead, the song, by Kim Noblitt, was a beautiful anthem about the glorious life we'll enjoy in heaven. The chorus says:

> If you could see me now,
> I'm walking streets of gold.
> If you could see me now,
> I'm standing tall and whole.
> If you could see me now,
> You'd know I've seen His face.
> If you could see me now,
> You'd know the pain is erased.

Then the song ends by saying,

> You wouldn't want me to ever leave
> this perfect place
> If you could only see me now.[3]

Isn't that fabulous? Those words transported all of us from that sad occasion of saying good-bye to our friend—to envisioning her frolicking through heaven. What a blessing to all of us it was to picture our friend "walking streets of gold" with happiness radiating from her because she had seen God's face! I don't know about the others attending that memorial service, but I left there almost feeling jealous of the one who had died! One of the first things I did after the funeral was to track down that beautiful song and study the lyrics. They thrill me, creating an image in my mind of what our life in heaven will be like. Reading over the words sends my spirits soaring skyward as I eagerly long for my turn to sit at Jesus' feet.

What a Way to Go!
Another thing that thrilled me recently was a story that appeared in our local newspaper describing the unusual death

of a woman in Santa Ana, California. While it's always sad for those of us who are left behind to say good-bye to a friend or loved one, this woman died in a way that many of us would envy.

> Giesela Lenhart was in full rapture as the Celebration Choir at Calvary Church reached the final verse of "Lord, We Lift Your Name on High." A tall woman, eyes closed, her outstretched arms seemed to reach higher than anyone else's in the riser's back row. Her clear, soprano voice rang out, "From the cross to the grave; from the grave to the sky; Lord, I lift your name on high."
>
> The words meant a great deal to Giesela, who had accepted Jesus as her savior Jan. 20, 1989. And who, at forty-one, may have known more than her share of loneliness and heartache.
>
> They were also her last words.
>
> The final notes sung, her arms still upraised, she fell backward off the riser, victim of a massive [fatal] heart attack.[4]

Reading that article, I couldn't help but think, *Wow! What a way to go!* The newspaper quoted one church member who expressed the same idea: "It would have to be . . . every Christian's ideal: to go 'home' while singing praises to God."

In that second, that "twinkling of an eye," this rejoicing Christian woman was transported from singing in an earthly choir with her fellow church members to rejoicing in the great celestial choir of heaven!

Have you ever thought about who's in that choir? Many of us probably imagine it as a vast angelic group. But as cherished as these angels are, consider that this woman, when she arrived in heaven, had experienced something that even the angels may never have known: *redemption!*

There's a beautiful old hymn, often called "The Angel Song," that makes this point. The chorus says:

Holy, holy, is what the angels sing,
And I expect to help them
Make the courts of heaven ring;
But when I sing redemption's story
They will fold their wings,
For angels never felt the joys
That our salvation brings.[5]

"ANGELS WE HAVE HEARD ON HIGH"

Al Smith's book of hymn histories explains how these beautiful lines came to be written by Johnson Oatman and John R. Sweeney: "One day Mr. Oatman and Mr. Sweeney were reading in the book of Revelation the thrilling word picture of a great choir which will assemble in heaven to sing praises and exalt the Lamb that was slain—the Lord Jesus. As they discussed this thrilling event, they realized that this would be a different choir than ever was heard in heaven before. This one was made up of the 'Redeemed' who had washed their garments white in the blood of the Lamb and, of course, angels couldn't be in this particular choir for they had never experienced the thrill . . . that comes into the heart and life through salvation."[6]

While we may envy the angels already enjoying the wonders of paradise, imagine that they may envy *us* the experience of salvation they can never know themselves! Can't you just picture them gathering around Giesela and saying, "Oooh! Tell us again about the day you were saved! We wanna hear all the details!"

Inspiring Hymns, Glimpses of Heaven

There have been many times in my life when I've wished God would just take me home to heaven right then and there. And what better way to go than in the midst of singing a glorious song of praise to Him? Such wishes often come in times of trouble. And I've had plenty of *that* in my life—my husband's devastating car crash, the death of two sons, and another son's eleven-year estrangement from us.

Sometimes it seemed unbearable. Those of you who have read my other books may remember my telling about a day when I decided to take things into my own hands and drive off a viaduct in an attempt to "fly away" to heaven on my own. But at the last moment I said the prayer of relinquishment—"Whatever, Lord!"—and turned the car around.

Since then I've said, "Whatever, Lord!" many times, knowing that God's plan for me is perfect. But I've also asked for help in living it out—and one of the helps God has given me is the beautiful music of heaven. From the ancient songs of the psalmist and the classic hymns of the Reformation to the modern ballads and praise music of the nineties, gospel music gives us a glimpse of the wonderful life that awaits us in heaven. Just think of all the beautiful songs that provide a preview of paradise:

"I've Got a Home in Gloryland That Outshines the Sun"
"Soon and Very Soon"
"Ivory Palaces"
"We Shall Wear a Crown"
"Lord, Build My Mansion"
"Finally Home"
"It Will Be Glory for Me"

A Funny Thing Happened

A cousin, a witty 85, asked a friend to handle her funeral arrangements and explained she wanted only women pallbearers.

"Why only *women* pallbearers?" the gentleman asked.

"Because," she replied, "men don't take me out now, so why should I let them take me out then?"

—Taylor Reese, author of *HUMOR Is Where You Find It*
Illustration reprinted with permission of *Christian Single* magazine.

Sometimes I join in singing one of these songs, and I'm moved to tears by the images the beautiful words create in my mind. At other times, the stories behind the hymns, like Al Smith's story about "The Angel Song," are as beautiful as the lyrics themselves. In another story about a beautiful hymn, Kenneth Osbeck tells how the third verse of the inspiring song "The Love of God" came to be: "The unusual third stanza . . . was a small part of an ancient lengthy poem composed in 1096 by a Jewish songwriter, Rabbi Mayer, in Worms, Germany. . . . The lines were found one day in revised form on the walls of a patient's room in an insane asylum after the patient's death. The opinion has since been that the unknown patient, during times of sanity, adapted from the Jewish poem what is now the third verse of 'The Love of God.'"[7]

Just imagine this person centuries ago having a mind so tortured that he was imprisoned in an "insane asylum." Yet at times the darkness apparently lifted so that the anguished person became an artist, painstakingly scratching with some unknown instrument these inspiring words into the cold, hard walls:

> Could we with ink the ocean fill
> And were the skies of parchment made,
> Were every stalk on earth a quill
> And every man a scribe by trade
> To write the love of God above
> Would drain the ocean dry,
> Nor could the scroll contain the whole
> Tho' stretched from sky to sky.

The timeless message of this song validates Martin Luther's comment about the power of music. "Next to theology no art is equal to music," he said, "for it is the only one, except theology, which is able to give a quiet and happy mind."[8]

Another Al Smith story tells the equally touching history of that familiar hymn "When the Roll Is Called Up Yonder." It began one day in the late 1800s when James M. Black of

"LET HEAVEN AND NATURE SING"

Williamsport, Pennsylvania, impulsively cut through an alley to save time on his way to the post office. As he hurriedly walked down the alley, he passed "a young girl sweeping the porch of a ramshackled house. She was dressed oh, so poorly, and in her young face were already the traces of worry and neglect," wrote Smith.

Black asked the girl, whose name was Bessie, if she went to Sunday school.

"No, sir," the girl replied. "I'd like to but I don't have anything fit to wear; but sir, how I'd love to go!"

Black and his wife and friends promptly brought the girl

some "church clothes," and she began faithfully attending both Sunday school and another church group called the Epworth League. "Each time there was a roll call, she was there to respond," Smith wrote.

Then came the day when Black called the roll and Bessie failed to answer. Black looked up from the attendance book, surprised. He called her name again, but she was not there. After the service he hurried to the alley, worried that Bessie's drunken father had forbidden her to come or that he had beaten her so severely she was unable to make her way to church. Instead, he found her dying of pneumonia. He summoned his own doctor to treat her, but all efforts failed to save her.

Black couldn't shake off the feeling he'd first experienced when he called the roll and Bessie didn't answer. He thought about how there would be "a roll call in heaven and oh, the sadness there would be for those whose names are not written in the Lamb's Book of Life," Smith wrote. A songleader, Black longed for a song that would "impress this truth upon the hearts" of the young people in his Sunday school class. But he couldn't find one. Later that day he was inspired to write one himself.

"I went into the house and sat down at the piano. Without any effort at all the words seemed to tumble from my mind. . . . The tune then came in the same manner. I felt that I was only the transcriber—I dared not change a note or word," he would explain later.

The song was first sung at Bessie's funeral after Black explained the circumstances leading up to it. "Never will I forget the effect it had upon the large audience of friends who had come. The Lord had taken little Bessie home, but in her place He had given a song to keep reminding all of us to be ready for that great roll-call day."

> When the trumpet of the Lord shall sound,
> And time shall be no more,
> And the morning breaks, eternal, bright and fair;

When the saved of earth shall gather over on the
    other shore,
And the roll is called up yonder, I'll be there.[9]

Cloud Busters

Theme Songs for Biblical Characters

Noah: "Raindrops Keep Falling on My Head"
Adam and Eve: "Strangers in Paradise"
Lazarus: "The Second Time Around"
Esther: "I Feel Pretty"
Job: "I've Got a Right to Sing the Blues"
Moses: "The Happy Wanderer"
Jezebel: "The Lady Is a Tramp"
Samson: "Hair"
Salome: "I Could Have Danced All Night"
Daniel: "The Lions Sleep Tonight"
Joshua: "Good Vibrations"
Peter: "I'm Sorry"
Esau: "Born to Be Wild"
Jeremiah: "Take This Job and Shove It"
Shadrach, Meshach, and Abednego: "Great Balls of Fire!"
The Three Kings: "When You Wish Upon a Star"
Jonah: "Got a Whale of a Tale"
Elijah: "Up, Up, and Away"
Methuselah: "Stayin' Alive"
Moses: "There's a Place for Us"
Nebuchadnezzar: "Crazy"

The trouble with doing something right the first
time is that nobody appreciates how difficult it was.

Laughingstock: Cattle with a sense of humor.

I don't suffer from insanity.
I enjoy every minute of it.

A Hymn for Every Calling

The dentist's hymn: "Crown Him with Many Crowns"
The contractor's hymn: "The Church's One Foundation"
The politician's hymn: "Standing on the Promises"
The boxer's hymn: "Fight the Good Fight"
The meteorologist's hymn: "There Shall Be Showers of
     Blessings"
The IRS's hymn: "All to Thee"
The gossip's hymn: "O for a Thousand Tongues"
The electrician's hymn: "Send the Light"
The baker's hymn: "I Need Thee Every Hour"
The telephone operator's hymn: "We've a Story to Tell to
     the Nations"
The airline captain's hymn: "Jesus, Savior, Pilot Me"
The dieter's hymn: "And Can It Be That I Should Gain?"
The UFO's hymn: "Come, O Thou Traveler Unknown"[10]

A person without a sense of humor is like a wagon
without springs—jolted by every pebble in the road.

Henry Ward Beecher

A woman taught the tiny tots in her Sunday school
class to sing her favorite hymn, "Oh, the Consecrated
Cross I Bear." Then came the Sunday morning when

a concerned mother questioned the teacher about the songs she was teaching the children. Her child told her she'd learned to sing, "Oh, the constipated, cross-eyed bear."[11]

Musical bloopers in church bulletins:

• The pastor will preach his farewell message, after which the choir will sing, "Break Forth into Joy."

• The concert held in Fellowship Hall was a great success. Special thanks are due to the minister's daughter, Gladys, who labored the whole evening at the piano, which, as usual, fell upon her.

• Twenty-two members were present at the church meeting held at the home of Mrs. Marsha Crutchfield last evening. Mrs. Crutchfield and Mrs. Rankin sang a duet, "The Lord Knows Why."[12]

Let the sea resound, and all that is in it; let the fields be jubilant, and everything in them! Then the trees of the forest will sing, they will sing for joy before the LORD, for he comes to judge the earth.[13]

Ring the bells of heaven!
There is joy today,
For a soul, returning from the wild!
See! the Father meets him out upon the way,
Welcoming His weary, wandering child.

Glory! glory! how the angels sing;
Glory! glory! how the loud harps ring!
'Tis the ransomed army, like a mighty sea,
Pealing forth the anthem of the free.[1]

May the Joybells of Heaven Ding-Dong in Your Heart Today

There's no biblical basis for the cherished image a friend planted in my mind recently when she merrily ended her letter, "May the joybells of heaven ding-dong forever in your heart." There's no mention of heavenly "joybells" in the Bible—no mention of regular bells in heaven, for that matter. The King James Version only mentions the word *bells* three times: twice in telling the Hebrews how to decorate the holy garment Aaron was to wear when he ministered to them as priest and once in Zechariah's prophecy about the inscription that would appear "upon the bells of the horses."[2]

Still, since bells have always been associated with worship services, we just naturally assume they will be among the many wonderful sounds we will hear when we arrive at the pearly gates. William O. Cushing's beautiful song lyrics, quoted in part on the opposite page, paint a glowing picture of heaven's bells pealing out as a sinner returns "from the wild." The image was made even more powerful for me when I read that Cushing, a powerful preacher during the 1800s, wrote the lyrics after he was forced to leave the pulpit because he "lost his power of speech."

Anguished by his disability, Cushing asked God for another way to serve Him. His prayer was answered when he discovered he had a gift for writing beautiful song lyrics. One of those songs was the thrilling hymn "Ring the Bells of Heaven." Others include "Under His Wings" and "When He Cometh."[3]

The Heavenly Sound of Church Bells

To me there's no more inspiring sound on earth than the heavenly *bonging* of the majestic bells that echo through the streets of small towns and cities everywhere, calling worshipers to church. And there's no more joyous noise than the cacophony of a tower full of church bells clanging away at the end of a worship service as the church doors are thrown open and Christians are released back into the world to spread the good news.

Someone told me about attending a holiday church service late on Christmas Eve in a beautiful old church in the midst of a large city's tall buildings and office towers. When the Christmas Eve service ended just after midnight the church-goers emerged through the old wooden doors to find snow-flakes swirling through the air and the heart of the usually bustling city extraordinarily quiet. Suddenly the church's bells pealed out through the darkness, filling the empty streets with the glad tidings of Christmas, their joyful sounds echoing off the neighboring structures of concrete and steel. It was, my friend said, a most extraordinary moment, one she doesn't expect to equal until she hears those joybells of heaven pealing out a welcome to her.

A recent newspaper story described another woman who'll be listening for the sound of joybells when she arrives in heaven. The article reported a multimillion-dollar donation to the Salvation Army from Joan Kroc, widow of Ray Kroc, who founded the McDonald's fast-food empire. In presenting her gift, Mrs. Kroc described how her billionaire husband "used to dress up as Santa Claus during the holidays and ring the bell for Salvation Army donations on the streets of San Diego. 'Right now, I bet there's a lot of bell ringing going on up there with Ray leading the chorus,'" Mrs. Kroc said.[4]

Maybe I love stories about bells so much because, frankly, I can identify with them. Bells can't help but be joyful, even when some people might not think it's appropriate. They just ring their hearts out, their uplifting tones merrily filling the air even when the situation would seem to call for a more restrained and dignified attitude. That's me!

For example, at Christians' funerals, I'm always *dinging* when everyone else is definitely in the *dong* mode. The normal funeral attire is somber black, but I like to wear bright green.

"RING THOSE CHRISTMAS BELLS"

You see, green is the color of new life, and while we who are left behind are mourning our loved ones' death, they are more alive than ever, dancing to the music of those glorious joybells in heaven! They are living proof of one of my favorite insights:

Death is not extinguishing the light.
It is turning down the lamp because the dawn has come.

Feeling this way, during mournful memorial services I generate a lot of raised eyebrows and feel a lot of elbows tapping against my ribs—the kind of jabs that silently say, *Stifle yourself, Barb! Don't you know death is serious business?* And I do mourn when a friend dies—but I mourn selfishly, feeling sorry for myself, knowing how I'll miss that person's friendship and wishing that I, too, could be strolling heaven's streets of gold with our beloved Savior.

Reminders of Heaven

At such times I feel a little like the church bells of London during the funeral procession for Princess Diana in 1997. The princess was loved all around the world, and we all mourned her death. Billy Graham noted that Princess Diana "set a wonderful example for all of us by her concern for the poor, the oppressed, the hurting and the sick." But he also noted another thing that her tragic death unintentionally gave us: a reminder "of how fragile life is, and how we should be ready to enter eternity and meet God at any moment."

In all the publicity surrounding Diana's death, one little sentence from a newspaper report has stayed with me longest and caused me to feel sympathy for those majestic London bells. The article said the bells' clappers were wrapped in heavy leather during the funeral procession lest their tones would sound too joyful.

When I read that description, I also couldn't help but think of the contrast between the bells' dull, somber *thuds* during Diana's funeral and the deliriously happy clamor of joybells we expect to hear in heaven. There will be no stifling of their happy sound inside those pearly gates! And if the beautiful old hymn is correct, the voices of angels will "swell the glad triumphant strain." It could be deafening—except there won't be any deafness there. Imagining the glory of it all sends my mind soaring heavenward—and wishing I could settle there *soon.*

Sharing Heaven's Glory

There are many stories about believers who, as they exit this life, manage to share with those they leave behind the joyful noise they hear as they're welcomed into glory. As they step through death's door and enter the portals of heaven, the ecstasy of the welcoming choruses they hear is obvious in the last earthly expressions that pass over their faces—expressions of awe and wonder.

In her book *Mourning Song,* my friend Joyce Landorf Heatherley shared someone's story about professional caregivers and even parents who avoid getting emotionally involved with a "bound-to-die child." As a result the children "die alone because adults deny death for fear of the hurt they might experience after the child has died." In contrast the story describes a mother "who was willing to put down her denial, pick up her own acceptance, and then beautifully prepare her little son for his death."

> She came every day to the hospital to visit her little five-year-old son who was dying of the painful disease lung cancer.
>
> One morning, before the mother got there, a nurse heard the little boy saying, "I hear the bells! I hear the bells! They're ringing!" Over and over that morning nurses and staff heard him.
>
> When the mother arrived she asked one of the nurses how her son had been that day, and the nurse replied, "Oh, he's hallucinating today—it's probably the medication, but he's not making any sense. He keeps on saying he hears bells."

Then that beautiful mother's face came alive
with understanding, and she . . . said, "You listen to
me. He is *not* hallucinating, and he's not out of his
head because of any medicine. I told him weeks ago
that when the pain in his chest got bad and it was
hard to breathe, it meant he was going to leave us.
It meant he was going to go to heaven—and that
when the pain got *really* bad he was to look up into
the corner of his room—towards heaven—and listen for the bells of heaven—*because they'd be ringing
for him.*" With that, she [hurried] down that hall,
swept into her little son's room, swooped him out
of his bed, and rocked him in her arms until the
sounds of ringing bells were only quiet echoes, and
he was gone.[5]

The mother had prepared her little son for death by helping him look forward to the happiness that awaited him.
Perhaps without knowing it, she had followed the advice
another author shares with parents:

Telling your children about life and death begins
with teaching them the wonderful truths about
heaven found in God's Word. Your goal is to fill
their hearts with the hope promised by Jesus in the
Gospels. The night before His own death, Jesus told
His disciples not to let their hearts be troubled,
because He was going to prepare a place for them
in heaven (John 14:1–4).[6]

That's good advice, not just for children, but for all of us!
We can face death with hope when we focus on the thrilling
happiness that awaits us, including the joy of seeing our
loved ones again. Imagining the young children who are gleefully frolicking in heaven's playground as they await the
arrival of their godly parents reminds me of one of Sam
Butcher's beautiful Precious Moments porcelain figures. Part

FAMILY CIRCUS

"Heaven is a great big hug that lasts forever."

of the "Hallelujah Square" mural in the Precious Moments Chapel, it depicts an adorable little girl arriving at heaven's gate, a tear sliding down her cheek. The comforting angel who greets her is pointing to a bucket labeled "Old Hankies."

Sam titled the scene "No Tears Past the Gate," and whenever I see it, I find myself wiping away tears of joy, just thinking of that marvelous place where Bill and I will be with our sons again and there will *never* be any more tears! What a thought!

A friend wrote a beautiful poem that describes my work with Spatula Ministries and all the ups and downs Bill and I have been through. The last two lines are my favorites. They say:

But when Gabriel blows his trumpet . . . and when Toot
    and Scoot is here,
Barb will jump the gate and grab her boys as Jesus
    dries her tears.

"NO TEARS PAST THE GATE"

That image is so precious to me, I've wallpapered it to my heart. Can't you just see me vaulting over that gate to get to Tim and Steve? Can you imagine the joy I'll know when I hold them in my arms again? (You probably can if you have deposits in heaven, yourself!) And then imagine the Savior joining us in our boisterous reunion, wiping away our tears of joy. Maybe, like Sam Butcher's little angel greeter, He'll remind us of one of the major benefits of our new home. He may point to a sign posted on the pearly gates, sort of like those restaurant signs that say, "No shirt, no shoes, no service." But the heavenly version would say:

> No troubles,
> No trials—
> No tears!

No Honking in Heaven

Yes, if there are bells in heaven, they will surely be joybells, and they'll ring out a glad welcome for our arrival there. Just imagine the difference in the sounds we'll hear as we breathe out our last earthly breath and the next moment draw in the sweet fragrance of heaven. One moment our earthly ears could be filled with the horrific noise of honking horns, screeching brakes, inflating airbags, and ambulance sirens—and the next moment we could be hearing the angelic choir sing music so beautiful it's beyond our comprehension here on earth.

One moment we could be surrounded by the poignant sounds of friends and family members weeping—and the next moment be the focus of exuberant rejoicing at the gates of heaven by loved ones who are waiting for us there.

One moment we could be irritated by the life-ending sounds of an IV alarm beeping, a heart monitor wailing out a "flat line," and a ventilator blasting out an emergency signal—and the next moment hear the blessed voice of the Savior saying, "You're home now, My child. Let Me show you the mansion I've prepared for you."

"I would have been here sooner, but I got hooked on oat bran muffins."

We know the sounds of heaven will be, well, *heavenly!* In our celestial home we won't be honked at, yelled at, beeped at, or bonged. We won't have to put up with the irritations of overeager smoke alarms (the signal at my house that dinner is ready), dental drills, jackhammers, barking dogs, or emergency exits left ajar.

When I think of all the noises, big and small, that clutter our days on earth, I'm amazed that we can get anything done at all—and I long for the soothing peacefulness of paradise. Our lives here sometimes seem to be completely controlled by various bells, beeps, and buzzers. For many of us, the day starts when the alarm clock awakens us. We stumble into the bathroom, where the latest invention is a battery-powered toothbrush with a timer that beeps when we've brushed the ideal two minutes. Next we head for the kitchen, where something gets shoved into the microwave. When the bell beeps, breakfast is done.

Some of us push a bunch of beeping buttons to arm a home security system before we go flying out the door. Others of us may have to beep another system to open our car doors. And once we're behind the steering wheel, another bell, beep, or buzzer reminds us to buckle our seat belts. (I'm holding out for one that reminds us to bring along the grocery list, too, and maybe check to make sure our shoes match.) Some cars beep when we put them in reverse (in case we can't tell which direction we're going, I guess); others have bells that chime when we leave the turn signal on too long without turning (which seems silly, because if it's been that long and we still haven't turned we've obviously forgotten where we wanted to turn in the first place, so what good does it do to remind us when we're two miles down the road?).

The modern world is full of emergency alarms, trouble signals, and warning bells. With all these gadgets reminding us to heed the warnings, how on earth do we get ourselves in so much trouble? Quite simply, for one reason or another, we ignore the signals. Or we don't hear them. Or we think they're meant for someone else.

Rise-Up Time
If only we would heed *all* warnings God sends our way! But too often in our busy lifestyles, we're so distracted by our myriad responsibilities that we don't hear the still, small voice that sounds urgent messages in our hearts. Even when we try to set aside time to study His timeless advice we speed on through His Word just like we zip past flashing lights and caution signals in our cars, sure we can squeak by one more time.

God uses all sorts of ways to get our attention, but sometimes we ignore Him, just as we've learned to disregard so many of the modern warning gizmos that have become routine in our high-tech world. When I think of the low-tech, wind-up alarm clocks that were all we had for so many years, I'm amazed at how things have changed. Those old rattletraps broke through the quiet morning sounds of nature with nothing more than a wind-up key that caused a mallet to hammer away at a couple of clanging bells on top of the clock.

For many years, Bill and I used that kind of trusty old alarm clock to start our day. Ironically, now that we've reached retirement age and no longer have jobs we must hurry to each morning, we wake up earlier than ever—usually around 4:30! We don't use an alarm clock at all unless we're traveling in another time zone and have appointments to keep.

Now that I don't *have* to get up at the crack of dawn, I enjoy doing just that. Those early morning hours are precious to me; they may be the closest thing to heaven I experience all day. The phone doesn't ring. There are no loud cars passing by on the street. No letter carriers or UPS deliverers are ringing the doorbell. The day's crises have not yet managed to intrude.

When someone sent me a list of early-risers in the Bible, I was cheered by the thought that the time of day I love so much has always been a special time for God's children. Now while I enjoy those quiet hours of the dawn, I think of my godly predecessors who worked and worshiped before the day began—without any kind of alarm clock to wake them up:

- Abraham got up early and "returned to the place where he had stood before the LORD."

- Moses and Aaron told the Israelites, "In the morning you will see the glory of the LORD."

- Moses climbed Mount Sinai early in the morning to meet God.

- In his last words, King David said a righteous leader who "rules in the fear of God . . . is like the light of morning at sunrise on a cloudless morning."

- Job's "regular custom" was to worship God "early in the morning."

- The psalmist wrote, "In the morning, O LORD, you hear my voice; in the morning I lay my requests before you and wait in expectation."

- Isaiah said, "In the morning my spirit longs for you."[7]

Jesus, Himself, used the early morning hours to communicate with God. The Bible says, "Very early in the morning, while it was still dark, Jesus got up, left the house and went off to a solitary place, where he prayed." And later we're told, "All the people came early in the morning to hear [Jesus] at the temple."[8]

How do you suppose the people managed to wake up early on those days when there were no clanging bells of alarm clocks to jar them loose from their slumber? Surely their excitement about hearing the Savior's words helped them spring up from their beds and hurry to the place where Jesus was speaking.

The Best Sound in Heaven

While heaven's joybells will certainly be wonderful to my ears, the heavenly sound I anticipate most eagerly is that one: Jesus speaking to me, the sound of the Savior calling my name. Can there be anything more blessed in all eternity? That image explains why I consider the events of the resurrection morning one of the most beautiful stories in the Bible.

A distraught Mary Magdalene sobbed outside the empty tomb on that early morning. She had gone there to care for the corpse, and now she was in such anguish, believing someone had stolen Jesus' body, that when the gardener asked her what was wrong she couldn't even turn to look at him as she answered. "They have taken my Lord away," she said, "and I don't know where they have put him."

Then the gardener spoke to her—just one word, her name: "Mary"—and her head jerked up at the sound of his voice. Her spirits soared as she realized he wasn't the gardener at all but Jesus Himself! Imagine the joy that swept through her heart and thrilled her soul to hear that sound: *her name,* coming from the lips of the risen Savior! That's the glorious sound that will awaken us to life eternal when we fall asleep on earth and open our eyes in heaven.

The late Peter Marshall, former chaplain of the U.S. Senate, told a story about a young boy who was dying from an incurable disease. He asked his mother, "What is it like to die? Does it hurt?"

His mother reminded him of what it was like when he had played hard all day and fell asleep on the sofa or in the car on

FAMILY CIRCUS

the ride home from his grandparents' house. "When you awoke in the morning you were in your own bed because your daddy came with his big strong arms and carried you home. Death is like that," the mother told him. "You fall asleep here, and you wake up and find that your Father has carried you home."[9]

The Mysterious Call

Until we wake up in heaven on "that great gettin'-up morning" to the sound of the Savior calling our names, we have to make the best of the mornings we wake up here on earth. For millions of people, that means being awakened by the jangling bell, beep, or buzzer of an alarm clock. And yes, there's a whole new generation of sounds to wake us up these days. Actually these modern alarms have distanced themselves so far from the good, old-fashioned, two-clanger alarm clock that they do everything but ring. Now you can buy clocks that awaken you with music, recordings, flashing lights, or, ironically, those same sounds of nature that for centuries have lulled people to sleep: ocean surf, wind sighing through the willows, frogs in the forest, creeks gurgling—and all sorts of other sounds. And not only that, but there are new alarms that *bing*, *bong*, and *beep* at us all day long.

I think of them as annoyance noises, those pesky reminders to take the clothes out of the dryer, fill the car's gas tank, and stand back so the lettuce can be sprayed with water in the grocery store's produce aisle.

My own home is full of these noisy gizmos. Friends give them to me for my Joy Room, and to be honest, it gets so crazy in there sometimes that I have to go outside and listen to the freeway to find a "piece of quiet." It seems that something is always ringing, dinging, or donging.

Recently I announced a moratorium on noisy doodads—just as Bill brought home yet another silly gift for me: an electric wind chime! "Look!" he said proudly, pointing to the wording on the box. "It chimes all by itself, so you can keep it INSIDE the house. You just plug it in."

Great! I thought, smiling through gritted teeth. *Now all we need is seventy-six trombones and a parade, and we can have round-the-clock mayhem!*

Each new noisemaker provides a splash of humor—at least the first few times we hear it. My friend Lynda gave me an alarm that made some kind of barnyard noise every time I opened the refrigerator. The idea was to keep me from getting into the ice cream so often. But, being a martyr, I selflessly gave the little loudmouth gadget to a friend who needed it more than I did! (And so that I could eat my ice cream in peace!)

Another friend had a different kind of alarm on one of her kitchen appliances. An intelligent, poised, retired schoolteacher, this woman—I'll call her Clara—was watching *Jeopardy!* one night when a crowing sound suddenly reverberated through the house: "Cock-a-doodle-DOOOOOOOO!"

Clara, absorbed in matching wits with the *Jeopardy!* contestants, was startled but couldn't find anything out of the ordinary in the house. She didn't hear the crowing again, so she assumed it was something on the television and settled back for the double-jeopardy segment. The next night, just as *Jeopardy!* was ending, the loud sound came again: "Cock-a-doodle-DOOOOOOOO!"

This time Clara was sure it hadn't come from the television. In fact, the crowing seemed to have come from the kitchen. But when she stood in the middle of the kitchen floor, perplexed, nothing seemed amiss.

The invisible rooster continued every night at exactly the same time, and eventually Clara figured out that it was the new microwave that was crowing. When she told me about it, I insisted on calling her at the appointed time to hear it for myself. Sure enough, at 7:45 P.M. she held the phone up to the microwave, and it crowed loudly: "Cock-a-doodle-DOOOOOOOO!"

By now, Clara's microwave had become quite a sensation among her friends and relatives. One of their favorite things to do was to come over and watch *Jeopardy!* and wait for the microwave to crow. She wrote to the manufacturer, asking if the crowing was a special feature that wasn't described in the owner's manual. The company responded by asking her to send the microwave back to them so they could determine whether a prankster at the factory had somehow programmed the microwave's components with this crowing. But by that time Clara had gotten rather attached to the feisty little rooster living inside the appliance. She decided to keep it as it was.

Eventually the excitement subsided, and Clara and the crowing microwave settled into a comfortable routine. Every night at 7:45, right in the middle of *Jeopardy!*, the microwave cock-a-doodle-DOOOOOOOOOOO-ed and Clara sighed and smiled, enjoying the cheerful greeting of the mysterious little bird. She had stopped trying to solve the mystery and instead claimed the verse from Proverbs, "It is the glory of God to conceal a matter" and those wise words from Deuteronomy, "The secret things belong to the LORD."[10]

Then one day when her grandson came over to paint her kitchen, he pulled the microwave away from the wall—and found a little round magnet stuck to the back of the appliance. There was a small talking alarm clock attached to the magnet, a gadget used by blind people. Like many such tools for the sight-impaired, instead of buzzing or beeping it crowed like a rooster.

Eventually Clara learned that the little magnet had been given out to those who had contributed to a local support group. She knew her husband had been a faithful supporter of the Society for the Prevention of Blindness, so she assumed the little magnet had been given to him before he died. How it got stuck to the microwave, we'll never know. Perhaps he left it in the cabinet and somehow it fell down the back wall when the new microwave was installed. However it happened, it added a spark to her life while it hid there, crowing away at 7:45 every night. Friends asked about the little bird whenever they called, as though it were a member of the family.

Now the mystery is solved—and *Jeopardy!* doesn't seem nearly as appealing to my friend. She might be the ideal candidate to try that new-fangled microwave described recently in the newspaper. The door doubles as a television and computer. So while the pizza is spinning around inside the oven she could shut the door and log on to the Internet, send an e-mail message, or even watch her favorite television show—*Jeopardy!* It probably wouldn't be as spirit-lifting as a *crowing* microwave, but it could run a close second!

Heavenly Bell-Ringers

We enjoy such stories because they make us laugh (especially when they're about someone else!), but at the same time it's reassuring to think that none of us will be embarrassed by false assumptions and silly scenarios in heaven. We won't be outwitted by crowing gizmos and stumped by mysteries. We'll surely be laughing in heaven—but we'll laugh for the sheer joy of being in the presence of God and our loved ones and all the other members of the heavenly host. As one century-old tombstone in London's Brompton Cemetery so simply but beautifully puts it, we'll be

WITH CHRIST, WHICH IS FAR BETTER.[11]

The sounds that perplex us on earth will be a thing of the past when we walk down those streets of gold. There won't be any irate drivers honking at us. No talking alarm clocks crowing at us. No computers beeping at some mistake we've made. No metal detectors ringing to stop us as we hurry to our offices or airplanes. We'll leave behind all the earthly sounds that frustrated us, as well as all those words that annoyed us. Never again will we hear:

- "Your appointment was yesterday."
- "This lane is closed."
- "Your application is denied."
- "Your account is overdrawn."
- "Your payment is overdue."

- "There's been an accident."
- "The principal wants to see you."
- "We've done all we can do."
- "I'm sorry."
- "Too late."
- "Too bad."
- "Good-bye."
- "Oops!"

Isn't it wonderful to think we're bound for glory, where there will only be joyful sounds and loving words? In that great choir gathered in Hallelujah Square we'll sing what Christians have predicted for decades in the majestic old hymns:

- "We'll sing and shout the victory."
- "Glory in the highest I will shout and sing."
- "Songs of praises I will ever give to Thee."
- "I'll sing with the glittering crown on my brow."
- "And there proclaim, my God, how great Thou art!"

I'm ready right now!

Cloud Busters

I never lay my head upon the pillow without thinking that maybe before the morning breaks the final morning will have dawned. I never begin my work in the morning without thinking that perhaps He may interrupt my work and begin His own. A person with that attitude is surely looking for the Lord's return. It's the only way to live!

G. Campbell Morgan

Days are scrolls:
Write on them only what you want remembered.

Bachya ibn Pakuda

There's nothing discreditable in dying. I've known the most respectable people to do it.

C. S. Lewis,
Letters to an American Lady

The youngest children enrolled in a church preschool always steal the show at the annual Christmas program. Last year the children—none of whom could yet read—held up brightly colored three-foot-high placards that spelled out Christmas words. The highlight came when one foursome walked onstage in reverse order and proudly spelled

RATS

Emergency operator: 911, what is your emergency?
Caller: Could you send the police to my house?
Operator: What's wrong there?
Caller: I called and someone answered the phone, but I'm not there.

It was one of Mother's hectic days. Her small son, who had been playing outside, came in with his pants torn. "You go right in, remove those pants, and start mending them yourself," she ordered.

Sometime later she went to see how he was getting along. The torn pants were lying across the chair, and the door to the cellar, usually kept closed, was open. She called down the stairs loudly and sternly:

"Young man, are you running around down there without your pants on?"

"No, ma'am," was the deep-voiced reply. "I'm just down here reading your gas meter."[12]

Don't you hear those bells now ringing?
Don't you hear the angels singing?
'Tis the glory hallelujah jubilee.
In that far-off sweet forever
Just beyond the shining river,
When they ring the golden bells for you and me.[13]

Hear, O my people, and I will warn you—if you would but listen to me . . . ![14]

I am thinking today of that beautiful land
I shall reach when the sun goeth down;
When thro' wonderful grace by my Savior I stand,
Will there be any stars in my crown?

Will there be any stars, any stars in my crown
When at evening the sun goeth down?
When I wake with the blest in the mansions of rest,
Will there be any stars in my crown?[1]

Stick a Geranium in Your Starry Crown

It's not unusual for women to tell me that my book *Stick a Geranium in Your Hat and Be Happy* has helped them learn to laugh again during the most miserable days of their lives. The book describes my own journey through the tunnel leading out of the cesspools of life. Most importantly, it shares the relief I found when I learned how God uses humor to hammer out our hurts. When we learn to laugh again despite our difficulties, we live out the premise that "pain is inevitable but misery is optional."

Since the book was published a few years ago, I've met thousands of folks, mostly women, who adopted the "geranium" philosophy and chose to laugh in the midst of heartache. And occasionally I hear about men who have benefited from the book too—usually pastors or Christian counselors. But as far as I know, Duward Campbell was the first cowboy. A tall, tough West Texas rancher, Duward stuck a geranium in his Stetson and looked for every opportunity to laugh in spite of life's difficulties. With a smile on his face and

a heart spilling over with God's love, he literally danced his
way to death's door.

Soon after he was diagnosed with terminal cancer, someone gave Duward a copy of *Geranium*, and he took it to heart.
Even now his wife, Gwen, chuckles when she remembers
Duward with a geranium stuck in the band of his cowboy hat
as he rode his horse or sipped coffee with his fellow ranchers
at the local Dairy Queen.

And when Duward became a "geranium cowboy," he didn't
just *wear* geraniums; he *raised* them. The flower beds around
the Campbells' home in Haskell, Texas, became his geranium
project and soon were spilling over with the bright red blossoms. To him, the geraniums weren't just flowers. They were
reminders to all who knew him that Duward Campbell, a
strong Christian, had consciously decided to laugh instead of
complain about his problems. You see, even though he didn't
talk about it much, Duward knew he was homeward bound,
and that calm assurance gave him the courage to be happy
even as he looked death in the face.

My friend Marilyn Meberg often talks about inspiring
people "who manage to add to others' cheer by how they exit
from life." When someone clipped Duward Campbell's long,
glowing obituary from the newspaper and sent it to me, I
knew he was one of those people. The eulogy said, in part:

> Cowboy tall at 6'2" and with rugged good looks,
> Duward was a commanding presence in his com-
> munity. Even amidst the ravages of cancer, his

indomitable spirit prevailed. Often he stuck a single geranium atop his cowboy hat and quoted the title of Barbara Johnson's book, *So Stick a Geranium in Your Hat and Be Happy*. . . . To his wealth of friends and family, he leaves a legacy of positive thinking, neighborly action and pervasive love.

Just as those red geraniums brightened Duward Campbell's life, he brightened the lives of others—especially his wife and their family, including their beloved grandchildren. He told them about the cancer, the doctor's prediction, and his own decision, despite the bad news, to be happy. And he told them matter-of-factly in his West Texas twang, "You can make up your mind: You can be miserable—you can just lie down and die—or you can stick a geranium in your hat and be happy."

It was obvious to all who knew him which choice Duward had made. He had learned the secret the apostle Paul talked about when he said:

> I have learned the secret of being content in any and every situation. . . . I can do everything through him who gives me strength.[2]

Like thousands of joyful Christians who have gone on to heaven before him, Duward Campbell laughed at death. He wasn't afraid to die. And in the fearless way he departed this life, he also inspired the loved ones he left behind.

One of the many happy memories that continue to encourage Gwen is remembering his determination to keep doing the things he enjoyed. One of them was dancing; they had enjoyed many a night doing the Texas Two-Step and the Cotton-Eyed Joe. Gwen laughs now when she remembers how, just a couple of weeks before he died, the two of them were out on the dance floor again, dragging Duward's oxygen tank along behind them as they swirled around the room.

Another bittersweet memory, ironically, is of the day when a Fort Worth doctor told them Duward's cancer had worsened.

"THIS TOO SHALL PASS"

Used by permission of Samuel J. Butcher, creator of Precious Moments.

When the oncologist came in with the results of the latest biopsy, his face was grim. "I'm afraid I have bad news," he began.

"Well, shoot," Duward answered impatiently. "I didn't need you to tell me that. I knew it wasn't good—all my geraniums are dyin'!"

Hearing him say that and fearing that his resolute joy might be weakening, Gwen slipped away and called one of their daughters back in their little hometown. "I don't know how you're going to do it, Honey," she said, "but you girls need to find your daddy some geraniums."

It was late fall, long past the first frost, and as Gwen and Duward made the four-hour drive home from Fort Worth late that evening, Gwen's mind raced ahead, hoping her daughters could find a few geraniums somewhere that were still blooming. As late in the day as she had called and as late in the season as it was, she wasn't sure they'd be able to find even one.

"But when we got home and opened the door," she recalled later, laughing at the memory, "there must have been a million of 'em. The house was full of geraniums."

Duward died in October 1997, and just as they'd filled his home with geraniums when he needed encouragement, his family and friends filled the church with geraniums for his funeral. The floral blanket on his casket was made of geraniums entwined with his cattle-herding rope, and laughter was entwined throughout the service, just as he had requested. When it was over, one of his favorite songs, "Waltz Across Texas," played as his friends paid their last respects.

Recently Gwen Campbell's little grandson, remembering his grandfather's last days, asked her, "Grannie, is PaPa in bed up in heaven?"

"Oh, no, Honey," Gwen said with a smile. "I'm sure he's not in bed. He's not sick anymore."

The grandson's face broke into a smile as he exclaimed, "Grannie, I'll bet he's teachin' Jesus how to do the Cotton-Eyed Joe!"

Getting Used to Wearing a Crown

It's silly, I know. But when I think of Duward Campbell and all the other merry Christians in heaven, dancing on those streets of gold, I imagine them wearing, not the majestic crowns described so beautifully in Scripture, but cowboy hats, baseball caps, firefighter helmets, sunbonnets, and all manner of head coverings—symbols of the work they did on earth. And of course when my imagination is really running wild, I see geranium blossoms bobbing on all the brims!

Some of us just don't seem sophisticated enough to wear heavenly crowns, but that's what the Bible says we'll have—"a crown that will last forever."[3] Here are some of my favorite promises of the crowns that will be available to us in heaven:

I have fought the good fight, I have finished the race, I have kept the faith. Now there is in store for me the crown of righteousness, which the Lord, the righteous Judge, will award to me on that day—and not only to me, but also to all who have longed for his appearing.[4]

Blessed is the man who perseveres under trial, because when he has stood the test, he will receive the crown of life that God has promised to those who love him.[5]

And when the Chief Shepherd appears, you will receive the crown of glory that will never fade away.[6]

For what is our hope, or joy, or crown of rejoicing? Is it not even you in the presence of our Lord Jesus Christ at His coming?[7]

Do you not know that in a race all the runners run, but only one gets the prize? Run in such a way as to get the prize. Everyone who competes in the games goes into strict training. They do it to get a crown that will not last; but we do it to get a crown that will last forever.[8]

A few years ago when Florence Littauer and I were both speaking at a women's conference, I was enthralled by her description of these five kinds of crowns: the crowns of righteousness, of life, of glory, and of rejoicing, and the imperishable crown. She told the audience she'd been a Christian fifteen years before she learned that crowns would be available to her in heaven. "That pepped up my whole Christian life," she quipped, explaining that she'd "always wanted to be a queen."

Florence said her study of the Bible had made her believe that we don't work our way to heaven, but through our work here on earth, some of us may earn these heavenly crowns.

For example, it may be that 2 Timothy 4:8 is telling us the crown of righteousness can be earned by being faithful throughout our Christian life and constantly looking forward to Jesus' second coming. Joni Eareckson Tada says this crown is "for those who are itching to have Jesus come back."

The crown of life may go to those who love God more than themselves and who don't just endure adversity but who rise above it, who show joy in the midst of trials. The old saying is true: There will be no crown-wearers in heaven who were not cross-bearers here on earth!

The crown of glory may be reserved for those who "humble [themselves] under the mighty hand of God" and who "feed [His] lambs" or support those who do.[9]

The crown of rejoicing may be waiting for Christians who share the gospel with others wherever they go.

Finally, the imperishable crown, said Florence, is waiting for those who are disciplined and well-trained in the Christian life. These are the believers who are devoted to prayer and faithful in their Bible study.

Royalty in Training

Now, for some of us, this idea of wearing a crown is going to take some getting used to. It's hard to imagine ourselves with the regal bearing of royalty. Maybe we need a little practice!

In my mind, one of the ways we can prepare ourselves for this royal duty is by setting a good example for our fellow earth-dwellers the way Jesus, our heavenly King of kings, sets an example for us. We know He reigns in love, extending grace to all His subjects. He thinks of us as His children, His sheep, and He nurtures us as we follow His pathway.

In the same way, we prepare ourselves to take our place beside His throne in heaven by practicing love here on earth. We set an example of Christian faith by enduring life's difficulties with courage and even joy, the way Duward Campbell and so many other devoted believers have shown us. And wherever we go, we spread God's care for His children so we can be a conduit of His love to others.

The King of creation wants us, His subjects, to be joyful and to love one another. In fact He has told us that His number-one priority is love: His love for us, our love for Him and for others. So our assignment as heavenly royalty-in-training here on earth is, above all, to spread His love.

Joy Begets Joy

Jesus also wants us to be joyful. But just as some of us have to accustom ourselves to the idea of wearing a heavenly crown, others have to *work* at being joyful until it becomes a habit. Do you know the difference between *joy* and *happiness?* Happiness depends on what is happening around us. But true joy just bubbles up from inside and is constant regardless of our circumstances.

One way to develop the joyful habit is to nurture an attitude of thankfulness. As someone said, God has two dwelling places—one in heaven and the other in a thankful heart. When God dwells in our thankful hearts we can't be anything but joyful. Science confirms that truth. After years of studying people with joyful temperaments, one researcher concluded, "The first secret is gratitude. All happy people are grateful. Ungrateful people cannot be happy."[10]

It's impossible to feel miserable while imagining ourselves wearing the crown Jesus has promised us and saying, "Thank You, God!" It's just as hard to stick a perky geranium in your hat (or your helmet or your ten-gallon Stetson) and be gloomy. If you're not as bold as Duward Campbell was to do it literally, you can at least do it in your imagination. Just envision yourself, no matter what your circumstances, joyfully adorned with a silly hat, or a heavenly crown—as you head out into the world each day. And let your first words of the morning be, "Thank You, God!"

Henri Nouwen offered some additional suggestions for being gratefully joyful. He wrote:

> It might be a good idea to ask ourselves how we develop our capacity to choose for joy. Maybe we

could spend a moment at the end of each day and decide to remember that day—whatever may have happened—as a day to be grateful for. In so doing we increase our heart's capacity to choose joy. And as our hearts become more joyful, we will become, without any special effort, a source of joy for others. Just as sadness begets sadness, so joy begets joy.[11]

RALPH

" THE TESTS ARE BACK, YOUR HIGHNESS, AND I KNOW WHAT'S CAUSING YOUR HEADACHES! "

A Spirit That Gravitates Toward the Light

When your heart is filled with God's love and your head is aglow with His crown, you can't help but express joy. And others invariably "catch" your joyful attitude because, as

Nouwen says, "Joy is contagious." He learned this from a friend who "radiates joy, not because his life is easy, but because he habitually recognizes God's presence in the midst of human suffering, his own as well as others." Nouwen's description of his friend creates a pattern we should all try to copy:

> Wherever he goes, whomever he meets, he is able to see and hear something beautiful, something for which to be grateful. He doesn't deny the great sorrow that surrounds him nor is he blind or deaf to the agonizing sights and sounds of his fellow human beings, but his spirit gravitates toward the light in the darkness and the prayers in the midst of the cries of despair.
>
> His eyes are gentle; his voice is soft. There is nothing sentimental about him. He is a realist, but his deep faith allows him to know that hope is more real than despair, faith more real than distrust, and love more real than fear. It is this spiritual realism that makes him such a joyful man.[12]

The more he was with this joyful friend, said Nouwen, "the more I [caught] glimpses of the sun shining through the clouds. . . . While my friend always spoke about the sun, I kept speaking about the clouds, until one day I realized that it was the sun that allowed me to see the clouds. Those who keep speaking about the sun while walking under a cloudy sky are messengers of hope, the true saints of our day."[13] By "catching" his friend's joy, Nouwen must have also learned the truth Helen Keller taught: "The best and most beautiful things in the world cannot be seen or even touched. They must be felt with the heart."

Crowns Aglow with Stars

We are children of God, members of Jesus' royal family—our Father's light shining through the clouds of others' sorrow. Pop

Blessed are the glad-hearted servants

who shine with the Master's joy!

May the God of hope fill you with all joy and peace as you trust in Him, so that you may overflow with hope by the power of the Holy Spirit. (Romans 15:13)

your imaginary (for now) crown on your head, unleash your brightest smile, and go spread some joy!

Have you ever noticed how one person with a bright smile can light up a room full of sourpusses? Think of the woman described as a "wondrous sign" near the end of Revelation, who was "clothed with the sun, with the moon under her feet and a crown of twelve stars on her head."[14] Just imagining the light given off by such an image makes me want to reach for my sunglasses! But that's the kind of impact we can have as we bring God's Word to those still struggling through their own cesspool.

Empowered by this image, we can walk confidently through life's darkest night. As Norman Vincent Peale often reminded his listeners, we're "not supposed to crawl through life on [our] hands and knees," with our faces in the mud.[15] Let your light shine! Deliberately choose to look for joy in every step of your journey through life and to share it with others. When you do, you will be blessed with happiness no matter what your circumstances are. Remember what Jesus told us to do: "Let your light shine before men, that they may see your good deeds and praise your Father in heaven."[16]

Just as one little pinch of salt can make all the difference in cooking, the light of one joyful Christian can radiate the love of Almighty God to the world. That reminds me of the story about the rich man who called his three sons to his bedside as he was dying. He told them, "I want to leave my fortune intact, so I will set each of you the same task to see which one is the most capable at managing money. In my warehouse there are three large storerooms, all of the same size. Here is a bag of silver each. Your task is this: Each of you fill one storeroom with as much as your silver will buy."

The first son thought long and hard about how he could get the most bulk for his money. He used his silver to buy sand. But even though his money could buy several wagonloads, when the silver ran out, the storeroom was only one-third full.

The second son spent all his silver on plain soil, but it filled only half of his storeroom.

The third son watched his brothers try unsuccessfully to fill their storerooms with the silver their father had given them. Then he spent just a few silver coins and bought some candles and matches . . . to fill his room with light.[17]

The Beginning of Prayer

Someone said a smile is the lighting system of the face and the heating system of the heart. And smiles can easily evolve into laughter, that sound only God's children can make. As Reinhold Niebuhr said,

> Humor is the prelude to faith,
> and laughter is the beginning of prayer.

At first glance, it might be puzzling to think of laughter as the "beginning of prayer." But remember that a happy heart springs from a grateful spirit. Each time you enjoy a hearty laugh see how natural it feels at that moment to chuckle out the beginner's prayer: "Thank You, Lord!"

Brighten the Corner Where You Are

There are so many ways we can wear Christ's light-giving, star-bedecked crown in this world, helping others see God's goodness shining through the clouds. Sometimes it just takes a moment to make a big impact on someone's life.

For example, there's this story about Dr. Albert Schweitzer, the famous missionary-doctor and Nobel Prize winner who spent his life helping "the poorest of the poor" in Africa:

> Reporters and officials gathered at the Chicago railroad station to await the arrival of the Nobel Prize winner.
> He stepped off the train—a giant of a man, six-feet-four, with bushy hair and a large mustache.
> As cameras flashed, the officials came up with hands outstretched and began telling him how honored they were to meet him. He thanked them and

then, looking over their heads, asked if he might
be excused for a moment. He walked through the
crowd with quick steps until he reached an elderly
woman who was having trouble trying to carry two
large suitcases.

He picked up the bags in his big hands and, smiling, escorted the woman to a bus. As he helped her
aboard, he wished her a safe journey. Meanwhile, the
crowd tagged along behind him. He turned to them
and said, "Sorry to have kept you waiting." . . .

Said a member of the reception committee to one
of the reporters, "That's the first time I ever saw a
sermon walking."[18]

The late Erma Bombeck, one of my favorite folks, had a real
gift for finding joy in every situation. One of her first jobs was
writing obituaries at a newspaper—surely a job that was
almost as dull as straightening staples and sorting golf balls!
But Erma found a way to laugh about her situation. She told
her friends how thrilled her mother was when she read the
obituaries Erma had written. "She was so impressed that I got
all the victims to die in alphabetical order," Erma joked. And
she once quipped that the epitaph she wanted on her own
gravestone was:

Big deal! I'm used to dust.

Oh, to have Erma's joyful attitude—the same joyful mind-
set of the little girl in another Henri Nouwen story. Nouwen
was studiously interviewing an artist when the woman's little
five-year-old daughter came bustling into the room. "I made
a birthday cake with sand," she told him sweetly. "Now you
have to come and pretend that you're eating it and that you
like it. That will be fun!"

The little girl's mother smiled at Nouwen and said to him,
"You'd better play with her before you talk to me. Maybe she
has more to teach you than I have."[19]

Some of us need to learn how to be God's joyful crown-wearers—and our teachers don't have to be Nobel Prize winners to teach us this lesson! They may even be innocent children, who so often seem to possess a natural gift for laughter. Our responsibility is to make ourselves teachable!

A Crown-Wearer's Duties

If we were royal heirs to an earthly monarch, we might have grand, attention-getting duties such as leading military campaigns or reigning over lavish ceremonial affairs. Instead, we are heirs to a servant King, whom we honor by serving others in humility and in love. Our responsibilities may not be glorious deeds that win us loud acclaim—at least not on this side of heaven. Here, our tasks may be something much simpler—and even more important:

> To speak a healing word to a broken heart.
> To extend a hand to one who has fallen.
> To give a smile to those whose laughter has
>   been lost.
> To encourage the dreamer who has given up.
> To share the painful solitude of one who is alone.
> To ease the burden of one bent low beneath a
>   thankless task.
> To reassure the doubter and reinforce the
>   believer.
> To light the candle of God's Word in the midst
>   of another's darkest night.

There's an inspiring story about a man who was disheartened by all the sorrow he saw in the world around him. Everywhere he looked he saw the evidence of our broken world: abandoned children, abusive marriages, desperate men and women suffering unspeakable pain.

In frustration, the distraught man cried out, "God, why don't You *do* something?"

"I have," God replied quietly. "I created you."

Crowns with Chin Straps

Our heavenly crowns may be glorious ornaments we'll wear while singing praises to our King when we get to heaven, but here on earth, Christ's crown of servanthood should come with a chin strap, because we have a lot of work to do! A friend sent me an essay recently that describes the "doodles" that appear on another woman's prayer journal. One of the drawings is a crown, drawn there to remind her, as she prays for her children, that "what they are today is not what they will be tomorrow." The same is true for all of us. And it just may be that WE are the instruments He's using to love or encourage someone else. As this writer said, "God Himself is at work in [all of us] and He will complete what He has begun." Her thoughts echo the wisdom of the apostle John, who wrote:

> If anyone acknowledges that Jesus is the Son of God, God lives in him and he in God. . . . God is love. Whoever lives in love lives in God, and God in him. In this way, love is made complete among us so that we will have confidence on the day of judgment, because in this world we are like him.[20]

God the Father is our King. Like Him, we will someday wear a crown of glory. We'll find it waiting for us when we arrive at the foot of His throne. There will be no need for fittings, no delay for customizing. God knows our head size!

Cloud Busters

For the LORD takes delight in his people;
he crowns the humble with salvation.[21]

"Oh, how I wish the Lord would come during my lifetime!" Queen Victoria of England told one of her advisers.

When he asked why, "her countenance brightened, and with deep emotion she replied, 'Because I would love to lay my crown at His blessed feet in reverent adoration.'"[22]

The Earliest Smile of Day

Oh, look! the Savior blest,
Calm after solemn rest,
Stands in the garden 'neath His olive boughs.
The earliest smile of day
Doth on his vesture play,
And light the majesty of his still brows;
While angels hang with wings outspread,
Holding the new-worn crown above his
    saintly head.

Jean Ingelow

In mansions of glory and endless delight,
I'll ever adore Thee in heaven so bright;
I'll sing with the glittering crown on my brow;
If ever I loved Thee, my Jesus, 'tis now.

William R. Featherstone

I've no idea when Jesus is coming back. I'm on the Welcoming Committee, not the Planning Committee.[23]

Soon after *Geranium* was published, I was invited to speak at David Jeremiah's large church in San Diego, where the "ticket" to get in was to wear some kind of crazy hat. What fun it was to stand at the podium and look out over that sea of zaniness crowning the heads of fifteen hundred ladies! One woman's hat was even battery-powered, with lights that blinked and flashed. But the idea that stole the show was one woman's portrayal of laughter in life's cesspools. On her head she wore an upside-down bedpan, decorated with geraniums!

It takes many hours to fill a pail of water if you're doing it drop by drop. Even when the pail seems full, it can take many drops more. Eventually, of course, one drop more makes the pail overflow.

So it is with kindness. Most people appreciate even one deed of kindness, but some find it difficult to show their appreciation. Don't let this stop you. Eventually you'll do some little thing that will make their hearts overflow.[24]

Finish then Thy new creation,
Pure and spotless let us be;
Let us see Thy great salvation,
Perfectly restored in Thee;
Changed from Glory into glory,
Till in heaven we take our place,
Till we cast our crowns before Thee,
Lost in wonder, love, and praise!

Charles Wesley, "Love Divine"

Never give up! The iron crown of suffering pre-
cedes the golden crown of glory.

According to your latest figures, if you retired today, you could live very, very comfortably until about 2 p.m. tomorrow.

The wealth of the wise is their crown.[25]

I've got a mansion just over the hilltop,
In that bright land where we'll never grow old;
And someday yonder we will nevermore wander,
But walk on streets that are purest gold.[1]

Finally, Fabulously *Home!*

The phone rang one day when my arms were loaded with mail and packages I'd just brought home from the post office. Grabbing the receiver off the wall phone as I passed it in the hall, I heard a voice say, "Oh, Barb! I've just got to talk to you! I've been trying to get your phone number for days, and finally I found you!"

Juggling my load of paperwork from one arm to the other, I squeezed the phone between my shoulder and chin. "Wait a minute," I said. "I've gotta get to another phone where I can sit down. Can you hang on a minute?"

"Okay," she replied.

Leaving the phone dangling by its cord, I hurried to unload the mail onto my desk. Then, on my way to the living room, my eye fell on some letters I'd intended to put outside for the mailman (we get mail both at home and at the post office). It just took a second to slip outside and stick them in the—Oops! The mail had already been picked up, and more had been delivered. Scooping the new stuff out of the box, I trotted back into the house and piled it on the table and suddenly remembered the finished cycle of clothes still waiting in the washer. Moving quickly, I loaded them into the dryer and then scooted into my Joy Room so I could ride my exercise bike while we talked on the phone.

"I'm back!" I panted into the phone, exhausted by all my running.

"How come it took you so long to go from one phone to the other?" the woman asked rather indignantly. "I thought you just lived in a mobile home!"

Folks have all sorts of images of mobile homes, I guess. This woman apparently imagined that Bill and I lived in a camper-sized trailer. It's not small—or at least it doesn't seem small when I have to clean it! And it's set in a lovely park that has a beautiful lake with sculptured landscaping and water fountains, and a large swimming pool and Jacuzzi. So it's not exactly what most people picture when they think of a "trailer park." We sold our home and moved here twenty-one years ago when the kids were gone so that we could have the comfort and convenience of a leisurely lifestyle. At that time we had no inkling that Spatula Ministries would be born and that we would be traveling constantly. But in God's economy, that was part of His plan for us, and we love the freedom we have here and all the pleasures that go with it.

We built a large Joy Room onto our home that makes a most unique guestroom with lots of toys and signs and hanging things designed to make us laugh.

A few years ago we welcomed into our Joy Room the heartbroken mother of a son dying with AIDS. She had traveled clear across the country to California for a special meeting of our local Spatula support group. She rode with us in our ten-year-old Volvo from the meeting back to our home that night and then settled happily into the Joy Room, thanking us profusely for making her feel so welcome. The woman was a most gracious guest, delighted with all the silly knickknacks surrounding her. Occasionally as she got ready for bed we could hear her out there, chuckling at something she'd just spotted in the corner or hanging on the wall.

A few months later, when I had a speaking engagement near her home in Florida, the woman invited us to spend a couple of nights with her so she could "return the hospitality," as she said. She picked me up where I was speaking and drove me to her home in a new, luxurious car. As soon as we turned into her neighborhood, I was amazed by the huge size of the homes there. They were MANSIONS!

When she welcomed us into her lovely home, I was nearly breathless with the wonder of the many large rooms, the lavish furnishings, and the exquisitely detailed decor. Her home had a gorgeous spiral staircase like you might see in the movies, and her dining room looked like the one I'd seen at the Hearst Castle. There were even servants who waited on us with sweet southern hospitality and provided every comfort we might want.

The most spectacular thing about her mansion was the atrium, which was larger than my entire mobile home. It had a huge ficus tree that had been specially designed just for that entryway. It was more than forty feet tall and had been crafted from a cypress trunk with three enormous branches. More than twenty-five thousand silk leaves had been individually attached with hot glue, making the tree spread out to fill the atrium. It sort of reminded me of the huge Swiss Family Robinson tree at Disneyland where kids can climb up and play. Thinking of all those silk leaves being glued on one by one just sort of overwhelmed me. Her whole mansion overwhelmed me!

As I unpacked in the spacious guestroom, I thought of how humble and appreciative my friend had been to settle in so contentedly, sleeping in a meager single bed in our Joy Room. She had her own bathroom at our house, but it was a miniature-sized cubbyhole adjoining the Joy Room, certainly nothing luxurious like she had at home. Still, she had bubbled with laughter, considering it lots of fun to visit with us. *Boy! What a far cry she was from her own deluxe furnishings,* I thought, looking at her fabulous home and remembering how graciously she had settled into my mobile-home Joy Room with all its tacky toys and signs.

Since then, these contrasting images—my friend's stay in our humble Joy Room and my incredulous arrival at her fabulous mansion—have dissolved into heavenly visions in my mind. When I think of my friend leaving her mansion to come visit me in my modest mobile home, I imagine Jesus leaving the glorious neighborhoods of heaven to come to a humble Bethlehem barn. Remembering the wonder of my friend's beautiful mansion, I realize that, as beautiful as it was, the mansion waiting for us in heaven would make her luxurious home seem like a tar-paper shack.

"Barb, we'll know how to find you in heaven. Your mansion will have geraniums all around it!"

Heavenly Homes

As different as they are from each other as well as from the palaces awaiting us in glory, my friend's mansion and my mobile home *do* have at least one thing in common with those divine domiciles in heaven: They're *both* filled with love.

If you grew up in a loving family, you're probably familiar with that strong, nurturing sense of welcome that wraps around you the instant you step inside the door. It's an atmosphere, a comforting feeling, that engulfs you like a soft cloud of warm, soothing mist. It's the sound of footsteps rushing toward you, the tinkle of laughter bubbling up from someone who's glad to see you. It's the light in a window and the sparkle in a loved one's eyes. In short, it's *home.*

That's surely the feeling, multiplied ten thousand times, that we'll have as we fly through the clouds and find ourselves in heaven. What joy we'll experience! What a welcome we'll receive! What love we'll know! All these glorious feelings will flood over us, and we'll be spellbound with the wonder of it all. Best of all, we'll finally hear the Master say those two precious words we've longed for through all of earth's trials: *"Welcome HOME!"*

Hallelujah Square

Yes, there's a welcome waiting for us in heaven that will exceed any reception we've ever known as human beings. It's beyond our imagination. Still, it's fun to think about, isn't it? One of the most heartwarming ideas about how heaven's entryway will look adorns the extraordinary, floor-to-ceiling "Hallelujah Square" murals in the beautiful Precious Moments Chapel near Carthage, Missouri.

The murals depict a "child's view of heaven" in the chapel built by Sam Butcher, the artist and creator of the adorable Precious Moments figures that have charmed millions of collectors around the world. Sam has graciously given me several of these delightful characters to share as illustrations in this book.

The idea of building the chapel occurred to Sam when he visited the magnificent Sistine Chapel in Rome several years ago. But standing in the famous church, Sam noticed that the tourists around him didn't seem emotionally connected to

Michelangelo's beautiful masterpiece that stretches across the ceiling. They simply admired the famous scene and then moved on, their faces expressionless. Sam was inspired in that great place to create a chapel himself to express his own gratitude to God. But he wanted it to be a place where visitors' hearts would be touched by the experience.

Soon after his visit to Rome, Sam was on the West Coast on business. He had a return airline ticket, but at the last minute he decided to rent a car and drive cross-country, sensing God directing him in this change of plans. He prayed as he drove, and by the end of the second or third day he was in the middle of America on his way back to Grand Rapids, Michigan. It was late at night, and as he traveled northeast on I-44 through the edge of the Ozarks, his headlights shone on an exit sign for highway HH.

Somehow that sign—highway HH—seemed significant to Sam, but he didn't understand why. Almost before he knew what was happening, he found himself turning the car around and heading back to the nearest motel to spend the night. Despite the late hour, he called a friend and said, "I think I've found a place for the chapel."

"That's great!" the friend replied. "Where are you?"

"Well," admitted Sam, "I don't really know."

The next morning he went to a real estate office. Several agents happened to be in the office that morning, all dressed in nice business suits. Sam was wearing faded blue jeans and a casual shirt. He explained to them that he was looking for a place to build a beautiful chapel. The agents, of course, wanted to know how he would pay for such a project. But they didn't wait for a reply. Instead, they basically ignored Sam, returning to their own conversation.

Sam was embarrassed. He knew he should leave, but somehow he just couldn't seem to make his feet move. Standing there in confusion, he caught the eye of the receptionist and could see that she was embarrassed for him. With a smile, he finally turned toward the door. But before he reached it he felt a hand on his shoulder. It was an older agent who'd overheard

Sam's description. "I think I know a place that's just what you're describing," he said. "C'mon. Let's go check it out."

Grateful to be rescued from the awkward predicament, Sam hopped into the car with the agent, and soon they were winding their way through the hills. As they rode, they got acquainted. And they learned that they shared the same strong Christian convictions. Soon the agent, Mel Brown, slowed the car to make a turn, and as he did, Sam looked hard at the road sign before them. They were turning onto highway HH.

"Where are we going?" Sam asked.

"This is where the property is that I want to show you," Mel replied.

"And what's this road HH? What does that mean?"

"Well, here in Missouri, we label the county roads with letters. This is a county road, and its name is HH. It doesn't really mean anything official. But I've always thought of it as 'heaven's highway.'"

All Sam could do was smile.

Soon they turned onto a winding dirt road and parked on a sloping hillside. They had walked only a short way when Sam stopped and scanned the landscape before him. At that moment he envisioned a chapel—the chapel that is now a reality and has drawn more than seven million visitors in its few years of existence.

Sam bought seventeen and a half acres that very day.

He wrote a check for the full amount.

Today the beautiful chapel, set amidst the rolling Ozark hills, welcomes visitors through its intricately carved doors. Inside, fifty-two biblical murals and thirty exquisite stained-glass windows inspire young and old alike. But the most remarkable thing about the sanctuary is that few people venture inside without having their hearts touched in some way. (Boxes of tissues are discreetly placed throughout the building for those who find tears mysteriously rolling down their cheeks. Judging by the reaction of the people who were there when I visited, the chapel staff must go through lots of tissues!)

The artwork lining the walls and stretching across the beautiful ceiling depicts the sweet little Precious Moments characters, and there's a story behind every picture. It is all so touching. But the most amazing feature of the chapel is that set of three magnificent murals at the front of the chapel—Hallelujah Square. It's an inspiring scene that quickly brought to my mind the chorus of a beautiful song:

> I'll see all my friends in Hallelujah Square.
> What a wonderful time we'll all have up there:
> We'll sing and praise Jesus, His glory to share,
> And we'll all live forever in Hallelujah Square.[2]

Many of the little Precious Moments figurines that have charmed so many folks around the world are based on actual people. That's also true of many of the Precious Moments angels depicted in Hallelujah Square; their namesakes are identified in photographs displayed in another room in the chapel. It's a touching symbol of how God uses the broken pieces of our lives, in this case it's often broken hearts, to create a beautiful comfort blanket of love.

For example, a little, dark-haired soldier-angel standing solemnly before the American flag was inspired by a decorated World War II veteran who was tormented for decades after the war by memories of the violence he believed he'd been forced to commit during the conflict. He wanted to believe in Jesus, but he felt unworthy. No one had ever told Sergeant Thomas about the wonderful gift of God's all-encompassing grace.

The sergeant's daughter had been led to the Lord many years earlier by Sam Butcher. So when, on his death bed, her father asked her, "Sissy, do you think Jesus loves me? Could He love even me?" she said she was "ready to tell him of God's love and of Jesus' sacrifice so that we can all be forgiven."

Now, when tour guides point out the features of the poignant mural, they sometimes tell the story of the little soldier standing with his comrades in Hallelujah Square. His presence there, inside heaven's gates, affirms the daughter's answer to her father's question: "Yes, Daddy, Jesus loves you. The Bible tells me so!"[3]

The mural shows the little angels doing things they loved to do—or weren't physically able to do because of disabilities—when they lived on earth. There is a comforting atmosphere of joy in Sam Butcher's portrayal of heaven as seen through the eyes of a child. When one of my friends saw the murals, she said the scene gave her a whole new attitude toward life in the hereafter. Before, she said, she had thought of heaven as a reverently majestic, praise-filled place. After seeing the little Precious Moments angels frolicking around Hallelujah Square, she also thought of it as a haven where we will share laughter—and *fun*.

Light and Love

Another mural in the Precious Moments Chapel depicts Sam Butcher's son, who was killed a few years ago in a car crash, arriving at those gates. The greeters there are holding another set of signs that say, "Welcome home, Philip." What a joy that will be to arrive in such a beautiful glorious place—and be greeted by name. Better yet, we'll instantly feel *at home*, immediately recognizing that enveloping *familiar* warmth of comfort surrounding us like a comfort blanket.

One of the familiar images I associate with memories of my childhood home is a porch light reflecting on snow. Growing up in Michigan, I'm on a first-name basis with snow and ice! One of my most cherished images is of walking home at night, strolling along the snowy sidewalks as we returned from church or some other outing. Nearing our neighborhood, I could spot my home from quite a ways off. Light would be streaming out the windows, making the snow glisten on our front lawn like transient diamonds scattered on the ground.

You probably have similar memories—of returning from someplace at night and seeing your home from a long way off or of turning a corner and suddenly seeing it there before you. To weary travelers—and even to those who've been away just a short while—the light of home can cut through the darkest night in a way that's different from all other sources of illumination. It flashes out a greeting of warmth, welcoming us back from the cold, winter night. Imagine that feeling magnified ten thousand times, and that's the light that will welcome us as we approach the gates of heaven.

Perhaps my memory of light beaming through the windows of our childhood home is why I appreciate so much the glowing houses and cottages in Thomas Kinkade's marvelous paintings. His pictures remind me of *home*. And right now I know I'm nearer my *heavenly* home than my childhood home.

In other words, to me,

Home is spelled H-E-A-V-E-N!

And we know that the light pouring out of heaven, extending a warm welcome to all those who know and love the Lord, is none other than God Himself. He is the *real* reason why heaven will be so wonderful. As fabulous as they'll be, our mansions will really be just dwelling places. The angelic choir, as much as it will resonate throughout the universe, will just be background music. The streets of gold, the pearly gates, and all those other beautiful images we may hold of paradise will just be window dressing.

A Home Made with Love
There will be beautiful things in heaven, but even if those things weren't going to be there, even if the only "thing" there was God, that would be enough. Because He loves us as no one else could ever love us. And when we're wrapped in that love, nothing else matters.

A clipping someone sent me provides a human illustration of the love Jesus is building into our heavenly mansions. It describes how a church and youth group in Iowa bought three hundred two-by-fours for a local Habitat for Humanity project. Before the lumber was used in framing the house, the thoughtful Christians "inscribed the lumber with messages of joy to the future homeowners."[4]

Knowing that the very framework of your home was inscribed with Scripture verses and messages of love and joy, how could you be anything but joyful each time you entered? That's surely how our mansions in heaven will feel to us as we step through the front doors, knowing that place is infused with love.

But even though we know in our hearts that, as someone said,

> Heaven's delights will far outweigh
> any difficulties we encounter here on earth,

we can't help but be distracted from that knowledge sometimes. It seems absurd that earthly worries could keep us from relishing the knowledge of what's in store for us in heaven—but they do. Sometimes it's the silliest notions that pull our focus off of what's important and set us on a truly trivial pursuit.

A story told by aviator Charles Lindbergh's daughter, Reeve Lindbergh, illustrates how easy it is to be consumed with insignificant things while ignoring something wonderful that's easily within our reach.

In 1997 Reeve was invited to give the annual Lindbergh Address at the Smithsonian Institution's Air and Space Museum to commemorate the seventieth anniversary of her father's historic solo flight across the Atlantic. On the day of the speech, museum officials invited her to come early, before the facility opened, so that she could have a closeup look at *The Spirit of St. Louis*, the little plane, suspended from the museum ceiling, that her father had piloted from New York to Paris in 1927.

That morning in the museum, Reeve and her young son, Ben, eagerly climbed into the bucket of a cherry-picker, a long-armed crane that carried them upward until the plane was at eye level and within their reach. Seeing the machine that her father had so bravely flown across the sea was an unforgettable experience for Reeve. She had never touched the plane before, and that morning, twenty feet above the floor of the museum, she tenderly reached out to run her fingers along the door handle, which she knew her father must have grasped many times with his own hand.

Tears welled up in her eyes at the thought of what she was doing. "Oh, Ben," she whispered, her voice trembling, "isn't this amazing?"

"Yeaaaaaah," Ben replied, equally impressed. "I've never been in a cherry-picker before!"[5]

Carrying Empty Freight

How often do we get distracted by some insignificant problem or event down here on earth and let our focus drift away from heaven and the One who waits for us there? As someone said, "We need to keep the Main Thing the main thing!" And the "Main Thing" is Jesus!

Yet, like Charles Lindbergh's grandson, we can be derailed by silly distractions that pull our focus away from what's really important. Or we can get hung up on activities and even worship schedules that, in the beginning, bring us closer to God. But when they're repeated exactly the same way over and over again, they can become monotonous. So our daily devotions become flat and uninspired, or we leave a church service and find that we can't even remember the lesson that was taught. But we just keep doing the same thing the same way because it's become a routine—a regimen we follow without thinking, a treadmill to nowhere rather than an elevator transporting our thoughts heavenward. That's when we have to shake ourselves awake and jump-start our worship, prayer time, or devotions.

At one of the Women of Faith conferences, the speakers had to climb three flights of steep stairs to go "the back way" from the floor of the arena up to the concourse where our books were being sold. Climbing all those stairs was no fun, so I looked around for an elevator. But the only elevator in the whole building was marked with a big, stern-looking sign that said, "This Elevator for Freight Only."

I looked at that sign, then I looked over my shoulder—and pushed the button! The oversized doors of the elevator yawned open vertically, like a huge whale swallowing up its prey. And I, feeling a little like Jonah, stepped inside.

The elevator carried me up and down between the arena floor and the concourse several times that day. Then, late in the afternoon, the elevator doors opened, and a workman and several boxes were waiting inside. As I'd been doing all day, I stepped inside, but the workman told me firmly, "Sorry, ma'am. This elevator is only for freight."

He had his hand on the control panel as if to clearly indicate which one of us was in charge.

"Oh, it's all right," I assured him with my brightest smile. "I've been riding it all day. You see, I'm one of the speakers, and I only have a few minutes to get upstairs to the book table before I have to be back on stage."

"Sorry, ma'am," he said again, pointing to the fine print under the "Freight Only" sign that explained it was the fire marshal's idea, not his. "You've gotta have freight to ride on this elevator. That's what the regulations say."

As in most situations where I'm not getting my way, my next step was whining. "Oh, please!" I moaned. "I've been using this elevator all day. It hasn't bothered anyone else."

"I'm really sorry, ma'am. It's the rule," he replied adamantly.

Obediently, I stepped out of the elevator. Then I spied something through the doorway of the nearby ladies room. "Wait a minute!" I yelled over my shoulder. Then, hurrying into the restroom, I grabbed a huge, *empty* cardboard box that once had held bathroom tissue. Folding the flaps down and holding them in place with my chin, I hurried back out to the elevator. Barely able to see over the top as I clutched the empty box in my arms, I stepped awkwardly into the whale's mouth and turned confidently to face the front, waiting for the jaws to snap shut. "Okay," I said merrily. "I got some freight! Now I'm qualified to ride!"

Apparently satisfied that I was now in compliance with the rules, the man pushed a button on the control panel, the elevator gate and jaws closed, and up we went!

As the metal beast rumbled upward through the elevator shaft to the concourse, the thought suddenly occurred to me that we're fortunate God doesn't require us to bring along any "freight" when we head toward heaven. As the beloved old song says, "Nothing in my hand I bring, simply to your cross I cling."[6]

Last year I noticed a touching photograph in a magazine that poignantly illustrated that fact. The picture accompanied a story about the powerful floods that had devastated parts of North Dakota and Minnesota in 1997. The focal point of the picture was a large sign leaning up against a pile of rubble—lumber, insulation, soaked carpet, and ruined appliances that had been pulled from one of the flood-stricken homes. In bold, black letters the sign said, "Store your treasures in HEAVEN!"[7]

Photograph © 1997 Ron Grosse, Lighthouse Christian Books, Green Bay, Wisconsin. Used by permission.

This sign outside an empty, flood-stricken house offered a lesson in faith.

That lesson reminds me of the quip that says:

> The average person probably hasn't stored up enough treasure in heaven to even make a down payment for a harp!

When I think of all the *things* we consider important here on earth and the luxury we'll enjoy in heaven not having to worry about all our *stuff* anymore, I feel like kicking up my heels and dancing a jig! Won't it be nice not to have to tend to all those dust-catchers and anxiety-inducers anymore? We won't have to worry about getting a dent in the minivan, a leak in the roof, or a bug in the computer. We won't have to fret about some cherished antique getting scratched or some inherited jewelry getting lost. No more frustration about snagged pantyhose or stained shirts. No more lost eyeglasses, misplaced hearing aids, or left-behind checkbooks. Why, just thinking about living in a place where I'll *never* have to search for my car keys again makes me downright giddy! What freedom we'll enjoy when released from bondage to all the *things* that have held us captive here on earth!

And even when we talk of storing our "treasures" in heaven rather than on earth, we know we're talking about two very different kinds of treasures. The thing we'll cherish most in heaven won't be a *thing* at all. It will be living in the presence of our loving Father and Creator. In fact, our palaces in heaven probably won't need any closets. After all, we're not going to bring any earthly treasures along with us. And we won't be bringing along any emotional baggage, either, when we're heading off for paradise, because Jesus says we're to lay down our burdens and let *Him* carry the freight!

> Come unto me, all ye that labour and are heavy laden, and I will give you rest.[8]

Just imagine living where love fills our lives so completely there won't be any empty spaces left in us to fill. Therefore we won't *want* anything. We'll be perfectly content—supremely satisfied. And since that will surely be the case, it seems quite likely that our heavenly palaces won't need to be very big because we won't have any *stuff* to store. They may be like the tiny little church shown in a newspaper photograph someone sent me. The caption says the minuscule Christ's Chapel Church, located in South Newport, Georgia, has welcomed passers-by for fifty years. Complete with peaked roof, beautiful stained-glass windows, and a stand-alone bell "tower," the little chapel in the photograph looks almost like a child's playhouse. The rows on either side of the center aisle are only two chairs wide, so it seems doubtful that even a dozen people could squeeze inside. But people do stop there, probably because the church's motto touches their hearts. The tiny chapel has proclaimed itself to be a place "where folks rub elbows with God."[9]

That photograph of the little church was the idea that made me rethink my vision of the palace awaiting me in heaven. Maybe it will be a *petite palace*—a wonderfully comfortable and inviting place—without being large and *palatial*. Maybe it'll be a small, warm, cozy place where I can rub elbows with God.

Whatever the Lord has prepared for me, I know it will be wonderful. As someone said, "I don't need to know the floor plan and decor. It is enough that [Jesus] has promised that He will come and take me to Himself. . . . There will be room for me, and it will be a bountiful homecoming."[10]

In heaven we won't be encumbered by all the material goods that clutter our lives here on earth. Whatever their size, our heavenly homes will be places of love set in neighborhoods where the peace is never interrupted by police or ambulance sirens, storm warnings, or blaring security alarms. How wonderful it is to picture the happy life we'll know for all eternity. How comforting it is to know we'll share it with our friends and loved ones who are waiting for us there.

One of my friends who shares my eager anticipation for heaven said she hopes we can be neighbors there. "Barb, I hope our mansions have kitchen windows that face each other," she said gleefully.

For years, I've shared a letter written by Dr. Harry Rimmer after he was on a radio show hosted by Dr. Charles Fuller. As far as I can tell, the story of the letter was first recorded by Al Smith of Greenville, South Carolina. Apparently, as Dr. Fuller was closing his radio program on the day Dr. Rimmer participated, he mentioned that the following week's show would focus on heaven. Later, Dr. Rimmer wrote Dr. Fuller this letter:

My Dear Charlie,

Next Sunday you are to talk about heaven. I am interested in that land, because I have held a clear title to a bit of property there for over fifty years. I did not buy it. It was given to me without money and without price. But the donor purchased it for me at tremendous cost.

I am not holding it for speculation, for the deed is not transferable. It is not a vacant lot, for I have been sending materials there for over fifty years out of which the greatest Architect and Builder of the universe has been building a home for me that will suit me perfectly and will never need to be repaired.

Termites cannot undermine its foundations, for it rests upon the "Rock of Ages."

Fire cannot destroy it.

Floods cannot wash it away.

No locks or bolts will ever be placed upon its doors, for no devious person can ever enter that land where my dwelling now stands, almost completed.

It is ready for me to enter in and rest in peace eternally without fear of being ejected.

There is a valley of deep shadow between the place where I live in California and that to which I shall journey in a short time. I cannot reach my home in that city of gold without passing through this dark valley of shadows. But I am not afraid, because the best Friend I ever had went through the same valley long ago and drove away its gloom. He has stuck with me through thick and thin since we first became acquainted fifty-five years ago, and I hold His promise in printed form never to forsake me nor to leave me alone. He will be with me as I walk through the valley of the shadows, and I shall not lose my way when He is with me.

I hope to hear your sermon on Sunday next from my home here, but I have no assurance that I shall.

My ticket to heaven has no date stamped upon it,
no return coupon, and no permit for baggage. I am
all ready to go, and I may not be here when you are
talking next Sunday, but if not, I shall meet you
there someday.

According to the story, this letter arrived at Dr. Fuller's
home on Wednesday. But "by that time, Dr. Rimmer was
already in that land which is fairer than day, the land he had
seen by faith for over fifty years."[11]

Like Dr. Rimmer, I've spent many years looking, by faith,
at the heavenly real estate that's waiting for me. How wonderful to know that I've got a "mansion just over the hilltop,
in that bright land where we'll never grow old." It won't be
long, now, before the housewarming committee welcomes me
to a moving-in party. And what a celebration that will be! This
beautiful poem says it so well:

When I Come Home to Heaven

When I come home to Heaven
How joyful it will be!
For on that day at last
My risen Lord I'll see.

No greater happiness than
To see Him face to face,
To see the love in His eyes
And feel His warm embrace.

I've done nothing to deserve
That perfect home above.
It was given freely through
The grace of Jesus' love.

Then why should earthly cares
Weigh down upon me so?

They'll be a distant memory
When home at last I go.

> Beth Stuckwisch,
> © 1984 Dicksons.
> Used by permission.

Cloud Busters

The way to heaven:
Turn right at Calvary and keep going straight!

This bumper sticker was punctuated with a bold cross:
No matter which direction I'm heading,
I'm homeward bound!

A woman was dying in the poorhouse. The doctor bent over her and heard her whisper, "Praise the Lord."

"Why, auntie," he said, "how can you praise God when you are dying in a poorhouse?"

"Oh, doctor," she replied, "it's wonderful to go from the poorhouse to a mansion in the skies!"[12]

A reporter watched a fire consume a house. He noticed a little boy with his mom and dad. The reporter, fishing for a human interest angle, said to the boy, "Son, it looks as if you don't have a home anymore."

The boy answered brightly, "We have a home. We just don't have a house to put it in."[13]

Home, where house ten thousand angels.
Home, where the most silent of prayers were heard.
Home, where my beloved Savior now awaits.
Finally, finally, home.

Roger Shouse

I am home in heaven, dear ones;
All's so happy, all's so bright!
There's perfect joy and beauty
In this everlasting light.

All the pain and grief are over,
Every restless tossing passed;
I am now at peace forever,
Safely home in heaven at last.

Did you wonder how I so calmly
Trod the Valley of the Shade?
Oh! But Jesus' love illumined
Every dark and fearful glade.

And He came Himself to meet me
In that way so hard to tread;
And with Jesus' arm to lean on,
Could I have one doubt or dread?

Then you must not grieve so sorely;
For I love you dearly still;
Try to look beyond earth's shadows,
Pray to trust our Father's will.

There is work still waiting for you,
So you must not idle stand;
Do your work while life remaineth—
You shall rest in Jesus' land.

When that work is all completed,
He will gently call you home.
Oh, the rapture of the meeting!
Oh, the joy to see you come!

Source Unknown

Thank heavens we won't have to decipher any "creative" real estate jargon (like the samples below) when we get to heaven!

Charming: Tiny. Snow White might fit, but five of the dwarfs would have to find their own place.

Unique City Home: Used to be a warehouse.

Daring Design: Still a warehouse.

Completely Updated: Avocado dishwasher and harvest gold carpeting.

One-of-a-Kind: Ugly as sin.

Must See to Believe: An absolutely accurate understatement.[14]

At dusk a little girl entered a cemetery. An old man who sat at the gate said to her, "Aren't you afraid to go through the cemetery in the dark?"

"Oh no," she replied. "My home is just on the other side."

Many folks buy cemetery lots in advance
but do nothing about preparing a home in heaven.

Think . . .
of stepping on the shore
and finding it heaven;
of taking hold of a hand
and finding it God's hand;
of breathing a new air
and finding it celestial air;
of feeling invigorated
and finding it immortality;
of passing from storm and tempest
to an unknown calm;
of waking and finding you're Home!

Source Unknown

Jesus was content to be born in a stable so that we may have a mansion when we die.

Death is the golden key
that opens the palace of eternity.

Milton

Let not your heart be troubled: ye believe in God, believe also in me. In my Father's house are many mansions: if it were not so, I would have told you. I go to prepare a place for you. And if I go and prepare a place for you, I will come again, and receive you unto myself; that where I am, there ye may be also.[15]

Holy, holy, is what the angels sing,
And I expect to help them
Make the courts of heaven ring;
But when I sing redemption's story
They will fold their wings,
For angels never felt the joys
That our salvation brings.[1]

Angels Watchin' Over Me

During the week of his eightieth birthday, Billy Graham appeared on *Larry King Live* to discuss "life after fifty." Midway through the interview, Larry King asked, "Billy, what happens when you die?"

Billy responded confidently, "I believe that an angel will take me by the hand at that moment and take me into the presence of Christ." And then he added, "I'm looking forward to it with tremendous anticipation."[2]

In His parable about the rich man and the beggar named Lazarus who lived beside the rich man's gate, Jesus said Lazarus "died and the angels carried him to Abraham's side" in heaven.[3] Jesus also said when the Son of Man comes "on the clouds of the sky, with power and great glory," He will "send his angels with a loud trumpet call, and they will gather his elect from the four winds, from one end of the heavens to the other."[4]

One way or the other, it sounds like angels are assigned to escort us from earth to eternity. Stories abound of persons who, as they sigh out their last earthly breath, die with the happiest expressions on their faces. Isn't it amazing to think perhaps they're greeting that heavenly messenger who's been sent to fetch them home to heaven? As C. S. Lewis's beloved wife, Joy, drew her last breath, "she smiled," he said, "but not at me."[5] The last words of another woman thrill me every time I read them. She exclaimed, as she stepped from this world to the next, "How bright the room! How full of angels!"[6]

THE FAMILY CIRCUS.   **By Bil Keane**

©1999 BKI

"If somebody dies in the hospital, angels move them to the eternity ward."

Just imagine seeing those celestial beings coming toward us, calling us by name, escorting us through the clouds to the throne of God! And when we get there, we'll find heaven *teeming* with angels. The Bible says there will be "thousands upon thousands, and ten thousand times ten thousand" of angels there.[7]

One Bible scholar speculates that "there may be as many angels as there are stars in the heavens, for angels are associated with the stars [in several Bible passages]. If this be so, there would exist untold *trillions* of these heavenly beings." And all of them, he believes, "possess separate and individual personalities, probably no two alike."[8]

And all those angels aren't there just to look pretty. They work! Their first "job" in heaven, just as ours will be, is to praise God. But, just as we'll inevitably do ourselves, they have other work too. One of their jobs, scholars say, is to "act as intermediaries between God and humans."[9] This is a role angels have performed since the beginning of time, when God "placed on the east side of the Garden of Eden cherubim and a flaming sword flashing back and forth to guard the way to the tree of life."[10]

What intriguing assignments angels have had since then! Working under God's orders, an angel brought messages to the slave Hagar and her master, Abraham; warned Lot to flee from Gomorrah; beckoned Moses to the burning bush; and protected and guided the children of Israel as they fled from Egypt and then wandered in the wilderness. God sent an angel to block the road in front of Balaam and his donkey as they trod a reckless path, and He sent an angel to instruct Samson's mother-to-be in prenatal care.

The most exciting part of angelic assignments must be those missions when angels are called upon to perform daring and exciting rescues. Can't you just picture God's army of angels up in heaven, waiting eagerly for a new mission, wondering what exciting, life-changing event they'll be part of? Maybe they're hoping they can walk, unscathed, into a fiery furnace like the angel who rescued Shadrach, Meshach, and Abednego. Or perhaps they're hoping to bed down with the lions like the angel who spent the night with Daniel in the lions' den.

It would scare the wits out of anyone who hadn't been trained by God Himself to hear, "One of you must go into that terrible prison, unshackle Peter, and lead him out," or, best of all, "You're going to have to walk into the darkest, most terrible tomb of death that's ever existed . . . and roll that stone away from the door." Can't you just see the angels rejoicing over such assignments?

On the other hand, think what a joyful assignment it must have been for the angel who led Dr. V. Raymond Edman home to heaven in 1967. Sharon Barnes, my friend and co-worker on the Women of Faith tour, told me how Dr. Edman, chancellor of Wheaton College, was admired and loved by the students. That's why they were overjoyed when he returned, after recuperating several weeks from a heart attack, to speak during the college's chapel service in September. Dr. Edman told the students that day, "Chapel is a time of worship, a time of meeting the King." And then, a few seconds later, Dr. Edman paused and slumped forward over the podium as Sharon and the other college students watched in stunned silence. Then he dropped to the floor—and fell into the arms of that waiting angel to be gently ushered into the presence of God.

What Will *Our* Assignments Be?

Thinking about the work of the angels over the centuries makes us wonder what *our* jobs will be in heaven. Of course there's nothing in the Bible that says we become angels in heaven. And there's no way to know whether we'll even have assignments while we're devoting ourselves to the full-time praise of God. But since heaven is going to be a fulfilling and wonderful place, it makes sense to assume we'll be given something fulfilling and productive to do.

In her book *Heaven . . . Your Real Home,* Joni Eareckson Tada says confidently, "We will have jobs to do. . . . We will serve God through worship and work—exciting work of which we never grow tired."

Joni, who has been confined to a wheelchair for many years, adds, "For me, this will be heaven. I love serving God." She cites Jesus' heaven parable in Luke 19:17, which concludes with the master telling his servant, "'Well done, my good servant! . . . Because you have been trustworthy in a very small matter, take charge of ten cities.'"

From that, Joni reminds us, we believe that "those who are faithful in a few minor things will be put in charge over multitudinous things. . . . The more faithful you are in this life, the more responsibility you will be given in the life to come."[11] Joni also notes that we're promised "new heavens and a new earth" in Isaiah 65:17.

"Did you get that?" she asks. "Heaven has our planet in it. A new earth with earthy things in it. . . . warm and wonderful things that make earth . . . *earth.*"

And if that's the case, Joni has plans to do some things in her spare time that she's been unable to do since she was paralyzed in the accident. She says she has made dates with friends and relatives to climb the mountains behind the Rose Bowl, ski the Sierras, play doubles tennis, and dance. She's also looking forward to "picnicking on the Hungarian plains" with a circle of Rumanian orphan friends and racing a friend on horseback. Oh, and she's planning to do some knitting too.[12]

All she really needs to know, says Joni, is that "heaven will feel like home. I will be a co-heir with Christ. . . . I will help rule in the new heavens and the new earth . . . and I will be busier and happier in service than I ever dreamed possible. And you will be too."[13]

While We're Waiting . . .

Meanwhile, our job here on earth is to love and praise God— and our neighbors. In striving to do that, we can certainly draw inspiration (and ideas!) by following the example Jesus left us and also by studying the work of His angels.

Of course, the only real record of angelic visits is in the Bible. But Scripture seems to predict that angels continue to work in our lives today by reminding us, "Keep on loving each other as brothers. Do not forget to entertain strangers, for by so doing some people have entertained angels without knowing it."[14] It also asks us, as though assuming it's a fact we accept without questioning, "Are not all angels ministering spirits sent to serve those who will inherit salvation?"[15]

With these words echoing in our minds, many of us are constantly on the lookout for suspected angel contacts in our lives today. One woman told me that every time she sees a feather lying on the ground she's reminded that there are angels among us. Sure, she's knows it's just a bird's feather. But she uses each feather as a reminder, like a string tied around her finger, that the Bible assures us God has sent His angels to earth as our helpers and friends—usually invisible but, perhaps, sometimes appearing in flesh and blood. Billy Graham has said, "Angels speak. They appear and reappear. They are emotional creatures. While angels may become visible by choice, our eyes are not constructed to see them ordinarily any more than we can see the dimensions of a nuclear field, the structure of atoms or electricity."[16]

FAMILY CIRCUS

"That angel's name is Harold."

© Bil Keane

One of the most reassuring verses to me is:

> For He shall give His angels charge over you,
> To keep you in all your ways.

One of my friends calls this her biblical 911 number because of its source: Psalm 91:11.

Angels Among Us

Angels are one of my favorite things to think about. In fact, I've been collecting angels for quite a while now. My favorites are the ones that are blowing trumpets. That's where the idea for *Toot 'n' Scoot* originated. Now my Joy Room—actually, my whole home—is full of angels, including wall hangings, rugs, scarves, bookends, Christmas stockings, wall plaques, and eight or nine figurines that sit on the television! Everywhere I look I'm reminded that he's gonna toot and I'm gonna scoot. And that fact keeps me going when my energy is sagging along with my pantyhose and I'm ready to throw in the spatula! Along with collecting trumpet-blowing angels, I love reading or hearing about the ways angels are believed to have intervened in people's lives.

Because the Bible assures us that angels do, in fact, exist and that they minister to us, Christians often look for ways they can do angels' work too. In the rest of this chapter, I'd like to share some stories about people who believe they've been helped by angels—and people who were perceived as earthly angels sent by God to comfort others.

One of my favorite stories comes from a newsletter published by my friend Ney Bailey, a missionary with Campus Crusade for Christ, who has graciously agreed to share the story here. She calls it "one of the most motivating true-life stories in the area of prayer that I have ever heard," and I agree. She noted that the details of the story were confirmed several years ago by the missions chairman of the Boston church that supported the missionary involved in the dramatic account.

The missionary, Dr. Bob Foster, worked in Angola, a country where conflict between guerrilla forces opposing the Marxist regime made parts of the country especially dangerous. The medical clinic run by Dr. Foster was in one of these areas. Here is his story:

One day Dr. Foster sent a co-worker on an errand to a city some miles away with the warning that he should be back by nightfall. The stretch of road between the clinic and the city went right through the jungle area where most of the guerrilla fighting took place, and it was very dangerous to travel through there at night.

The co-worker went on his way, finished his errands in plenty of time, and began his return. Much to his dismay, however, his van developed engine trouble and broke down in the middle of the contested jungle area. With no other cars on the road, he had no choice but to lock the doors, pray, and attempt to get a little rest.

Amazingly, he slept through to morning without a problem. He caught a ride into town for some spare parts, fixed the van, and completed the trip back to the clinic. He was greeted by a relieved Dr. Foster and other co-workers. "We are so thankful to see you!" Dr. Foster told him. "We heard sounds of heavy fighting from the area you were in." Dr. Foster's assistant said he had heard and seen nothing.

Soon after that, a guerrilla officer came to the clinic to be treated. Curious, Dr. Foster asked him if he had seen a van stalled along the highway the previous night. "Yes, of course," replied the officer.

"But why didn't you move in to take possession of it?" queried the doctor.

"We started to," said the officer, "until we got closer. Then we saw that it was heavily guarded.

There were *twenty-seven* well-armed government soldiers surrounding it."

Needless to say, Dr. Foster and his co-worker were amazed.

The incident remained a mystery until Dr. Foster's assistant returned to the States on furlough. Here, person after person on his prayer team came up to him. . . . in fact, *twenty-seven people* in all [told him] the Lord had given them a special burden to pray for him on such-and-such a day previously. It was *the very day* he had been stranded in the jungle.

The story reminds us of that wonderful verse that says:

The angel of the Lord encamps around those who fear Him, and rescues them.[17]

Ordinary, anonymous people who appear in our lives, do something wonderful, and then seem to vanish without a trace are assumed by many believers to be angels. Many such encounters are described in the Habitat for Humanity book, *The Excitement Is Building.* One of my favorite stories tells of an all-volunteer crew that was building a house in Fort Myers, Florida.

The volunteers arrived at the lot early one Saturday morning to assemble the prefabricated walls, door frames, and trusses. But when the walls were up and it was time to set the trusses—the big Vs that give the roof its peaked shape—"they simply would not fit," the authors wrote. The workers tried again and again to find ways to recalculate or relocate the trusses so they would fit, but it soon became apparent that the problem was impossible to remedy.

"About that time, a rather nondescript passerby stopped and looked over the situation. After a minute or two of thoughtful observation, he asked if he could survey the scene in more detail. Because everyone was so frustrated by this time, the man was hardly noticed as he scurried nimbly up the framework to examine the layout. He soon came down and gave all the dejected volunteers a jolt. He explained a detailed but basic solution to the seemingly unsolvable problem. The volunteers quickly set about doing just as he suggested, and his plan worked to perfection.

"And then they noticed that their 'Divine Engineer' had vanished."[18]

Being Angelic

The idea that angels are real, that they intercede in our world to minister to God's children (that's us!), should inspire us to do a little angel-work ourselves whenever the opportunity arises. The deeds we do don't always involve amazing mathematical calculations, like the work of the Habitat workers' "Divine Engineer." They can be as simple as a gentle word of encouragement or as quiet as a smile.

One thing I've learned is that God sometimes uses the smallest gestures of kindness to touch a life of torment, ease a broken heart, or light a spark of hope. My helpers and I see this happen at every Women of Faith conference when we give away the flat, shiny marbles I call "splashes of joy."

To be honest, these little gifts have gotten to be quite a job for us. They're shipped to each conference site by the manufacturer from Wichita, Kansas, and the boxes are *really* heavy. At the work space where my books will be sold, we risk wrenching our backs every time we lug one of the boxes up on the table—and there are usually several boxes of them.

Then, if we're lucky, we get the boxes open without breaking all our fingernails (the boxes are apparently sealed with the same glue that holds the space shuttle together). Next we get to rip open the dozens of net bags the marbles are packed in. Finally, we lug the boxes around again, spreading out the marbles over the books and the corners of the table. If we have time, we wipe off the resin dust before the doors open on Friday night and the women start coming in—sometimes fifteen to twenty thousand of them! That's when the *real* joy-splashing work begins!

As the women stream by the table, my helpers and I say to those passing near the table, "Would you like a splash of joy?" Then, even though we also hand out little papers that explain the marbles, we have to say approximately 2,887,922 times (or at least it seems that way!), "Put it on your windowsill. When it sparkles it will remind you of all the ways God blesses your life . . . Yes, they're free . . . No, we don't have a different color . . . Yes, you can take one for your sister (friend, mother, daughter, coworker, pastor's wife, or bus driver) too . . . No, it doesn't stick to anything. It's not a magnet."

Then, after a couple of hours of this, our "speech" changes to, "No, I'm sorry. They're all gone . . . No, there's really no way to order them; Barb just has them sent to each conference site, and we give them out there . . . Yes, they're really all gone. I know . . . Just a little while ago we had a whole mountain of them—in fact we had nearly two hundred pounds of them. But they're all gone now."

Believe me, there comes a time during every conference when you don't dare mention the words "splash of joy" around my helpers! They're liable to flash you a look that will frost your face for days! That's why we all laughed until we cried (*really* cried!) when a woman wrote me recently suggesting that we "extend" the splash-of-joy idea by selling *jars* of the marbles to conference attendees. We could call them "jars of joy," she suggested.

Now, I have to admit that her idea is really a good one—from a marketing standpoint. But the mere thought of shipping *jars* and *more* marbles everywhere we go just about sent us all into hysterics. Feeling a little mischievous, I shared the woman's letter with one of the gals who works at my table. She laughed too. And then she cried. And then she said, "Barb, I quit!"

No, the splashes cause us enough problems already. We won't be selling them in jars anytime soon. In fact, by the end of a conference, we have the firm opinion that we don't ever want to hear the phrase "splash of joy" again!

Then we go home, and inevitably the letters arrive . . .

"Dear Barb," one might say, "this has been an awful year

for me. I didn't want to come to the conference, but my friend from church insisted. We stopped by your book table and one of the women there smiled at me and said, 'Do you need a splash of joy?' She held out this little, flat marble and said it would remind me of all my blessings. I dropped it in my pocket and planned to forget about it. But every time I stuck my hand in my pocket, I felt it there. And gradually, the fact hit me: Despite all that has happened to me, I have many blessings to be thankful for. I'm healthy. My husband loves me. I have good friends who care about me. Thanks, Barb, for helping me remember."

The woman who suggested that we sell jars of splashes added that she had come to the Women of Faith conference "feeling anything but joyful." She was involved in a very stressful legal separation from her husband, she said, and her life "felt out of control, frustrating, unfair." Then she picked up "the silly little thing" at my book table.

> I put it in my coat pocket and fingered it all day, and for the few days following. It truly did remind me of God's love for me and kept me looking for those small but precious splashes of joy He is so faithful to inject into every day if we will but look for them, acknowledge them, and receive them. As I drove home from the conference that day, I asked the Lord to help me find some of these "splashes" to share with others as you had done.

She eventually found something similar and started handing them out.

> First, I explained to my husband and children what "splashes of joy" were and gave them each one to keep and one to share. Over the next few days I consistently put "splashes" in my pockets and shared them with others . . . a little boy in my son's first grade class who was discouraged, my doctor, my

dear friend . . . , a lady at the checkout in the grocery store, my babysitter and her daughter, complete strangers whose path I providentially passed. Not one person was anything less than thrilled, blessed, and encouraged.

Finally, my thoughts turned to my mother. . . . She is a widow, must work full-time at a stressful job to make a living, and is frequently prone to being discouraged. . . . I sent her a bag of "splashes," explained the idea to her, and urged her to buy a pretty jar for her desktop to put them in. My children and I made a little sign to put inside the jar that said "splashes of joy." She loved the idea and is now using these splashes, as I am, to encourage others in her environment.

Another letter writer said she gave her sister the little blue splash she picked up at the book table when the Women of Faith tour was in Pittsburgh in September 1996. The sister, a happily married mother and grandmother, was in a battle against breast cancer that would continue another two years. She put the little marble on her stereo, where it often brought a smile to her face.

The sister was in the hospital in November 1998 when the doctors gave her only a few days to live. What happened next was an incredible act of love that grew out of adversity. The woman's letter described it beautifully:

She wanted to die at home. As the doctors and nurses made preparations for her to be discharged a few days later, she made preparations for her funeral.

That's when she remembered the splash of joy. She had her daughter go from store to store until she could find more of those little flat marbles! She bought a bunch of them, all different colors, and filled a deep, clear glass bowl with them. As the doctors and nurses came, changed shifts, etc., she asked them to dip their hands into the bowl and take a splash of joy with them. She had them all in tears by the time she was discharged! But they won't forget her . . . or the joy she infused them with! . . .

She died a few days later at the age of forty-five. At her funeral, bowls full of splashes of joy were placed around the church, and everyone was invited to take some home along with a little paper explaining what they were. All her life, the sister had been allergic to flowers. But for her memorial service the sanctuary was overflowing with flowers "from everyone who never could give her any while she was alive!" the letter continued. "It was everyone's last gesture of love to her. And the splashes of joy were her last gesture of love to those she left behind."

Reading the letter, I was so touched by this woman's beautiful story. Then came the part that made my tears flow:

> Barbara, you just have no idea how very much your little idea has turned into a huge thing. Your splashes of joy have been shared all over Steuben County, New York now. Even people who didn't personally know my sister have requested a splash after hearing about the little marbles. I'm sure there are hundreds of stories people from all over could tell about how the splashes of joy have touched their lives.
>
> I apologize for making this such a lengthy letter when all I really wanted to tell you was "thank you" for the joy you share. Hopefully you have been touched yourself by the joy that is now being "boomeranged" back to you!

More than you'll know, Honey . . . more than you'll ever know.

"HEAVEN MUST HAVE SENT YOU"

Too Blest to Be Stressed

From these letters you can understand how these "silly little things" I call splashes of joy are not only boomerang blessings to those of us who hand them out. They're also pebbles in a pond, generating ripples of blessings that radiate in all directions. Certainly, some of them get dropped into purses or pockets and are quickly forgotten. But once in a while, that little piece of polished glass touches a life in a way no one could have expected. And the result is simply awesome.

Being an angel lover, I like to think my coworkers and I (the "splashers") are doing angel work when we toss these little marbles into the sea of ladies who attend the Women of Faith conferences (the "splashees"). In response, we (along with the others they share the idea with) receive the most heartwarming encouragement. As one letter-writer put it, "the splashes of joy become showers of blessing" to *all* of us.

The goodness generated by those colorful little marbles boomerangs back to us. It revs us up and charges our batteries so that we can lug those boxes around and repeat our little speeches another few thousand times a week or so later!

Temporary Assignments

A suspicion of angel activity occurred to me last year when the Women of Faith conference was held in Buffalo, New York. During the afternoon before the event began, Bill and I visited Niagara Falls. (We laughed all the way up there, recalling how I'd told one of the conference workers that Bill and I were taking the afternoon off to "do the Niagara thing" and she'd misunderstood and thought I'd said we were doing the *Viagra* thing, referring to the new drug that had just come out for men.)

What a breathtaking place Niagara Falls is! Riding the little *Maid of the Mist* boat right up to the foot of the majestic falls and feeling the power of the thundering water as it plunges over the precipice, I was spellbound by the extraordinary beauty of this natural wonder. Gazing up at the white curtain of foam, crystals of light seemed to sparkle in the sunlight, and I was suddenly overwhelmed, realizing how the falls symbolize God's outpouring love that refreshes us.

The Niagara Falls story that made me think of angels concerns two children who fell into the river above the falls during a boating accident several years ago. The boat was destroyed, its operator was killed, and a seven-year-old boy was swept over the falls. Miraculously, he survived and was rescued by the *Maid of the Mist*.

His little sister was near the brink of the falls when a New

Jersey tourist spotted her. The tourist climbed over the guard rail, stepped into the water, and reached out over the murderous current toward the child. At the last possible moment, the little girl grasped his thumb. But the additional weight added to his precarious position in the current caused the rescuer, himself, to lose his balance and wobble dangerously close to the precipice. He called for help, and a second tourist, a man from Pennsylvania, climbed over the guard rail and helped both the man and child back to shore.

The rescuers were just two "ordinary" men, two tourists. And it might be that they simply found extra adrenaline that day to pull the little girl back from plummeting over the falls. But many who saw them risk their lives for a stranger compared them with angels.[19]

Just as the Bible instructs us to "entertain strangers" because they might be angels in disguise, we should also be ready to "rescue strangers" if God decides to use *us* in angelic ways. Most of us probably hope He won't send us out to lean over the edge of Niagara Falls and pull someone back from the brink of death. Instead He might send us to, say, Omaha—assigned, unknowingly, to the airplane seat next to a brokenhearted mother or a hard-hearted father. It could be someone who's trying to run away from God. Perhaps He might plant us in a crowd where one person, quietly standing up for what's right, could make all the difference. He might send us to a hospital or a prison or a nursing home to clasp the hands of someone there who is desperately reaching out for God.

Boomerang Blessings
Opportunities to do good are everywhere, but they're sometimes fleeting. We move on by and later tell ourselves, *I should have done this or that.*

There's a wonderful story about how this kind of decision to do good can boomerang blessings back to us. The tale describes a king who wanted to know what kind of people inhabited his kingdom. So he had a huge boulder rolled into the middle of a major roadway, then he hid among the trees, watching to see what would happen. A merchant, his wagon piled high with goods, rolled to a stop before the huge boulder. Briefly, he considered moving it but decided it wasn't worth his time or effort. He guided the horses around the rock, creating new ruts in the grass beside the road. Next a coach came along carrying a kingdom dignitary. When the driver stopped, the official stuck his head out the window and impatiently demanded that the driver hurry on around the obstacle. A farmer appeared next, pulling a hay wagon. He, too, detoured around the boulder without trying to remove it.

Finally, a single rider approached. He could easily have ridden around the boulder on his horse. But he stopped, looked around for a tree limb to use as a lever, and managed to pry the stone from its resting place and send it rolling into the ditch. As he started to mount his horse and ride away, he noticed a leather pouch lying in the road where the stone had been. Inside was a hundred gold pieces and a note from the king, explaining that the gold was for the person who took the time to remove the boulder.[20]

That story reminds me of another boomerang blessing that came to us because of something that happened at a Women of Faith conference. We accept only cash and checks at my book table, no credit cards. When women want to buy books and don't have their checkbooks or enough cash, we tell them to take the books and send the cash later. Folks are usually astonished to believe we would trust them this way, but as far as we know, we've never had anyone who took the books and didn't eventually pay.

The special blessing came last summer, when the conference was on the West Coast. We told a woman who had brought only a credit card to take the books she wanted and mail a check later—and she did. The blessing came when the woman went home and told her husband, a non-Christian, how we had trusted her with the books. He was so amazed he told her to send a check to me, not for the amount of the books she bought, but for five hundred dollars to support our work with hurting families!

Of course, there's no guarantee that every good deed we do will result in that person returning the favor. But I'm convinced that, sooner or later, one way or another, a blessing will come. But even if there were no possibility of a boomerang effect, we know by being kind to one another we are doing God's will—and for Christians, that should be blessing enough.

Wherever we go, we should be aware of the possibilities to do the work of angels—not to preach and quote Scripture but to serve and minister to others, even those who can never repay our kindness. Perhaps, in time, they'll pass the blessing on to someone else and not to us.

Whenever we can, we should follow the example of the kind-hearted woman who spotted a little boy, ten years old, standing in front of a New York City shoe store, barefooted, on a cold November day. The woman stopped and asked him, "What are you looking at?"

"I was asking God to give me a pair of those shoes," the little boy replied.

The woman stepped toward the door of the store and held out her hand. "Come with me," she said.

She took a half-dozen pairs of socks off the rack as they walked toward the back of the store. There she asked a clerk to bring her a basin of warm water and a towel. The man quickly complied.

Removing her coat and gloves, the woman knelt down and washed the boy's little feet and dried them with the towel. She eased the socks over his cold toes and then asked the clerk to find him the shoes he'd been eying in the store window. The boy watched in wonder as her requests were fulfilled. Finally the clerk dropped the extra socks in a bag, totaled the bill, and accepted the woman's money.

"You'll be a lot more comfortable now," she told the boy, smiling, as they walked together through the doorway. As she turned to go, the astonished lad caught her hand and looked up in her face.

"Are you God's wife?" he asked.

As Christians we are Christ's bride, His church. When we

do angel work in His name, we demonstrate His love to others. These kindnesses don't have to be daring or costly. An encouraging word—or simply an attitude of joy—can often make all the difference to someone who's given up hope. A little smile can brighten someone's day. And while you're smiling you might as well go one step further and share a chuckle or two. You know what they say: A laugh is just a smile with a sound track.

C. S. Lewis said, "The best argument for Christianity is Christians: their joy, their certainty, their completeness." Lewis also warned, however, that Christians can be "the strongest argument *against* Christianity . . . when they are somber and joyless, when they are self-righteous and smug, . . . when they are narrow and repressive, then Christianity dies a thousand deaths."[21] Let's resolve to be angels of joy and missionaries of mirth wherever we go today—and every day!

Cloud Busters

An angel is someone
who brings out the angel in you.

People with a heart for God
have a heart for people.[22]

Remember:
Each of us can decrease the suffering of the world
by adding to its joy.[23]

Make a friendship kit:

Rubber band: To hold friends close
Tissue: To dry a tear
Recipe: To make and share
Stationery: To write a note of encouragement
Band-aid: A reminder that friends help heal a
　　　　　hurting heart
Poem: To express your love
Prayer: To lead your friend to God

We are each of us angels with only one wing.
And we can only fly by embracing each other.

Luciano de Crescenzo

PUT YOUR ARMS AROUND EACH OTHER

(This page 1 banner headline appeared in The
Tennessean *on April 18, 1998, quoting Mayor
Phil Bredesen the day after a devastating tor-
nado ravaged much of East Nashville.)*

Always deal reasonably [with others] and don't be
rude. Consider that the stranger with whom you
are dealing may very well be the visitor sitting
beside you in church next Sunday![24]

When Jesus died on the cross and saved you from
sin, He did so not only to get you into heaven but for
an even more important reason. . . . Jesus saved you
. . . in order to make you into a person who could do
magnificent things for others in His name.[25]

It doesn't take great wisdom to energize a person, but it does take sixty seconds. That's the amount of time it takes to walk over and gently hold someone we love.[26]

On Valentine's Day a wrinkled old man sat on the bus seat holding a bunch of fresh roses. Across the aisle was a young girl whose sad eyes seemed to be locked on the floor—except for moments when she glanced back again and again at the man's flowers.

The time came for the old man to get off. Impulsively he thrust the flowers into the girl's lap. "I can see you love the roses," he explained. "I was taking them to my wife, but I know she would like for you to have them. I'll tell her I gave them to you."

The girl accepted the flowers with a delighted smile then watched the old man get off the bus . . . and walk through the gate of a cemetery.

He who overcomes shall thus be clothed in white garments; and I will not erase his name from the book of life, and I will confess his name before My Father, and before His angels.[27]

"YOU MAKE MY SPIRIT SOAR"

Used by permission of Samuel J. Butcher, creator of Precious Moments.

Blow ye the trumpet!
Blow it loud and clear.
Blow it so that everyone can hear.
God's people now listen for the final sound
To leave this world and live on holy ground.[1]

Ain't a Gonna Need
This House No Longer

One night about 1916, Harrison Mayes, a young coal miner, was nearly killed by a runaway coal car deep inside a Kentucky mine. Struggling to survive his terrible injuries, Mayes promised God he would dedicate himself to the Lord's work if his life could be spared. God apparently accepted the offer; the coal miner lived to be eighty-eight years old.

It never occurred to Mayes not to keep his end of the bargain with God, but it took awhile to find his own humble niche in God's kingdom of workers. He couldn't carry a tune in a bucket, so gospel singing was definitely out. He was a failure at preaching too.

Ah, but he could use his hands. Soon he began painting signs with Christian slogans on them. His first printed message was "sin not," which he painted on both sides of the family pig! Next he made wooden crosses, and then, as one writer described his zeal, "like an evangelical Johnny Appleseed, he planted them across the Southeast."

Although he kept his job in the coal mine—in fact, he often

worked double shifts to fund his work as God's messenger—his real focus was on planting his crosses all over the country. In the 1940s he began casting concrete signs in the shape of hearts as well as crosses, and he cut biblical messages into the molds: "Prepare to Meet God," or "Jesus Is Coming Soon," or "Get Right with God." Each sign weighed fourteen hundred pounds.

Mayes, who didn't drive, hired a flatbed truck to haul the signs to sites along America's roadways. Then he dug holes and gently "planted" the signs. By the time he was too old to plant any more of his hearts and crosses, thousands of the sturdy cement monuments were standing along highways in forty-four states.

While his focus was on planting roadside crosses, Mayes also used a more ancient means of carrying God's messages. It's estimated that he tucked little Bible verses and other religious notes into as many as fifty thousand bottles of all shapes and set them bobbing down creeks and rivers all over the country.

His son, interviewed for a newspaper article a few months ago, recalled that his father never sought donations but was nevertheless supported by many miners and their churches. If his father had six dollars, the son said, he gave the family three—and spent the rest on his signs.[2]

Now, you might think Harrison Mayes was a little eccentric. In fact you might question his sanity as he carried out his single-minded campaign to crisscross America with crosses. But you could never doubt his devotion to God.

When he died in 1988, he left no fortune for his family to inherit. He had accumulated no earthly treasures to speak of. He seemed to understand the wisdom that says when you go to heaven the only thing you take with you is what you leave behind. What Harrison Mayes left behind was a legacy of love for the Lord—and several thousand simple roadside markers, directing those who came after him toward salvation. A handful of Mayes's crosses and signs are still standing; perhaps you've seen one of them and been reminded: "Jesus Saves."

Can't you just imagine the stoop-shouldered little coal miner standing humbly before God's mighty throne as the Father reviews his good works? Surely Harrison Mayes will see a twinkle in God's eye and hear Him say, "Well done, my good and faithful servant!"

"THIS WORLD IS NOT MY HOME"

Used by permission of Samuel J. Butcher, creator of Precious Moments.

The Narrow Road to Heaven
Heaven will be a spacious place, and all sorts of treasures will be available to us there. But the entryway is too small for a moving van; we can't take anything with us to paradise

except the love we carry inside our hearts. Harrison Mayes knew that lesson well.

Jesus said, "The gate is small and the road is narrow that leads to true life."[3] When we read this verse we usually think of how easily we can stumble off the narrow beam of light that illuminates the route to heaven. But it also reminds us there's a parking area outside the gate and a sign that says, "Wide Loads Exit Here." That's the drop-off area where we lay down all those things that have meant so much to us on earth: the bank deposits, jewelry, lavish homes, and luxury cars. None of it will fit through the narrow way to heaven.

But that's not all we leave in the parking area outside the pearly gates. All our worries are to be dropped off there, too, along with our broken hearts and our tears.

My daughter-in-love Shannon has so beautifully described to me the way she saw one of her and my son Barney's friends "gradually let go of the things of the world and grasp the things of heaven" as he neared the end of a ten-year struggle with cancer. It was a gradual process, she said, and it illustrated to her how people "struggle to come into this life and struggle to go out of it."

As time passed, the friend made a remarkable transition, letting go of the concerns of the world, letting go of the initial anxiety he'd felt when first diagnosed, releasing the frustration that had tormented him, and taking hold of the peace that seemed to flow out of heaven and wrap him securely in God's comfort blanket. Finally, when he died, it was clear he understood that he was taking nothing with him, Shannon said, "nothing except the love of those whose lives he had touched."

The beautiful words of Ecclesiastes teach us there is "a time to get, and a time to lose; a time to keep, and a time to cast away."[4] There are occasions in life when we must hang on— grip the hand of God tightly and struggle fiercely to hold on to His promises. And then, at the end of our lives, there is a time to let go of the struggles and simply fall into those everlasting arms of the Father.

Just think of what America was like when the Europeans first began exploring the New World. On land, they walked or rode horses over nothing more than simple footpaths—routes worn by Indians or wildlife moving single-file through the forests. As more settlers felt the urge to move westward, the single paths became double to accommodate the wheels of the wagons that hauled families and their belongings. When the pioneers left home, they packed their Conestogas with everything from pearls to pianos—the treasures they were certain they would need in their new home.

But something interesting often happened as the days passed and the hardships began. Gradually, the priorities of many of the pioneers changed as their journey continued. Beside a river swollen by flood waters, they might discard the piano that threatened to sink the wagon as they prepared to ford the stream. At the foot of the mountains, many of them abandoned the heirloom chests, trunks, and other furniture that had been handed down for generations. In the middle of the desert, they left behind the wagon and all it contained so that when they emerged on the other side—*if* they emerged—they sometimes had nothing left but their lives. And once again, they needed only a narrow trail, one person wide.

That's kind of like the way we will approach heaven: standing alone, empty-handed, with all our "important" earthly priorities littering the roadway behind us as it narrows down to a path just one person wide. When we stand at the foot of God's throne, we'll have nothing to show for our toil on earth except the life we've lived for Him. That's what folks mean when they say we can't take anything with us to heaven but we can send it on ahead. We do so by investing ourselves and our love for God in the hearts and lives of others.

> As for man, his days are like grass,
> he flourishes like a flower of the field;
> the wind blows over it and it is gone,
> and its place remembers it no more.[5]

While we can take nothing with us to heaven, we can leave a lot of important things behind to encourage our friends and loved ones—and very few of them have anything to do with material goods.

Do Others See God in Us?

All we can take with us to heaven is what we leave behind in the lives we touch. A minister's words at a memorial service also illustrate this kind of legacy: A woman died shortly after moving to the city where her only child, a woman named Cathy, lived, far from the old hometown. Because Cathy was so beloved in her own church, she decided to have her mother's memorial service there, among her own closest friends, instead of back in the hometown she and her mother had shared.

At the service, the minister said, "I didn't know Cathy's mother. But I know Cathy, and I'm sure I saw her mother in her—just as I know I see Jesus in her. Cathy was her mother's child, and she is Jesus' child. And in her life we see the love they both invested in her."

Trust funds can be handed down. Family heirlooms can be passed on. But sooner or later whatever earthly treasures we leave to our loved ones will wind up in that pile of rubble alongside the narrowing pathway to heaven. The only legacy worth anything is our footprints for them to follow . . . right up to God's throne. In the light of eternity, nothing else matters.

When a man was moving to a new town, his friends bought a tiny young sapling, a flowering tree, for him to plant at his new home as a reminder of all the good times they had shared. The man nurtured the tree in the lawn of his new home, and soon it was taller than he was. Each spring its growing array of blossoms lifted his spirits and reminded him of his friends back "home."

But then he had to move again, and this time it was to another part of the country. He couldn't bear to leave the tree behind because it meant so much to him. So he called a tree expert and insisted, "No matter what the expense, I want to take this tree with me."

But the specialist just shook his head. "This tree won't live where you're going," he said. "It can't survive that climate. All you can do is tell the new owners its story and help them understand how special it is."

That's how many of us ended up with the Tree of Life taking root in our hearts. Its seed was a gift from someone else, someone who had nurtured its growth in his own life—and then passed the gift on to us. What a privilege it is to receive such an awesome inheritance! Its value is beyond any earthly comparison. It is Jesus' gift to us of eternal life, something we don't deserve, didn't work for, and can't buy for any price.

The New Me
While it's important to think of the spiritual legacies we leave behind, it's downright fun to think about the inheritances awaiting us in heaven. Imagining myself in God's constant presence, joyfully enveloped in His eternal love, I get really excited. And I can hardly wait to move into my own mansion, walk the streets of gold, and join the heavenly chorus!

But there's something else that makes me positively giddy just to think about. It's the new body I'll have instantly when the rapture is complete. The Bible says, "It will take only a second—as quickly as an eye blinks—when the last trumpet sounds. The trumpet will sound, and those who have died will be raised to live forever, and we will all be changed."[6]

An old, old hymn describes the process so joyfully:

> On that resurrection morning
> When the dead in Christ shall rise
> I'll have a new body, praise the Lord, I'll have
>   a new life.
> Sown in weakness, raised in power, ready to live
>   in paradise,
> I'll have a new body, praise the Lord, I'll have
>   a new life eternal![7]

Now, the Bible doesn't say anywhere that we get to *choose* what kind of new body we get, but just in case we do, I plan to order something in a petite size! For years I've said my body's a perfect ten but I keep it covered with fat so it won't get scratched. Maybe in heaven my "inner" dream body will finally be revealed! If it is, I imagine I'll be cute—like the caricature of me that W Publishing Group included in a promotion.

It's fun to pretend we'll be able to pick and choose specific body parts in heaven rather than being assigned a whole new model at once. Let's see . . . I might ask for a dynamic voice like Billy Graham's, a caring heart like Mother Teresa's, and tireless feet like John the Baptist's. Maybe while I'm at it I could request the patience of Job, the artistic ability of Michelangelo, the wisdom of Solomon, the insight of C. S. Lewis, and hands like Noah's—or perhaps hands like the Master Carpenter's . . .

When we get our new bodies and our new, eternal lives in heaven, inevitably there will be some tears among those we leave behind. (At least we hope there will! As someone said, "Parting is such sweet sorrow—unless you can't stand the person!") But any tears that are shed here on earth will simply reflect the light of heaven's joy when we move into our new bodies and our eternal life in heaven begins. Then we'll look back and understand the meaning of the observation that "God's most precious gems are crystallized tears."

Moving Day
Yes, I'm looking forward to moving into that new body God has promised me. No more aches and pains, no more groans, no more corns or calluses. How wonderful to think of moving out of my earthly body that is quickly becoming like the dilapidated house described in the wonderful old song:

> This old house is a gettin' shaky,
> This old house is a gettin' old,
> This old house lets in the rain,
> This old house lets in the cold;
> On my knees I'm a gettin' chilly
> But I feel no fear or pain,
> 'Cause I see an angel peekin' through
> A broken window pane.
>
> Ain't a gonna need this house no longer,
> Ain't a gonna need this house no more;
> Ain't got time to fix the shingles,
> Ain't got time to fix the floor,
> Ain't got time to oil the hinges nor to mend
>   no window pane;
> Ain't a gonna need this house no longer,
> I'm a gettin' ready to meet the saints![8]

The song's grammar isn't exactly exemplary, but the attitude it expresses thrills my heart every time I hear it. Every now and then, I imagine there's an angel peeking through a broken part of my heart, winking at me and nodding his little head, reassuring me that I'm "gettin' ready to meet the saints" up there. Knowing what wonders await me in heaven, I have absolutely no fear of death, because I know . . .

When they drop these bones down in the ground
I'll be livin' on the other side.[9]

Just thinking about trading in our worn-out earthly bodies for new models gives me a little boost. As Joni Eareckson Tada says, "This thought alone makes the earthly toil not only bearable, but lighter." Joni compares our new lives in heaven with the way her horse used to feel when the mare was finally headed home:

> I can remember how, after hours of riding my horse to check gates and fences, my weary mount would be wet with sweat, her head hanging low. I had to urge her to put one tired hoof in front of another. Then as soon as she caught a whiff of home or recognized the fences of her own pasture, her ears would pick up and her pace would quicken. The nearer we came to the barn, the more eager her trot. After a quick unsaddling, she would joyfully roll in the dirt and take long, deep drinks from the trough. How good it feels for a beast to be home, to be able to rest.
> How good it will feel for us to rest, to be at home.[10]

Guaranteed a Winner

For Christians, no matter what happens to us here, we're gonna come out winners on the other side! As someone said:

> God believes in me, so my situation is never hopeless.
> He walks beside me, so I am never alone.
> God is on my side, so I can never lose.

That promise really came alive for me last year because of something that happened at a Women of Faith conference on the East Coast. When it was my turn to speak to the sixteen thousand women attending the conference, I showed a little button that says, "Someone Jesus loves has AIDS."

Someone
Jesus loves
has AIDS

The button is really a corollary to another succinct idea that's become a nationwide trend—the initials "WWJD?" that adorn everything from jewelry to license plates, asking "What would Jesus do?" Tying together the two ideas, I asked the audience, "What would Jesus do?" when it came to dealing with those who might be considered outcasts, especially homosexuals and others afflicted by HIV and AIDS. Of course the answer was that He would love them.

It is so easy to glibly *say* that we apply the "WWJD?" principle to our lives. Maybe we point to the time we spend volunteering in the church nursery. Or maybe we let someone cut in front of us in rush-hour traffic, or we drop a dollar in the Salvation Army's red bucket at Christmastime. It might even be possible to get a little smug, thinking we're doing what Jesus would do. But what about those situations that aren't so pristine and noble? What about our dealings with those down-and-out people who are outside the mainstream? That's the issue that arose for several of us at the recent conference.

Right after I had spoken and had shown the AIDS button and talked about "WWJD?" being the guideline for all of life, I was hustled down to the speakers' lunchroom to grab a bite to eat. Suddenly our darling conference director, Christie Barnes, came bounding into the room, her beautiful brown eyes as big as saucers. She blurted out that a woman was upstairs on the main concourse threatening suicide unless she got help! The suicidal woman, Toni, was a prostitute in that city, Christie explained, and she also had full-blown AIDS. Toni was afraid that her pimp, who had already shot and cut her previously when she had tried to leave him, was trying to find her.

Evidently Toni had slept in a dumpster the night before and had walked a couple of miles to get to the conference. A nice, well-dressed woman outside the coliseum had befriended her and another woman gave her a ticket to get in to hear the program.

After she heard me speak about "WWJD?" and loving those with AIDS, Toni became agitated, insisting on seeing me. When she learned that I wouldn't be coming back up to my book table because we'd sold out, she started loudly insisting that she *had* to see me. Women of Faith staff members on the concourse tried to talk with her, but Toni would have none of it. She began raising a ruckus and threatening suicide.

The coliseum's security force responded, counselors at the New Life Clinics table made themselves available, and the city police were summoned. Yet with all the professional people who COULD help, the woman was apparently determined to talk to ME, of all people! Eventually a staff member contacted Christie, who scurried to relay the woman's demands.

Quickly I gathered some other Women of Faith workers plus my own helper, and we dashed into one of the coliseum's locker rooms where Christie had led the tall, unkempt, slovenly dressed woman. She was about thirty-five years old, wearing ill-fitting shorts, a dirty T-shirt, and a baseball cap. We settled onto a couch in the lounge area, and I asked Toni to tell us what was wrong. It took awhile for her to settle down, but eventually the story came pouring out about her hard life as a prostitute and her desperate need to escape from her violent pimp. She was sure if he found her he would kill her. Then she pulled up her pant leg and showed us the bullet wound where he had shot her once before. It was a hole about the size of a plum; it looked like a small funnel that had been embedded in her thigh. Then she showed us a scar along the side of her face, the result of his recent knife attack.

Knowing she had full-blown AIDS, I looked around at the other women, who were listening in horror to her story. During the twenty years I've been involved with Spatula Ministries, I've had plenty of contact with AIDS victims, and I've met people with some incredibly brutal stories. But I suspected that none of those other women had even talked with a prostitute before, let alone one with AIDS. Seeing their faces touched by gentle compassion and watching as they repeatedly reached out to hug the trembling woman, I was amazed to see what was happening to them.

Toni said she desperately wanted to get out of her life of prostitution. She wanted to become a Christian, but she had to get away from her pimp. She hoped to make it to Chicago where she had family to shelter her and she would be safe.

When she'd finished her story, I offered my most encouraging smile and gave her the little button I'd shown during my talk, the one that said, "Someone Jesus loves has AIDS." With shaky hands, she fastened it to her dirty T-shirt, and we began to talk about how she could come out of that life. We reminded her that Jesus loved her and that she could have a new heart and a new life. She obviously grasped these ideas wholeheartedly, and right then and there she prayed with us to accept Christ as her Savior. We all jubilantly joined her in saying a loud "Amen!"

But there was more work to be done, and it had to be done quickly. Toni was smelly and dirty, having slept in the dumpster the night before. So a shower was top priority. The other women rushed out to find the things she would need. One of the gals hurried off to find soap, shampoo, and towels and to collect enough money to buy her a bus ticket to Chicago. Another rushed up to the concourse to get some clothes from the conference venders—T-shirt, chambray shirt, sweatshirt, and anything else that would fit a medium size.

Meanwhile, I took her into the shower room to get started

on the cleanup mission. My old Baptist habits came out while we were in the shower, and for a moment I thought perhaps I could baptize her right there. But things were just too crazy, with water flying everywhere from about fifty shower jets protruding from a big pole in the center of the room.

As Toni stepped into the shower, I saw a huge, gaping wound that ran from her neck down under her breast to her sternum; it looked fresh and untreated. "You really need to have a doctor look at that," I told her, but she protested, saying if she didn't get out of the city, she would have more injuries than just a knife wound. After that she sat quietly on a little stool while I shampooed her hair and helped her scrub down.

Now, I have to insert a personal note here. Bill and I had been away from home two weeks when this conference began, and when I left home I knew I probably wouldn't have a chance to have my hair done. So I had brought along a wig, just in case of an "emergency." When I had looked in the mirror that morning, I'd decided this was an EMERGENCY day (little did I know!). So there I was in the shower room with Toni, wearing my wig and darting in and out of the squirting water. And do you know what a wig does when you wear it in a shower room with hot water shooting down on it? Well, it shrinks up into little frizzy sausages! But at the time I didn't even notice, because I was so intent on getting Toni scrubbed clean and headed out on her new life.

In a few moments the other gals came running back with all the necessities—clothes, a hairbrush, and enough money to buy the bus ticket. Before long, Toni had clean hair, a clean body, and clean clothes emblazoned with "Women of Faith." Then we gathered around her again, our arms entwined around each other's shoulders, and prayed. We asked God to give Toni a clean heart. "Thank you, dear Lord, for giving *all* of us a fresh start and a new beginning each and every day," we prayed. "And thank you for bringing Toni to us so we could share in the fresh start she's beginning in You right now."

At that moment, the (former) prostitute was in a win-win situation. If she escaped and got on the bus and rejoined her family in Chicago, she had a brand-new start, a forgiven past, and a new life to serve the Lord. She could know that God could no longer see her sin, because He had removed it "as far as the east is from the west." She could begin a new life in a bright, clean future.

But if the pimp caught her again—and even if he killed her, as she feared—she would be *safe in the arms of Jesus.* From that moment on, her life was hidden in Christ. If she died, she would go immediately into the presence of God as her new faith in Christ transported her into heaven for eternal life. EITHER WAY SHE WAS A WINNER!

"If you get to heaven before I do," I told her with a smile, "you start polishing up those pearly gates, because I'll be coming too before long."

Then it was time to go. We all started for the door, but Toni suddenly stopped, her eyes wide. "My pin!" she said, patting her chest where the AIDS button had been attached to her old T-shirt. She ran over to the trash can and pulled the pin off the old, dirty shirt we had discarded when she got into the shower. She smiled through her tears as she fastened it to her new Women of Faith blouse, and we all hugged her one more time.

We walked her through the little crowd of people who had gathered outside the locker room—the security guards, counselors, and Women of Faith workers who were waiting to see what would happen. The police officer who had been summoned when the suicide threat was made was still waiting too. He had told one of the workers that he had arrested the woman before for prostitution and knew she had had "trouble with her pimp." We assumed he thought we were pretty foolish for scurrying around so excitedly to assist this poor, degenerate woman.

A taxi had been called, and we helped Toni limp across the coliseum plaza and climb into the seat, instructing the driver to take her directly to the bus depot. Then the cab pulled away, and we waved her off, overwhelmed by the transformation that had taken place right before our eyes: clean body, clean clothes, clean heart, NEW WOMAN!

All this had taken some time, and I had to hurry back up on the platform to join the other speakers saying our final good-bye to the women at the conference. It was then that I realized what had happened to my "hair." It was quite a sight to behold, I'm sure—half of my wig fluffy and full and the other side shrunk up into tight, fuzzy little sausage curls.

The program ended, and we filed out through an exit reserved for the speakers. The same police officer was standing there. As I walked past him, he put his arm out as if to stop me, and I thought, *Oh no! Now what?* But his words were so special. He leaned down and said into my ear, his voice raised so I could hear him above the loud music, "Thank you for what you did for that woman. You probably saved her life."

His words came as such a surprise, because we had assumed he thought we were silly to try and help her. And here he was, as touched by the whole thing as we were!

We may never know the final outcome of this story. We don't know if Toni made it to Chicago or if she was killed by her pimp. God only gives the final score when the game is over. And for Toni the game *isn't* over. But we DO know that the lives of the other women who were in that locker room, exhibiting the "WWJD?" message, were changed that day. None of the other women had ever had the opportunity to embrace such a down-and-out person, a woman with AIDS who came out of a dumpster to touch their lives. Some of them may not even have known what a pimp is, and they had certainly never embraced a prostitute! But there they were, ministering to her with love and concern, praying for her, hugging her, and sending her off with great sympathy for her needs.

When God can take a broken, fractured life and transform it through others who are doing what Jesus would do . . . that is the real test of "WWJD?" I know it changed things in MY life, and all those other helping women experienced a change as well. They appreciated the opportunity to really DO something Jesus would do for that wounded, hurting soul.

Only God knows the final result. Deuteronomy 29:29 says, "The secret things belong to the LORD." We may not know the full story until we get to heaven. The whole thing could have been a scam, just a way to take advantage of others' kind hearts. But I firmly believe that no matter what happens to Toni, God has already used the experience for something good. The impression that incident made on those darling helpers at the Women of Faith conference—as well as many of those who were gathered outside the locker-room door—will last a lifetime. They've had a real taste now of doing what Jesus would do under stressful conditions—and they will never be the same.

Ready to Go!

The experience with the prostitute also reinforced in us the fact that as Christians, we're ready for *anything!* If life serves us up a challenge we cannot overcome here on earth—we still come out on top in heaven! We win, no matter what! That's the gift we shared with Toni in the locker room: the assurance that victory is hers, no matter who (or *what*) wins the race down here in the cesspools of life. The secret is to be ready. For years, I've treasured a poem that carries just that warning. It's appeared in a previous book, and I wanted to include it for you one more time in this volume that's focused on being ready for the Lord's return:

> 'Twas the night before Jesus came and all through
>   the house
> Not a creature was praying, not one in the house.
> Their Bibles were lain on the shelf without care
> In hopes that Jesus would not come there.
>
> The children were dressing to crawl into bed,
> Not once ever kneeling or bowing a head.
> And Mom in her rocker with the babe on her lap
> Was watching the Late Show while I took a nap.
>
> When out of the east there arose such a clatter,
> I sprang to my feet to see what was the matter.

Away to the window I flew like a flash
Tore open the shutters and threw up the sash!

When what to my wondering eyes should appear
But angels proclaiming that Jesus was here!
With a light like the sun sending forth a bright ray
I knew in a moment this must be THE DAY!

The light of His face made me cover my head
It was Jesus! Returning just like He said.
And though I possessed worldly wisdom
        and wealth,
I cried when I saw Him in spite of myself.

In the Book of Life, which He held in His hand,
Was written the name of every saved man.
He spoke not a word as He searched for my name;
When He said, "It's not here," my head hung
        in shame.

The people whose names had been written
        with love
He gathered to take to His Father above.
With those who were ready He arose without
        a sound
While all the rest were left standing around.

I fell to my knees, but it was too late;
I had waited too long and thus sealed my fate.
I stood and I cried as they rose out of sight;
Oh, if only I had been ready tonight!

In the words of this poem the meaning is clear;
The coming of Jesus is drawing near.
There's only one life, and when comes the
        last call
We'll find that the Bible was true after all![11]

The Second Coming

To the warning of the poem, these ancient words from the Book of Revelation echo a loud "Amen!"

> Look, he is coming with the clouds, and every eye will see him, even those who pierced him; and all the peoples of the earth will mourn because of him. So shall it be! Amen.[12]

When Jesus comes again, every person on earth will see "the Son of Man coming on the clouds of the sky, with power and great glory. And he will send his angels with a loud trumpet call, and they will gather his elect from the four winds, from one end of the heavens to the other."[13] As Charles Wesley's lyrics so vividly describe the scene:

> Lo! He comes, with clouds descending,
> Once for our salvation slain;
> Thousand thousand saints attending, swell
> the triumph of His train;
> Alleluia! Alleluia! God appears on earth to
> reign. . . .
>
> Yea, Amen! Let all adore Thee
> High on Thine eternal throne;
> Savior, take the pow'r and glory,
> Claim the kingdom for Thine own.
> O come quickly, O come quickly!
> Alleluia! Come, Lord, come!

Don't you love those last lines? Sometimes when I'm humming that beautiful tune, I add my own little petition: *Come quickly, Lord! It's not that I haven't enjoyed this life You've given me. Oh, I have! Despite all the hard times, the bumps in the road, and the times I've been splattered on the ceiling, I've enjoyed it all, and I've tried to wring every bit of joy out of it that I could. I'm thankful, Lord, but I'm ready. I'm keeping my spiritual ears tuned*

to the heavenly frequency, so that as soon as I hear those first notes
from Your mighty trumpet, I'll be on my way.

Meet Me at Heaven's Gates

The Lord is coming soon. And there's a part of me that wants
to hurry and be first in line at heaven's gates. But there's
another part of me that wants to cherish every moment of that
transition from earth to heaven. Sometimes I think I'll shoot
up to heaven like a rocket, and other times I hope I can float
up gently, like steam rising toward the sun. Ruth Bell Graham
expressed those feelings so beautifully in one of her poems
that I've asked her permission to use it to close out this book.
Read the words slowly and let the awesome image form in
your mind . . .

And when I die
I hope my soul ascends
slowly, so that I
may watch the earth receding
out of sight,
its vastness growing smaller
as I rise,
savoring its recession
with delight.
Anticipating joy
is itself a joy.
And joy unspeakable
and full of glory
needs more
than "in the twinkling of an eye,"*
more than "in a moment."
Lord, who am I
to disagree?
It's only we
have much
to leave behind;
so much . . . Before.

These moments
of transition
will, for me, be
time
to adore.[14]

*1 Corinthians 15:52

How eagerly I'm anticipating the "unspeakable joy" of heaven! How about you? Are you ready for that trumpet to sound? Surely it won't be long now! As one friend told me, "I'll see you here, there, or in the air!"

Someday soon, *He's gonna toot, and I'm gonna scoot right outta here!*

Acknowledgments

Many thanks for the jokes, poems, song lyrics, and zany "splashes of joy" in this volume that have been shared by other writers and friends. We have made diligent effort to identify all the original sources, but sometimes this is an impossible task. Other times, our research turned up multiple sources for the same item. Many jokes and stories were found in collections such as *The Best of Bits & Pieces,* and *More of the Best of Bits & Pieces,* both published by Economics Press, Fairfield, New Jersey, and *The Speaker's Quote Book* from Kregel Publishing, Grand Rapids, Michigan. Whenever the source of an unattributed item in this book can be *positively* identified, please contact W Publishing Group, P.O. Box 141000, Nashville, TN 37214, so that proper credit can be given in future printings.

Grateful acknowledgment is also given for:

"Hallelujah Square," © 1969 by Ray Overholt Music. Used by permission.

"How Great Thou Art," © 1953 S. K. Hine. Assigned to Manna Music, Inc., 35255 Brooten Road, Pacific City, OR 97135. Renewed 1981. All rights reserved. Used by permission (ASCAP).

"If You Could See Me Now," © 1992 Integrity's Praise! Music/BMI. All rights reserved. Used by permission.

"I'll Fly Away," © 1932 in *Wonderful Message* by Hartford Music Co. Renewed 1960 by Albert E. Brumley & Sons/ SESAC (administered by ICG). All rights reserved. Used by permission.

Notes

Dedication Page

Sam Butcher's additions to the Precious Moments illustration of "This World Is Not My Home" are the trumpet (how appropriate for a book titled *He's Gonna Toot, and I'm Gonna Scoot*) and the boomerang labeled with my motto: *Joy*. Sam knows I'm a believer in the principle of boomerang blessings. In this book, he's helping me toss out a boomerang of love and joy to you!

Chapter 1. We've Got a One-Way Ticket to Paradise!

1. Albert E. Brumley, "I'll Fly Away," © 1932 in *Wonderful Message* by Hartford Music Co. Renewed 1960 by Albert E. Brumley & Sons/SESAC (administered by ICG). All rights reserved. Used by permission.

2. Herbert Buffum, "I'm Going Higher Someday," arr. Alfred B. Smith. Copyright © 1981 by Alfred B. Smith. All rights reserved. Used by permission.

3. Oswald Chambers, *My Utmost for His Highest* (Grand Rapids: Discovery House, 1935), July 29.

4. Matthew 24:30, Revelation 1:7 (KJV), emphasis added.

5. Chambers, ibid.

6. Joni Eareckson Tada, *Heaven . . . Your Real Home* (Grand Rapids: Zondervan, 1995), 198.

7. H. L. Turner, "Christ Returneth."

8. 1 Thessalonians 4:16–17.

9. Charles Ryrie in *Ten Reasons Why Jesus Is Coming Soon: Christian Leaders Share Their Insights*, comp. John Van Diest (Sisters, Ore.: Multnomah, 1998), 190.

10. Tim LaHaye and Jerry Jenkins, *Left Behind* (Wheaton, Ill.: Tyndale, 1995), 16.

11. Joni Eareckson Tada, quoted in *A Place Called Heaven*, comp. Catherine L. Davis (Colorado Springs: Chariot Victor, 1997).

12. Psalm 71:14, emphasis added.

13. Kay Hively and Albert E. Brumley Jr., *I'll Fly Away* (Branson, Mo.: Mountaineer Books, 1990), 134.

14. Psalm 90:10 (RSV), emphasis added.

15. *St. Petersburg* (Fla.) *Times,* 7 September 1998, 10.

16. Dion De Marbelle, "When They Ring Those Golden Bells."

17. Someone sent me this quote from Randy Alcorn's sermon "What Does the Bible Say About Heaven?" posted on his Internet web site.

18. Peggy Andersen, "Seattle company taking rocket-ship reservations," Associated Press article in an undated clipping from the *Orange County Register.*

19. Adapted from *The Best of Bits & Pieces*, comp. Arthur F. Lenehan (Fairfield, N.J.: Economics Press, 1994), 16.

20. Clifford Pugh, *Houston Chronicle,* "Patience wears thin in today's on-the-go society," published 9 July 1997, in the *Denver Post.*

21. Frederick Buechner, *Whistling in the Dark,* quoted in *The Answer to Happiness, Health, and Fulfillment in Life: The Holy Bible Translated for Our Time* with *Selected Writings by Leading Inspirational Authors (The Answer Bible)* (Dallas: Word, 1993).

22. Billy Graham, *Storm Warning* (Dallas: Word, 1992), 312.

23. Stuart K. Hine, "How Great Thou Art!" Copyright 1953 S. K. Hine. Assigned to Manna Music, Inc., 35255 Brooten Road, Pacific City, OR 97135. Renewed 1981. All rights reserved. Used by permission. (ASCAP)

24. Adapted from *Reader's Digest,* June 1998.

25. *The Last Word: Tombstone Wit and Wisdom,* comp. Nicola Gillies (Oxford, England: Dove Tail Books, 1997).

26. *Prairie Home Companion's Pretty Good Joke Book,* vol. 3 (St. Paul: Minnesota Public Radio, 1998), 5.

27. Ibid., 7.

28. "The Good, Clean Funnies List," P.O. Box 12021, Huntsville, Alabama 35815.

29. *More of the Best of Bits & Pieces,* comp. Rob Gilbert, Ph.D. (Fairfield, N.J.: Economics Press, 1997), 40.

30. Psalm 55:6.

Chapter 2. Transposed by Music

1. W. O. Cushing, Ira D. Sankey, "Under His Wings."

2. Mrs. Will L. Murphy, "Constantly Abiding."

3. Kim Noblitt, "If You Could See Me Now," © 1992 Integrity's Praise! Music/BMI. All rights reserved. Used by permission.

4. Robin Hinch, "Giesela Lenhart went 'home' while praising God," *Orange County Register,* 21 March 1998, Metro-6.

5. Johnson Oatman and John R. Sweeney, "Holy, Holy Is What the Angels Sing."

6. Al Smith, *Treasury of Hymn Histories,* published in 1982 by Praise Resources, 2200 Wade Hampton Blvd., Greenville, SC 29615.

7. Kenneth Osbeck, *Amazing Grace* (Grand Rapids: Kregel, 1990), 47.

8. Martin Luther, *What Luther Says,* quoted in *The Answer Bible.*

9. Smith, *Treasury of Hymn Histories.*

10. Source unknown.

11. Adapted from a story by Kirsten Jackson in *Christianity Today.* Date unknown.

12. Source unknown.

13. 1 Chronicles 16:32–33.

Chapter 3. May the Joybells of Heaven Ding-Dong in Your Heart Today

1. W. O. Cushing, "Ring the Bells of Heaven."

2. See Exodus 28:33, 39:25, and Zechariah 14:20.

3. Kenneth W. Osbeck, *101 Hymn Stories* (Grand Rapids: Kregel, 1982), 76–77.

4. "Salvation Army gets $80 million from Kroc," *Orange County Register*, September 1998.

5. Joyce Landorf, *Mourning Song* (Grand Rapids: Baker, 1974), 52–53.

6. Joey O'Connor, *Heaven's Not a Crying Place: Teaching Your Child about Funerals, Death, and the Life Beyond* (Grand Rapids: Revell, 1997), quoted in *Focus on the Family* magazine, August 1998, 7.

7. Genesis 19:27; Exodus 16:7, 34:4; 2 Samuel 23:3–4; Job 1:5; Psalm 5:3; and Isaiah 26:9.

8. Mark 1:35 and Luke 21:38.

9. Adapted from Peter Marshall's story retold by Jeanne Hendricks in *A Place Called Heaven,* comp. Catherine L. Davis (Colorado Springs: Chariot Victor, 1997), 70.

10. Proverbs 25:2 and Deuteronomy 29:29.

11. This epitaph utilizing a portion of Philippians 1:23 (KJV) is quoted in Gillies, *The Last Word*, 25.

12. *The Best of Bits & Pieces*, 130.

13. Dion De Marbelle, "When They Ring Those Golden Bells."

14. Psalm 81:8.

Chapter 4. Stick a Geranium in Your Starry Crown

1. E. E. Hewitt and John R. Sweeney, "I Am Thinking Today."

2. Philippians 4:12–13.

3. 1 Corinthians 9:25.

4. 2 Timothy 4:7–8.

5. James 1:12.

6. 1 Peter 5:4.

7. 1 Thessalonians 2:19 (NKJV).

8. 1 Corinthians 9:24–25.

9. 1 Peter 5:6 (KJV) and John 21:15.

10. Dennis Prager, "A Simple Truth about Happiness," *Reader's Digest*, June 1998, 99.

11. Henri Nouwen, *Here and Now* (New York: Crossroad, 1994, 1997), 28.

12. Ibid., 28–29.

13. Ibid., 29.

14. Revelation 12:1.

15. Norman Vincent Peale, quoted in "Quips, Quotes, Quibbles, & Bits," *Tampa Tribune*, 2 June 1998.

16. Matthew 5:16.

17. Adapted from Stephen Cassettari, *Pebbles on the Road* (New York: HarperCollins/Angus & Robertson, 1993), reprinted in *Bits & Pieces*.

18. *More of the Best of Bits & Pieces*, 33–34.

19. Nouwen, 31.

20. 1 John 4:15–17.

21. Psalm 149:4.

22. Roy Zuck, ed., *The Speaker's Quote Book* (Grand Rapids: Kregel, 1997), 340.

23. Tony Campolo, quoted in *From A to Z Sparkling Illustrations*, comp. Graurorger & Mercer (Grand Rapids: Baker, 1997), 114.

24. *The Best of Bits & Pieces*, 103.

25. Proverbs 14:24.

Chapter 5. Finally, *Fabulously* Home!

1. "Mansion Over the Hilltop," copyright 1949, Singspiration Music (administered by Brentwood-Benson Music Publishing, Inc.). All rights reserved. Used by permission.

2. Ray Overholt, "Hallelujah Square," copyright 1969 by Ray Overholt Music. Used by permission.

3. Adapted from *Chapel Bells* magazine, Fall 98, 6–7.

4. "Even the Lumber Carries Words of Love," *Episcopal Life*, June 1998.

5. Someone told me about this story in an interview with Reeve Lindbergh on Morning Edition, National Public Radio, 21 October 1998, discussing her book, *Under a Wing* (New York: Simon & Schuster, 1998).

6. Augustus Montague Toplady, "Rock of Ages."

7. The photo accompanied a report by Region 9 CBA board member Karen Grosse in *CBA Marketplace*, August 1997, 26. It is used here with the permission of Karen and Ron Grosse.

8. Matthew 11:28 (KJV).

9. Associated Press photo, *Baton Rouge* (La.) *Advocate*, 20 February 1998, 18A.

10. Margaret Guenther, "God's Plan Surpasses Our Best Imaginings," *Episcopal Life*, July/August 1993, 20.

11. This story, originally told by Al Smith, is used here with his permission.

12. *The Christian*, quoted in Zuck, *The Speaker's Quote Book*.

13. *Parables, Etc.*, quoted in Zuck, *The Speaker's Quote Book*.

14. "Un-Real Estate" in the "Off the Wall" column, *San Juan* (New Mexico) *Sun*, 2–8 July 1997.

15. John 14:1–3 (KJV).

Chapter 6. Angels Watchin' Over Me

1. Johnson Oatman and John R. Sweeney, "Holy, Holy Is What the Angels Sing."

2. Billy Graham's statements come from a transcript of CNN's 26 October 1998 broadcast of *Larry King Live*.

3. Luke 16:22.

4. Matthew 24:30–31.

5. Brian Sibley, *C. S. Lewis Through the Shadowlands* (Grand Rapids: Revell, 1985, 1994), 154.

6. Martha McCrackin, quoted in Zuck, *The Speaker's Quote Book.*

7. Revelation 5:11.

8. "The Doctrine of Angels," in Dr. H. L. Willmington, *Willmington's Guide to the Bible* (Wheaton, Ill.: Tyndale, 1981), 776. Scriptures cited include Job 38:7; Psalm 148:1–3; Revelation 9:1–2; 12:3, 4, 7–9.

9. George Howe Colt, "In Search of Angels," *Life* magazine, December 1993, 65.

10. Genesis 3:24.

11. Tada, 66–67.

12. Ibid., 54–55.

13. Ibid., 70.

14. Hebrews 13:1–2.

15. Hebrews 1:14.

16. Billy Graham, *Angels: God's Secret Agents* (Dallas: Word, 1975, 1986, 1994, 1995), 37.

17. Psalm 34:7.

18. Millard and Linda Fuller, *The Excitement Is Building* (Dallas: Word, 1990), 85–86.

19. Based on information in Joan Colgan Stortz, *Niagara Falls* (Markham, Ontario: Irving Weisdorf & Co., 1994, 1995, 1998), 28.

20. Adapted from *Bits & Pieces,* a publication of Economics Press, 6 November 1997, 24.

21. Quoted in Sheldon Vanauken, *A Severe Mercy.*

22. *Our Daily Bread,* 17 June 1998.

23. *Random Acts of Kindness,* intro. by Dawna Markova (New York: Fine Communication, 1997).

24. Mary Hunt, *The Financially Confident Woman* (Nashville: Broadman & Holman, 1996), 170.

25. Tony Campolo, *It's Friday, but Sunday's Comin'* (Dallas: Word, 1993), 88.

26. Gary Smalley with John Trent, *Love Is a Decision* (Dallas: Word, 1996), 70.

27. Revelation 3:5 (NASB).

Chapter 7. Ain't a Gonna Need This House No Longer

1. Charles Wesley, "Blow Ye the Trumpet."

2. This story comes from information in a Scripps Howard News Service article by Fred Brown, "The Way of the Cross," *Cape Coral* (Fla.) *Breeze*, 4 November 1998, 8.

3. Matthew 7:14 (NCV).

4. Ecclesiastes 3:6 (KJV).

5. Psalm 103:15–16.

6. 1 Corinthians 15:51–52 (NCV).

7. "I'll Have a New Life," copyright 1940 Stamps/Baxter Music (administered by Brentwood-Benson Music, Inc.). All rights reserved. Used by permission.

8. Stuart Hamblen, "This Ole House" © 1954 Hamblen Music, renewed 1982. Used by permission. Music available from Hamblen Music, Box 1937, Canyon Country, CA 91386.

9. Rich Cook, "Buried Alive." Used by permission.

10. Tada, 203.

11. "'Twas the Night Before Jesus Came," © 1985 Bethany Farms, Inc. Used by permission of Jeffrey Cummings, Bethany Farms, Inc., St. Charles, Missouri.

12. Revelation 1:7.

13. Matthew 24:30–31.

14. Ruth Bell Graham, *Sitting by My Laughing Fire* (Waco, Tex.: Word, 1977). Used by permission.

BARBARA JOHNSON

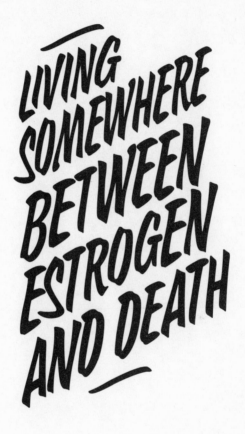

W PUBLISHING GROUP™

www.wpublishinggroup.com

A Division of Thomas Nelson, Inc.
www.ThomasNelson.com

To Gopher Bill,
my perfectionistic engineer husband.

I call him my joy-robber, but the truth is he has
made me look so hard to find the hidden joys in life
that I've found *more* joy than I ever dreamed possible!
He is the solid, practical anchor who keeps his airhead
wife grounded; I love to hear him say I'm his best
friend. He's my invaluable helper, facilitator,
and coworker, and without him none of my
books would ever have been completed.

Contents

The Wonder Years

*When we wonder how we got this old
and why we didn't save for a facelift!*

Bill and I went on a cruise recently that left us both feeling younger than our years—and exhausted too! When our tour group assembled on the first day and we got a chance to look each other over, Bill and I were surprised to discover that we were apparently the youngest ones there! When you consider that we're no spring chickens (closer to Geriatric Junction than we like to admit), you can imagine how old those other folks looked!

I wondered if the trip had been described as a senior citizens special somewhere in the fine print (which we never read because neither one of us can *see* fine print anymore). But we weren't upset about it. At first it was sort of fun to be the "youngsters" of the group; I figured that would give me an excuse for any mischief I might get into.

But by the second day, the newness of being "young again" had worn off as the flip side of the situation became obvious. Every time we left the boat for some sort of bus excursion, again and again we heard:

"Uh-oh! I left my sweater back on the boat."

"Has anyone seen my pocketbook? Oh, no . . . I must have left it in the restroom."

"I can't see a thing without my glasses. I must've put 'em down when I looked through those pay-binoculars back at the scenic view."

After each one of these announcements, all the old eyes seemed to turn expectantly to Bill or me. Sagging faces would wrinkle up into a hopeful smile. "Oh, honey, that's so nice of you to go get it for me," they would say as Bill or I heaved a patient sigh and headed back to retrieve the lost items.

We assisted them as they slowly hobbled up and down stairs; we waited outside restrooms holding their purses, scarves, sweaters, totebags, and half-eaten sandwiches entombed in fast-food boxes. After every stop, we loudly guided them as their feet struggled to find the steps of the bus. "Just a little higher . . . okay . . . good . . . up a little more . . . you're almost there. That's it." And then we pushed and shoved to get them to the top of the steps and back to their seats.

Then, back on the bus, we suffered through the same sort of confused conversation with at least one of them:

"Here you go! Here's your seat."

"Are you sure this is my seat?"

"Yep, this is it, all right. Just scoot on in, and we'll be on our way."

"It sure doesn't *feel* like my seat . . . I had mine fixed just right, and this one is tilted back too far."

"Well, just lift that little lever and—oops! Too fast. Your teeth still in?"

"I don't think this is my seat. I was sitting closer to the front. Now I can't see anything."

"No, you were right here. You'll be able to see as soon as

Marcus takes off his hat. See? Here's your crocheting, and there's Agnes's magazine that you borrowed."

"That's my crocheting? I thought I was making a pink *sweater.*"

Finally, everyone would be seated—usually with one or two of them still fussing that someone else had their seat and a few not even certain they were on the right bus—and off we'd head for our next stop, where we'd go through it all over again.

At mealtimes, Bill and I read the menus out loud for our companions, who couldn't seem to make heads or tails of it. We cut up their meat, spread mayonnaise on sandwiches, fetched extra napkins, and tracked down the hot water to dilute too-strong coffee.

Sometimes when one of these feeble, confused, white-haired tourists was asking for help, I'd smile what I hoped was my patient-looking smile and hope the old lady couldn't read my mind, which wanted desperately to say, *For goodness' sake! This is so simple. Can't you figure this out for yourself?*

Of course when these feelings got close to the surface, I would stuff them back inside.

Not too long after this "vacation," Bill and I headed out on a speaking engagement, this time to Canada. In Montreal we boarded a tiny plane (it only held twelve people) to fly to the city in Quebec where I was to speak. As we boarded the plane we were given a rather complicated form having to do with customs legalities as we crossed the Canadian border.

The paper didn't make any sense to me; I looked at it until I was cross-eyed and still couldn't make heads or tails of it! Meanwhile, out of the corner of my eye, I could see a darling little white-haired lady across the aisle rapidly filling in the blanks on her form.

In frustration, I sighed, huffed, clucked my tongue, and tapped my pencil on the irritating paper. But she didn't look up, too busy writing out her own answers on the form. Finally I admitted loudly, "I can't *read* this. How can I fill it out?"

The old lady smiled patiently then returned to her writing

as she said slowly, as though I would have trouble hearing her, "Well, the first line is asking your *NAME*. The next line is for your *ADDRESS*. The third line is your *BIRTHDAY* . . ."

Dutifully I wrote down my name and address as she instructed. We were halfway through the confusing form, with the old lady carefully pronouncing the information each line wanted. At that moment, I felt old, feeble-minded, and confused. How could this be so difficult for me when she was whizzing through her form like a court stenographer? I paused and sighed again. Then I said, "You're so smart. Now, what does this next line want?" And then I added, "Thank you for helping me with this."

She smiled that same patient smile again. She told me later she was eighty years old. She reached across the aisle and gave my arm a little pat. "Oh, I'm glad to help," she said. But in her twinkling eyes at that moment, I could read her mind. It was saying, *For goodness' sake! This is so simple. Can't you figure this out for yourself?*

It was at that moment, however, that she actually looked over and saw my form.

"Oh, honey. You're on the *French* side. If you'll just turn the paper over, the other side is in *English!*"

We had a good laugh over that incident, and that darling gal taught me a valuable lesson that day: Old age depends more on how you feel and act than on how many years you've lived. That charming old lady had several years on me, but my inability to figure out the form made me feel decrepit while her good-natured laughter made her seem like a breath of fresh air.

Living Joyfully . . . Deep in Denial

The fact is, I've always said I don't really like being around old people—so it's a little tough realizing that *now I AM one!* It's easy for me to slip into the mind-set that portrays most of them as being like that group of befuddled senior citizens on our cruise: endlessly forgetful, hopelessly confused, and, in general, a pain to be around. When that image comes to mind,

I can't help but whisper a prayer, begging, *Please, please, PLEASE, Lord! Don't ever let me be old!*

Of course the only way to avoid getting old is to die young, and that just wasn't God's plan for me. If you've read my other books, you know there were times when I *wanted* that to happen; I argued with God that I'd suffered enough and it was time for me to come home and get some heavenly rest. But He apparently had other things in mind for me.

They say that the best way to grow old is not to be in a hurry about it—and Lord knows, I've put it off as long as I could. But the other thing about old age is that it happens to us without any effort at all on our part. We blow out the candles on our twenty-first birthday cake, and *poof!* The next thing we know, we're wearing goofy party hats and singing "Auld Lang Syne" in some old folks home in Florida and wondering, *How did this happen?*

Laughing through the Ages

Yes, according to my birth certificate, I am living somewhere between estrogen and death, or, as someone said, between menopause and LARGE PRINT! But I don't have to *act* my age because, thank God, I've discovered a wonderful anti-aging remedy. It won't actually turn back the clock, and it's certainly not a new wonder drug. In fact, it's been promoted since biblical times as a cure for a wide variety of problems (see Proverb 17:22). And it's no secret, either; lots of people use it. *(They're* the ones I'd like to take my next cruise trip with!)

If you know anything about me, or if you've read any of my seven other books, you can already guess what I'm talking about. It's the same God-given gift that's kept me functioning through some previous tragedies.

What is it?

Laughter.

A sense of humor.

An attitude expressed by Oscar Wilde's motto: "Life is too important to be taken seriously."

A tendency to look for joy throughout the journey, to find a way to laugh at *everything* life throws my way—even death. How could anyone laugh at death? Well, consider what the late Dorothy Parker suggested for the epitaph on her own tombstone:

Excuse my dust.[1]

Don't you love it! This is the same attitude that caused comedian Bill Cosby, as he approached his fiftieth birthday, to laugh when he quoted his grandfather's advice, "Don't worry about senility. . . . When it hits you, you won't know it."[2]

For Better or For Worse by Lynn Johnston

For Better or For Worse © Lynn Johnston Prod., Inc.
Reprinted with permission of Universal Press Syndicate. All Rights Reserved.

That attitude is the same sparkling joy that *other* old lady shared with me on the little plane in Canada as we laughed together about my struggles with the silly customs form. That wonderful eighty-year-old "youngster" reminded me that our age truly is just a number, nothing more. It's how we feel inside that determines how old we really are.

It's the way we live our lives—our attitudes and our actions—that determines what stage of life we're in. You may have a husband in the throes of a midlife crisis, parents who are struggling to remember what decade they're in, and adult children who are giving you fits, but if you can keep breathing and laughing, you'll survive (at least until it's *your* turn to move into the home for the bewildered and try to remember what decade it is!).

Anyone can laugh—whether you're mobile or bed-ridden, active or lame, whether you're equipped with single or double eyes, arms, ears, legs, and kidneys! No physical limitation can prevent you from laughing. Even if some problem has robbed you of your voice, you can still laugh with your eyes. And if for some reason your eyes can't sparkle anymore, you can still smile in your heart.

Laughing at Life

My all-time, tried-and-true method for lightening up any situation is to laugh at it! Fortunately, I have a lot of kindred spirits out there who share their funny experiences with me, including hilarious stories about their health problems.

One of my favorites is about a daughter who was concerned that her elderly mother hadn't had a Pap smear in several years. She finally persuaded her mother to let her make an appointment for an exam with her own doctor. "You can spend the night with me, and I'll drive you to his office in the morning," she told her mother. "Then we'll go out for a nice lunch."

The mother reluctantly agreed and spent the night in her daughter's apartment. The next day they went together to the doctor's office, and while the daughter waited in the lobby the mother nervously undressed, climbed up on the table, and, with the nurse's assistance, slid her heels into the stirrups.

The doctor came in, greeted her pleasantly, then settled onto his stool.

"My, aren't we FANCY today!" he exclaimed as he lifted the sheet draped over the old lady's upraised knees.

Shocked, she had no idea what the doctor meant. When the exam was over, she hurriedly got dressed and rushed out to meet her daughter in the waiting room. In a panic, she repeated what the doctor had said.

"What in the world do you think he meant by that?" the mother asked, bewildered.

"I have no idea, Mother. What did you do to prepare for the exam?"

"Well, I showered, and I used some of that feminine deodorant spray in your bathroom," the mother replied.

There was a slight pause as the woman looked her mother in the eye.

"I don't HAVE any feminine deodorant spray, Mother."

"Yes you do—that tall pink-and-gold can."

"Mother! That's not deodorant. That's *gold-glitter hairspray!*"

That charming old lady sure gave that doctor's day a lift, didn't she? Of course she didn't really mean to . . . but that's what makes the story so funny!

Some people spread joy wherever they go—whether or not they mean to! And some of us have to put forth a little effort to keep a smile in our hearts. Others are never happy unless they're complaining about something. I got a note from a woman who had a friend like that. Luckily, the woman who wrote to me could see the humor even in having such a pessimistic friend. She wrote, "My friend Irene is *always* complaining! I took her to a greeting-card store the other day, and she looked and looked and looked.

"Finally, I said, 'Irene, what in the world are you looking for?'

"She replied, 'I'm looking for a card that says, "I had what you've got—only WORSE!"'"

This is the same witty woman who told me her horoscope

predicted one morning that she was going to have an adventure involving water. "And then," she continued, "I dropped my false teeth in the toilet!"

Surviving the Change

It's easy to find things to complain about as we grow older, but it's so much healthier to *laugh* instead. Of course, sometimes it's not easy to *find* those laughable situations. One of the least funny things about growing older is menopause.

With our hormones raging, our emotions swinging wildly

© 1996 Randy Glasbergen

"Having nine lives is cool, but if I have to go through menopause again, forget it!"

to and fro, our memory shot, and our bodies flashing with enough heat to bake the Thanksgiving turkey, we NEED to laugh—but often find ourselves crying instead.

I'm not sure how a MAN could ever understand menopause, but I think Dave Barry came pretty close when he wrote this hilarious definition:

> [The change] is the stage that a woman goes through when her body, through a complex biological process, senses that the woman has reached the

stage in her life where her furniture is much too nice for her to have a baby barfing on it. So the body stops producing estrogen, which is the hormone that causes certain distinct female characteristics such as ovulation and the ability not to watch football.

This bodily change is called "menopause," from the ancient Greek words *meno* (meaning "your skin sometimes gets so hot") and *pause* (meaning "that it melts Tupperware").

Also some women tend to become emotional and easily irritated by minor things that never used to bother them, such as when their husbands leave a partly used meatloaf sandwich in bed, as though the Meatloaf Sandwich Fairy were going to come along and pick it up for him.

The traditional way to cope with menopause is to ask your physician to prescribe costly pharmaceuticals, but of course these can cause harmful side effects. . . . So more and more health experts are recommending a "holistic" approach, in which you develop a deeper understanding of the natural process that your body is going through and then, with this newfound knowledge as your guide, you stick the meatloaf sandwich into the breast pocket of your husband's best suit.[3]

An article in *Today's Christian Woman* put a really uplifting slant on menopause. Citing Ecclesiastes 3:1—"There is a time for everything, and a season for every activity under heaven" —it said:

Menopause is a season, not a disease. It's not fatal. In fact, it's a good time to take stock. In the same way that a harsh winter is always followed by spring and new life, menopause can be a precursor to a fresh beginning to the rest of your life. Take time to reflect on what you did *right* the first two-thirds of your life, and dare to dream about your next twenty-five years or so.[4]

Lambasting the Labels

If you're like me (that is, if some people would consider you to be *old* too), you dislike those labels the rest of the world wants to put on us, even the one that says we're no longer old—we're "chronologically gifted"! No matter how well-intentioned they are, these names just seem to go from bad (old people, senior citizens, golden agers, and mature Americans) to worse (elderly, geezers, seasoned citizens, and old biddies).

And I know I'm not alone in resenting being categorized this way. My eye doctor, Dr. Robb Hicks, was kind enough to share an anecdote about this problem of "name-calling" that occurred within the medical profession.

After surgery one day, Dr. Hicks joined another doctor in the hospital physicians lounge, where they had gone to wash the surgical powder off their hands, look for donuts, and then dictate their patients' medical records into the recording system while the procedures they had just completed were still fresh in their minds.

The other physician, "Dr. Tom," had just been given a birthday card signed by all the surgical nurses "congratulating" him on reaching his sixtieth birthday. He feigned pleasure over the attention, but back in the physicians lounge with his friends, Dr. Tom was obviously not excited about reaching this milestone.

The doctors settled into their cubicles to dictate the medical reports. Dr. Hicks heard Dr. Tom begin dictating the history and physical status of the patient whose gallbladder he had just removed:

"This well-nourished Caucasian *elderly* man . . . ," Dr. Tom began. Then he paused for a few seconds. Dr. Hicks heard a slight sigh, and then Dr. Tom backed up the recorder and commenced again: "This well-developed, well-nourished Caucasian man *of sixty-two years* . . ."

Like Dr. Tom, I don't want to be thought of as elderly. Instead, I want to be like those women described by another physician, plastic surgeon Harvey Austin, who said, "There is no such thing as an old woman! We've been conned. My [plastic surgery] patients are not vain. They only want to let the little girl out!"[5]

© 1991 by Ed Fischer and Jane Thomas Noland. Reprinted from
What's So Funny about Getting Old? with permission of Meadowbrook Press, Minnetonka, MN.

That's us, isn't it? We're not old; we're just mature little girls. We have a little something extra, now that we're heading toward the sunset. Unfortunately, that little something extra is often in the worst possible place. I love the little quip that says,

> With age a woman gains wisdom,
> maturity, self-assurance . . .
> and ten pounds right on the hips.[6]

When I go around the country speaking for conferences, I often say, "Actually, I'm a perfect ten under here. I just keep it covered with fat so it doesn't get scratched!" For many of us that perfect-ten body is attached to a thirty-year-old mind encased in an antique display case! As Ashleigh Brilliant says,

> Inside every older person,
> There's a younger person,
> Wondering what happened.
>
> Ashleigh Brilliant
> Pot-Shot 1390, © 1978

No matter how incongruously our youthful minds fit into our aging bodies, we can refuse to be old. We can celebrate our youth—no matter how many decades we've been youthful!

For Women Only!

Before we go any further, I need to make one small request. If you're a man, would you please stop right here? Don't turn another page. I don't mean to hurt your feelings, but, you see, this book is FOR WOMEN ONLY! So just close the cover and put the book back where you found it. If you're a man and you bought this book without noticing the warning right there on the cover that says FOR WOMEN ONLY! (in bright letters) and if you don't have a wife, mother, sister, or friend to give it to, then you have my permission to return this book to the store where you bought it. Just show the salesclerk your receipt, hand over the book, and say, "Barbara says on page 13 that I'm not allowed to read this book, so would you please give me my money back?"

If they're reluctant to give you a refund, try whining. This usually works.

It's not that there are any big secrets hidden in these pages. And except for the chapter that pokes fun at men in my usual *kind and educational way*, there's nothing controversial here— no putdowns or backstabbing. It's just that, well, I'd like to talk about *women* things in this book. That's why we put *estrogen* right there in the title. Testosterone problems are NOT for us!

Actually I've looked forward to writing this book for several years, but I never felt old enough! My previous books have been aimed at hurting parents who have suffered a loss through death or a broken relationship; those books contain many experiences shared by families who are part of Spatula Ministries, the organization Bill and I started many years ago. Spatula's goal is to peel hurting parents off the ceiling with a spatula of love and set them on the road to recovery.

In writing those earlier books, I always felt I had to share my "credentials," my own painful experiences. But while I was doing that, in the back of my mind I was thinking, *Oh, it would be so nice just to write a book for the sheer fun of it and not have to include my credentials!*

Finally, I realized that if I wanted to write that kind of book I'd better do it now—while I can still remember what I wanted to say! So here it is, a book of zaniness that pokes fun at the way many of us are right now: frazzled by life's knock-out blows, staggering down that inevitable road to the home for the bewildered, fighting fifty or enduring our sixties—but still looking for those little splashes of joy that brighten our pathway like transient diamonds.

If you're one of the estimated forty-three million women "in peri-menopause (the term designating the transition phase between having regular periods and no periods at all), in menopause, or past menopause,"[7] this book is for you. We're in or nearing that stage the late Margaret Mead whimsically described as the "PMZ: post-menopausal ZEST"![8] Actually, I prefer to think of it as a time that's ripe for post-menopausal ZANINESS!

Think of this book as a cookbook of PMZ "recipes." You won't find any sad stories here, no harrowing tales of brokenness. This book is just a journal of joy. Sometimes it makes sense; sometimes it doesn't. My goal is not to help you lose twenty pounds, control your raging hormones, or find the right hairstyle for your funeral debut; instead I just want to share some bursts of joy with you. And I'm not just talking about mindless giggles here, either. I mean the kind of humor my friend Marilyn Meberg talks about—humor that releases us "from the bondage of our circumstances and ourselves so that the inherent capacity to laugh, which lives in us all, can bubble to the surface and carry us through those times that are tension-producing and spirit-breaking."[9]

If I *do* feel the need to remind you that I'm offering this light-hearted encouragement after a lifetime of "tension-producing and spirit-breaking" experiences, I hope you'll just let me blurt out some code words for heartache, perhaps DYNA-ANGINA! Then you can pause to remember my credentials—and we'll get back to our silliness.

Part of the goofiness I plan to share has grown out of a story included in an earlier book, *Mama, Get the Hammer! There's Fly on Papa's Head!* The story, from an unidentified newsletter, described a modest woman trying to buy a box of Tampax at a supermarket. As luck would have it, she picks up a box with no pricetag, and the cashier makes a storewide announcement on the PA system, asking the stock person to look up the price. The stocker misunderstands and thinks the cashier is talking about *thumbtacks*. He asks, again on the PA system, "Do you mean the kind you push in with your thumb or the kind you pound in with a hammer?"

I loved the story but was reluctant to put it in my book. After all, this is not a subject one would expect in a book written for hurting parents by a post-menopausal woman! I was afraid the shock might be too much for some folks.

But just the opposite happened. Of all the stories in all the books I've written, that tampon story is one of the favorites that's often mentioned by readers when I'm out on speaking appearances. If I've heard it once, I've heard it a zillion times: "I *loved* that story about the Tampax! I laughed 'til I cried!"

And then the women say, "Have you heard . . . ?"

That's where the next round of "female" stories came from—jokes, quips, and real-life stories that women could only tell to other women.

For example, at one meeting I mentioned the tampon story—then added that that kind of experience would never happen to me now because I'm living "somewhere between estrogen and death, or, to put it another way, between the *Blue Lagoon* and *Golden Pond!*" A woman came up to me afterward and said, "Barbara, we're living *somewhere between training bras and support hose!*"

But then another woman added the clincher: "Let's face it, Barb," she said. "We're living *somewhere between Tampax and Depends!*"

Then, along those same lines, someone else showed me a greeting card with suggestions for what to do with a diaphragm you no longer need. One of the suggestions was to use it as a "rainhat for a cat"![10]

Girl-Talk

That's the kind of silliness you're gonna find in this book. I think you'll agree these aren't *naughty* jokes and stories—you won't find any foul language in these pages; there's certainly nothing here about immorality. The things I want to share are, well, personal. Girl-talk. Jokes and anecdotes from women about women that are just too good not to share.

When we were putting this book together, I tried out a few of the jokes on the folks at W Publishing Group, asking, "Could I put this in the book?" Then, I suppose, a memo probably went throughout the corporate offices: "Barbara Johnson wants to know if it's okay to talk about tampons and adult diapers in her next book."

Next I asked, "Could this book be just for women?"

I've already caused those good folks more headaches than they deserve. It seems every time we agree on a new book project, I throw out some ridiculous request, and somebody somewhere within the organization—usually the one with the most common sense and the greatest experience—says, "Why, we can't do *that!*"

But, as I said earlier, I've found that whining works wonders. In the end, they've always had the kindness (and courage) to do things my way. So this time, when I asked if we could put the disclaimer on the cover, they just rolled their eyes, said their prayers, and hoped for the best. And the result is right here in your hands. I hope you have as much fun reading it as I've had in collecting all these little jewels of joy and putting them together for you!

I've figured out why people get gray hair.
It's from worrying about their teeth falling out!

Some women fight old age until the day they die. Lady Nancy Astor said, "I refuse to admit I am more than fifty-two, even if it does make my sons illegitimate."[11]

Fulfilling a friend's request that he scatter her husband's ashes from a small airplane, the Rev. Robert Fulghum dutifully carried the ashes aloft and tossed them out the open door of the little plane—only to have the wind send the ashes right back in the door, "filling the cockpit with the final dust of Harry, the deceased husband. Covering the widow, the pilot, and me," he wrote in his book *Uh-Oh*. "We flew back to the field in silence. . . . I can now add a practical paragraph to the *Minister's Manual*: 'If the ashes of the deceased are blown back into the cockpit, return to the airport and borrow a vacuum cleaner from the airport janitor and vacuum the deceased from the plane. NOTE: It is *very* important first to put a clean bag into the vacuum cleaner!'"[12]

Being tickled to death is a great way to live. Jumping for joy is good exercise.[13]

Signs you're getting old:
Dialing long distance wears you out.
You know all the answers,
but nobody asks you the questions!

You know it's time to throw in the towel
when you'd fall apart completely
if it weren't for static cling![14]

Many people's tombstones should read:
"Died at thirty. Buried at sixty."

Nicholas Murray Butler

There are three stages of life: youth, maturity, and
"My, you're looking good!"

President Dwight Eisenhower[15]

Those who love deeply never grow old; they may
die of old age, but they die young.

—English playwright
Sir Arthur Wing Pinero

Age gracefully? I think not! Age ferociously
instead. Seize everything valuable within reach.
Extend. Question. Give. The face will follow. All the
cosmetic surgeons in the world could never produce such a face.[16]

You know you're getting older when . . .
"Happy Hour" is a nap!

People who need to get older
Are much luckier
Than people who need to get younger!

Ashleigh Brilliant,
Pot-shot 2927, © 1983

A feeble, elderly woman, all hunched up and using a cane, limped into a doctor's office. Five minutes later, she came out, walking erect and without a limp.

A guy in the waiting room asked, "Gee, what did the doc do? You're doing just great."

The lady replied, "He gave me a longer cane."

Overheard at the beauty shop: "I knew her forty years ago, and she looked just like she does today: OLD!"

Stop the Conspiracy!

Have you ever noticed that when you're over the hill, everything seems *uphill* from where you are?

Stairs are steeper. Groceries are heavier. And *everything* is farther away. Yesterday I walked to the corner and was dumbfounded to discover how long our street had become.

And that's not all. People are less considerate now, especially the younger ones. They speak in whispers all the time, and if you ask them to speak up, they just repeat themselves, endlessly mouthing the same silent message until they're red in the face and exhausted. What do they think I am, a lip-reader?

And they drive so fast you're risking life and limb if you happen to pull onto the freeway in front of them. All I can say is, their brakes must wear out awfully fast, the way I see them screech and swerve in my rearview mirror.

Even clothing manufacturers are becoming less civilized these days. Why else would they suddenly start labeling a size 6 dress as a 12? Do they think no one notices that these things no longer fit around the waist, hips, thighs, and bosom?

The people who make bathroom scales are pulling the same prank but in reverse. Do they think I actually *believe* the number I see on that dial? Ha! I would *never* let myself weigh that much!

Just who do these people think they're fooling? I'd like to call up someone in authority to report what's going on—but the telephone company is in on the conspiracy. They've printed the phonebooks in such small type that no one could ever find a number there!

All I can do is pass along this warning: Maturity is under attack! Unless something drastic happens, pretty soon *everyone* will have to suffer these awful indignities.

Courtroom lawyer, questioning a potential juror:
Q: Have you lived in this town all your life?
A: Not yet!

Once you pass forty, your "big break" will probably be a bone.[17]

Beauty is only skin deep . . .
but fortunately, I have very deep skin.

Ashleigh Brilliant,
Pot-shot 4614, © 1988

"As far as the east is from the west, so far has He removed our transgressions from us." (Ps. 103:12 NASB)

Now, if God would just do that with our gray hair and wrinkles, we'd be in great shape!

Nancy L. Jackshaw[18]

If you can read these words without a magnifying glass, you have no business reading this book! You're obviously much too young and probably wouldn't understand the humor anyway! Go buy a comic book and come back in thirty years!

What's the difference between a terrorist and a menopausal woman?

You can negotiate with the terrorist!

Lord, deliver us from war, pollution,
and cellulite buildup.

© 1989 Remarkable Things,
Long Beach, California

Bumper Sticker:
SO MUCH WORK . . . So few women to do it.

No wonder I feel so tired—
I'm older now than I've ever been before!

Ashleigh Brilliant
Pot-shot 358, © 1972

Real Life Adventures by Gary Wise and Lance Aldrich

The first time you're offered a senior citizen discount.

Real Life Adventures © GarLanco. Reprinted with permission of
Universal Press Syndicate. All rights reserved.

Sign posted in a customer service department:
Suppose we refund your money,
send you another one without charge,
close the store, and have the manager shot.
Would THAT be satisfactory?!

You were taught, with regard to your former way of life, to put off your old self, . . . to be made new in the attitude of your minds; and to put on the new self, created to be like God in true righteousness and holiness. (Eph. 4:22–24)

Fat Farm Failures . . . and Other Excuses for the Middle-Age Spread

You have a heart of gold. That would explain why you weigh two hundred pounds!

After I had a hysterectomy several years ago, my doctor assured me it was just a myth that women automatically put on extra weight after menopause. "There's no reason why you should gain weight if you eat a sensible diet and get sufficient exercise," he said. The problem is . . . eating sensibly has never seemed like much fun to me!

For nearly a year after my surgery, I steadily gained a pound or two every month. My friend Mickey was experiencing the doctor's idea of the "myth" in the same way. So she and I decided we were never going to lose weight on our own; instead, we agreed we would splurge and have ourselves admitted to a fat farm—a spa located some fifty miles north of Los Angeles, out in the desert. Friends warned us we wouldn't get much to eat at this place, so we stopped at a fried chicken restaurant on the way for a bucket of reinforcements. We also took crackers and snacks in our luggage and sneaked everything into our room at the spa.

Sure enough; our friends were right. The food wasn't just scanty—it was almost microscopic! It did have nice names, however, like souffle of this and fillet of that. They served a lot of weak tea and fancy little cubes of gelatin with fingernail-size portions of whipped cream. One especially memorable dessert was called "tofu supreme."

We would have starved except for the fried chicken and crackers we ate in our room that first day. For dinner that night they served a small wedge of lettuce and a spoonful of fluffy yogurt.

The next day we had veggie burgers. Have you ever had a veggie burger? At this fat farm, a veggie burger was two very THIN oblong crackers with some strands of carrots, a pile of ground-up broccoli, and some bean sprouts smashed between the crackers! As we studied this sorry excuse for a lunch, Mickey and I had fun wondering what McDonald's might name this concoction if it were added to their menu. I thought they might call it the McSprout or the McSproccoli. Mickey opted for the Quarter-Ouncer.

But just thinking of McDonald's when our stomachs were so desperate for some real nourishment (that is, something fried and fattening) made us want to make a break for the nearest golden arches (which were at least a half-hour's drive away). So we couldn't play that game for long!

We were all expected to dress up for dinner each night. So there we sat, looking beautiful and starving to death. We were supposed to stay for four days, but the fried chicken only lasted until the first night, and we ran out of crackers and cheese the next afternoon. It was then that we decided to escape that place while we still had enough energy to make the drive home.

On the way back to LA we stopped at that same fried chicken place. Faint with hunger, we staggered up to the window and ordered the REALLY big bucket.

When someone sent me the following menu, it reminded me of those two long days at the fat farm. I don't know where it came from, but I think you'll quickly see why it's "guaranteed" to make you lose weight:

MONDAY
Breakfast: Weak tea
Lunch: Bouillon cube in 1/2 cup water
Dinner: 1 pigeon thigh
            3 ounces prune juice (to be gargled only)

TUESDAY
Breakfast: Scraped crumbs from burnt toast
Lunch: 1 doughnut hole
Dinner: 2 canary drumsticks

WEDNESDAY
Breakfast: Boiled-out stains of tablecloth
Lunch: Bellybutton from navel orange
Dinner: Bee's knees and mosquito knuckles

THURSDAY
Breakfast: Shredded eggshell skins
Lunch: 1/2 dozen poppy seeds
Dinner: 3 eyes from Irish potato (diced)

FRIDAY
Breakfast: 2 lobster antennae
Lunch: 1 guppy fin
Dinner: Fillet of soft-shell crab claws

SATURDAY
Breakfast: 4 chopped banana seeds
Lunch: Broiled butterfly liver
Dinner: Jellyfish vertebrae

SUNDAY
Breakfast: Pickled hummingbird tongue

Lunch: Prime ribs of tadpole
Dinner: Tossed paprika salad
         Aroma of empty custard pie plate
*Note: All meals are to be placed under a microscope while eaten—
to make them more filling.*

Source Unknown

Obviously, Mickey and I were big failures at abiding by the
rules; instead, we decided to leave the fat farm and farm our
fat ourselves! We probably shouldn't have gone together,
because neither one of us had enough will power, when it
came to food, to turn down a single morsel. We reminded
each other of the friend Erma Bombeck described when she
said it was just her luck to go to a fat farm and share a room
"with the only person there who had sewn Reese's Pieces into
the hem of her jacket."

**"My burger's still a little pink on the inside.
Hold the cigarette lighter up to it for a
couple of minutes, would ya?"**

Since then, I've been very good about watching my weight. I watch it go up and down and up and down. I heard some- one call this "the rhythm method of girth control!"

Actually I *do* watch what I eat—until I get it in my mouth; then I lose sight of it.

The Portly Majority

The only good thing about being plump, or well-upholstered, as I like to say, is that we're not alone. Despite all the diets, weight-loss clinics, fitness clubs, and self-help books, *millions* of us are overweight. In fact, the results of the most recent National Health and Nutrition Examination Survey show that "for the first time, overweight people outnumber normal- size ones in the United States."[1]

THIS IS *NOT* YOU AND IT'S *NOT* ME . . .

BUT JUST LOOKING AT HER MAKES ME FEEL BETTER.

Well, to those of you living "in the fat," I say, *Hang in there!* It may be true that "your bellybutton should not be touching your knees when you're standing,"[2] but there are ways to disguise your flab. You could always learn to alter your clothes so they fit your body more comfortably. But one problem with that, as Erma Bombeck predicted, is, "If you get a dress to fit your hips, you have enough material left over from the hem and sleeves to slipcover Brazil."[3]

Another alternative is the new body slimmers (the things we used to call corsets and girdles). And get this: In addition to squeezing your thighs, derriere, and torso into excruciatingly tight undergarments that are two sizes too small, you can now wear a girdle to control bat-wing arms. Someone sent me a newspaper clipping that described it as "a Lycra band to slip onto your arm and make it look firm under all those snug-fitting dresses and blouses."[4]

Totally Distracted

It just doesn't seem fair, does it? By the time we've reached this age, we've survived so many trials, failed at so many diets. About the only one I could ever follow was the Stress Diet.

Breakfast
1/2 grapefruit
1 slice whole wheat toast
8 oz. skim milk

Lunch
4 oz. broiled chicken breast
1 cup steamed zucchini
1 Oreo cookie
herb tea

Midafternoon Snack
Rest of the package of Oreos
1 quart rocky road ice cream
1 jar hot-fudge sauce

Dinner
2 loaves garlic bread
large pepperoni and mushroom pizza
3 candy bars
entire frozen cheesecake eaten directly from the freezer

Pamela Pettler[5]

This silly regimen reminds me of the diet Erma Bombeck described. She said, "One January I went on a seven-hundred-calorie-a-day diet. By the end of the month, I had eaten all my allotted calories through June 15." Erma liked to say that in two decades she'd lost "a total of 789 pounds. I should be hanging from a charm bracelet."

GLASBERGEN

© Randy Glasbergen

**"It's a low-cholesterol ice cream cone—
a scoop of mashed potatoes with sprinkles."**

Food Links

Now that we've passed the halfway point in life, many of us could use a breather—a brief respite between the exhaustion of getting our children to adulthood and the prospect of dealing with our parents' (or our own!) slide into la-la land. Sure there are other sources of comfort available to us: We could call a friend, go for a walk, or read our favorite passages of Scripture. But in all likelihood, our friend would have a new recipe to share, and if you're like me your favorite place to walk is to the donut shop! And, while Scripture is certainly a balm for my soul, it can also be a stimulant to my appetite. Maybe that's how some beloved passages get contorted like this one:

The Twenty-Third Cupcake

My doctor is my shepherd; I shall not weigh more.

He maketh me to lie down in green sweatpants; he ordereth me to do situps. He specify-eth my goal. He sendeth me down jogging trails of endless length for my heart's sake.

Yea, though I stroll by the door of the bake shop, I will not enter; my sweetrolls and crumbcake I secretly buy elsewhere.

I eatest my cupcakes in the presence of no one. I feast on rich Twinkies and Ding-Dongs. My cup's full of ice cream.

Surely huge hips and thunder thighs will haunt me all the days of my life, and I will live in a body of cellulite forever.

Ann Luna

You see, for some of us, everything we do reminds us of food, even reading Scripture! Or we see a baby's cute little toesies, and we think of bite-size Tootsie Rolls. We notice the wrinkles in an old man's smile and think of prunes. We pull our pantyhose over our thighs and think of cottage cheese. We gaze at majestic, snow-capped mountain peaks and see chocolate-marshmallow sundaes topped with whipped cream. And every time we look at the night sky we think of Milky Ways and Starbursts. It never ends! We can't even look at a traffic light in December without wondering whether the red and green M&Ms are in the stores yet.

A Fanatic for Food

It's a constant challenge for me to keep my mind off food—but I'm not quite as bad as those people who equate eating with a divine encounter! In a newspaper interview one person said, "Food is the closest thing to God because it brings everyone together and puts a smile on everyone's face."[6]

Another expert, the director of an eating disorders center, said, "For many women, loving food has become safer than loving a man. Food never breaks a date, doesn't criticize or reject you."[7] No wonder when we think of a "gorgeous hunk" these days the image of a refrigerator comes to mind! But that brings to mind the little quip someone sent me. It says:

> Diet Rule #2:
> Never weigh more than your refrigerator.[8]

We love to eat—but there's a downside: a big backside! So we go on a diet, but if food is "the closest thing to God" and "safer than loving a man," when we diet we're not just declining a second helping of mashed potatoes—we're destroying our whole psyche! Maybe that's why a fitness trainer put his finger right on the problem when he astutely announced:

> One of the problems with diets is the first
> three letters spell "die"![9]

Food can easily become the center of our lives, and when we try to break its hold on us, we sometimes feel like we're coming as close to death as we want to get on this side of the pearly gates!

You Know It's Time to Diet When . . .

There have been times in my life when I didn't worry about

STAYSKAL

"You weighed yourself on three scales and
none registered over 63 pounds?
Your diet must be working."

my weight; I had plenty of other worries to distract me! But
now that Bill and I have settled into our golden years, there
are fewer distractions—and more tempting things to eat.

And we may soon be tempted to eat even those things
we've never liked—because now they're being genetically
engineered to taste like something we *do* like. I read somewhere that scientists have already developed green peppers
that taste like apples. Next they may try to make Brussels
sprouts taste like grapes.[10] If only they could make strawberry
shortcake taste like anchovies and sweetrolls taste like
Limburger cheese—now *that* would be helpful to us perpetual
dieters!

There's rarely any good news about my favorite foods these
days. But someone did send me some wonderful news about
asparagus the other day (and I love asparagus!). It said, "Your

body expends more energy digesting asparagus than it takes in—four spears have thirteen calories, no fat, and considerable nutrients."[11] Now *that's* something to celebrate!

Unfortunately, asparagus is not the main staple of my diet. And although I don't *think* I'm overeating, and even though I try to be careful about making the right choices, somehow, like old age, the extra pounds just seem to magically appear. One day we're a sleek, size 10 glamour girl, and the next thing we know we're the mother of two kids, the grandmother of five, and the final resting place for about ten million fat cells! That reminds me of a little note sent to me recently by a friend who, like many of us, is constantly struggling with her weight. She said, "The beaded belt I wore years ago around my hips is now my necklace, and my rear end looks like an inflated parachute." Still, this darling woman can laugh at these challenges. In the note she said our friendship makes her "fat cells vibrate with laughter."

This lighthearted attitude seems to be the best alternative when it becomes obvious that those fat cells are *not* transients—somehow they're trying to take up permanent residence on our bodies. For many of us, that's a moment of great revelation—THE moment when we know it's time to diet. Some of the other indicators, according to clippings friends have sent me, are:

- You take a shower and nothing below your waist gets wet.

- You get a pedicure and have to look in a mirror to see what color the manicurist painted your toenails.

- You get out of breath just blinking your eyes in bright sunlight.

- Your finger gets stuck in the holes of the telephone dial.

- Tollbooth operators on the expressway suggest that next time you use the lane marked "WIDE LOADS."

- On hot days, small children flock to you to stay in the shade.

- Bus drivers ask you to sit up front to serve as an airbag for the rest of the passengers in case of a crash.

Losing Weight without Losing Your Mind

Actually, experts say that weight control is quite easy if you keep in mind these first two rules of successful dieting:

> There are only two things you need to avoid in order to lose weight: *food and drink!*

And . . .

> If it tastes good, spit it out!

If those guidelines are just a little too stringent for you, consider this more reasonable advice from Dr. Gabriel Cousens, a California physician and author of *Conscious Eating*, who suggests that at mealtime you eat a few bites with your eyes closed and focus on the food in your mouth. Focus on enjoying the meal "instead of considering it another task to be done efficiently."

I think Dr. Cousens's advice may be especially appropriate for us older folks, because many of us now have the luxury of time to try his suggestions. Most of us no longer have to eat in a rush; our days of holding the steering wheel in one hand and a Big Mac in the other while trying to control a rowdy Little League team in the back of the minivan are (we hope) over. So if we're eating in a hurry these days, it may be because it's a habit rather than a necessity.

Missing Motivators

Perhaps one reason why we women tend to gain weight in our later years is that we've run out of motivation. In past years, we went on crash diets for our prom, graduation, or

YOU'VE HEARD OF THE
ESTROGEN PATCH?

© 1997 Barbara Johnson.

NOW THERE'S SOMETHING NEW...
THE DIET PATCH!

wedding, then we tried to shed a few pounds for our children's baptism, twenty-five-year homecoming celebrations, or family reunions. But when all of those milestones are behind us, we develop other priorities—breathing, for example, or trying not to lose our minds while we wrestle with parents who need to be in a nursing home but refuse to go, or holding our families together when one of us struggles through a health crisis.

Sure we'd like to be thinner, but it just isn't happening. At that point, we have two options:

1. Lie.
2. Learn to live with it.

Despite Christian teachings, a lot of women choose the first alternative. In fact, a recent newspaper article said, "More of us lie about our weight (34 percent) than anything else—shaving off a few pounds to make ourselves feel better." If this is your choice, you might as well fudge a little on your age while you're at it. According to the same article, 20 percent of all American women do![12] If ever I have to give my weight, I just say, "I weigh one hundred and *plenty!*"

A woman has reached middle age
when the only pinches she gets
are from her girdle!

I like to think of banana cream pie as a fruit.

Pat Prints calendar, 1993

EXERCISE AND DIET
TO FIGHT HAZARDOUS WAISTS!

Class Reunion

My class reunion's coming,
    and I don't know what to do.
My weight and chins have doubled
    since the year of '42.

I look into the mirror and—
    Good grief! How can this be?
Gray hair, false teeth, thick glasses—
    It's my mother's face I see!

But I head out to the party.
    No sense moping, I decide.
I'll just have to grin and bear it.
    (But I'm dying, deep inside.)

Then I walk into the banquet hall
    And stop. There's some mistake.
Not a single classmate do I find.
    Did I confuse the date?

Still, the faces seem familiar,
    As each one I keenly stare at . . .
Then I realize I'm looking at—Good grief!
    My classmates' parents!

Ann Luna

A Dieter's Malapropisms:
    It's on the fork of my tongue.
    Take it with a bag of salt.
    May a mighty oak grow from these tiny mustard
seeds of faith.

You can't have your chicken and eggs too.

People who live in glass houses shouldn't throw sour grapes.

How to Plant a Special Garden

First, plant five rows of peas: Preparedness, Promptness, Perseverance, Politeness, and Prayer.

Next to them, plant three rows of squash: Squash Gossip, Squash Criticism, and Squash Indifference.

Then five rows of lettuce: Let us be faithful, Let us be unselfish, Let us be loyal, Let us be truthful, Let us love one another.

And no garden is complete without turnips: Turn up for church, Turn up with a smile, Turn up with determination.[13]

Keep smiling!
The luscious plum forgot to—
and became a wrinkled prune.[14]

Wouldn't it be wonderful if there were a delicious, "all-natural" food that is nutritious, fat-free, has no cholesterol, and promotes good health?

There is! You'll find it described in Galatians 5:22–23—the "fruit of the Spirit." This fruit is wholesome and beneficial—and it's even better when shared![15]

Middle age
is when you choose your cereal
for the fiber,
not for the toy.

I've reached the age
where it's harder and harder
to think of my body as a temple.
(It's more like a building project
that got out of control!)

If there is a fountain of youth,
it is almost certainly caffeinated.[16]

Beauty is skin deep,
but stupid goes all the way through.[17]

No one is lonely while eating spaghetti.
It requires too much attention!

I'm not fat . . .
I'm calorically gifted!

The cheerful heart has a continual feast. (Prov. 15:15)

A Fact of Aging:
What You Lose in Elasticity
You Gain in Wisdom

It's not that I'm against exercise.
It's just that when I look at my body
I feel it's already been punished enough!

Until a few years ago, my favorite thing to exercise was my right to vote! The only time my heart rate got into the "workout zone" was while I was waiting in the checkout line, nervously wondering if I'd have enough money to pay for all the groceries I'd piled in the cart for Bill and our four perpetually hungry sons. My idea of *strenuous* exercise was, as someone said, to fill the tub, pull the plug, then fight the current!

It's not that I sat around grooming my collection of dust bunnies or eating bonbons. As the years have gone by, Bill and I have stayed busy by traveling for speaking appearances and running Spatula Ministries. We used to get our weight-training experience by delivering industrial-size bags of catfood for a ninety-year-old neighbor lady who had thirty-five cats and was no longer able to go to the store herself.

Actually, I thought we were in pretty good shape. No, we weren't going to be asked to pose as models for any fitness gyms, and you won't find my portrait in that new pinup calendar that features shapely models who've lived at least half a century, but we managed to meet the World Health Organization's definition of fitness: We were "able to meet the challenges of daily life."[1] That attitude changed when I was diagnosed a few years ago with adult-onset diabetes. At that

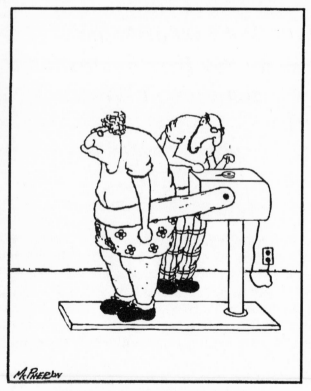

"You want it set on low, medium, high, or industrial strength?"

point, exercise—*real* exercise—suddenly took on new impor-
tance. My doctor told me exercise was absolutely essential if I
planned to stay attached to all my fingers and toes.

Somehow I just couldn't see myself squeezing my sixty-
year-old body into one of those svelte leotards and jogging off
to a gym. There had to be another way. Finally I came up with
what seems to be the perfect solution—for me, at least.

When we're at home, the things that consume most of my
time are the mail and the telephone. The mail to Spatula
Ministries is delivered in big rectangular tubs that we pick
up at the post office. (I've decided our address should be a
post office TUB number, rather than a box number, because
BOX sure doesn't describe the barrel-size bin where our mail
ends up.)

Because it's so much faster, I try hard to respond to as
many letters as possible with a phone call instead of a letter.
That's lots of phone calls! But while I'm on the phone, I'm also
on my exercise bike. (So if you get a phone call from me someday and I sound a little out of breath, it's *not* because I've
exhausted myself dialing those long-distance numbers, as
some jokester said about old people.)

Bill set up my exercise bike in my Joy Room, an addition to
our mobile home that's filled with funny plaques, pictures,
toys, gadgets, dolls, and all manner of hilarious stuff folks have
sent me over the years.[2] As I pedal my bike, I enjoy all those
goofy things in the Joy Room while talking on the phone.

While I'm riding the bike, I'm also touring the country—
making imaginary trips along a big, colored map of the
United States Bill posted on one wall of the Joy Room in front
of the exercise bike. As I cycle along, I stick a pushpin into the
map every twenty-five miles so I can keep track of how many
miles I've accumulated. Seeing those pins march across the
map helps keep me motivated! It's been a couple of years now
since I started this routine, rolling out of our home here in
California while staying put right in my Joy Room. I try to
ride the bike ten to fifteen miles every day we're home, so by
the time you read this, I should be closing in on Philadelphia!

But following a cross-country route is not the only thing I do to stay motivated. On a table by the exercise bike I keep a list of Spatula friends so that, as I near a city, I can look to see who lives there. Then I pray for that person, asking God to be especially close to her that day and to wrap her in His big comfort blanket of love and let her feel His presence that day.

My goal is to cover all fifty states this way. (It might take awhile to pedal to Alaska and Hawaii, but I'm determined!) As I look at the route on the map and check my address list to see who lives along the way, I also pay attention to the weather reports. If the weather is cold, I may put on some earmuffs—just to get into the spirit of things; as I cross the desert I may sip iced tea while I pedal along.

EXERCISE IS VERY IMPORTANT AS YOU
GET OLDER...MY GRANDMOTHER
STARTED WALKING FOUR MILES
A DAY WHEN SHE TURNED 60...

SHE'S 97 NOW, AND WE DON'T KNOW
WHERE THE HECK SHE IS!

This method works for me. While I strengthen my heart and lungs I'm also strengthening my spiritual life—putting some zing into my conversations with God by praying for specific friends (maybe one of them is YOU!).

Find Something Fun to Do

Of course, my system won't work for everyone—and I don't follow the same routine every day. Sometimes I ride a *real* bike; Bill and I even have a tandem bicycle we pedal around the neighborhood. (The problem with this is that Bill rides in front and can't really tell what's going on behind him, so it's tempting for me to just relax and enjoy the ride without putting out much effort!)

As many of you know, we live in a mobile home park where there are lots of retired folks (some of us are more retired than others). One day I was out riding my ten-speed around the park and stopped to let a little old white-haired lady cross the bike trail. As she hobbled in front of me, she smiled and said, "My, honey, it's sure nice to see someone around here with dark hair for a change!"

Of course, she didn't know that I call my hair my "convertible top." No one else besides my hairdresser and God knows what's underneath! But the old lady's comment lifted my spirit and made me feel much younger than my years. That's one advantage of exercising out in the neighborhood— I may encounter someone who offers a friendly hello or a word of encouragement.

So now, in the same way that dear little lady's comment motivated me to keep going, I encourage you to exercise so you can enjoy these later years in life. The experts say that exercise has more than just physical benefits; it not only helps us control our weight and maintain good circulation, it also adds to our sense of well-being by helping us fight stress, be hopeful, and stay young at heart.

Dr. James Rippe, author of *Fit Over Forty*, says, "It's hard to find a better prescription than staying physically active and optimistic." Staying active, he says, improves our chances for a healthier, more enjoyable life.[3]

You might be surprised to discover how easily you can work moderate exercise into your daily routine. If you can't picture yourself pedaling an exercise bike, consider working out with one of those large rubber bands while you talk on the phone. You can find them at most sporting-goods stores, and they're usually less than ten dollars for a package of three. Just loop one end of the band around your foot and hold the other loop in your hand, and you can work your leg and arm muscles while you're working your jaws! (Just be sure to take it off before you try to get out of your chair so you don't fly through the house like you've been fired out of a slingshot!)

Even washing windows or waxing the car is good exercise, if you happen to enjoy that kind of thing. If you don't stay too long at the bargain tables, shopping can be beneficial too. And of course, dancing is another way many older people get their exercise. All over the country, gray-haired dancers are breezing through classes at places ranging from Dance Masters to Jazzercise.

One of the easiest but most effective ways to exercise is just to walk. Experts say this (and most other forms of exercise) are especially effective after dinner. By exercising after your evening meal, they say, you not only burn extra calories, you get yourself out of the house, where you might be tempted to settle onto the sofa and continue eating as you watch TV.

Know the Enemy!
There's a little quip that says:

> Over the years, I've learned who is my friend and who is NOT my friend.
> GRAVITY is NOT my friend!

Well, for some of us, that sofa is the enemy too! A newsletter from the Baylor College of Medicine in Houston said, "The most exhausting part of exercising is the mental argument that takes place when you try to talk yourself into getting up off the couch and *just doing it!*"⁴ Remember: "All glory comes from daring to begin."⁵

But *when* to begin? That's the question. I love columnist Dave Barry's answer to that perplexing question: "Not today, certainly. You've done enough today! I would rule tomorrow out, also, seeing as how it comes so soon after today. You rush into these things, and the next thing you know you've strained a ligament or something. So I would say the best time to begin would be first thing after Easter, although not the one coming up."⁶

Barry also points out another advantage of exercise you may not have realized: A growing familiarity with PAIN!

> People who exercise regularly are prepared for . . . pain. Take joggers: you see them plodding along, clearly hating every minute of it, and you think, "What's the point?" But years from now, when you're struggling to adjust to the pains of the aging process, the joggers, who have been in constant agony for 20 years, will be able to make the transition smoothly, unless they're already dead.⁷

All right, now. That's enough foolishness. Let's get back to the challenge at hand: finding a form of exercise that works for you. Remember, it doesn't even have to involve activities that have traditionally been considered exercise. For example, one article I saw said that even *fidgeting* can play a role in keeping off the pounds. That's terrific news for those restless types who can't sit still for more than a minute without popping up to water a plant, straighten a picture, or adjust the mini blinds.

I'll bet you never realized you were becoming more fit while you fidgeted! But that's possible. The article said that researchers from the National Institutes of Health estimated that "people who paced the room, moved arms and legs frequently, or changed seated positions burned 138 to 685 extra calories per day."⁸

INSIDE ME THERE'S A THIN WOMAN STRUGGLING TO GET OUT...

How To Starve and Sweat

© Randy Glasbergen

BUT I CAN USUALLY SEDATE HER WITH 4 OR 5 CUPCAKES!

There's a new-fangled idea that just might be more appealing than fidgeting. It's called belly-rolling, and while I haven't tried it yet, it *sounds* like something that could certainly make me laugh whether or not it works as a fitness aid.

The gadget is a GIANT, sturdy ball about three feet in diameter that's supposed to be a real boon for "those who haven't worked out in a while or have back problems." According to one report, it's used to increase flexibility and strength, especially in folks in their forties and fifties. One way to use it is to "drape yourself over the ball, facedown, arms at sides, knees bent, toes touching the floor, and ball positioned directly beneath the midsection. Hang there thirty seconds or more, allowing back and shoulders to stretch and relax. Exhale and gently lift head and chest until completely off ball, holding two to three seconds."[9]

Just picturing myself draped over that giant beachball makes me laugh. It's so easy to imagine all sorts of silly scenarios—like the ball rolling over with me still attached to it, arms and legs flying out in every direction, clearing a broad path through our mobile home park! Now THAT would give the old folks something to talk about around the shuffleboard court!

Blazing Birthdays

Sometimes, as hard as we try to stay in shape, birthdays still take their toll on us. And other times, birthdays themselves can be disastrous, as this silly letter describes:

Dear Esther,

I'm sorry you couldn't make it to my recent birthday party. Apparently, it was quite an event—not that I remember much about it.

They tell me the problems started when I drew in a big breath to blow out the eighty-four candles someone had set afire on top of my birthday cake and, blinded by the glaring blaze and disoriented by the merciless heat, I forgot why I was holding my breath and temporarily lost consciousness.

Luckily, my daughter and her family had decided to host the party beside their swimming pool, so instead of breaking my hip in a disastrous fall to the kitchen floor, I toppled backward into the pool. The water was so cold, I instantly awakened from my faint, screaming at the top of my lungs and, as a result, losing my dentures in the deep end of the pool.

Without a moment's hesitation, my nephew Joey

dived in and swam to the bottom to retrieve my teeth, but when he tried to resurface, he accidentally became entangled in the billowing fabric of my tent-shaped housedress, and together we kicked and flapped and squawked, undulating repeatedly until my wig finally let go and floated off, ghost-like, in the churning water.

Thinking one of her puppies was drowning, the old dog Sparky jumped in next, swimming determinedly into the fray to rescue the wig.

It was about that time that my birthday cake, with all seven dozen candles still burning, suddenly ignited like a sparkler and set the paper tablecloth on fire.

Fortunately, the firefighters arrived within minutes, and if the firetruck had been hauling water I suppose everything would have turned out okay. But the truck's tanks were empty, so one of the firefighters, his yellow rubber coat popping and squeaking loudly as he ran, dropped a pumper hose in the pool.

I thought for sure he would rescue us, as we were still flapping and squawking in the icy water, but Sparky apparently mistook him for some sort of monster—perhaps a loud and lurching fire hydrant—and she suddenly began barking so ferociously that the poor man dropped the hose and never looked back. He said later he wondered why the old dog was so zealously guarding that undulating mass of inflatable beach toys.

Eventually, the pumping lowered the water level in the pool until our feet could touch bottom. But by then the whole backyard was a swirling vortex of flames and smoke. I couldn't see a thing, what with all the haze and chaos—and the fact that one lens of my bifocals had popped out when I hit the water. But Sparky obviously has either sharp eyesight or a keen memory despite her many years. She took off like a rocket after that same poor firefighter and took a big chunk out of his thigh before he scrambled up the only tree in the yard that wasn't burning.

I guess Joey and I looked a little bedraggled as we groped our way out of the pool and through the swirling curtain of smoke and chaos. We tried to slip, unseen, out of the growing crowd, but the firefighters mistook us for arsonists trying to avoid detection and quickly called the police, who were already in route in response to another call about a crazed and rabid dog wreaking havoc on our property.

I tried to explain what had happened, but since Joey had left my dentures back in the pool, no one could understand a word I was saying. They hauled us both off to jail, bringing Sparky along as a material witness.

It was nearly midnight before my daughter and her husband finally came to bail us out. I was surprised when they dropped me off at the YWCA, saying I would have to stay there for a little while. It was a little sad to think I had completely missed celebrating my birthday.

I hope you're doing well. Please give my regards to everyone at the nursing home. I'll try to give you plenty of notice next year so you can join me for a piece of birthday cake—if my daughter's house is rebuilt by then.

                                            Gertrude

Look in the Mirror

A lot of us are at that awkward age when Father Time starts catching up with Mother Nature. We can always claim that old age is about ten years older than we are, but let's face it: We're at that point in life when everything starts to wear out, fall out, or spread out.

Sometimes I'm tempted to adapt a line I see every day on my car and transpose it onto the full-length mirror in my bedroom. It would say:

IMAGES IN MIRROR ARE SMALLER
THAN THEY APPEAR.

You see, just like so many things, fitness and exercise are affected by our attitudes about ourselves. As someone said, "Attitude is the mind's paintbrush. It can color any situation."

When you look in the mirror, you can still see your smooth, unlined face just the way it was twenty or thirty years ago—unless, that is, you insist on wearing your glasses while you're looking in the mirror! (Let's face it, many of us have eyesight that's deteriorating faster than our faces!) The point is, don't be too hard on yourself. And look on the bright side. That's the attitude of the woman who reported that she looked in the mirror each morning and said, "Thank you, dear Lord, that wrinkles don't HURT!"

The Older the Better

There are a lot of things that can make you feel old, and looking into the mirror (if you're wearing your glasses and the WRONG attitude) is one of them. But there's good news. An article I saved from several years ago suggests if we can get past sixty-five, we usually feel BETTER about getting old. It's that stretch between sixty and sixty-five that seems to be the problem.

For example, one study showed that significantly more people between ages sixty and sixty-four visit the doctor than those who are sixty-five to sixty-nine. It seems that people in their early sixties are nearing the transition time that will pole-vault them into retirement. They begin to feel age "creeping up on them," and they start worrying about their health.

This theory says that how old you feel also depends on who you spend your time with. People in their early sixties may still be dealing quite a bit with younger friends and peers, particularly in the workplace, and they may feel slower than those who are in their fifties or even younger. But when retirement happens, people over sixty-five tend to spend more time with those their own age, and they're comfortable with that group because, in many cases, they may even feel a bit stronger than their peer group.[10]

Maybe it's all a matter of perception. At sixty you can get up in the morning and decide you feel weak "because you're getting older." But at sixty-six, you get up in the morning and conclude that you feel pretty good for your age.

Stay Flexible

This choice illustrates the two basic ways we can deal with aging: Negatively, by letting it wear us down, or POSITIVELY, by choosing to see how the pluses far outweigh the minuses. One way to deal positively with the advancing years is to stay as fit as we possibly can. And, of course, it always helps to be able to laugh. As Ashleigh Brilliant says,

> Life becomes much easier,
> once you get through
> youth, middle age, and old age.

> Ashleigh Brilliant
> Pot-shot 2584, © 1982

When you're old, the challenge is not in bending down to touch your toes.

It's in remembering what you're there for once you arrive.

Two old ladies in a rest home were talking. One of them said to the other, "It's my birthday. I'm eighty years old, and, by George, I want to do something shocking, so I'm going to streak the cafeteria today."

Sure enough, she runs by the cafeteria with nothing on.

Two old men, eating sloppy joes, see her. One of them says to the other, "Say, Alma's jogging clothes are looking kinda wrinkled today, aren't they?"[11]

Erma Bombeck said when she went to sign up for an exercise class, they told her to wear loose clothing.

"I said, 'Are you kidding? If I had any loose clothing I wouldn't need to take the class!'"

They say life begins at fifty.
It begins, all right—
it begins to DISINTEGRATE!

It's tough to be at the age at which,
when you go all out,
you end up all in.

Remember, you may be OLDER today than you have ever been before, but you are YOUNGER than you will ever be again!

Time may be a great healer . . .
But it's a lousy beautician!

I've reached that point in life where
the only thing I can exercise is CAUTION!

Great news: Laughing one hundred times is the physiological equivalent to working out on a rowing machine for ten minutes! The problem is, once I get going, I'm afraid I won't be able to stop, and I'll laugh myself into anorexia![12]

Thank you for calling the Weight Loss Hotline. If you'd like to lose half a pound right now, press 1 eighteen thousand times.[13]

At our age, forget the natural ingredients.
We need all the artificial color and
preservatives we can get!

The show is really over when you find yourself picking your teeth out of the popcorn.

Finish each day and be done with it.
You have done what you could;
Some blunders and absurdities no doubt crept in.
Forget them as soon as you can.
Tomorrow is a new day;
You shall begin it well and serenely.

Ralph Waldo Emerson

WOMEN: It's easy to go for the burn—
just sit around and wait for a hot flash.

Those who hope in the LORD
    will renew their strength.
They will soar on wings like eagles;
    they will run and not grow weary,
    they will walk and not be faint. (Isa. 40:31)

Growing Old Is Inevitable;
Growing Up Is Optional

Wild in the spirit—twinges in the hinges.

To tell the truth, I didn't pay a lot of attention last year when news reports said American astronaut Shannon Lucid was breaking the world record for a woman in space. But when she came back home after spending more than six months aboard the Russian space station *Mir*, I was awestruck by the pictures.

Fascinated, I watched as Dr. Lucid waved to the crowds as she returned to Florida. Later, I watched again as she was greeted by the president upon her arrival back in Houston. While the rest of the world was probably marveling at her courage and intelligence, I watched it all and couldn't get over one wonderfully startling fact: *SHANNON LUCID HAS GRAY HAIR!*

Of course, that was after 188 days in space. I'm not sure *what* color her hair was before she moved in with the Russians! But that's not the point. The wonderful thing is that when most people think of astronauts they think of YOUNG, athletic daredevils with movie-star looks and cocky attitudes. Instead, here's the holder of an incredible space-endurance record, and SHE'S A MIDDLE-AGED WOMAN!

Shannon Lucid set this extraordinary record at the age of fifty-three on her FIFTH mission into space! So I hope she continues to let that gray hair show; I hope she's still breaking space records when she becomes a grandmother. It's such an inspiration for the rest of us who are over fifty and, like Shannon Lucid, continue to face challenges.

In the welcome-home ceremonies, President Clinton said when Shannon was in eighth grade, she told her teacher she wanted to be a rocket scientist. Her teacher replied that "there was no such thing and that if there were it wouldn't be a woman," the president said.[1]

Keep on Dreaming!

In these later years of our lives, some of us may be confronted by the kind of long odds and tall roadblocks that little Shannon ran into when she shared her dream with that rather narrow-minded teacher. In the same way, it may seem that we're running out of time to accomplish the dream we have for ourselves. Perhaps we're starting to think it will never be anything more than a dream—and that even if the dream were "do-able," someone else would *do* it, not us. After all, we may tell ourselves, we're getting on in years, and dreams are for younger people.

For many women in what I like to call "the second half of our first century," the challenge is not to accomplish some life-long dream but just to cope, to survive one more day. During these years, we may be struggling with children who are still giving us fits even though they're adults, or maybe we're trying to survive the loss of a child. Many women in this age bracket have parents whose health—or sanity—is fading, and they're also coping with husbands who are enduring all these same problems plus their own midlife crises. Or we may be dealing with a break in a family relationship due to death, divorce, or alienation of some sort. Or perhaps you're at a point when life seems to be whizzing by and leaving you in the dust. Maybe just getting up in the morning is a challenge for you.

Well, here's a statistic that should nudge you right off that mattress and onto your feet: "In an ordinary year, about 130 Americans—or one out of every two million—will die from falling out of bed. Over the same period, one out of four hundred will be injured just lying in bed, generally because of the headboard collapsing, the frame giving way, or some other mechanical failure!"[2]

Tight Corner by Ken Grundy and Malcolm Willett

**When catching a falling star, make
sure it fits in your pocket.**

See? You're not safe in bed anyway, so you might as well get up and get going. Climb up out of your rut, pull yourself upright—and do something courageous!

As I was accumulating material for this book, I tagged the folder for this chapter "risk-taking" because that's what I'm urging you to do in these pages: Be bold, take a chance, do something different, push back a barrier, or, in those cases when you think you're at the end of your rope, KEEP BREATHING! Whether it's something as simple as attending church again after a lapse or something as potentially frightening as dating again after your marriage ends due to death or divorce, I hope you'll take a good look at what's left of your life and choose to make it meaningful.

Choose Life

The sentiments expressed by the late Douglas MacArthur still hold true today. He said, "Whatever your years, there is in every being's heart the love of wonder, the undaunted challenges of events, the unfailing childlike appetite for what comes next, and the joy of the game of life. You are as young as your hope, as old as your despair."

In other words, it's your choice. You can choose to "grow young" and hopeful—or you can wallow in your despair and age quickly. I know it's scary to take risks, to try something new, because we can't help but wonder, *What if we fail? What if we get into this and realize we've made a HUGE mistake?* Well, you have to figure . . . at this point in your life, this won't be the FIRST mistake you've ever made, and no matter how bad it is, it probably won't be the WORST mistake you've ever made. And unless you fail at something REALLY adventurous (like swimming the English Channel or attempting an Evel Knievel–style motorcycle jump over the Grand Canyon), it probably won't be your LAST mistake, either! And in all likelihood, what you GAIN in wisdom, experience, and character by taking this risk will far outweigh any problems that occur, even if things don't go exactly as you hoped. And you'll become a better person for having tried.

Somewhere I saw a line that said:

THE PERSON WHO RISKS NOTHING
DOES NOTHING, HAS NOTHING, IS NOTHING!

Max Lucado puts it this way:

> Life has rawness and wonder. Pursue it. Hunt for it. Don't listen to the whines of those who have settled for a second-rate life and want you to do the same. Your goal is not to live long; it's to live.
>
> Jesus says the options are clear. To be safe, you can build a fire in the hearth, stay inside, and keep warm and dry. You can't get hurt if you never get out, right? You can't be criticized for what you don't try, right? You can't fail if you don't take a stand, right? . . . So don't try it. Take the safe route.
>
> Instead of building a fire in your hearth, however, you can build a fire in your heart. Follow God's impulses. Adopt a child. Move overseas. Teach a class. Change careers. Run for office. Make a difference. Sure it isn't safe, but what is?
>
> You think staying inside is safe? Jesus disagrees. "Whoever seeks to save his life will lose it." Reclaim the curiosity of your childhood. Just because you're near the top of the hill doesn't mean you've passed your peak.[3]

Laughter Brings Blessings

Many older women, especially those who suddenly find themselves alone, hesitate trying something new because they might look foolish. Thank heaven for braver souls— like the friend of Spatula Ministries who had a very clever and generous idea for helping her church raise money for a new building. At a "service auction" held by the church fund-raisers, she sold eight singing telegrams, which she merrily "delivered" for the purchasers. Then something magical happened:

> Soon I began receiving calls. I went to the post office for a sixtieth birthday. To the park for an aunt's eightieth birthday. To a nursing home to sing for a mother's eightieth birthday, and so on. The more I went out the sillier I dressed. Usually I used the same song but individualized it for the occasion. Everyone received me so graciously and I had great fun. Laughter brings such blessings!

Now, you know this darling gal probably felt foolish the first time she arrived at the post office and announced that she was going to SING for someone! But she overcame those fears and earned a blessing while spreading joy to others.

The Magical Mix of Laughter and Tears

Risk-takers' lives are enriched, not just by the joy we experience, but also by the tears we shed. Remember, it takes both sunshine and rain to make the rainbow. That's a principle of life the Disney studios discovered when they began making feature-length animated cartoons.

One of the first such cartoons, *Snow White*, was a huge commercial success, but subsequent animated features didn't do as well. When the Disney experts analyzed failures and compared them to *Snow White*, they discovered that "the films that people would pay to see again and again had two ingredients—laughter *and* tears! Everything they did from that point had to have both elements before it was released."[4]

Don't be afraid! As one writer said, "Confident people are not afraid of suffering, for suffering brings experience, and experience, wisdom. Sufferings of this present time will seem insignificant as we keep our eyes on the future."[5]

Step out in faith and do what you feel led to do, whether it's something simple, like volunteering for a new outreach ministry with your church, or something more complicated—like applying for astronaut training!

And if you need help in venturing out of your shell, here are ten steps that will help give you a friendly little boost of confidence—a gentle push out the door—as you set off on your journey:

1. Begin the day in a calm and cheerful mood. Say, "This is going to be a good day. I will be calm and cheerful today."

2. Try smiling at others. A smile is contagious and you will feel better as others smile at you.

3. Count your blessings. List them one by one. Do you ever realize the real wealth you have?

4. Enjoy this day with beautiful thoughts, pleasant memories. Live life one day at a time.

5. Be adventurous. Try walking and see new neighborhoods, new buildings and parks, new scenery.

6. Give a friend a phone call or write a letter. Let that person know he or she is in your thoughts and prayers. Offer a word of encouragement—the oxygen to the soul.

7. Be a happy person. See the bright side of life. Having a cheerful, loving attitude lends itself to your best health.

8. Do a good deed or give something beneficial to a loved one.

9. Give of yourself; offer your services to a hospital or church. Help people. The law of giving will reward you tenfold.

10. Do the best you can each day. You are really living only when you are useful and constructive.[6]

Stepping Out in Faith
My life has been sprinkled with many kinds of "risks"—mostly ridiculous pranks I've pulled to ward off my own

brushes with insanity! One of them occurred back in 1980 when the beautiful Crystal Cathedral was about to open here in Orange County, California. Dr. Robert Schuller had invited several dignitaries to be a part of the dedication ceremonies: Billy Graham, Los Angeles mayor Tom Bradley, the late Norman Vincent Peale, and opera singer Beverly Sills, to name a few. It was a very elaborate event, and admission was by invitation only.

We had a houseguest at that time—Andy, a darling college student who was visiting us. He had read all about the big, gala event, and he said to me, "Let's go!"

I explained that in no way could *we* ever get in because it was for dignitaries—important folks and invited guests—not little peons like us. But he was determined to get in; he even made a bet with me that he could figure out a way to get us *both* inside.

We drove down there—it's just about a fifteen-minute ride from our home—and parking was almost impossible. We had to leave the car far down the street and walk back to the entrance. The ceremonies were just about to commence; flags were fluttering high, and the orchestra was playing as the VIP guests were being seated in their special places of honor.

In my purse I carry a little telephone beeper that clicks and whirs to let me retrieve telephone messages when I'm away from home. Andy had seen me use it; as we neared the front entrance, he asked for the gizmo. Then, grasping it firmly in front of him, he hurriedly approached a red-coated usher who had been greeting guests and passing out programs at the front door.

With me hurrying to stay up with him, Andy stepped up close to the usher and said in a low tone that only she could hear, "We're from security, and we have to check out the platform for a possible bomb."

Immediately the usher hustled us inside the door, and we proceeded at a rapid pace down to the front of the Crystal Cathedral, where the audience was eagerly anticipating the beginning of the program. Andy thrust the little beeper into the potted palms and flower arrangements situated around the platform, pressing the clicker to make it beep. He moved around with a concerned look on his face while I struggled not to laugh. After all, we were in plain view of *everyone* in the audience, and we were *definitely* not dressed for this! Andy was in blue jeans and a sport shirt, and I was wearing slacks and a blouse.

After several beeps and clicks with his head down in the planters, Andy whirled around to signal a thumbs-up to the startled usher, who had returned to the door. Then he briskly walked back up the aisle and out the side door, with me hot on his heels. I did spot a few familiar faces in the audience as we retreated; their bewildered expressions nearly did me in. It was all I could do to keep from guffawing as we tripped back up the aisle. But I managed to get outside before we both erupted into gales of laughter—and Andy quickly reminded me that he had won the bet.

Now, before we go any further, I need to say emphatically that security at the Crystal Cathedral today is very sophisticated; it would be impossible now to do what Andy and I did that day. Someone trying to pull off such a prank would be courteously escorted to a holding room until the authorities could come and transport him to the nearest mental hospital!

The really amazing thing is that the Crystal Cathedral has welcomed me many times since then; in fact, I've been invited to speak at women's conferences there, and my Spatula group has been meeting there regularly for the past twelve years! A couple of years ago, I was the guest on *Hour of Power*, a nationally televised program from the Crystal Cathedral that airs every Sunday morning. Decked out in a big straw hat covered with red geraniums, I was interviewed by Dr. Bruce Larson, who talked about my book, *Stick a Geranium in Your Hat and Be Happy*. He told the audience about three of my books being on the bestseller list at that time, and he spoke supportively about our work with hurting parents.

As I stood there, looking out over that vast audience and taking in the beauty and the overwhelming spectacle of that glorious place, suddenly an image ignited my mind: Andy and I, nosing through the palms on the edge of the platform, looking for fictitious bombs. If you ever see a tape of that interview, you'll see that I appear to be on the verge of uncontrollable laughter at one point in the program—that's when I remember Andy's and my first visit to that fabulous place.

Dr. Schuller has been most kind to our ministry in the years since the Crystal Cathedral opened. Recently he wrote me a letter, congratulating me on the success of my last book, *I'm So Glad You Told Me What I Didn't Wanna Hear*. He ended the letter by saying, "Your life is blessed to be a blessing!"

What a wonderful phrase—"blessed to be a blessing." Surely if this is true then I'm expected to take a few risks here and there to make sure that blessing gets passed on! That thought pushed me to risk saying yes to an "extra" invitation I received last year when Bill and I were in New Orleans for a conference. Usually when we travel the timing is pretty tight and we don't have any free time for side trips, but a Spatula friend had heard I was going to be speaking in New Orleans, and she called and asked if we could come to her small town in Mississippi and join her and her husband for lunch.

Her hometown is more than a two-hour drive from New Orleans, so arranging a quick visit wasn't easy. But she is a precious friend who has been through a difficult loss, and I was delighted to be able to arrange our schedule so we could have lunch with her.

When we arrived at her home, we were expecting a quiet, simple lunch with just the four of us. But when our friend greeted us at the door with her beautiful smile and her melodious southern drawl, she said, "*Bah-bra*, the most unusual thing has happened! We have to go to the Ramada Inn for lunch, because we have more than 450 ladies wanting to meet you!"

"What!" I answered, aghast. The astonished look on my face made her rush on with an explanation. She said her husband had mentioned to his Sunday school class that we were coming . . . and after that the calls quickly came pouring in. The next thing they knew, they were calling the hotel to arrange a banquet-size luncheon!

As we drove up to the hotel, the ladies were lined up around the entrance. In any other situation, what happened next might have been ugly, but these lovely women were so patient it didn't seem to matter that the bookstore, which had quickly set up a table to sell my books, ran out. Nor did anyone get upset when the serving staff ran out of food . . . and eating utensils . . . and chairs. Despite all the shortages—and the big change in plans—we had a terrific time of fellowship and sharing. One lady told me the last "important" person to visit there was Barry Goldwater!

We took a little risk in going there—our schedule was tight, and we were already exhausted as we made that two-hour trip. But what a boost those merry women gave to us. It was a real splash of joy for my memory treasure chest.

Plunging into Public Speaking

One of the risks that quickly grew out of Spatula Ministries was the public speaking appearances. At first it was a little scary to think of standing up in front of an audience and telling my story. The first few times, I was afraid I might forget what I wanted to say . . . that I would cry at the sad parts or that no one would laugh at the funny parts . . . or that someone might be offended by something I said. But I felt God's love pushing me up to the microphone—and the rest was easy. Now I've done it so often I feel confident the Lord will propel the story each time I step up to the podium.

Still, you just never know how accommodating the facility will be or what kind of response an audience will have. At several gatherings in the last couple of years, the facility has been overcrowded and women had to be turned away or shuttled into cramped "overflow" rooms. At one luncheon gathering recently, the church sponsoring the event had ordered box lunches for all the attendees—but there were many more people than they had planned for, and they ran out of food. Being resourceful women, the conference organizers called the city's Rescue Mission, which sent over delicious meals for the two hundred hungry women who hadn't gotten served. There wasn't a single complaint; some women even said the Rescue Mission's lunches were tastier than the catered ones!

My years of public speaking have rewarded me with many blessings. One of them is that I've met *many* very creative women like the ones who found food at the Rescue Mission; for me, this is one of the greatest rewards of undertaking this rather risky adventure. For example, soon after my book *Splashes of Joy in the Cesspools of Life* came out, I was invited to speak at a large banquet at a mega-church in Arizona. As we walked into the banquet room, we were shocked—and delighted—at what we saw.

The room had been decorated "cesspool-style," one of the clever women laughingly told us. Rolls of pink, yellow, blue, and white toilet tissue had been gracefully draped all around the banquet room, and streamers of the tissue formed a wistful curtain to hide the edge of the speakers platform. And *on* the platform were three complete toilets covered with gold paper and sparkly stuff—truly, a sight to behold. Each of the fifty tables was set with a rubber-plunger centerpiece covered with pink feathers, white pearls, and toilet-tissue bows. Can you imagine the fun we had in such a setting?

To start things off, the director of women's ministry stood up and said, "Let's plunge right in, ladies!" Then she taught us a little song: "Flush away, flush away, flush away all," and the place fairly rocked with all the gals laughing, singing, swinging, and swaying.

The crowning joy of the day was the farewell gift the ladies gave us—a lovely toilet seat encrusted with pearls and trimmed with feathers, sprayed all over with more sparklies. Bill hand-carried it all the way back to California, and you can believe he was the talk of the airport that day! Of all the places we've been and all the conferences we've been a part of, THAT was certainly the most memorable decor. It still makes me laugh just to think of it.

After another speaking appearance, we got a splash of joy from a letter written by one of the women attending. She commended the organizers of the Joyful Journey tour, a nationwide series of women's conferences that I participated in. The woman said she appreciated how everything had been planned right down to the smallest detail—even to having Scripture verses taped to the back of the restroom doors! She noted, however, that the Scripture verse she had found in *her* restroom stall had been "a little unsettling." It read, "YOU ARE SURROUNDED BY SO GREAT A CLOUD OF WITNESSES"!

Pots of Thoughtfulness

The women I've met on my travels have not only shared laughter with me, they've also taught me what thoughtfulness is all about. Soon after *Geranium* was published, we were in Canada attending a booksellers convention in August. A local bookstore had invited me to stop by and sign some books while we were there, and I was happy to do it. What a nice surprise to learn, as we arrived, that one of the bookstore employees had started back in March to grow geraniums from seeds in little pots nestled under special lights in her basement—in cold-weathered Canada!

She had lovingly tended eighty of these little seedlings, and by the time I arrived there to sign the books, they were robust and ready for adoption. She generously presented them to me, each little pot wrapped in shiny gold paper, so that I could give them to customers who came to have their books signed. What a treat it was for all of us that day to see those little geraniums going out of the store to spread a bit of joy in someone's window!

Surprises on the Speakers Platform

These are just a few of the ways I've been blessed during all these years of public appearances. Actually, I've been "performing" in front of audiences since I was a young child.

When I accompanied my pastor father to tent revivals around Michigan I was so small I had to stand on a chair to sing "specials" for the gathered congregation. To this day, the smell of wood shavings brings those memories rushing back to my mind.

One of my first performances was as a tiny child wearing a huge, flower-covered hat (visions of things to come, I guess) while singing "Just a little pansy, velvety and brown. On each tiny blossom, God is looking down." Things went well, and I got pretty good at this little number—until the time my mother forgot to STARCH my pansy hat—and the brim flopped pitifully over my eyes. I looked more like a wilted petunia than a perky pansy!

Since then I've rarely felt a moment of stagefright, but I *do* tend to wonder whether something unexpected is going to happen in the middle of my presentation or if I'll commit some inadvertent goof (as I did when I drank the holy water from a baptismal chalice, thinking it was the drinking water I'd requested).

Writing with God's Hand on Mine

The public speaking goes hand-in-hand with another risk I encountered several years ago when, out of the blue, a publisher invited me to write a book about our family's experiences—Bill's devastating accident, the death of two of our sons, and another son's alienation and disappearance. I had just turned FIFTY, and I had never written anything, let alone a book! But the publisher assured me the Lord would propel the book forward, and the result was *Where Does a Mother Go to Resign?* It poured out of me in just eight weeks, and—miracle of miracles—it's still selling well today, eighteen years later, so I know that God's hand was, indeed, guiding mine.

Soon after that project was completed, my friend Lynda sent to a different publisher another manuscript I'd prepared. It had grown out of the journal I'd been keeping throughout the painful years we were struggling to survive. In no time, back came a rather curt letter from the publisher saying my material wasn't suitable for publication. I felt pretty foolish and a little intimidated. Yet I knew God was guiding me, and somehow I continued writing but with more determination to inspire others through my own experiences.

And guess what! The publisher who rejected that proposal was none other than Word, Inc., the wonderful company that's become like a family to me and has published my last five books as well as this one! If ever there was an illustration of "the stone the builders rejected" (Ps. 118:22), I'm it! No one could have been less likely to become an established author than I was when we sent in those pages from my journal all those years ago. And no one could have felt more rejected than I did after that proposal was labeled "unsuitable."

Plenty of other folks were rejected before their efforts succeeded. Author Irvin Stone reportedly collected seventeen rejection letters before a publisher accepted his book *Lust for Life*—which sold twenty-five million copies!

Julia Child's first cookbook was rejected, too, and "Dr. Seuss" got turned down twenty-four times before a publisher finally told him yes.[7]

Abraham Lincoln was defeated in his first run for the Illinois legislature in 1832. Thank goodness he didn't give up politics after that first discouraging failure!

Babe Ruth STRUCK OUT more than thirteen hundred times!

Mother Teresa spent most of her life devotedly working for the poor in Calcutta in relative anonymity. It was only when she was in her seventies that recognition came her way.

Col. Harland Sanders, a seventh-grade dropout, opened his first Kentucky Fried Chicken franchise when he was in his sixties.[8]

Recently I learned that Charles Schulz, the cartoonist who created the "Peanuts" comic strip, was turned down for employment by Walt Disney many years ago because Disney said Schulz's work was just not good enough. Now, there's a star on Hollywood Boulevard with Charles Schulz's name on it. And guess whose star is right next to it: Walt Disney's!

As one editorial writer urged, "Remember that big success is always a possibility, regardless of your age or status. Perseverance is all."[9] Just in case you run out of perseverance before you run into a brick wall on your first attempt at risk-taking, write this verse on an index card and carry it with you wherever you go. Better yet, memorize it, and recite it to yourself regularly:

> [We may be] confident of this, that he who began
> a good work in [us] will carry it on to completion
> until the day of Christ Jesus. (Phil. 1:6)

Retiring Your Retirement

Many retired people are finding innovative ways to "unre-tire." Instead of spending their golden years in "drydock," just waiting for Gabriel to blow his horn, they're going back to work, choosing to be productive instead of consumptive!

You think you're too old to walk into a business and apply for a job? You're not! If that's what you want to do, you're not alone. Millions of Americans over age fifty are taking up new careers, especially in areas that welcome "mature workers."

One article I saw said that banks like to hire older workers because "when customers see dignified tellers . . . they see their money in good hands." Hotels like people in our age bracket because we're dependable. Travel agencies are favorite employers of older people who enjoy traveling and who enjoy the enticing perks of discount hotel rates and airfares.[10]

Furthering God's Kingdom, One Step at a Time

If you just can't bring yourself to take a risk on your own behalf, perhaps it would give you courage to remember that everything you do, you're doing for the Lord. If HE asked you for help, how could you turn Him down?

Well, He's asking! And that doesn't necessarily mean He's asking you to apply to seminary and lead a mission trip to China. There's plenty of work right in your own backyard for those who are willing to do it. Many schools welcome volunteers of all ages. A friend in Florida told me about a gray-haired grandmother who has volunteered at the elementary school in her neighborhood for more than thirty years—long past the time when her own children were students there. In August she calls the school, asking if there are papers to be copied and collated—and there always are. She's been honored several times by that school as one of its otherwise-unheralded "angels."

Another woman didn't even have to venture outside her home to do her good deed. She simply volunteered to be her church's publicity chairman. Every week she typed up a one-paragraph news item describing her church's regular services or special programs that were coming up. She mailed them in to the local newspaper and radio stations to use in their weekly "bulletin board" listings.

Her church was fairly large, with several services during the week, so she never really knew if those little notes that appeared in the paper were effective. Then came the day when the pastor pulled her aside one morning before the service began. He said, "Ann, I'd like you to meet Diane. She and I have met together quite a few times this past month, and she's decided she wants to be a part of our congregation. In fact, she's planning to come forward to be baptized today. And Ann, she started coming to our church because she saw one of the little items you put in the newspaper."

Well, you can imagine how excited Ann was about that news. "I felt almost like a new mother!" she exclaimed. "Diane and I hugged each other, and I'm not sure which one of us was happier."

Volunteers who work with Habitat for Humanity share a similar sense of leading others to Christ in a rather unlikely way. There are hundreds of stories about the lives touched by these home-builders—many of whom are middle-aged women who have never held a hammer in their lives before showing up at a worksite to volunteer. One of my favorite stories is about the Habitat for Humanity work project in Charlotte, North Carolina, that was led by former President

Jimmy Carter in July 1987. In just one week, Carter and his wife, Rosalynn, along with dozens of volunteers, built fourteen houses in a Charlotte neighborhood.

Two years later, Habitat founder Millard Fuller was back in Charlotte and asked a friend to go with him to see the Habitat houses built during the Carter work project. According to Fuller's book *The Excitement Is Building,*

> As they turned around in the cul-de-sac and started driving slowly back up the street, they saw the house Jimmy and Rosalynn Carter had worked on. In the front yard a little boy, maybe six years old, was playing. They stopped the car momentarily, so the boy ran over to greet them.
>
> "Hey," he said, "you got a pretty car."
>
> "Yes, and you have a pretty house. Which one is yours?"
>
> He waved a finger back toward the house.
>
> "What's your name?" Millard asked him.
>
> "D.J."
>
> "Well, D.J., I want to ask you a question. Who built your house?"
>
> Millard thought he would say, "Jimmy Carter." Instead, D.J. quietly replied, "Jesus."[11]

What an honor it would be to have someone feel that Jesus had touched his or her life because of something WE did! Don't let your fears and inertia keep you from reaping these blessings. Remember that God is with you when you venture outside that door.

Someone sent me a little clipping from some unknown source that says,

> The Christian life is a life of faith. . . . I have noticed that God regards faith highly and has a strategy for developing it. He gets us climbing after Him and then when we are committed to the path, He points down and we notice there's no safety net.

God's best moments for us are when we dare all on Him alone, when all our usual ropes and nets have been removed and all we have is Him. "By faith Abraham heard God's call and went . . . even though he didn't know where he was going."

Real faith loves tough situations, for that is where God works most often. Faith laughs at impossibilities and cries, "It shall be done!"

Laugh at Impossibilities

Speaking of Abraham . . . relocating wasn't the only "tough situation" he and his wife, Sarah, risked in their old age. I love the Genesis passage that tells the story of Sarah's risky "adventure," perhaps because Sarah reminds me so much of myself, laughing at the wrong time—and getting caught!

> Then the LORD said [to Abraham], "I will surely return to you about this time next year, and Sarah your wife will have a son."
>
> Now Sarah was listening at the entrance to the tent, which was behind him. Abraham and Sarah were already old and well advanced in years, and Sarah was past the age of childbearing. So Sarah laughed to herself as she thought, "After I am worn out and my master is old, will I now have this pleasure?"
>
> Then the LORD said to Abraham, "Why did Sarah laugh and say, 'Will I really have a child, now that I am old?' Is anything too hard for the LORD? I will return to you at the appointed time next year and Sarah will have a son."
>
> Sarah was afraid, so she lied and said, "I did not laugh."
>
> But he said, "Yes, you did laugh." (Gen. 18:10–15)

Can't you just hear God saying, "Oh yes you did laugh, Sarah!" This old woman may be the only character in the Bible who heard God's voice—and thought He was joking! Thank heaven she didn't do what I would probably want to do if I found out I was pregnant at age ninety—throw myself off a cliff! Instead, Sarah was courageous. And in fact she was delighted by her pregnancy. She seemed to cherish her condition.

When the baby was born Sarah named him Isaac and predicted, "God has brought me laughter, and everyone who hears about this will laugh with me" (Gen. 21:6). She was right; thousands of years later, Sarah's laughter is still contagious.

"...THE ONLY REAL PROBLEM IS I KEEP GETTING HIS 'PAMPERS' MIXED UP WITH MY 'DEPENDS'..."

Reprinted with permission of the *Kansas City Star*.

How Long Since YOU'VE Laughed?

How long has it been since YOU did something outrageous? Maybe not as outrageous as getting pregnant at age ninety . . . but how long has it been since you ate watermelon and tried to see how far you could spit the seeds? Or gathered big armfuls of lilacs and brought them to friends so their homes would smell like spring? Or marched in a parade or climbed *up* the down escalator? Take a chance. Break out of your little plastic mold and become a DINGY person (not din-gee but DING-ee) even if people think you are fresh out of the rubber-room situation.

Did you ever watch a child swat madly at specks of dust hanging suspended in a shaft of sunlight? Children delight at such innocent, simple things—and so can you. Become a child again. Laugh! It's like jogging on the inside. Look for ways to enjoy your day—however small or trivial. Have a joyful attitude, the kind that makes you celebrate every good thing that happens, no matter how trivial—even finding a convenient parking space! Look at a field of flowers and see FLOWERS, not WEEDS!

That kind of positive attitude is vividly expressed in these charming Christmas letters from Bruce and Rose Bliven that appeared in Ann Landers's column in 1976 and 1977:

> At 86, Rose and I live by the rules of the elderly:
>
> If the toothbrush is wet, you have brushed your teeth. If the bedside radio is warm in the morning, you left it on all night. If you are wearing one brown shoe and one black shoe, you have a pair just like it somewhere in the closet.
>
> Try not to mind when a friend tells you on your birthday that a case of prune juice has been donated in your name to a retirement home.
>
> I stagger when I walk, and small boys follow me, making bets on which way I'll go next. This upsets me. Children shouldn't gamble.
>
> Like most elderly people, we spend many happy hours in front of the TV set. We rarely turn it on.

The next year, Ann published this "sequel":

> Dear Friends:
>
> Rosie and I are now 87. Would we care to try for 174? The answer is no. I'm 46 percent as old as the United States and still can't spell "seize."

Rosie has aged some in the past year and now seems like a woman entering her 40s. She chides me about the little elf who regularly enters our house in the middle of the night, squeezes the toothpaste tube in the middle and departs. Last May, we celebrated our 63rd anniversary.

As for me, I am as bright as can be expected. I remember well the friend who told me years ago, "If your IQ ever breaks 100—sell!"

I walk with a slight straddle, hoping people will think I just got off a horse. On my daily excursions, I greet everyone punctiliously, including the headrests in parked, empty cars. Dignified friends seem surprised when I salute them with a breezy "Hi!" They don't realize I haven't enough breath for a two-syllable greeting.

When we are old, the young are kinder to us and we are kinder to each other. There is a sunset glow that radiates from our faces and is reflected on the faces of those about us. . . .[12]

Wouldn't you love to have friends with a lighthearted attitude like that? The next best thing to having a friend like that who can boost your spirits is to BE A FRIEND who helps others see the laughter in life.

Making a Fresh Start

Does your "sunset glow," like that of Rose and Bruce Blivens, reflect on those about you? Or is your light slowly fading while you huddle at home, feeling sorry for yourself?

As Dr. Samuel Johnson said, "If a man does not make new acquaintances as he advances through life, he will soon find himself left alone." Adds author Sherwood Eliot Wirt, "We seniors should never let pass an opportunity to meet [new friends]." And he insists, "It's a major blunder for us to make friends exclusively among people our own age. If we do that we let the world segregate us!"[13]

© Dana Summers. Reprinted with permission.

Now, it may take some practice to become sociable again. As you overcome your reluctance to reach out to others, you'll have to remember the little adage:

> Hospitality is making your guests feel at home
> even though you wish they were!

In case you're out of practice at making friends, here's a list of excellent tips on how to do that:

Spend time. The best way to get to know someone is to do things you both enjoy together and talk. Look for others who share your interests.

Make eye contact. Looking directly at someone, rather than toward the floor or ceiling, demonstrates your interest in what the person is saying.

Investigate. Ask questions. Discover what someone likes or dislikes. Find out about her job situation, family background, and dreams.

Listen. Interactive conversation shows you care. Learn from the different perspectives others have on issues.

Express esteem. Treat the other person with kindness. Show that you value and respect what he does or thinks.[14]

Did you notice what the first letters of the items in this list spell? SMILE! That's really the first step in reaching out to anyone in friendship.

Cut on dotted line.
Then when you meet someone who needs a smile,
give her one of yours.

Winston Churchill said, "We make a living by what we get. We make a LIFE by what we GIVE." What have you given away to a friend lately?

Have you given someone your smile?

Have you shared your laughter?
How about a hug?
Have you paid someone a compliment lately?
Have you told a friend how special he or she is?
Have you listened with your eyes and your ears?
Have you been there for someone who was hurting?
Did you go out of your way just to be kind?
Were you willing to share your time and your life?[15]

As someone said, "It takes no light away from your own candle to light another." Take a chance! Do something risky. Make a new friend. Do a good deed. Even if you got a late start, it's never too late to do something meaningful with your life!

Do all the good you can by all the means you can in all the ways you can in all the places you can and all the times you can to all the people you can as long as ever you can.

John Wesley

Fill your life with experiences, not excuses.[16]

He who laughs last thinks slowest!

Life is a matter of choice.
You can choose to be thirty years old
or seventy years young.
YOU decide!

Church Bulletin Blunders:
"Don't let worry kill you—let the church help!"
"The ladies of the church have cast off clothing of every kind, and they may be seen in the church basement on Friday."
"The service will close with 'Little Drops of Water.' One of the ladies will start quietly, and the rest of the congregation will join in."

"What does man gain from all his labor at which he toils under the sun?" (Eccles. 1:3)
WRINKLES![17]

As I pulled into the parking lot of a church where I was to speak at an "area-wide women's seminar," I spotted the large, bold sign that had been placed on the church marquee—and HOPED the words had been transposed.
The sign said: WIDE WOMEN'S AREA SEMINAR.

Anything can happen to me tomorrow,
But at least nothing more can happen to me yesterday.

Ashleigh Brilliant
Pot-shot 4374, © 1988

Middle age is when you want to see how long your car will last . . . instead of how fast it will go.

Two sets of grandparents arrived at the hospital together to see their newborn grandson. Just getting out of the car was quite an ordeal since all four were in various stages of recovery from knee operations and hip replacements. As the foursome hobbled toward the hospital entrance, brandishing canes and walkers, one of them quipped, "Mercy! I hope they don't admit us before we get to the maternity ward!"[18]

Suddenly Mine

O Lord
May I believe in the darkness
When all hope has vanished
When waves beat with fury
And no star lights my sky.
May I believe without
Feeling or knowing or proving
Till one shining moment when
You shatter the darkness
And all I believed for
Is suddenly mine.

Ruth Harms Calkin[19]

Classified Ad

For sale: antique desk suitable for lady with thick legs and large drawers.

Then I heard the voice of the LORD saying, "Whom shall I send? And who will go for us?"

And I said, "Here am I. Send me!" (Isa. 6:8)

Precious Memories—
How They Leave Us

Young at heart—
slightly older in other places.

When we are out speaking at seminars and conferences, Bill and I take along several pounds of flat, iridescent marbles about the size of a half-dollar. We give them to the women who visit our book table, telling them the marbles are "splashes of joy" to put on the window sill so that when the sun shines on the shimmering glass, they'll be reminded of God's blessings. It's such fun to give away these smooth, flat sparkles; there's probably more than a ton of them out there in circulation by now!

When the marbles are shipped to me from the manufacturer in small bundles of single colors—red, lilac, blue, amber, purple, and green—they have a powder residue on them. So I have to undo each bundle and place the marbles in the towel-lined kitchen sink and rinse them off. Then I spread them out on a large towel and dry them so they're clean, shining, and lustrous when we hand them out at the book table.

Recently a reporter from some publication called me while I was busy at this task. She said she was calling various authors and other people to find out *precisely* what they were doing at that exact moment.

"Well," I said, wondering how this was going to sound, "I'm washing my marbles in the sink."

She didn't answer for a moment. Then she asked, "Who is this again?"

"It's Barbara Johnson." (I'd already told her that when I first answered the phone.)

"The Christian author?"

"Well, yes, I . . ."

"And you're washing your marbles?"

By this time I'm sure she was wondering if she'd dialed the wrong number and reached the home for the bewildered. Finally she gave me time to explain that I always rinse the splashes of joy we give away at meetings and other gatherings. We had a good laugh about her first reaction. Then I told her that washing my marbles helps me remember how God washes us and cleanses our lives. Our robes of righteousness get caked with grime and grit, and God cleans us. His love washes away all the residue we pick up in life so our robes are white again, clean and shining.

Many of my friends know I love to joke about my marbles—washing them and occasionally *losing* them. In fact, one friend sent me a little plaque that said:

All My Marbles Certificate
This is to certify that I,
Barbara Johnson,
am in possession of All My Marbles.
I can never again be accused of not having All My Marbles.

At the bottom of the certificate, this zany friend had written, "If everyone had All Their Marbles—the world would be a nicer place to live!"

Living in La-La Land

Keeping all our marbles gets harder as we get older, doesn't it? Actually, from our side of our faces, it probably seems that we're still cruising along normally through life, but others notice that we occasionally slip into temporary goofiness—losing our reading glasses when they're on top of our heads, unloading the groceries after a shopping trip and putting the *TV Guide* in the refrigerator and the milk in the closet, forgetting where we parked the car at the mall. These things can happen to anyone, of course, but they seem to happen to us older folks a little more often than to younger people.

This poem sums up the situation perfectly:

> Just a note to send my greetings,
> Let you know I'm still alive,
> Though I'm getting more forgetful.
> Things just seem to slip my mind.
>
> I fuss and fret and try to think,
> But all that comes to me
> Is pain between my eyeballs—
> My head hurts terribly!
>
> I walk into the bathroom
> To retrieve a headache pill.
> There I stand, listing my options,
> Wondering what I'm doing here.
>
> I back into the hallway,
> "Start all over," I suggest.
> Then, remembering what I needed,
> I head back toward the shelf.

But once more, memory fails me.
"Why am I here?" I ask.
Then my eye falls on my toothbrush,
And I take my dentures out.

Still, it seems like there was something else . . .
"What could it be?" I pose.
Then I fill the tub with water
And sit down awhile to soak.

"This isn't it," I tell myself.
"I came for something more."
Then I spy the scales and, dripping wet,
Stride quickly 'cross the floor.

I step onto the circular disk
And struggle hard to see
The numbers on the dial below—
"Where could my glasses be?"

I step into the bedroom,
Where I'm sure my specs I'll find.
But standing there beside the bed,
I just cannot decide

Why I've come there—did the phone ring?
Then I see the looking glass.
Good heavens! I'm stark naked!
I'd better get dressed—fast!

I step up to the closet,
Pull the chain to flick the light.
My nightgown hangs before me.
"Oh! It's time to say good night."

I slip into my nightie
As I hum a sleep-tight song,

Pull the covers up around me—
But wait! There's something wrong.

It's the sun. It's at my window!
How could day arrive so soon?
Then I spy the clock and blink my eyes.
"For heaven's sake! It's noon!"

I hurry to the bathroom,
Since I'm running far behind.
There I stand, listing my options,
Wondering what I came to find.

I see this note I started—
Now I can't remember when.
"I'll finish it, right now, right here—
If I can find a pen."

I shuffle to the kitchen,
Where by chance I come upon
A recipe for turnips.
But, my stars! The type is small.

I squint and try to read it,
But my focus is so bad,
A pain streaks o'er my temples—
Creates misery in my head.

I walk into the bathroom
To retrieve a simple pill . . .
It all seems so familiar—
What AM I doing here?

                    Ann Luna

One of the biggest problems we have with forgetfulness is forgetting what we've already said. We repeat ourselves— but, after all, that's one of the prerogatives of aging, isn't it? I saw a little cartoon with an old man saying to a friend, "At my age, I realize I've already said everything I ever wanted to say, so from here on out, I'll just be repeating myself."

Guess what I lost this week...

© 1997 Barbara Johnson.

My glasses.

The danger, of course, is that some of us think we really do know EVERYTHING when we've gained a little seniority over the rest of the world. As somebody said:

I KNOW IT ALL.
I JUST CAN'T REMEMBER IT ALL AT ONCE!

Memory Mischief

For some of us, the biggest challenge of our advancing years is not remembering names, faces, and events that occurred decades ago. It's remembering what happened a couple of hours ago. With each footstep we take into the future, some of us loosen our grip on our SHORT-TERM memory. To put it bluntly, we can't remember what we just said.

And another problem we have is that we can't remember what we just said! (Just kidding!)

Have you seen the glaze slide over someone's eyes when you start in on a story about some exciting adventure you've had? Some bargain you found? Some delicious feast you enjoyed? Sure you've seen it—it's the disengaging message that says, *I've already heard this story two dozen times.* If only we could REMEMBER what that eye-glaze means when we see it, but no! We just keep prattling away, laying out all the little details about who said what and who did this and—

Now what was I talking about? Oh yes, remembering what we just said. Well, the important thing is, if we're going to repeat our stories endlessly, we owe it to our friends and relatives to at least make the stories HAVE A POINT and, even better, BE ENTERTAINING.

This is a real challenge for some of us, because we start off in one direction and remember something even more earth-shaking. As Ravi Zacharias said, quoting an unknown sage, "Old age is signaled when everything you hear reminds you of something else."[1] You start off on a tale about your cruise down the Mississippi, and before you know it, you're giving your shoe size and the recipe for baked apples, but . . . now, where was I going with this? Oh yes, making our stories interesting and STAYING ON TRACK!

Well, my only REAL advice on this topic is to hang on to your sense of humor as you lose your grip on reality.

Someone sent me a little piece of advice that said, "What I know from having lived a long life is . . . a sense of humor helps. Memory helps. You can get by with one or the other, but when you lose both, you're vegetation."[2]

A friend wrote me a wonderful letter that said:

> Since I've become a grandmother, I guess I'm in the golden years. I try to keep an upbeat attitude and laugh a lot. Sometimes I don't remember what I'm laughing about, but it must have been funny, so I keep on.
>
> It seems memory loss is a big factor in growing older. The neat thing is that my friends are all in the same boat, so their feelings won't be hurt when I forget because they don't remember either! If I do something stupid, I won't remember long enough to stay embarrassed.

Mental Aerobics

Experts say one of the best ways to hang on to your memory is to exercise your mind. That doesn't mean you have to learn a new language or try to memorize the names of everyone in the House of Representatives. It just means "staying mentally active."

And how do you do that? Memorizing beautiful Scripture verses is one of the best ways. Being able to repeat those soothing, comforting messages is not only good mental experience, it's good for our souls as well! In times of trouble, it can be a lifeline back to sanity.

One expert suggests "reading and participating in such challenging activities as carpentry, piano-playing and games like chess [or] backgammon. . . . Some studies show that bridge players have better memories than non-bridge players. Others suggest that doing anagrams and crossword puzzles may amount to mental maintenance. Favor the complex over the simple, the active over the passive. Chess is better for your brain than checkers. But checkers is better than watching television."[3] Here are some other tricks for jump-starting your memory:

- **Get all the gadgets.** Beepers, computers, and electronic daily planners can remind you to take your medicine or mow the lawn. . . . So go ahead, get one of those key rings that chirps when you clap your hands.

- **Make notes.** Rather than write a list you could forget to look at, try putting Post-It notes in places where you can't possibly miss them. If you have to call your daughter in the morning, post a note on something you use every morning—like the coffeepot or shower head.

- **Block the doorway.** If you need to return *Now, Voyager* to the video store, don't put it on the kitchen counter where you'll forget it. Drop it on the floor, right in front of the door.

- **Create memory prods.** Remember how the sentence Every Good Boy Does Fine helped you recall the treble notes (E,G,B,D,F) in music class? Use this technique with a shopping list. If you need lettuce, sugar, napkins, chicken, rice, and soup, keep in mind that Little Serpents Never Climb Rickety Stairs. If you come up with an odd enough visual image, you'll be surprised how often you'll remember it.

- **Rely on state-dependent recall.** Remember when you marched into the kitchen, a [woman] on a mission, only to arrive there and forget what the mission was? Well, sit back down in the La-Z-Boy whence you came. Studies indicate that returning to the state you were in when you had the thought often gives your memory just the jump start it needs.

- **When in doubt, stall.** Many memory problems are momentary. So, . . . buy yourself a moment. How?

Take a sip of coffee. Cough and feign a frog in your throat. You might even stop mid-sentence and compliment someone in the room about his necktie.
Many times, a few extra seconds is all you need to come up with an elusive name.[4]

This last tip reminds me of a darling little white-haired lady I met last year at a retreat in Texas. Her eyes always had a merry twinkle, and the smile never left her face. She wasn't at all perturbed at her own occasional memory lapses. At one point someone asked her a question, and she paused, blinked a few times, and raised an index finger to her lips in an effort to remember the answer. Finally, she said:

"Do you need to know right now,
or could you wait a little while?"

This lady may have had a slow memory, but she more than compensated for it by exhibiting a wonderfully quick wit. Little zingers like that help the people around us realize that the QUALITY of our minds (for the most part, at least!) is as good as ever. It just takes us a little longer to kick-start our brains into action!

We've all struggled to put a name with a face that seems so familiar. Other times the NAME is familiar, but the face is a mystery. That kind of situation brought a laugh to us recently when I was speaking at a women's retreat and a beautiful African American woman came up to me after lunch. She had the brightest, widest smile that flashed from her dark face, and her shiny black hair was carefully braided into dozens of tiny braids that swung merrily as she walked.

With a mischievous giggle, she pointed to her nametag and laughed about the fact that her name was BARBARA JOHNSON too. She said, "Barbara, when I came through the lunch line, they saw my nametag and thought I was you. They gave me my lunch for free!"

Slow Memory, Quick Wit

One of the good things about modern technology is all the wonderful little gadgets that have been developed to help us deal with the challenges of aging. One of the best gifts I've ever received is a tiny little gadget on a keyring that I can speak into to record thirty-second reminder messages to myself. My friends Marilyn Meberg and Pat Wenger bought it for me so when I park my car at the mall, I can just raise the keyring to my lips and say, "Row E, space 12," and later, when I'm out on the pavement, wondering where on earth my car is, my little keyring will tell me exactly where it is (IF I CAN JUST REMEMBER TO PRESS THE BUTTON!).

"I'm always losing my car keys, my temper, my memory and my patience... so losing weight should be a breeze!"

It's a wonderful aid for those times when it's close to suppertime and Bill's not home and I have that sneaky feeling I've forgotten something. When I push the button, I hear my own voice reminding me, "Don't forget to pick up Bill at the car-repair place at 5:30!"

My friends got me this great little gadget because we've spent a lot of time together during the last year as part of the Joyful Journey tour. Being in many airports and changing planes and schedules, they have seen me jot down on my hand the flight number or the phone number for whoever is picking me up. Truly this little device has been a godsend for me. It's like having a second mind! Now I can wash my hands without erasing all my important notes!

Reliving the Good Times

Another way to exercise our memories—if we don't overdo it and get STUCK in the past—is to reminisce. Recall happy memories as often as you wish; they never wear out. Experts say remembering beloved memories helps us preserve our identities and maintain our self-esteem.

We joke that our memories deteriorate as we age, but the truth is that unless we're afflicted with TOTAL memory loss due to Alzheimer's or dementia, our brains serve as amazing libraries of information for us. One writer suggests that we use the incredible gift of memories for pleasure—as a means of soothing and comforting ourselves. She writes:

> Even if you regularly lose your keys, forget where you parked your car, or misplace important papers, your memory stores more information than all the libraries in the world. Your brain is far more sophisticated than any computer. You may have forgotten an incident, and then twenty years later something cues that memory—a smell, a sound, a person, a picture—and instantly your mind recalls massive details about an event.
>
> Think of how many voices you recognize on the telephone. One time, a friend whom I hadn't talked to in twenty years called me. All he said was "Hello," and before he said his name I knew who it was. . . .
>
> Someone starts reciting a nursery rhyme or a story you knew as a child, and it all comes back.

Another way to marvel at your amazing memory is to pull out old photos. As you look at them, notice how images burst upon your conscious mind. . . .

Reminisce with people about past times. Before I moved from Minnesota, one of the most healing ways to ease the separation . . . was to talk about turning points, the ways people had been helpful to each other, the times someone had been mad or wanted to leave. Often someone would say, "Oh, I had forgotten that." We ended up laughing, crying, and appreciating the richness of our experience together—as if everyone had brought an ingredient for a cake and we put it all together. And somehow, with all the memories more alive in our minds, it was easier to part because we knew the memories would stay with us.[5]

Sharing Special Memories

Memory is a form of immortality. Those we remember never die; they continue to walk and talk with us, and their influence is with us as long as we remember them. Shared memories can also be a bridge that brings us to new acquaintances. That's what happened for us recently when I was speaking at a women's conference in Boston.

A darling gal came up to me, obviously thrilled about something. I could hardly wait to find out what it was. She excitedly told me that she had lived in Anchorage, Alaska, several years ago, and now she lived in Boston. She had never read any of my books or heard anything about me, but she had decided to come to the women's conference.

During my presentation, I told the audience about the car crash many years ago in a remote part of Canada that had killed our son Tim and his friend Ron as they were driving back after spending several months in Alaska. Tim had called me just a few hours before he was killed; he'd told me he had undergone a spiritual rebirth, that he'd come to know the Lord in a new and invigorating way, and that he couldn't wait to get home and tell me all about it. The next long-distance phone call I received was from the Royal Canadian Mounted Police, telling me both boys had been killed by a drunk driver. As I described to the audience how our family struggled through this heartbreaking time, I held up a picture of Tim's smiling face.

That's when this darling gal realized *she had known Tim in Alaska!* In fact, she had been at the prayer meeting he attended the night before he left Anchorage to drive back home to California. She had been part of the group that had prayed for him and shared the excitement he'd felt about returning home to share his new-found joy with his family.

The young lady said when I'd held up his picture and she saw Tim's face, "everything fell into place." Suddenly she remembered sitting there with Tim, singing and raising their hands in praise, Tim's leaving with excitement and joy, anticipating the journey back to California, obviously with his new relationship with the Lord. The girl was overjoyed to be able to share this memory with me; suddenly, she said, it was as if it all had happened yesterday instead of more than twenty years ago.

What a bittersweet moment that was for us both, and how refreshing it was for me to see her joy in sharing this memory with someone (me!) for whom it meant so much. Later she even sent me photographs of that prayer meeting, and once again, I see my son's smiling face in the midst of a group of enthusiastic young folks.

Truly, memory is a mental bank account. In it we deposit the treasures of our lives so that, in time of need, we can withdraw hope and courage. These treasures are memories large and small: splashes of joy ranging from a pat on the back, the beauty of a full moon on a special evening, finding an empty parking space when we were in a terrible rush, enjoying a glorious sunset with someone we love. Remembering all these happy memories can make us feel like mental millionaires!

Laughter in the Cemetery

For Tim and me, one special memory was feasting on fast food from the In-n-Out Hamburger stand. We would often stop there when he was learning how to drive. Bill was recovering from the devastating effects of an accident[6] at that time, so the driver's training was left up to me. During those weeks I sure learned the truth of the little ditty that says:

> My nerves are a-twitter; my hair has gone white.
> My knees, they are knocking; I'm quaking with fright.
> My whole life is streaking in front of my eyes.
> "Dear Lord, please be with me!" I urgently cry.
> My heart's in my throat, but at least I'm alive.
> The problem? I'm teaching my son how to drive!

It may seem strange to those who've never tried to find a quiet, safe place in the city where a kid can learn how to drive without fighting rush-hour traffic and multi-lane freeways, but Tim and I chose a nearby cemetery. It was beautiful and peaceful, and my favorite part was that the speed limit was only fifteen miles per hour! We would drive around the beautiful grounds for a while, then we'd head for In-n-Out, where I would recover from the experience while Tim stuffed himself with burgers and fries. Then we would go back to the cemetery and try negotiating all the curves again.

It seems like only yesterday that we spent those lovely afternoons together. As Psalm 90:4 puts it:

> For a thousand years in thy sight are but as yesterday when it is past, and as a watch in the night. (KJV)

Someone has said, "Yesterday is a secret room in your heart where you keep the memories of other years." In this secret room we cherish the laughter from another time and again hear the melodies of half-forgotten songs. Today is filled with hurried hustle-bustle, and tomorrow is a mystery, but our yesterdays are treasures from the past to be cherished and enjoyed again and again. There's a lovely little verse that says:

> The heart is like a treasure chest that's filled with sou-
>   venirs;
> It's where we keep the memories we've gathered
>   through the years.

Years have passed since Tim and I slowly wound our way through that beautiful cemetery around and around as he learned to drive. Now Tim's grave is right there next to the curving road where we drove together. Recently I was there, standing beside his grave, remembering how we laughed as we rode along that cemetery trail, enjoying the day together.

While I was reliving those bittersweet memories, I could see a little car wending its way along that same path where Tim and I had been so many years ago. In the passenger seat was a young mother, probably about thirty-five, and steering the car I could see a nervous young boy who must have been about fifteen. As the car was coming closer to where I was standing, I wanted to call out to that mother, "Enjoy your ride with him now, while you can. Make a memory of your experience—and go get a hamburger to celebrate!"

Before I knew it, my heart was smiling and a great feeling of peace flowed through me. I was thankful for that bittersweet memory of long ago.

The Tapestry of Our Lives

Reminiscing helps us put our lives into perspective. As we get older, we can see how each stage, every memory, fits into the grander scheme of things. My life has included sorrow as well as happiness. And all those emotions, all those bittersweet memories, have created what I like to think of as a bright, colorful, firmly woven tapestry.

The happy times are the golden threads that catch the sunlight, warming the soul. The bright pattern was created by our children and then the grandchildren, whose sparkling threads added a nubby texture, a splash of vivid color, to the fabric. The black, somber woof threads that subdue the tapestry's gaudiness were painstakingly woven as we endured hardships in life.

Some of the threads in my tapestry are frayed. Others are broken. But the tapestry remains intact because other threads, as invisible as love yet as strong as the everlasting arms, are woven amongst the weakened ones, holding the delicate fibers together.

As I reminisce, I think of how we wove our way through joys and sorrow, good times and bad, glorying in each other's triumphs and supporting each other in times of trial. And in every loop and knot of our lives together, I see the hand of God.

AGE is mostly a matter of mind.
If you don't mind it, it doesn't matter. [7]

TODAY'S FORECAST: Partly rational with brief periods of coherent thought giving way to complete apathy by tonight.[8]

What goes around, comes around . . . and will whack you on the back of the head when it does.[9]

GOOD NEWS: I've finally discovered the Fountain of Youth.

BAD NEWS: At my age, I've forgotten what I wanted to do with it.[10]

The only good thing about the decline of my memory is that it has brought me closer to my mother, for she and I now forget everything at the same time.[11]

I'm not confused, I'm just well-mixed.

Robert Frost

Never ask old people how they are if you have anything else to do that day.

Joe Restivo

Menopause is a mother's revenge for all the times you tried her patience after age fifty.[12]

My mind not only wanders,
sometimes it leaves completely.

One of the side benefits of forgetting names and faces:
You keep meeting new people every day![13]

A little old lady had to go to a gynecologist. Her husband took her to the doctor's office and waited in the waiting room.

When the old lady was settled in the examining room, the doctor asked, "Are you sexually active?"

"Just a minute," the woman replied, looking rather confused and starting to head for the door. "I'll ask my husband."

"No, no," said the doctor. "Let me put it another way. Do you and your husband still have intercourse?"

"I'll ask my husband," the woman said, jumping up from her chair and heading down the hall. She opened the door into the waiting room and hollered, "George, do we still have intercourse?"

Her husband snorted in exasperation and hollered back, "How many times do I have to tell you, Martha? We still have BLUE CROSS!"

It's no use having a good memory,
Unless you have something good to remember.

Ashleigh Brilliant
Pot-shot 3227, © 1985

Hello, welcome to the Psychiatric Hotline.

If you are obsessive-compulsive, please press 1 repeatedly.

If you are co-dependent, please ask someone to press 2.

If you have multiple personalities, please press 3, 4, 5, and 6.

If you are paranoid-delusional, don't do anything. We know who you are and what you want. Just stay on the line until we can trace the call.

If you are schizophrenic, listen carefully and a little voice will tell you which number to press.

If you are depressive, it doesn't matter which number you press. No one will reply, and nothing will really ever change anyway.

If you have an Oedipus complex, have your mother help you press two.

If you have attention deficit disorder, we can't help you because you have probably already hung up by now.[14]

Behold, thou desirest truth in the inward parts: and in the hidden part thou shalt make me to know wisdom. (Ps. 51:6 KJV)

Grandmothers
Are Antique Little Girls

*Grandkids are God's reward for
our having survived parenthood!*

The day I first felt old is burned like a bittersweet image that haunts my memory. We were visiting with our youngest son, Barney, and his adorable wife, Shannon—and enjoying the cute antics of our precious granddaughter, Kandee. As she played with the new toy we had brought her, little Kandee, who had just celebrated her first birthday, suddenly looked up and flashed her two-tooth smile at Barney. She toddled over and grabbed his knee, excitedly patting it and proclaiming, "Daaah! Daah! Daaah-DEEE!"

That was the moment when old age settled on my doorstep—when this wonderful little creature called my youngest son "Daddy."

It just didn't seem possible. After all, Barney was the

youngest of our four boys, the one I'd brought home from the hospital in a bright red Christmas stocking just a few short years ago—or at least it *seemed* like a few short years. Somehow it had been easy to accept his getting married and moving out of the house. In fact, having him out on his own had given Bill and me a new sense of freedom for the many opportunities that awaited us in the years ahead.

Sure, there were a few moments of mixed feelings later when Barney and Shannon told us we were about to become grandparents. We were joyous, of course, but there was just a momentary pause in our celebration as we considered the new titles we were about to acquire. When Kandee was born, however, any hesitation was forgotten as we snuggled her in our arms and practiced up on forgotten baby-talk.

But now here she was, a toddler, moving on her own and obviously starting to think on her own. AND SHE WAS CALLING *MY SON* "DADDY"! Yes, at that moment I felt old.

Now, each of us responds differently about being a grand-mother. One writer said:

> I wanted to be a grandmother, and I was teetering between senility and death. My interest span was becoming limited, patience was in short supply, and I was beginning to forget all the cute games and nursery rhymes. . . . In a few years, I'd throw the baby up into the air and forget to catch him. . . . I wanted people to stop me in a supermarket and say, "Your baby is beautiful!" and I would fan myself with a pound of bacon and protest, "Oh, puleeese, I'm the grandmother."[1]

Wouldn't that be wonderful, to be mistaken for our grand-children's parents? It's so much better that way than when the opposite occurs. My friend Sue had that horrifying experience when she had just turned thirty and had given birth to a darling baby girl.

On her first solitary trip out of the house after the baby was

born, she admittedly looked a little frumpy—prematurely
gray, she was still carrying a few extra pounds and had been
too rushed to put on any makeup. She hurried into a baby
boutique to buy something frilly for her daughter. She picked
out a beautiful little dress and took it to the counter.

"Oh, isn't this sweet!" exclaimed the saleswoman. "Are
you buying this for your GRANDBABY?"

Sue said she was so shocked she called her husband and told
him she would be a little late getting home. Then she drove
directly to the beauty shop in tears, burst in the door, and
wailed, "This is an emergency! This gray hair has got to go!"

THE FAMILY CIRCUS   By Bil Keane

"Mommy, when you get old how many grandchildren are you gonna have?"

Forgotten Joys

As someone said, grandchildren "give us pause on the way to heaven." With their arrival, they bring a rush of emotions that sweep over us, temporarily detouring us off the aging track. As soon as we get over the shock of being called "Grandma" many of us find ourselves consumed with new, youthful energies and interests we never would have dreamed we'd have: watching cloud formations change or throwing pebbles into ponds or watching squirrels frolic in the treetops.

We look in those little faces and see a miraculous blending of generations and genes: a grandfather's cheekbones, a mother's eyes, a sibling's dimples. And that fresh new face composed of familiar parts reminds us of loved ones living and gone and of all the emotions and history we've shared with them.

Grandchildren are truly a joy!

BUT . . .

They're also exhausting.

And they (and their parents!) can be quite demanding.

And sometimes they live too far away to visit often.

And sometimes they live too close to give us any privacy or "time off."

And sometimes our other responsibilities or problems—continuing careers, our own needy parents, or strained relationships—can make grandparenting a very trying situation.

Whatever our situations are, we must pray for patience—and strive to be the best grandparents we can be, modeling Christlike love to our grandchildren at every opportunity.

Max Lucado wasn't talking specifically about grandparenting when he wrote the following encouragement for those who "want to make a difference in the world," but it's easy to see how living this kind of "holy life" could be a powerful example for the little ones who might be watching us. He wrote:

> You want to make a difference in your world?
> Live a holy life.

Be faithful to your spouse. Be the one . . . who refuses to cheat. Be the neighbor who acts neighborly. Be the employee who works and doesn't complain. Pay your bills. Do your part and enjoy life. Don't speak one message and live another.

Note Paul's words in 1 Thessalonians 4:11–12: "Do all you can to lead a peaceful life. Take care of your own business, and do your own work as we have already told you. If you do, then people who are not believers will respect you."

A peaceful life leads nonbelievers to respect believers. If John the Baptist's life had not matched his words, his message would have fallen on deaf ears.

So will ours. People are watching the way we act more than they are listening to what we say.[2]

Children are especially prone to "watch the way we act more than they listen to what we say." What a gift we give them when we show them this kind of role model. Many children these days have two working parents and a lifestyle that's always in a rush. Each day they may be hurriedly shuffled from home to school to soccer practice (or dance class) to daycare to supper to homework to bed. Whew! And to think that many of them have this schedule all their lives!

A Haven in Grandmother's Garden

Think of the haven we provide these grandchildren when we invite them to share a peaceful, unhurried afternoon at the zoo or "working" in our gardens or looking for butterflies in the park. To make them the center of attention for even a brief while lets them know—more than mere words could do—how much we cherish them.

Imagine what it's like for a little one to be held in a grandmother's arms and hear her lovingly pray, "Thank You, God, for this dear child, for the joy he brings me and the pride I have in him! Thank You for giving me such a wonderful gift to cherish!"

Of course, merely imagining such a scene doesn't do much good. Instead, try your best to DO IT whenever you can!

Supergrannies

Indeed, many grandmothers these days struggle with the same time pressures as the grandchildren and their parents are coping with. Most of us grew up with the stereotypical image of a grandmother as that cute little woman with her white hair pulled up into a bun, wearing an apron while she sits in her rocking chair, peeling apples to put in a homemade pie, but that image is probably much more accurate in depicting OUR grandmothers than in describing our grandkids' grandmothers (us!).

Someone sent me a little clipping from an unidentified source that comes closer to describing many grandmothers today. It says, "Move over, Superwoman. Here comes Supergranny, that fifty-plus ball of fire who has a pilot's license, a law degree, and a doctorate in political science!"

It's true. Many women sail through the half-century mark on their way up the corporate ladder—or Mount Everest. Astronaut Shannon Lucid isn't the only gray-haired woman who's setting records and making stunning achievements in what used to be called middle age (or even OLD age!). I think this little poem sums it up pretty well:

Supergranny

Don't look for her in the rocking chair,
Granny isn't in it.
She's off to fight a fire somewhere
Or serving in the Senate.

She might be in a cockpit
Or removing an appendix,
Or checking test tubes in a lab
Or speaking from a pulpit.

She could be on a book tour
Or working as a chef.
Or running a big company
From behind a corporate desk.

A lot has changed in granny's world;
She studies to keep up.
But one thing still comes naturally:
That special Granny LOVE!

Ann Luna

Grandmother Show-and-Tell

Just imagine what it's like these days in grade-school class-rooms on Grandparents Day as the proud students introduce

their guests. Can't you just hear the students saying, "My grandmother is a banker," or "My grandmother is a doctor," or "My grandmother is a professor"? The most amazing introductions—and they're surely coming—will be, "My grandmother is PRESIDENT!" or "My grandma is a TRAPEZE ARTIST!"

Actually, while these titles would surely impress the adults in the room, they probably wouldn't mean all that much to the kids. In front of their classmates, they might like to brag that their grandmothers are airline pilots or firefighters, but in all probability that's NOT the thing they care most about. The important thing to most young grandchildren is not TITLES but TIME. That seems to be the sentiment in the following essay. I don't know who wrote it, but she obviously had a wonderful grandmother.

What Is a Grandmother?

A grandmother is a lady who has no children of her own. She likes other people's little boys and girls. A grandfather is a man grandmother. He goes for walks with the boys and they talk about fishing and tractors and stuff like that.

Grandmothers don't have to do anything but be there. They are old, so they shouldn't play hard or run. Instead they drive us to the market where the mechanical horse is and have lots of dimes ready. Or they take us for walks, and they slow down past things like pretty leaves and caterpillars. They never say "Hurry up."

Usually grandmothers are fat, but not too fat to tie your shoes. They wear glasses and funny underwear. They can take their teeth and gums off.

It is better if grandmothers don't typewrite or play cards, except with us. They don't have to be smart, only answer questions like, "Why do dogs chase cats?" or "How come God isn't married?"

Grandmothers don't talk baby talk like strangers

do because it's hard to understand. When they read to us they don't try to skip pages, and they don't mind if it's the same story over again.

Everybody should try to have a grandmother, especially if you don't have TV, because they are the only grown-ups who have time.

Kids have a knack for getting right to the heart of things, don't they? That reminds me of the story I heard about a little boy who was being cared for by his grandma. The little boy had lots of questions, which his grandmother tried patiently to answer. But when he asked, "How old are you?" she replied, "Honey, you're not supposed to ask ladies their age."

Then he said, "Well, how much do you weigh?" to which she gently replied with the same answer.

Then he said, "How come you and Grandpa got a divorce?"

Finally becoming exasperated, she said, "That's nothing for you to be concerned about. Now, go out and play."

Later in the day, the little boy found his grandmother's purse. He dug through it, looking for candy, and instead found her wallet, including her driver's license. Excitedly, the little boy ran to his grandmother and said, "Grandma, I know how old you are and I know how much you weigh . . . and I even know how come you and Grandpa got a divorce!"

She asked him how he could possibly know that, and he answered proudly, "You got a divorce because you got an F in SEX!"

Holiday Hilarity

One of the most important roles we grandparents play is sitting in the audience, watching from the grandstand, and leading every round of applause when our grandchildren are performing somewhere, whether it's horse shows, debate tournaments, or gymnastics meets. Kids love to have us there —so we ought to try to stay awake and act interested!

Some of the funniest stories I've ever heard describe children's antics in Christmas pageants. Of course, at the time they may not be quite so funny—but a few years later they're the highlight of any family gathering.

One of our family's favorite stories is about Larry, our lighthearted son, who was always looking for a little mischief. One year when he was scheduled to appear in our church's Christmas program to sing "As Shepherds Watched Their Flocks by Night," he jokingly "practiced" for weeks at home, singing, "As shepherds washed their socks at night."

The whole family was in stitches every time he broke into that chorus; in fact, at one point, I offered him five dollars if he would get up in front of the church and, like Frank Sinatra, do it "his way." (I guess I've always been one who's perpetually looking for a little mischief too!)

Well, he acted horrified that I even suggested it—and accused me of bribing him to "commit a crime." On the night of the Christmas program, his stomach was full of butterflies, and his little heart was racing because he was so nervous. He shakily stepped up to his "spot" on the platform, took a big breath, and—you guessed it—unintentionally burst out with, "As shepherds washed their socks at night"!

That was the most memorable Christmas program for our family. But we weren't alone in having some unintentional holiday gaffs. Someone gave me this little collection of Christmas-pageant antics, and I enjoy them all over again every time I read them:

- A few days before Christmas I walked into the room where my small son was playing, just in time to hear him singing, "Ho-ly infant, so tenderfoot ride . . ."

- While the art class was setting up a Christmas scene on the school lawn, one of the boys asked uncertainly, "Where do we put the three wise guys?"

- Then there were the four youngsters in the Christmas pageant each carrying a letter to form the word "S-T-A-R," but they went up in reverse order, accidentally spelling "R-A-T-S."

- After the Sunday school class had sung "Silent Night" and had been told the Christmas story, the teacher suggested they draw the nativity scene. A little boy finished first. The teacher praised his drawing of the manger, of Joseph, of Mary, and the infant Jesus. But she was puzzled by a roly-poly figure off to one side. "Who is this?" she asked.

   "Oh, that's Round John Virgin," the little boy replied.

Antique Grandmothers

A friend told me about some grandparents who were showing their little grandson an antique fire engine. The grandfather explained to the little guy that "antique" meant the fire engine was OLD. The boy thought about it a moment then asked, "So are YOU a GRANTIQUE?"

Isn't that a great title? Sort of spiffs us up and puts a higher "market value" on some of us, don't you think? It's certainly pleasanter to think of ourselves as "grantiques" rather than OLD! And anyway, some of the things sold as antiques these days really are quite young. It's amazing to go into antique shops and see things we used only a few years ago (at least it SEEMS like just a few years ago) being sold as highly collectible treasures!

A little news item recently announced the rather surprising age of a product many of us wish we had had when we were new mothers: disposable diapers. The article said Pampers turned thirty-five years old last year, having been invented in 1956. Ironically the inventor was a MAN who came up with the idea while he was babysitting his granddaughter and "was introduced to the joys of changing and washing diapers."[3]

Special Times with Grandma

Grandparenting is probably the most fun when the grandkids are little, when some of the best times we can have come by DOING things with the little ones. Una McManus shared several good ideas in "Grandma, Let's Play," an article she wrote for *A Better Tomorrow* magazine. Some of her suggestions are:

- **Write love letters.** As soon as a grandchild is born, write letters to him or her regularly. . . . Tell your grandchild about himself, his birth, and his development. . . . Store the letters in an attractive box until the child is old enough to appreciate them. . . . [Then] bind your letters into a "love book."

- **Keep a "little things" drawer.** During their early years, your grandchildren will love to have a drawer of their own in your home. Fill it with little things you collect for them, such as free soaps, toys from cereal boxes, sample jellies, free novelty pencils, homemade crafts, and small souvenirs or postcards from trips.

- **Create homemade cards together.** When a grandchild comes to visit, sit down together at the kitchen table and make a list of family birthdays, anniversaries, graduations, and other celebrations. Then get out construction paper, crayons, old magazines and cards, . . . glue, and scissors and go to work making homemade greeting cards. . . .

- **Share a photo memory.** Develop extra copies of photographs and make reprints of old snapshots. Then create a family photo album for each grandchild. . . . Take an evening or a Sunday afternoon to go through the album with the child. Use each photo as a springboard for sharing thoughts about the person and the place. . . .

- **Decorate pancakes.** When grandkids spend the night, make breakfast fun in the morning by creating "funny face pancakes" together. Raisins, cherries, cake decorations, and pieces of cut-up fruit can serve as eyebrows, mouths, and noses. . . . Let the child pour, decorate, and taste to his heart's content. . . .

- **Teach a skill.** . . . Perhaps you can take lessons with your grandchildren to learn something new for both of you such as skiing, calligraphy, or puppet making. . . .

- **Create a "Grandparents' Week" tradition.** Invite the grandchildren for a week during the summer and devote that week to their interests.[4]

The Adolescent Years

While the younger years may be the most fun, many grandmothers enjoy an even more meaningful relationship with their grandchildren as they reach adolescence and the teenage years. These are the times when children typically tend to rebel against parents and expectations. So they often turn for solace during these turbulent times to their grandparents, especially if the elders have shown them unconditional love during the children's growing-up years.

Recently I heard someone reminisce, saying that as a teenager he had fled many times to his grandmother's kitchen after an argument with his parents. There he had found unquestioning acceptance.

"She never asked a lot of questions," the young man said. "She didn't take sides. She really didn't talk much at all. She just opened her door—and her heart—and took me in. Maybe part of the relief I felt by being with her was that my parents had always expected so much of me—and Grandmother expected NOTHING of me, except that I let her love me."

This grandmother had probably never read any of the self-help books that are out there these days, offering wise advice on how to reach out to teens when they're going through family crises. But she showed great wisdom in opening her heart and especially by LISTENING nonjudgmentally.

One expert recommends a twelve-word limit for parents (and it would surely work for grandparents too) during conversations with their kids. The article said, "Teens are all too accustomed to parents' rapid-fire interrogation and long dissertations about the mistakes their kids are making. . . . Keep your comments to your kids (including adult children) to twelve words at a time—or fewer. The same holds true for answers to their questions. It prevents your children from tuning out what you're saying, as well as increases their curiosity, and that raises more questions from them. Because you're responding to their inquiries (not the other way around, as usual), you won't wear them down with too much talk and you'll actually listen better."[5]

Grandma's Love Bank

Being a grandparent doesn't mean we're old, of course. In fact, there are a lot of grandmothers out there who haven't even hit forty yet! But being a grandmother DOES mean we have a special opportunity. We can be a source of unfailing, unquestioning, nonjudgmental, nonstop, full-powered love for these children. And while it's true that it can be detrimental to children to give them too many material things, it's absolutely impossible to give a child too much love. Someone sent me a little clipping—I have no idea where it's from—that made this point so clearly. It said:

> Extra love from grandparents goes into a child's psychological bank account, which draws interest and can be used for an emotionally rainy day.

What a comforting thought—to imagine our grandchildren facing some tough decision someday or feeling lonely in some far-off place and suddenly remembering a grandmother's love—and being comforted by it. Surely there's no greater legacy we can leave to our grandchildren than this constant, enduring gift—the kind of love modeled by Jesus and described so beautifully in 1 Corinthians 13: a love that never ends.

GRANDPARENT: A thing so simple, even a small child can operate it.[6]

If you want to be loved,
don't criticize those you want to love you.[7]

Bouquets of Gold
"Grandma, I have flowers for you."
She held them up for me to view.
I took them from her little hand
And vaguely tried to understand
Emotions stirred anew.

Leafing back through 40 years,
A yellow meadow scene appears.
The little girl from whom I grew
Picked flowers for her grandma, too . . .

Glowing hemispheres.

Did Grandma pause and meditate,
Like me, begin to contemplate,
Recalling scenes with etched designs
When she picked golden dandelions
According to childish trait?

And will my grandchild someday hold
A bright bouquet of meadow's gold
Placed there by one as yet unborn?
And will she then recall this morn
And this story be retold?

Adeline Wiklund[8]

How far you go in life depends on your being tender with the young, compassionate with the aged, sympathetic with the striving, and tolerant of the weak and the strong—because someday in life you will be all of these.

George Washington Carver

Kids are like sponges.
They absorb all your strength and leave you limp.
Give 'em a squeeze, and you get it all back.

Bumper sticker: DON'T BUG ME! HUG ME![9]

A young boy, some six years old, was studying his grandmother. Soon he asked, "Grandma, are you a lot older than my mom?"

"I sure am, honey, lots older," she replied.

The boy nodded. "I figured that," he said, "but I got to tell you that her skin fits a whole lot better than yours."[10]

Grandma Brown took her two grandchildren to the zoo. . . . They stopped before a huge cage of storks. Grandma told the two youngsters that these were the birds that brought both of them to their dad and mom.

The two children looked at one another, then the oldest leaned over and whispered in his sibling's ear, "Don't you think we ought to tell Grandma the truth?"[11]

Life is like riding a bicycle.
You don't fall off unless you stop peddling.[12]

A grandmother took her three-year-old granddaughter into her lap and began reading to her from Genesis. After a while, noticing the little girl was unusually quiet, the grandmother asked, "Well, what do you think of it, dear?"

"Oh, I love it!" answered the child. "You never know what God is going to do next!"

Another grandmother took her four-year-old granddaughter, Amanda, to the doctor's office because she'd been running a fever. The doctor looked in her ears and said, "Who's in there, Donald Duck?"

Amanda said, "No!"

Then the doctor looked in her nose and said, "Who's in there, Mickey Mouse?"

Again Amanda answered, "No!"

Finally he put his stethoscope on her heart and asked, "Who's in there, Barney?"

Amanda replied indignantly, "No, Jesus is in my heart. Barney is on my underwear!"

Even when I am old and gray,
    do not forsake me, O God,
till I declare your power to the next generation,
    your might to all who are to come. (Ps. 71:18)

MENacing MENstrual Cramps, MENopause, MENtal Failure . . . Is There a Connection Here?

Men are like parking spaces.
All the good ones are already taken—and the rest are
handicapped or their meters are running out!

Bill was reluctant to let me replace our old, flattened bed pillows, but I finally talked him into it. We had had them for several years, and even when they were washed and dried, they were still too FLAT to suit me. They had lost their newness, and I insisted they needed to be replaced.

He wasn't eager to get new ones because he likes his bed pillow all squashed down and not puffed up. He clung like a child to his old, matted-down pillow, but the old ones didn't LOOK good and I kept insisting we needed new ones. Finally, he gave in.

I found some pillows on sale, and they were just terrific—big, fancy, blown-up poufs that looked really nice when the bed was made up. They weren't sagging and squashed down like the old flattened out ones.

Well, I was really proud as I carried those old, sorry-looking pillows to the trash can and stuffed them down into the bag that lined the can. But Bill didn't share my joy. He complained that he couldn't sleep because his new pillow was "too hard, too big, and too uncomfortable."

Since I was the one engineering this big transfer, I hated to admit it, but I woke up with a crick in my neck, too, and felt as though I'd been sleeping on a pile of rocks. It was sure hard to admit that perhaps I'd made a mistake in replacing those old, soft eiderdown pillows that had served us so well for many years. Bill was right. The new ones *were* too stiff. They wouldn't mold to our heads and necks the way the old ones did.

After two nights of this disturbed sleep (and after listening to Bill's continuing complaints) I knew I had to make the situation right . . .

By now the old pillows that I'd stuffed into the trash were buried under a couple days' accumulation of other garbage, and our garbage truck comes through our neighborhood early in the morning. So after the second sleepless night, I sneaked out of the house right at dawn and tiptoed out to the trash can, which Bill had set out on the curb the night before. Still dressed in my housecoat and slippers, I gently lifted the noisy lid off the can—then gasped as the stench of a week's collection of trash escaped from the container.

Where we live there are lots of older people who get up with the sun and go for morning walks. I knew I would have to take the risk that being caught digging through those bags of trash would earn me the neighborhood nickname of "BAG LADY." But I was a woman on a mission!

Hurriedly I tried to undo the little twistie on one of the bags. Bill always puts them on so tight, as though worried that something in there would try to ESCAPE! Well, I completely dug through that first bag of garbage, and it wasn't there—but in going through all the refuse, I'd spilled a bunch of OTHER trash. (Bill really packs a lot of trash in each bag because he's so neat about how he collects his trash, flattening every milk carton and cereal box and sometimes even tearing up the cardboard into little pieces!)

It took awhile, but after an eternity of pushing and shoving through the trash, I finally decided which bag the pillows were in. By this time, several couples had walked past me and nodded good morning (looking rather astonished to see me knee-deep in refuse).

Finally I pulled out both pillows, which were now stained with drops of grape juice, bleach droplets, and who knows what else, and hugged them to my heart. They felt so soft and comforting!

I dashed inside and immediately dropped both of them in the washer with LOTS and LOTS of soap (still moving as quietly as I could, mind you, so Bill wouldn't know what I had done).

Then I put them in the dryer with LOTS and LOTS of fabric-softener sheets. Of course, the dryer had to go through several cycles to get them dry because down and feathers take a LONG time to dry—nearly six hours in this case!

Finally they were dry, and I slipped them into the pillow-cases and remade the bed, really proud of myself that I had done all this without Bill's ever knowing what was happening.

It was dark that night when he finally climbed into bed and fell asleep, never realizing the switch that had been made.

The next morning as he was making up the bed (this is one of his little ways of showing love—he always makes the bed for me), I figured that he must surely know what I'd done. But he said not a word. As he finished up, he smoothed the bedspread over the pillows and said, "Well, you know, I guess those new pillows are okay. Maybe it just takes awhile to get used to them."

When he saw the crinkled smile I was trying to hide, I had to confess what I'd done. That old verse, "He that covereth his sins will not prosper" kept bouncing around my mind—and anyway, I was going to have to do some fast talking to explain why I had two BIG new pillows taking up a whole shelf in our closet. So I told him about diving into the trash can the day before. ("Oh," he said, a rather worried look on his face. "Did you get it all put back in the bags okay? Did you remember to put the twistie on tight?")

Anyway, now we have nice, matted-down, well-worn, OLD pillows, but they are COMFY and he is WUMPHEE (my long-time nickname for him), and we have one more thing to laugh about as we lay our weary heads on those old, familiar pillows each night.

"Look, I know you hate it, but until I get a chance to put some non-slip decals in the tub, I'd feel a lot better if you'd just wear the helmet."

Growing Old Together

If you've read my other books, you know I like to poke fun at men. Please understand that these jokes and anecdotes and wisecracks have nothing to do with FACT! They're just for fun. And since this book is FOR WOMEN ONLY, I want to add an extra helping of silliness here to celebrate these creatures God gave to us so we'd always have something to laugh about!

And just so you know, I love and respect Bill, my husband and soulmate through DECADES of fun and adventures. He's always been my anchor as well as the wind in my sails, whichever one I needed most at the time!

We work together well, and I'm blessed by his love and companionship. We've helped each other survive so many challenges that the other day, when I saw a startling scene, I thought it depicted our relationship perfectly. In the street before me, a tow truck was towing another tow truck.

Picture the strong person in your midst, the one you would call if you had a problem, the one who encourages you and builds you up. If you're like me, that person is your husband.

But what happens when that stable force needs help himself? That's what Bill and I went through many years ago when he was disabled due to an almost-fatal car crash. Then, for a little while, I was the tow truck towing the tow truck. Now we're both back on track and going strong—and laughing every chance we get.

Men, Women, Old Age, and Technology:
A Dangerous Mix

Bill is always looking for little gifts for me. Last year he got me the best gift yet: a lava lamp! He knows that I love things that move and chime and light up, and this bright red lava lamp is the highlight of my Joy Room. I love watching it ooze and swirl around. It's so soothing and peaceful.

Even though it's rather a "new" invention (actually I think they're making a comeback after first appearing in the sixties), somehow my lava lamp reminds me of simpler times, when clocks ticked and tocked, dishwashers had two arms and two legs instead of four "cycles," and telephones came with built-in helpers whose voices greeted you as soon as you gave the bell a crank: "Number please!"

The truth is, technology has just about left me behind. But the amazing thing is that it's leaving Bill behind too. He's just as confused as I am about some of the new computerized "advancements."

I'm finding this is true for lots of folks in our generation. Age is the great leveler when it comes to coping with advancing technology. It used to be when we couldn't figure out how to run some gadget or gizmo, we could call our husbands and they'd size up the situation in no time, press a few buttons, and send us on our way. But that's changing.

No longer are we the only ones who can't figure out how to turn on the air conditioner in a hotel room—or even to get into the room in some places with computerized locks! Now things are so complicated some husbands can't figure them out, either! One woman told me her husband bought a new large-screen television that came with a SIXTY-FOUR-PAGE instruction manual! (And we know what he did with that, right? Used it as a coaster.)

The woman said, "By trial and error, he learned how to turn it on and change the channel—and didn't even attempt to learn the zillions of other things this monster can do."

Maybe the problem is that these machines are rushing us, leaving us feeling disconcerted. Maybe that's why we can't catch on (or catch up!). A few years ago, *Parade* magazine published a little table of listings that explained why we no longer have time to catch our breath and figure things out. Technology is pushing us to do everything faster and faster— just when most of us would be content to snooze along on the SHOULDER of life's highway, stopping occasionally to smell the flowers—and sip some tea!

The table in *Parade* was titled, "The Vanishing Pause,"[1] and it looked like this:

SLOW MOTION	CRUISE CONTROL	FAST FORWARD
buttons	zippers	Velcro
stove	pressure cooker	microwave
washboard	wringer-washer	washer-dryer
pen	typewriter	word processor
abacus	adding machine	calculator
operator	rotary dial	touch-tone
U.S. Mail	Federal Express	fax

Looking at these lists, you can start to understand why so many of us older folks feel so tired all the time. We no longer have the tried-and-true excuses we used to use when something wasn't ready when it was expected. That's certainly been true for me since I began writing books. It used to be that if I didn't have a manuscript in to the publisher on exactly the deadline, I could say, "Oh, it must have been held up in the mail. I mailed it on . . . let's see, was it Tuesday or Wednesday?" when the truth was I hadn't gotten it into the mail until FRIDAY! Now when things are due on Friday, the publisher sends me a form for OVERNIGHT SHIPPING—or worse yet, a FAX NUMBER! So when something is not on time, I can't blame anyone but myself!

One woman told me she and her husband were planning a cross-country trip in their elaborate motor home and were hoping their eight-year-old grandson would come with them for part of the trip. "He's the only one who can program the satellite dish and figure out how to run the microwave," she confessed.

And even some of the younger husbands are having trouble with all the new-fangled gadgets on the market these days. At a meeting I attended recently, I met Bryan Eckelmann, a wonderfully warm and delightful minister in Massachusetts who has given me permission to share his hilarious story:

> It was the first spring of my life away from the suburbs—a small farming community in Ohio. Timberly, my farm-savvy wife, eager to plant a big

garden, was thrilled when one of the church members loaned us his roto-tiller.

After he dropped it off, Timberly raved, "Bryan, this isn't just any roto-tiller, this is the best—a Troy-Bilt Pony!"

I tried to act impressed and educated at the same time. "Yes, I know. I've seen them in the magazines."

I *had* seen the ads praising this tiller's power and ease of use. The words were always accompanied by a photo of a woman in an A-line skirt effortlessly guiding the tiller around the garden with only her index finger. What could be easier!

So easy that I was happy to help. Our infant son had colic and was only happy in the front pack Timberly wore *while* she tried to run the tiller. After one long row and an aching back, she asked me to finish the job when I came home.

No problem! I changed clothes and got to it.

But no guiding this tiller with one finger for me—after one hour I was hot, aching, and cursing false advertisers everywhere. I had only tilled two rows when Timberly came out and asked, "What's the problem?"

"It's just slow going," I yelled over the engine roar of this two-hundred-pound monster. "This isn't working well at all—maybe something's broken." I was trying to act brave, but she knew I was exasperated.

"Broken? It can't be! We just borrowed it!" Timberly stepped behind the machine, reached down to a lever I had not seen before, and pulled up. The tiller lurched forward under its own power.

Shocked, I yelled, "How'd you do that?!"

She stopped the machine and stared at me for a moment, both of us taking in the fact that I'd spent an hour *pushing* a two-hundred-pound self-propelled

tiller around our garden without engaging the driver mechanism. For three months both of us were
too embarrassed to tell a soul!

Bryan, being the fine pastor he is, was quick to apply his
roto-tilling lesson to his ministry: "That day was a great lesson for me," he said. "Since then, I've come to recognize those
all-too-frequent times when I've tried in vain to push and pull
my life in the right direction, ignoring the limitless power of
God's Spirit so easily available to me, His child."

It's about time men experienced some of the technological
torture we women have faced for so long! Actually, I agree
with something Erma Bombeck wrote many years ago. She
said, "Men have a reputation for being mechanical. This is not
true. Occasionally, Christmas has to be postponed while a man
in a closet tries to put together a bicycle, following instructions (in Japanese) and looking for the E wing nut."[2]

**"I couldn't afford to get airbags as an option. If it looks like
we're going to hit something, start blowing these up."**

Car Trouble

Bryan's story reminds me of how silly my sister and I felt when we borrowed a friend's car during a weekend conference in another state. It was a very nice car, just the right size and easy to drive, but throughout the long weekend we were unable to get the windows to roll down. There seemed to be lights and colors and levers for everything else, but there was no button to roll down the windows.

We returned the car on Sunday, and as we were thanking the owner, I happened to mention that we hadn't been able to find the button to lower the windows.

"Oh," she said, surprised. She opened the car door and pointed to a rounded crank in front of the armrest. "It's right here—you just turn this handle."

Janet and I, both accustomed to power windows, had been looking for a button to push when the BIG lever to roll the windows down manually was RIGHT THERE! We had probably bumped it a dozen times as we were feeling around, trying to find the button. We laughed until we cried, thinking how "modern" we were when all that was needed was a little old-fashioned common sense!

Last year I had a similar "splash of joy" when I was speaking in North Carolina at the church Billy and Ruth Graham attend. What an honor it was when Ruth Graham called the place I was staying and invited me to go to church with her.

Billy was out of town and her car was in the repair shop, so she came to pick me up in his car. She immediately explained all that to me and apologized for not being familiar with the rather elaborate controls. In fact, she had to speak over the blaring of the radio because she didn't know which knob to turn to get if off—and of course I was no help. The car is specially equipped with phones and security devices, so just a small thing like turning off the radio seemed to be a big deal—at least to us non-mechanically inclined women!

Soon another problem became obvious. It was an unusually warm day, and the car was getting hot. Ruth asked me to turn on the air conditioner while she was driving to the church. I looked at all those little knobs and gizmos and couldn't read ANY of the tiny letters identifying each one. Hesitantly, I tried pushing one lever across a slot, but it quickly became apparent that instead of turning on the air conditioner I had accidentally revved up the HEATER!

Finally, Ruth stopped the car, and we asked a passer-by if he could turn off the heater and get the air conditioner going for us. It must have been a funny sight: two mature women, pulling up to the curb with the radio blasting and heat pouring out of the car. We both had some good laughs about how ridiculous we felt that day; it really broke the ice (in more ways than one!) and made getting acquainted a joyous experience.

Deceiving Tendencies

Space-age technology isn't the only thing that puts us old-age men and women on the same level. It seems to me there are many ways that men and women mellow out and become more alike, more compatible, as we toddle off toward the sunset. One article said that becoming grandparents often enriches a couple's marriage and gives their relationship a new depth. In other situations, the relaxed pace of traveling together with no schedule, no itinerary, gives retired couples a new sense of shared adventure.

For Bill and me, our work with Spatula Ministries and all the traveling we do to far-flung speaking engagements has given us a new purpose in life. The boomerang joy we receive as we meet new people all over the country has enriched our lives beyond measure.

One of the things Bill and I do together is the monthly shopping. Someone once said, "The only thing worse than going shopping with a husband who doesn't like to shop is going shopping with a husband who DOES like to shop!" Because he's a retired engineer, Bill can really get into the DETAILS of shopping, comparing prices and carefully deciding which is the best buy. It used to drive me nuts when I was always in a hurry, but now that our lives are a little more relaxed, I enjoy having him along.

Recently we were at one of the big warehouse stores; somehow we got separated, and I came out ahead of Bill while he was occupied with something else in the store, and for a change I pushed the cart to the car and unloaded it (a job he always does for me). When we got home and I began to put things away, I realized I had apparently LEFT two huge boxes of stuff in the bottom of the cart! We had shoved them onto the bottom of the cart, and apparently I had just overlooked them as I transferred our purchases from the cart to the car.

When I told him what had happened, he just said, "Well, it's down the drain now. You can consider that stuff totally lost." His pessimistic opinion frustrated me so much that I decided to drive the fifteen miles BACK to the store just to show him he was wrong.

I just wish you guys had given some thought to what you were going to do after you retired...

ED FISCHER

Bill refused to go with me, pooh-poohing the idea that I would ever find those lost boxes. "Why bother?" he asked. "You're just wasting your time—and gasoline too."

But I was thinking to myself, *If I don't get the stuff back (which I probably won't) I will just go back in and purchase everything again and tell Bill I found them after all!* He would never know the difference, I rationalized, and I would have the great satisfaction of proving him wrong.

This thought persisted as I got closer to the store; I began mentally plotting my route up and down the aisles, collecting all the lost items, re-buying them, and then bringing them home and letting him think I had miraculously FOUND them.

When I pulled into the crowded parking lot and started to make my way to the entrance of the store, I must have had a frantic, searching look in my eyes because when I stopped a cart boy and hesitantly began to explain my problem (*couldn't hurt to ASK,* I reasoned), he immediately said, "Oh, you're the lady who left the big boxes in the bottom of the cart. They're inside the store. We have a whole closet full of things people leave in their carts and we keep them there, safe and sound."

Astonished, I sputtered, "Does it happen THAT often?"

"Oh yeah," he replied. "We have a lot of people who drive off and leave stuff in their carts." He smiled at me and added, "But they're usually OLD PEOPLE."

Well, that made my day! After loading my stuff in the car, carefully making sure this time that I hadn't left anything in the cart, I drove home wondering whether I should be flattered or humiliated by the boy's remark. Then I thought about my plan to re-buy all the stuff I thought I'd lost and never let Bill know what I'd done. That verse from Jeremiah kept popping into my head: "The heart is deceitful above all things, and desperately wicked" (17:9 KJV). Yet, I had to admit it would have been a lot more fun to pull that kind of prank rather than just returning home and saying, "Look what I found!"

The sad part is that when Bill saw me coming in with all the stuff, he said, "I'll bet you just went back and re-bought all the stuff to make me look bad!"

Pretending to be shocked that he would even *have* such a thought, I denied—at least for a little while—that I would even consider such a scheme.

Men are wonderful creatures; they truly are. They compliment us—and complement us! They can make us cry; they can build us up—or leave us flattened. They support us and nurture us and console us. In short, they're nice to have around! But one of their most valuable gifts to us women, in my rather lop-sided opinion at least, is that they give us so much to laugh about. Here are some of my favorite quips and jokes about our struggles with the new technology—and especially about men. If you are married, it might be better to enjoy this little collection while he's out playing golf or getting the car tuned-up!

An elderly gentleman went to the doctor for a health checkup. The doctor gave him a good going-over then pronounced him in fine shape.

"So, how do you stay so healthy?" the physician asked him.

"Doc, God is with me day and night," the old gent replied.

"That's nice," the doctor replied, hardly looking up.

"No, Doc. I mean He's with me *everywhere* I go. Even at night, when I get up out of bed to use the bathroom, God is right there to help me. He even turns the light on for me."

"He turns the light on for you?" the doctor asked, puzzled.

"Yep! Every night when I go to the bathroom, God turns the light on for me."

The doctor stepped into the waiting room to speak privately to the old man's wife.

"Your husband seems to be in good health physically," the doctor said. "But he might be slipping mentally. He said something peculiar. He said God Himself turns the light on for him when he gets up in the night to use the bathroom."

"Why, that old coot!" the wife retorted. "He's been piddlin' in the refrigerator again!"

"I'm a walking economy," a man was overheard to say. "My hairline's in recession, my waist is a victim of inflation, and together they're putting me in a deep depression."[3]

Generally speaking, men and women respond to situations quite differently.

Ask a man where he got a cake, and he'll tell you, "At the grocery store." Ask a woman the same question, and she'll ask, "What's the matter with it?"

But ask a woman how she bruised her toe, and she'll say, "I kicked a chair." Ask a man the same question, and he'll reply, "Somebody left a chair in the middle of the room!"[4]

Growing old is only a state of mind . . . brought on by gray hairs, false teeth, wrinkles, a big belly, shortness of breath, and being constantly and totally pooped.[5]

Men don't really lose their hair—
it just goes underground and comes out their ears!

Morning memory jog, upon arising:
It's gotten so I have to put a sign beside my bed:
"First the pants, THEN the shoes!"[6]

Youth looks ahead,
Old age looks back,
Middle age looks TIRED.[7]

Lewis and Clark were not really meant to explore the West for all those months. They simply did not want to admit (especially in front of Sacajawea) that they were lost.[8]

An eighty-year-old lady was complaining to a friend that she had a lot of trouble during the night because a man kept banging on her door. When her friend asked, "Why didn't you open the door?" the lady replied, "What? And let him out?"[9]

Dave Barry's advice on how to drive like a geezer:

1. The geezer car should be as large as possible. . . . If necessary you should get TWO cars and have them welded together.

2. You should grip the wheel tightly enough so

that you cannot be detached from it without a surgical procedure, and you should sit way down in the seat so that you're looking directly ahead at the speedometer.

3. You should select a speed in advance—23 miles per hour is very popular—and drive this speed at all times, regardless of whether you're in your driveway or on the interstate. . . .

4. If you're planning to make a turn at any point during the trip, you should plan ahead by putting your blinker on as soon as you start the car.[10]

Two ninety-year-old men, Herb and Herman, were at the funeral service for another ninety-year-old pal. After the benediction, they lingered, looking at the open casket of the deceased brother. Finally, Herb said to Herman, "You know, it's hardly worth going home."[11]

Congressman Claude Pepper, at age eighty-seven: "At my age, I don't even buy green bananas."[12]

In buying a gift for your wife, practicality can be more expensive than extravagance.

Max Lucado[13]

Have you ever wondered why it takes MILLIONS of sperm and only one egg to make a baby? Maybe it's because not one of those little surfers will stop and ask for directions!

Gary Smalley[14]

Father

4 years: My daddy can do anything.

7 years: My dad knows a lot, a whole lot.

8 years: My father doesn't know quite everything.

12 years: Oh, well, naturally Father doesn't know that, either.

14 years: Father? Hopelessly old-fashioned.

21 years: Oh, that man is out-of-date. What did you expect?

25 years: He knows a little bit about it, but not much.

30 years: Maybe we ought to find out what Dad thinks.

35 years: A little patience. Let's get Dad's assessment before we do anything.

50 years: I wonder what Dad would have thought about that. He was pretty smart.

60 years: My dad knew absolutely everything!

65 years: I'd give anything if Dad were here so I could talk this over with him. I really miss that man.[15]

The perfect man met the perfect woman, and they got married. One Christmas Eve, they were driving down the highway and noticed a man stranded by the side of the road. This was no ordinary man. It was Santa Claus!

Being the perfect people they were, they offered Santa a ride because he was in a hurry to get his toys delivered. Alas, the roads were slippery, and there was a terrible car crash. Two of the three people were killed. Do you know who survived?

(The perfect woman. Everyone knows Santa Claus and the perfect man don't really exist.)

Author and pastor Max Lucado says he used to be a "closet slob" with the attitude, "Life is too short to match your socks; just buy longer pants!"

Then, he says, he got married![16]

CURE FOR BALDNESS IN MEN
Epsom salts
Persimmon juice
Alum

Combine all ingredients and rub mixture on head daily. (It won't keep your hair from falling out, but it shrinks your head to fit what you have left!)

Getting a husband is like buying an old house. You don't see it the way it is but the way it's going to be when you get it remodeled.

Do you know what a dirty old man is?

A middle-aged father with three daughters and one bathroom!

A retired husband is a wife's full-time job.[17]

Jesus was walking on the water and came up to a boat with three men fishing. As Jesus climbed into the boat he saw that one of the men wore thick glasses and had poor vision. Jesus took the man's glasses and threw them into the water. As soon as they hit the water the man's eyesight was restored.

The next man held out a withered hand. Jesus touched his hand and the man's flesh was restored.

Jesus then turned to the third man. The man held out his hands and said, "Lord, don't touch me! I'm on disability pension!"[18]

A friend who is bald says he will *never* wear a turtleneck sweater. He's afraid he'll look like a roll-on deodorant!

This is the same friend who said he used to use Head & Shoulders—but now he needs Mop & Glow!

After a canceled flight at an unspecified airport, passengers mobbed the reservation counter. Airline personnel were doing their best to rebook passengers quickly. But a demanding passenger pushed to the front of the line, pounded on the counter, and shouted repeatedly, "You have to get me on this plane."

The reservations agent remained accommodating and unrattled.

The passenger's tirade became even more incensed and insulting. "Do you know who you're talking to?" he shouted. "Do you know who I am?"

The agent calmly took the microphone and announced over the intercom, "Ladies and gentlemen, we have a passenger here who doesn't know who he is. Will someone who knows this passenger please come identify him?"

And with that, the other passengers broke into applause.[19]

Mirth is God's medicine. Everybody ought to bathe in it. Grim care, moroseness, anxiety—all this rust of life ought to be scoured off by the oil of mirth. It is better than emery. Every man ought to rub himself with it. A man without mirth is like a wagon without springs, in which everyone is caused disagreeably to jolt by every pebble over which it runs.

Henry Ward Beecher

Rebuke a wise man and he will love you.
Instruct a wise man and he will be wiser still; teach a
    righteous man and he will add to his learning.
The fear of the LORD is the beginning of wisdom,
    and knowledge of the Holy One is understanding.
    (Prov. 9:8–10)

Ready for Liftoff!

*I'm a child of the King . . . still living in
palace preparation mode.*

Last year I was honored to be a guest in the home of a very
wealthy woman. As we pulled into the driveway, I was
amazed at the size of her beautiful mansion. It rose elegantly
from the carefully manicured grounds, a stately structure
with a wide, columned porch that opened into a foyer featuring a grand, winding staircase. Standing at the front steps I
had to lean way back and rest the back of my head on my
shoulders just to see the top of the house.

Frankly, I was a little intimidated by the size and opulence
of this majestic home. But then a uniformed maid opened the
front door for us, and there was our gracious hostess, welcoming us with outstretched arms and a warm heart and
making us feel right at home in the luxurious surroundings.

She showed us around, and each room was more beautiful than the one before it. Finally, she guided us into a grand dining room, where the table was set with some of the prettiest china I had ever seen; in fact, someone told me later this woman had several different sets of exquisite china.

Everything in her home was lavish, from the crisp linen napkins and glittering silverware to the dainty dessert plates and the sparkling chandelier.

It was lovely, but as I sat there in the vast dining room, enjoying our hostess's hospitality, the words to that old, old song drifted into my mind: "A tent or a cottage, why should I care? He's building a PALACE for me over there."[1]

It was all I could do to keep from blurting out suddenly, "You know, I'VE GOT A PALACE TOO!"

Actually, Bill and I now live in a comfortable mobile home.

"I'm getting so old that all my friends in heaven will think I didn't make it."

But we've got a MANSION waiting for us in heaven—and I'm dancing on tiptoes in my eagerness to get there!

Recently I've started collecting angels—but not just *any* angels. I collect trumpet-tooting Gabriels! They're everywhere around our home—little ceramic figurines and colorful banners depicting angels dressed in flowing gowns, mighty wings majestically spread. And each one holds a long, slender horn. Everywhere I look I see an angel and that little joke I saw somewhere comes to mind:

> DUE TO THE SHORTAGE OF
> TRAINED TRUMPETERS,
> THE END OF THE WORLD
> WILL BE POSTPONED THREE MONTHS!

Well, if all my angels could suddenly become real, there would certainly be no shortage! They're there to remind me of that joyful day when Gabriel will sound his horn, and we'll all move into our mansions in heaven. On that glad moving

"A Child of the King" by Marilyn Goss

day, we'll slip into our heavenly robes, adjust our heavenly crowns atop our heads, and hurry eagerly, arms outstretched and faces aglow, toward our heavenly Host: Jesus! Won't it be fabulous to have Him show us around and point out which mansion is our own!

Imagining that day, I picture heaven as a place filled with beautiful mansions that glow like the light-filled homes in artist Thomas Kinkade's radiant scenes. Have you seen his work? It's . . . well, it's heavenly! He has an incredible talent for creating scenes that are both splendid and inspiring. Light seems to spill out of the homes' windows and doorways, reminding me of that line that says:

Sunset is heaven's gate . . . ajar.

Having Thomas Kinkade's lovely pictures in my home, along with all my happy angels, keeps me constantly filled with joyous anticipation of what's waiting for me in heaven. These reminders keep me focused on what's REALLY important in this life. They help me remember the message my friend Dick Innes put in the form of these inspiring words:

Time
We enter it at birth.
We pass through it in life.
We exit it at death.
It was our preparation for eternity.

Until that day comes and Gabriel blows his horn, we're living in palace preparation mode, folks!

When my editor saw the theme of this chapter, she said, "But Barb, you wrote about that in your LAST book."

My answer was, "Yes, I did. But the Lord hasn't come yet, has He? So we're STILL living in palace preparation mode!"

Don't ever forget it! Our life here is nothing more than preparation for the next one. Surround yourself with reminders of that heavenly promise.

The angel figurines scattered in every room of our home and the striking Thomas Kinkade pictures hanging on my walls do more than hint of heaven; they reassure me that none of my problems are here to stay. As the Bible says, they "came to pass"! No matter what trials beset me here, I've got a reservation in a much better place.

A luxurious palace is waiting for me. My name is already painted on the mailbox! The lights are on, and the table is set. (Just think of that when you hear the quip, "Death is God's way of saying, 'Your table is ready'!") And best of all, the Lord Himself is standing in the doorway, waiting to welcome me! One of these days, I'm gonna move in there and spend eternity in glorious praise of the One who created it all for me.

What a happy day that will be! Thinking of it reminds me of that little Christian comment that says:

> When I was born, people were happy and smiling. I was the only one crying.
> When I died, people were sad and crying. I was the only one happy and smiling.

When I go, I'm going out with a laugh. No matter what my outward appearance, you can believe on the inside I'll be singing and shouting hallelujah. It won't be anything like the little item someone contributed to the newsletter published by Joel Goodman, director of the Humor Project. It said:

> I work on an obstetrical floor in a hospital. Someone recently posted an article at our nursing station which said, "Recent research shows that the first five minutes of life are very risky." Underneath that, someone else had penciled in the words, "The last five minutes aren't so hot either!"

As Christians, we can LAUGH at death. For us, death is not the joyless end of our lives; it's the *beginning* of endless joy.

Our final exit here will be our grandest entrance there! That encouraging fact is the lifeline we cling to every day of our lives; it's the secret that empowers us to face with courage *anything* that comes our way because we know (1) God is with us; we're His; we're engraved on the palms of His hands, and (2) better days are ahead—if not in this life then in the next. As someone said,

For Christians, *nothing* is the end of the world!

Dying to Get to Heaven

When Bill and I were meeting recently with our insurance agent, he consulted some actuarial tables and told me my life expectancy was another nineteen years. The poor man probably expected me to be a little sad to hear this prediction. I was sad, all right, but not in the way he expected. As he delivered this bit of news, my face automatically wrinkled up into a frown, and I spouted off, "Ugh! I don't wanna wait *that* long!"

It's not that I'm living a miserable life. On the contrary, I've made it a habit to wring out of every single day all the fun and love I can find. Sometimes it seems I have the best of both worlds—overflowing joy here and the promise of eternal happiness in paradise. Still, I know that my pleasantest day here on earth is *nothing* compared with the unfathomable joy that awaits me in heaven.

Someone told me about an elegant fashion show organized several years ago by a church women's group. The guests were rewarded with several door prizes, and one frail but spirited ninety-year-old lady burst into laughter as she opened the gift she'd won—a *twenty-year* goal-planner. Shaking her head and laughing happily, she quickly handed it to a much younger woman at her table. "Honey, I hope to heaven I won't be needing this!" she said with a merry twinkle in her eye.

That woman didn't need a place to write down her goals for the next twenty years; at that point her main goal was arriving at heaven's gates and moving into her mansion—and her new, perpetually youthful body!

No Luggage Allowed

Can you imagine how glorious our lives in heaven will be? No, probably not—it's simply beyond our comprehension. Heaven will be so wonderful that the material things we cherish most on earth will be meaningless because our days will be filled with an exuberant joy that comes merely from being in God's presence.

Have you heard the story about the rich man who was determined to "take it with him" when he died? Here's how it goes:

> [The] rich man prayed until finally the Lord gave in. There was one condition: he could bring only one suitcase of his wealth. The rich man decided to fill the case with gold bullion.
>
> The day came when God called him home. St. Peter greeted him but told him he couldn't bring his suitcase.
>
> "Oh, but I have an agreement with God," the man explained.
>
> "That's unusual," said Saint Peter. "Mind if I take a look?"
>
> The man opened the suitcase to reveal the shining gold bullion.
>
> Saint Peter was amazed. "Why in the world would you bring pavement?"[2]

When we're heading for a place where the streets are paved with gold, we won't need to bring any carry-on items! Someone once said, "The only thing we can take with us is the love we leave behind." That's so true.

Lifting Up Others with Love

Where does this love legacy come from? When we welcome Jesus into our lives, He fills our hearts with love—packed down, overflowing. Then we invest it in others—and our investment multiplies!

Several years ago, I saw an essay by J. Anne Drummond that pointed out how "the real treasures, the lasting treasures, are not here on earth. The ones that matter are those that are stored in heaven. . . . One day all the keepsakes we store in the backs of our closets will be taken by our loved ones to save in *their* closets or sold to someone else or thrown away. But the treasures of love and personal friendship with Jesus Christ can never be taken from us."[3]

In my childhood home, a plaque hung on the wall to remind all of us, "Only one life, 't will soon be past. Only what's done for Christ will last." Somehow those lines still help me today to get a better perspective on my life here on earth and remember that what we do in this short life counts toward ETERNITY! We can't take anything WITH us, but we can send love on ahead—by sharing Christ's love with those who are in need here.

Noteworthy Encouragement

One of the ways we share God's love is through encouragement. Someone said the word *encourage* means "to fill the heart, to puff it up, to enlarge it." By encouraging a friend, we give that person a special gift—a boost that is aptly described in this little essay by an unknown writer:

> One of the most powerful things one person can share with another is *encouragement*. Encouragement can stop a suicide, a divorce, and countless other tragedies. A word of encouragement can heal someone who is broken and wounded. It can give someone the courage to keep trying. . . .
>
> The people of God should be a radiant contrast to the people of the world. We should bubble over with the joy of the Holy Spirit. We should find it easy to be positive and uplifting. Are you an encouragement to those around you? Don't let someone die from neglect and lack of encouragement. Share your Christian joy!

Our sin-tainted world delights in discouragement; negative people pollute our outlook and weaken our hope. But Christians know the antidote for discouragement; it's spelled out again and again in Scripture: "Anxious hearts are very heavy but a word of encouragement does wonders!"[4] The address book from my old college days is imprinted with this reminder: "As cold waters to a thirsty soul, so is good news from a far country."[5] When others write to encourage me, I reread their notes several times before depositing them in my Joy Box—to be read many times in the future.

So many hearts need to be filled up with hope. As I speak around the country, I look out over the audiences and imagine hearts that are squashed down, stamped on, flattened out from lack of care or from thoughtless deeds done to them, or shriveled and dying from lack of encouragement. What happiness it brings ME to share a glad word with those hurting hearts and help bring restoration with an infusion of God's hope! When something is restored it pops back in place, like an out-of-joint bone that is popped back into alignment, relieving the pain. Encouragement works like an emotional chiropractor—and both "doctor" and patient benefit from the treatment. As someone said, "Encouragement is a double blessing. Both giver and receiver are blessed."

Becoming an Encourager

It's easy to be an encourager. We can encourage someone with a cheery phone call, a quick visit—or just a smile. One of my favorite ways to encourage others is by writing a quick note. Usually I jot something down on a silly cartoon I've seen somewhere. The message doesn't have to be long. Brief and sincere notes can uplift the receiver as much as a bouquet of flowers—perhaps more. If you find it hard to express yourself, begin by telling your friend about some kindness she has done for you. Remind her how much her friendship means to you, then offer your own encouragement to her.

Note-writing has always been a part of our family life. Perhaps that's why the little "Memo from Jesus" at the front of this chapter means so much to me. Like the angel figurines and the Kinkade pictures, copies of this memo are posted around my house to remind me Jesus is coming back for me.

We had as our guest a young man from Canada who lived with us for a year while he attended high school. He came from a rather uncommunicative family, so it took awhile for him to get used to our family's constant chatter and joking—and especially to all the notes we left each other.

The boys had learned always to check the refrigerator for notes from me. Typing has always been faster than handwriting for me, so I would type out the list of chores I expected of each of them. Even though I tried to divide the work evenly, one day Larry complained that he had too much on his list. "I'll *never* get all this stuff done!" he pouted.

When we compared all the boys' notes, the problem quickly became apparent. Barney, who was then ten, had redone all the notes, laboriously retyping them (with one finger) and redistributing all of HIS chores to his three brothers! Then he signed the notes "MOM" and even put on some of my lipstick and blotted his lips to imprint a "kiss" on the notes, just as I always did!

Luckily, our Canadian guest missed out on this prank. Before he returned home he said the *one thing* he really loved about living with us was our "note system." He said getting a note telling him what chores were expected of him, where everyone was, what to do to prepare for dinner, and what activities were planned for that evening was like having his own private mail system.

A Gift of Hope

An encouraging note can mean a lot, even to those who are accustomed to receiving them. Mark Twain, who was known to be a vain man, confessed that he could "live for three weeks on a single compliment."

Encouragement is the gift Chuck Swindoll describes as a "hope transplant" to someone in need.[6] Erma Bombeck was a talented encourager. For decades, she encouraged millions of us as she simultaneously entertained us with her syndicated newspaper column and her books. She kept on encouraging and entertaining us right up until the end. When she died last year, the whole nation paused to reminisce at the love and laughter she had shared. One writer described her as "a national treasure in a world and age that desperately needs to lighten up."[7]

Erma was one of my role models. We met—briefly—only one time, but she touched my life—and the lives of millions of others—through her words, her humor, and the Christian kindness she showed to all who knew her. She encouraged others to wrap themselves in happiness and to endure hardships by focusing on the "big picture" rather than getting bogged down in drudgery. One of her best columns, published several years ago, described how she would do things if she could live her life over:

> There would have been more I love yous . . . more I'm sorrys . . . more I'm listenings . . . but mostly, given another shot at life, I would seize every minute of it . . . look at it and really see it . . . try it on . . . live it . . . exhaust it . . . and never give that minute back until there was nothing left of it.[8]

Many would say that Erma, by her writing, helped us live the way she said she would have relived her own—with gratefulness for the blessings right under our noses. And finally, there was Erma's farewell. Published in her last column just five days before she died, it was used to introduce her last book, *Forever, Erma*. It said:

> My deeds will be measured not by my youthful appearance, but by the concern lines on my forehead, the laugh lines around my mouth, and the chins from seeing what can be done for those smaller than me or who have fallen.[9]

If *my* spirit is wrinkled and lined, I hope those crinkles are from being pressed against God. That's where I've tried to stay throughout my life, no matter what circumstances beset me. As Hudson Taylor said, "It doesn't matter how great the pressure is. What really matters is *where the pressure lies*, whether it comes between me and God or whether it presses me nearer His heart."[10] Romans 8:39 says this so clearly: "NOTHING can separate us from the love of God." He *WALLPAPERS* our hearts to His.

Nothing can happen to us in this life without coming through God's filter. As someone said, citing Romans 8:18, "Heaven's delights will far outweigh earth's difficulties." Whatever we must endure here is only temporary. When God permits His children to go through the furnace experiences of our lives, He keeps His eye on the clock—and His hand on the thermostat!

This life is only temporary; it's the next one that lasts forever. We have only a few allotted years between eternities to do God's work here on earth. As someone said, "Heaven will mean the most to those who have put the most into it." While we're here in God's waiting room, living in palace preparation mode, each of us has a role to play, a job to do.

Some save lives; others save souls.

Some raise children; others comfort the dying.

Some feed the hungry; others clothe the poor.

Some help the needy; others encourage the fearful.

Many times in my life, I've been lifted out of a cesspool by others' kind, encouraging words; in their notes and voices I have heard God speak. When I landed on the ceiling, God handed others a spatula of love to scrape me off and send me on my way again.

And then it was my turn. God set me down on the shores of the cesspool and handed me the lifeline I now gladly throw to others. The lifeline is God's loving encouragement, which pulls us into God Himself.

Clinging to one end, I throw the other end to someone who's recently landed in the muck. And then God lifts both of us out of the cesspool and wraps us in His comfort blanket of love.

Sharing Heaven's Hope

There is *nothing* in your life that God and you cannot handle together—if you get out of the way and let HIM be in control. He can turn your troubles into blessings, and then He can use those blessings to add depth to your spirit so that your praise for Him is even more fervent and joyous and your life is an inspiration to others.

My friend Rose Totino, founder of Totino's Frozen Pizza, lived that kind of inspiring life. She faced a lot of challenges during her seventy-nine years. But she never took her eyes off heaven. In fact, when I look at the enthralling photograph of Rose on the next page, I see a marvelous joy radiating from that exuberant smile, don't you? That sparkle of joy we saw in Rose was the reflection of God's glory.

This photograph was used by American Express in an advertising campaign featuring American heroes. Several years later, it was printed again in a much more touching way. It appeared on the front of the leaflets given to guests at Rose's memorial service in 1994. Inside the leaflet, the tribute to Rose noted how she would want to be remembered: "as a woman whose face was always turned to God and as one who knew so well that when the day came for Jesus to take her home, there would be, as she often said, 'no U-Haul behind the hearse.'"

This was followed by a beautiful little essay—one Rose had spotted on a bulletin board at the Mayo Clinic. It said:

> Cancer is limited.
> It cannot cripple love.
> It cannot shatter hope.
> It cannot corrode faith.
> It cannot eat away peace.
> It cannot destroy confidence.
> It cannot kill friendship.
> It cannot shut out memories.
> It cannot silence courage.
> It cannot invade the soul.
> It cannot reduce eternal life.

It cannot quench the Spirit.
It cannot lessen the power of the resurrection.

Author Unknown

Many beautiful words have described Rose, but it is the photograph that touches my heart most deeply. It's as if, in that ecstatic smile, Rose is responding to the joyously welcoming chorus she hears as she nears heaven's gates.

For Rose—and for all Christians—death isn't something to be feared. It's precious! It's our grand entrance into heaven, our arrival at the foot of God's throne. What a happy time that will be! When I think of the joy and peace that await me there, I can hardly wait!

Rose W. Totino
Photo reprinted with permission of the American Express Corporation.

Permission Acknowledgments

Mail addressed to Spatula Ministries arrives by the basketfuls, and each day's letters bring new anecdotes, cartoons, poems, jokes, and maxims my thoughtful friends have clipped or quoted from unidentified magazines, newspapers, church newsletters, and bulletin boards. Many of these little gems are too good not to share—but in many cases, despite diligent effort, I've been unable to identify the original source. Please contact the publisher if you can help identify the creators of these little treasures so that proper attribution can be given in future printings.

As always, I especially appreciate the help of those writers, agencies, artists, and friends whose names are listed below. They have graciously agreed to share with me—and with you, the reader—something they created in order to give all of us a little boost.

American Express Corporation and the Rose Totino family for allowing me to reprint the inspiring photograph of Rose that concludes the last chapter of this book.

Ashleigh Brilliant of Brilliant Enterprises, 117 W. Valerio Street, Santa Barbara, California 93101, for his clever Pot-shots that are sprinkled through the book.

Ruth Harms Calkin for sharing her poem "Suddenly Mine" in chapter 4.

Mary Chambers and InterVarsity Press for the funny cartoon in chapter 8.

J. Anne Drummond for allowing me to quote from her essay "Estate Sale" in chapter 8.

Gallant Greetings for letting me reprint the greeting card in chapter 3.

Randy Glasbergen for sharing five of his clever cartoons that appear throughout these pages.

Marilyn Goss and Arts Uniq' for Marilyn's beautiful rendering of "A Child of the King" in chapter 8.

Dr. Robb Hicks, Dick Innes, Sue Nichols, Dorothy Petersen, Rev. Larry Potts, Marilyn Shilt, Rev. Roger Shouse, and Sherrie Weaver for sharing their anecdotes, jokes, poems, and experiences with the readers of this book.

Nancy L. Jackshaw and Leaning Tree Publishing for sharing the witty lines from one of the company's greeting cards.

The *Kansas City Star* for permission to reprint the Schorr cartoon in chapter 4.

Bil Keane for sharing one of his clever "Family Circus" cartoons in chapter 6.

The King Features Syndicate for Wayne Stayskal's "Ralph" cartoon in chapter 2.

Carol L. Leet for letting me reprint the story about her granddaughter in chapter 6.

Ann Landers and Creators Syndicate for the delightful letters from her column that appear in chapter 4.

Meadowbrook Press for allowing me to use cartoons from Jane Thomas Noland and Ed Fischer, *What's So Funny about Getting Old?* and Mary McBride, *Grandma Knows Best But No One Ever Listens!*

John McPherson for generously sharing four silly cartoons in chapters 2, 3, and 7.

Pamela Pettler for sharing "The Stress Diet" in chapter 2—and a special thanks to the Pettler family members scattered coast to coast who helped me find Pamela.

The nice folks at Recycled Paper Greetings for letting me reprint in chapter 2 that dancing fat lady from one of their clever cards.

Dana Summers for his witty cartoons in chapters 1 and 4.

TON Communications for allowing me to use the words from an "It's in the Bible" greeting card in chapter 4.

Universal Press Syndicate for efficiently granting my requests to use an item from a "Dear Abby" column and for these cartoons and comics: "For Better or For Worse" by Lynn Johnston, "Real Life Adventures" by GarLanco, and "Tight Corner" by Grundy/Willett.

Sherrie Weaver for again sharing her clever witticisms scattered throughout the book.

Adeline Wiklund for allowing me to reprint her touching poem "Bouquets of Gold" in chapter 6.

Notes

Chapter 1. The Wonder Years

1. Dorothy Parker, quoted in Lois L. Kaufman, *Old Age Is Not for Sissies* (White Plains, N.Y.: Peter Pauper Press, 1989), 57.
2. Bill Cosby, quoted in Kaufman, Ibid., 55.
3. Dave Barry, *The World According to Dave Barry* (New York: Wings, 1994), 237.
4. Verla Gillmor, "Managing Menopause: Help and Hope for Facing the Change," *Today's Christian Woman*, January 1997, 49.
5. Dr. Harvey Austin, quoted in Kaufman, *Old Age Is Not for Sissies*, 42.
6. Rob Scott and Mike Wallard, designers, *Girls Just Wanna Have Facelifts: The Ugly Truth about Getting Older* (Kansas City, Shoebox Greetings, 1989).
7. This description appeared in an excerpt from Gail Sheehy, *Silent Passage* (New York: Random House, 1992), in the *Austin American-Statesman* Lifestyle section, 16 June 1992, D-1.
8. Margaret Mead, quoted in *Family Circle*, 14 May 1996, 52.
9. Marilyn Meberg, *Choosing the Amusing: What Difference Does It Make?* (Portland, Oreg.: Multnomah, 1986), 24.
10. From a Sylvia greeting card © Nicole Hollander and © The Maine Line Company, Rockport, Maine.
11. Lady Nancy Astor, quoted in Erma Bombeck, "At Wit's End," 15 February 1995, the *Orange County Register* Accent section, 5.
12. Robert Fulghum, *Uh-Oh: Some Observations from Both Sides of the Refrigerator Door* (New York: Villard, 1991), 184.

13. Norene Firth, *A Bowl of Cherries: Looking at Life Through Homespun Homilies* (Norwalk, Conn.: The C. R. Gibson Co., 1980).
14. Martin A. Ragaway, *Don't Even Think of Retiring Until . . .* (Los Angeles: Prince/Stern/Sloan, 1982).
15. President Dwight Eisenhower, quoted by Jacquelyn Benfield in a column titled "Age Clues" in an unidentified newspaper clipping sent by a friend of Spatula Ministries.
16. Roger Rosenblatt, "Secret Admirer," *Modern Maturity*, August 1993.
17. Sherrie Weaver, *Stress or Insanity* (Glendale Heights, Ill.: Great Quotations, 1996).
18. This Scripture verse and Nancy L. Jackshaw's clever line are part of a beautiful greeting card published by Celebration Greetings, Boulder, Colorado. Used with permission.

Chapter 2. Fat Farm Failures . . . and Other Excuses for the Middle-Age Spread

1. Associated Press, "Thin may be in, but fat's where it's at," *St. Petersburg Times*, 16 October 1996, 1A.
2. Pam Pavlik's "Upfront" column in the *Philadelphia Inquirer*, "The real skinny," date unknown.
3. Erma Bombeck, *A Marriage Made in Heaven or Too Tired for an Affair* (New York: HarperCollins, 1993).
4. *Tampa Tribune*, 25 September 1996, Baylife 2.
5. Pamela Pettler, "The Stress Diet" in *The Joy of Stress* (New York: William Morrow, 1984). Reprinted with permission.
6. Chef Leonardo DiCanio, quoted in "A Taste of Gold," *Tampa Tribune* Food & Health section, 5 September 1996, 1.
7. Mary Anne Cohen, director of the New York Center for Eating Disorders, quoted in *Tampa Tribune* Baylife section, 23 September 1996, 2.
8. This little quip appeared on—what else?—a refrigerator magnet by Linda Grayson, produced by Printwick Papers.
9. Fitness trainer Chris Reichart, quoted in *Tampa Tribune* Business & Finance section, 11 March 1996, 4.
10. "Veggies That Taste Like Fruit?" *Tampa Tribune* Baylife section, 20 September 1996, 2, citing an article in *Child* magazine.
11. *Tampa Tribune*, 27 June 1996.
12. Bernice Kanner, "Americans admit lying is a daily habit," Bridge News, reprinted in the *Tampa Tribune*, date unknown.

13. Taken from a Dear Abby column by Abigail Van Buren. Distributed by Universal Press Syndicate. Reprinted with permission. All rights reserved.
14. *Weight Watchers Little Book of Wisdom: Words to Lose By* (Weight Watchers International, 1987, 1995).
15. Thanks to pastor Larry Potts, First Christian Church, Gainesville, Missouri, for sharing this insight.
16. Sherrie Weaver, *365 Days of Life in the Stress Lane* (Glendale Heights, Ill.: Great Quotations Publishing, 1994).
17. Weaver, *Stress or Insanity*.

Chapter 3. A Fact of Aging: What You Lose in Elasticity You Gain in Wisdom

1. WHO definition of fitness, cited in Susan H. Thompson, "Benefits of exercise are easy to attain," *Tampa Tribune*, 5 September 1996, 3.
2. My Joy Room started out as a shoebox-size Joy Box that I quickly outgrew. For details, see my book *Stick a Geranium in Your Hat and Be Happy* (Word, 1990).
3. Dr. James Rippe, *Fit Over Forty* (New York: William Morrow, 1996).
4. "Vitality, Vim, and Vigor, Six Steps to More Energy," a pamphlet published by the Baylor College of Medicine Office of Health Promotion, One Baylor Plaza, Houston, TX 77030.
5. Eugene F. Ware, quoted in John C. Maxwell, *Leadership 101: Inspirational Quotes & Insights for Leaders* (Tulsa: Honor Books, 1994), 34.
6. Dave Barry, *Stay Fit and Healthy Until You're Dead* (Emmaus, Penna: Rodale, 1985), 15.
7. Ibid., ix–x.
8. "Don't just stuff and veg," *Tampa Tribune* Food and Health section, 26 September 1996, 3.
9. Fitness expert Candice Copeland-Brooks of Mammoth Lakes, California, in a *Living Fit* article quoted in "Get on the ball," *Tampa Tribune* Food and Health section, 26 September 1996, 3.
10. Randolph Schmid, the Associated Press, "Feeling Your Age a Matter of Mind," undated clipping sent by a friend of Spatula Ministries.
11. Adapted from William Van Wert, *What's It All About?* (New York: Simon & Schuster, 1996), 128.

12. Sanford University School of Medicine Psychiatrist William F. Fry, cited in "Fit notes," *Tampa Tribune* Food and Health section, 14 November 1996, 6.

13. From a cartoon by Randy Glasbergen. Used by permission.

Chapter 4. Growing Old Is Inevitable; Growing Up Is Optional

1. Associated Press, "Clinton praises Lucid's space feat," 28 September 1996.

2. Larry Laudan, *The Book of Risks* (New York: Wiley & Sons, 1994), cited in Jeffrey Kluger, *St. Petersburg Times*, 9 June 1996.

3. Max Lucado, *He Still Moves Stones* (Dallas: Word, 1993).

4. Carol Kent, *Speak Up with Confidence* (Nashville: Thomas Nelson, 1993), 47.

5. Ingrid Trobisch, "Losing a Loved One," *A Better Tomorrow Magazine*, Winter 1993, 89.

6. Adapted from Alfred A. Montapert, "Ten Steps to Brighten Your Life." Publishing source unknown.

7. Reported by Charles Osgood, "Newsbreak," CBS Radio Network, 22 September 1980.

8. *Tampa Tribune*, 17 September 1996.

9. Ibid.

10. Marc Silver, *U.S. News & World Report*, 4 June 1990, 76.

11. Millard and Linda Fuller, *The Excitement Is Building* (Dallas: Word, 1990), 34–35.

12. Ann Landers, 13 December 1995. Permission granted by Ann Landers and Creators Syndicate.

13. Sherwood Eliot Wirt, *I Don't Know What Old Is, But Old Is Older Than Me* (Nashville: Thomas Nelson, 1992), 87.

14. Dave Veerman, ed., *How to Get Along with the Opposite Sex: Book 2 of the Ready for Life Series* (Wheaton, Ill.: Victor Books/ Scripture Press, 1994).

15. Donna Watson, Ph.D., *101 Ways to Enjoy Life's Simple Pleasures* (Austin, Tex.: Bard and Stephen, 1994), 17.

16. H. Jackson Brown Jr., *Live and Learn and Pass It On* (Nashville: Portal Publications, 1992).

17. From an "It's in the Bible" greeting card, the copyright of TON Communications Inc., Newark, Delaware. Used by permission.

18. This funny story was submitted by Janice S. Walsh to "Lite Fare," *Christian Reader*, September–October 1996, 76.

19. "Suddenly Mine" from *Lord, You Love to Say Yes* by Ruth

Harms Calkin, Pomona, California. Used by permission. All rights reserved.

Chapter 5. Precious Memories—How They Leave Us
1. Ravi Zacharias, *Deliver Us from Evil* (Dallas: Word, 1996).
2. Van Wert, *What's It All About?* 230.
3. Hugh O'Neill, *New Choices* magazine, October 1996, 72.
4. Ibid.
5. Charlotte Davis Kasl, Ph.D., *Finding Joy: 101 Ways to Free Your Spirit and Dance with Life* (New York: HarperCollins, 1994), 84–85.
6. The story of Bill's accident and miraculous recovery is told in *Stick a Geranium in Your Hat and Be Happy*.
7. This little gem was credited to *Railway Employees Journal* in an unidentified clipping sent by a Spatula Ministries friend.
8. Weaver, *365 Days of Life in the Stress Lane*, October 1.
9. Adapted from Weaver, ibid., August 31.
10. Martin A. Ragaway, *Good News, Bad News* (Los Angeles: Price/Stern/Sloan, 1984).
11. Bill Cosby, quoted in Kaufman, *Old Age Is Not for Sissies*, 56.
12. Erma Bombeck, *Star News*, Hendersonville, Tennessee, 12 November 1993, 2A.
13. Ed Fischer and Jane Thomas Noland, *What's So Funny About Getting Old?* (Minnetonka, Minn.: Meadowbrook Press, 1991).
14. Adapted from a joke in "Laughter, the Best Medicine," *Reader's Digest*, April 1996, 77, and combined with other contributions sent by friends of Spatula Ministries.

Chapter 6. Grandmothers Are Antique Little Girls
1. Bombeck, *A Marriage Made in Heaven*.
2. Max Lucado, *A Gentle Thunder* (Dallas: Word, 1995).
3. "35 years behind baby boomer bottoms," *St. Petersburg Times*, 8 September 1996, 6H.
4. Adapted from "Grandma, Let's Play," *A Better Tomorrow* magazine, winter 1993, 74–77.
5. John Crudele, CSP, and Richard Erickson, Ph.D., *Making Sense of Adolescence* (Liguori, Mo.: Triumph Books, 1995), quoted in *Servant Life*, February 1996, 5.
6. Adapted from Charles L. Allen, *Grandparents R Great* (Uhrichsville, Ohio: Barbour, 1992), 8.

7. Ibid., 60.
8. Used with permission of Adeline Wiklund, Shelley, Idaho.
9. Jack Canfield and Mark Victor Hansen, *Chicken Soup for the Soul* (Deerfield Beach, Fla.: Health Communications, 1993), 12.
10. James E. Myers, *A Treasury of Senior Humor* (Springfield, Ill.: Lincoln-Herndon Press, 1992), 180.
11. Ibid., 181.
12. Ibid., 173.

Chapter 7. MENacing MENstrual Cramps, MENopause, MENtal Failure . . . Is There a Connection Here?
1. "The Vanishing Pause," *Parade* magazine, 16 February 1992, 23.
2. Erma Bombeck, "Erma Bombeck's Life Secrets. For such a young person, I've learned a whole lot," *Family Circle*, September 1982, 60.
3. Milton Segal, quoted in "Quiplash," undated column from *Christian Reader*.
4. Martha J. Beckman, *Meditations to Make You Smile* (Nashville: Dimensions for Living, 1995), 117.
5. Original source unknown. Adapted from Allen, *Grandparents R Great*, 48.
6. Attributed to "RTN" in Fischer and Noland, *What's So Funny About Getting Old?*
7. *Over the Hill: Humorous Thoughts on Growing Older* (Lombard, Ill.: Great Quotations, 1986), 33.
8. Adapted from Weaver, *365 Days of Life in the Stress Lane,* June 9.
9. Lucille Nahemow, Kathleen A. McCluskey-Fawcett, and Paul E. McGhee, eds., *Humor and Aging* (San Diego: Academic Press, 1986), 114.
10. Barry, *The World According to Dave Barry*, 275.
11. Reggie the Retiree, *Laughs and Limericks on Aging—in Large Print* (Fort Myers, Fla.: Reggie the Retiree Co., 1991).
12. Kaufman, *Old Age Is Not for Sissies*, 8.
13. Max Lucado, *When God Whispers Your Name* (Dallas: Word, 1994), 43.
14. Gary Smalley, *Making Love Last Forever* (Dallas: Word, 1996).
15. This essay appears in Ann Landers, *Wake Up and Smell the Coffee!* (New York: Villard, 1996) citing the Danbury, Conn., *News-Times* and a Dutch magazine.
16. Max Lucado, *In the Grip of Grace* (Dallas: Word, 1996), 116.

17. Kaufman, *Old Age Is Not for Sissies*, 62.

18. Thanks to Roger Shouse, Indianapolis, Indiana, for sharing this little joke.

19. Adapted from a Knight-Ridder Newspapers article appearing in the *Tampa Tribune* Baylife section, 25 June 1996, 2.

Chapter 8. Ready for Liftoff!

1. Harriett E. Buell, "A Child of the King," 1877.

2. The Rev. Warren Keating in *The Joyful Noiseletter*, reprinted in *Reader's Digest*, December 1995, 63–64.

3. J. Anne Drummond, "Estate Sale," *Decision* magazine, September 1986. Used by permission of J. Anne Drummond.

4. Prov. 12:25 TLB.

5. Prov. 25:25 KJV.

6. Charles Swindoll, *Hope Again* (Dallas: Word, 1996).

7. *National Catholic Reporter*, 10 May 1996, 2.

8. Erma Bombeck, "At Wit's End." Used by permission of the Aaron Priest Agency.

9. Erma Bombeck, *Forever, Erma* (Kansas City: Andrews and McMeel, 1996), xiv.

10. Hudson Taylor, quoted in Swindoll, *Hope Again*.

More *joy from the*
Geranium Lady!

BARBARA JOHNSON

Plant a Geranium in your Cranium

Sprouting Seeds of Joy in the Manure of Life

Best-selling humorist Barbara Johnson is back—and getting back to her roots—with a candid look at life and discovering joy in the midst of trials, including her own unexpected battle with cancer. Using excerpts from inspiring articles and extraordinary letters from her mailbag, Johnson presents one big package of humor, comfort, and encouragement that her beloved audiences have come to expect.

W Publishing Group™

God's Most Precious Jewels are Crystallized Tears contains the stories of twelve extraordinary women as they journeyed through incredible hardship to become sparkling jewels of joy and encouragement to others. Barbara includes her own story of grief turned to blessing with her signature touch of hope and humor. Woven throughout these inspiring stories are descriptions of real gemstones—their origin and their traditional meanings.

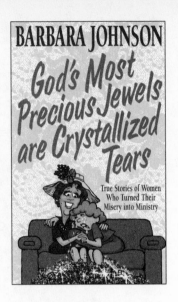

If you need a fresh breath of joy in your life, Barbara's 365-day devotional will help you look for life's little sparkles, even in the midst of life's most crippling sorrows. Love and hilarity bubble through these pages in equal doses as Barbara dispenses her unique blend of wisdom and zaniness to help thousands of hurting readers learn to laugh again. Each day's devotion features a Scripture passage and encouraging thought all wrapped up in Barbara's trademark style of offering firsthand advice about handling life's hardest hurts while dispensing infectious laughter and outrageous joy.

W PUBLISHING GROUP™

Bad news about your children carries a triple whammy of pain, worry, and "where did we go wrong?" Drawing on her own personal experience and the letters she has received from hundreds of hurting women, Barbara shares hope and humor to encourage parents in seemingly hopeless situations.

This is the book that started it all for the Geranium Lady! Sharing her own difficult experiences, Barbara proves that while pain is inevitable, misery is optional. If you need a fresh breath of joy in your life, this book is just the prescription for you. Barbara can help you look for joy, even in the midst of life's harshest challenges. This powerful book has sold one million copies and made Barbara a perennially best-selling author.

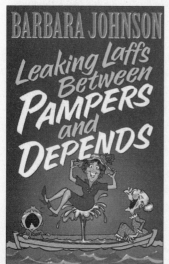

Between the years of childbearing and grandparenting, a woman has a lot to juggle! Barbara Johnson shows how the road from marriage to menopause is filled with more than a few potholes . . . but provides women with more than enough hope and humor to make it through the journey.

W PUBLISHING GROUP™

For women only, this is one of Barbara's most unique books. With her zany collection of observations about "life between the Blue Lagoon and Golden Pond," Barbara jumps right in, showing women how to survive growing older with courage and joy.

Barbara insists that laughing in the face of adversity is not a form of denial but a proven tool for managing stress, coping with pain, and maintaining hope. She zeroes in on the spiritual benefit of a smile, a giggle, and a good, old-fashioned belly laugh.

Pack Up Your Gloomees is filled with bittersweet stories of Barbara's journey through the minefields of life and her wise and encouraging responses to letters from hurting parents. Each chapter ends with a laughter-packed collection of Gloomee Busters.

W PUBLISHING GROUP™

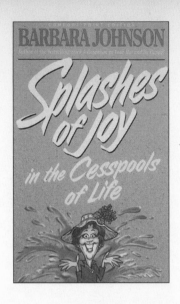

Barbara's approach to life is positive, uplifting, therapeutic and fun. *Splashes of Joy* offers an invigorating spurt of encouragement and a gentle reminder to splatter joy into the lives of others.

Sharing outrageous humor, rib-tickling insights, and inspiring, real-life examples, Barbara shows readers how to put life's trials into heavenly perspective. While we wait on Gabriel's horn to sound, Barbara gives women an external telescope with which to view their often difficult world.

W PUBLISHING GROUP™

This book has been enjoyed by and shared with:

_____

_____

_____

_____

_____

_____

_____

_____

_____

_____

_____